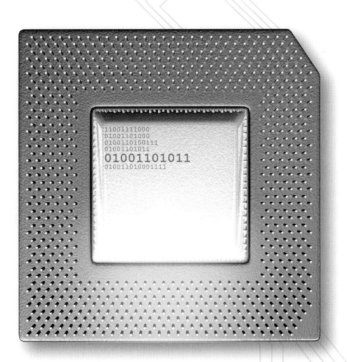

Introduction to Computers

ISBN 978-1-934920-63-3

For permission to use material from this text or for general questions about permissions, submit a request on line to http://www.wordsofwisdombooks.com/contact.asp

Publisher: Words of Wisdom, LLC — Schaumburg, IL
Book Title: Introduction to Computers
Author: Editorial Board
Rights: Words of Wisdom, LLC
Publication Date: 2012
Edition: 1

Acknowledgments

We would like to thank the Editorial Board for their time
and dedication to the creation of this book.

Debby Telfer
Myles Vogel
Dr. Stephanie McWilliams

TABLE OF CONTENTS

Chapter 1: Introduction to Computing 2

The Power of Basic Computing 2

A Brief History of Computing 3

What Is a Computer? 4

Definition...4

Types of Personal Computers 4

Basic Operations 5

Computer Hardware 5

Components in General 5

System Unit..5

Peripherals 6

Input Devices 7

Output Devices 7

Storage Devices 8

Communications Devices...12

Computer Software 13

Definition...13

User Interfaces..13

Installing Software 13

Software Upgrades...14

Software Licensing 15

Types of Software 15

Networks...18

Types of Networks 19

Buying a Computer..20

Desktop versus Portable?...20

What About Software?...21

The Basics..21

Where and How to Purchase?..21

What Size Laptop Computer?...21

Summary..22

Chapter 2: The Internet 24

The Power of the Internet...24

Entertainment 25

Electronic Commerce 25

Electronic Communication 25

Research and Problem Solving 25

A Brief History of the Internet and World Wide Web.........26

Accessing the Internet 26

Internet Service Providers 27

Online Service Providers 27

Wireless Internet Service 27

The World Wide Web 28

Web Pages and Sites 29

Web Servers 29

Web Browsers 29

Standards for Use 30

Web Addresses 31

Web 2.0...32

Social Networking 33

Blogs 33

Web Research 33

Procedures 33

Search Engines 33

Successful Searching..33

Browsing 35

Sources: Credibility 35

Citing Sources Found on the Internet 36

Internet Issues 37

Social Issues 37

Security 39

Protection: Surfing Securely 39

Summary..40

Chapter 3: Productivity Software: Navigation 42

The Power of Software..42

What Is Software?..42

The Operating System 43

Starting and Operating the Computer..44

Turning on the Computer 44

Shutting Down the Computer...44

Using the Mouse...44

Starting Microsoft Windows 7® 46

The Windows 7 Welcome Screen 46

Optional Log-in to Windows 7 48

Overview of the Windows 7 Desktop 50

Starting a Program with the *Start* Menu..52

Menus, Commands, and Dialog Boxes..52

Using Windows 7 Help..53

Working with Windows 7 54

Opening, Closing, Maximizing, Minimizing, and Restoring Windows..............54

Moving and Resizing Windows 55

Switching Between Windows...55

Using Scroll Bars 55

Status Bars..56

Using Windows Explorer..56

The Windows Explorer Window...56

Working With Files and Folders..59

Organizing Files within Folders 59

Creating a Folder...61

Parts of a Folder Window 62

Expanding and Collapsing a Folder..62

Saving a File into a Folder...63

Example Procedures 64

Using Application Software...68

Managing Office Files...69

The Application Interface...74

Conventions for Working
with Dialog Boxes 77

Commonly Used Office Commands 78

Summary..80

Chapter 4: Productivity Software: Word Processing 82

The Power of Word Processing 82

Common Business Tasks That Use Word Processing 83

A Brief History of Word Processing..83

Word Processing Basics 84

Creating a New Document 84

The Word Window 85

How to Use the Help Feature in Word.......................................87

Status Bar Options 89

Entering Text...92

Selecting Text 95

Editing Text...97

Formatting Text...100

Advanced Topics...121

   Graphics..121

   Tables..124

   Columns...128

   Track Changes 130

   Envelopes and Labels 132

Summary...136

Chapter 5: Productivity Software: Spreadsheets **138**

The Power of Spreadsheets 138

Common Business Tasks That Use Microsoft Excel®.....................139

A Brief History of Spreadsheets...139

The Basics of Excel 140

   How to Use the Help Feature in Excel 141

   The Excel Window...142

   Worksheet Design Considerations...147

   Entering and Editing Data in Excel..148

   Inserting and Deleting Rows and Columns 149

   Formatting 151

   Formulas 158

   Copying and Pasting in Excel 164

   Printing Worksheets..169

Advanced Topics in Excel 173

   Working with Lists..173

   Charting and Graphing 174

   Conditional Formatting 179

   Using IF/THEN Functions to Control
   for Conditions...181

   Working with Dates in Excel 182

   Named Ranges 182

Fast Track Project: Monthly Billing Report 184

Summary 186

Chapter 6: Productivity Software: Presentations 188

The Power of Presentations 188

Common Business Tasks That Use Microsoft PowerPoint® 189

A Brief History of Presentation Application Software 190

PowerPoint Basics 190

    Planning a Presentation 190

    Creating a New Presentation 193

    The PowerPoint Window 196

    Entering Text in PowerPoint 203

    Selecting in PowerPoint 203

    Editing Text in PowerPoint 204

    Formatting in PowerPoint 206

    Adding New Slides 212

    Graphics in PowerPoint 214

    Using the Notes Pane 223

    Working with Slides 223

    Adding Transitions 224

    Viewing a Slide Show 225

    Printing a Presentation 226

Advanced Topics in PowerPoint 228

    Custom Animations 228

    Copying, Importing, and Exporting Slides 230

Fast Track Practice: Creating a Sales Presentation 233

    Slide 1: Title 233

    Slides 2, 3, 4: Medical Equipment Suppliers 233

    Slide 5: Sales from Medical Equipment 233

    Slide 6: Recommendations for Next Year to Save Money 233

Slide 7: Closing 233

Summary 234

Chapter 7: Productivity Software: Managing Personal Data 236

The Power of Personal Information Management Systems 236

Widespread Business Use 236

Automated Reminders 237

Central Point for E-mail Access 238

A Brief History of Personal Information Management Systems 238

The Rise of Microsoft Outlook 239

Common Business Tasks That Use Outlook 240

Overview of the Outlook Window 241

Navigation Pane 241

Preview Pane 241

Reading Pane 242

View Settings 242

E-mail 242

Procedures 242

Conversations 249

Address Book and Contact Groups 251

Security Concerns 252

E-mail in a Business Setting 254

Calendar 256

Basic Procedures 256

Tasks 260

Syncing Outlook, Facebook, Google Calendar, and Yahoo! 261

Summary 262

Chapter 8: Computing in the Future 264

What to Expect in the Next Five Years 265

What Will Future Industrial and Personal Computing Needs Require? 266

Nanotechnology 267

Data Storage..267

Innovations in Information and Entertainment Delivery 268

Cloud Computing..268

Portable Devices and Cloud Computing 269

Businesses and Cloud Computing..269

Concerns About Cloud Computing.......................................270

Virtualization and iPv6 270

Trends in Information Technology and Health 270

The Medical Homes Model...270

Electronic Record Keeping 271

Telemedicine 271

Increased Need for Health Information Technology Specialists.............................272

Electronic Record Security and Cloud Computing..272

Trends in Information Technology and Other Industries 273

Construction Management...273

Leadership in Energy and Environmental Design Certification 273

Certification 274

Trends for Future Certification in Information Technology 274

Vendor-Specific Certification 275

Online Education 275

Wireless Magazine and Newspaper Subscriptions 276

Online Access to Print Publications 276

Loss of Advertising Revenue...276

Hardware Personal Computing 277

Smartphones 277

The Future Smartphone Network...278

Smartphone Availability 278

Summary 279

Appendix A: File Management Essentials: File Management Shortcuts......... A-2

Appendix B: Internet Essentials: Internet Shortcuts...................................... B-2

Appendix C: Word Essentials: Word Shortcuts.. C-2

Appendix D: Excel Essentials: Excel Shortcuts D-2

Appendix E: PowerPoint Essentials: PowerPoint Shortcuts...........................E-2

Glossary G-2

Photo Credits..P-2

Index I-2

Preface: Why Should I Learn About Computers?

COMPUTERS ARE EVERYWHERE

In today's fast-moving world, it is hard to imagine life without computers. They appear almost everywhere and inside all kinds of things—everything from the personal computer on your desk to the microwave in your kitchen and the smartphone in your pocket.

Not very long ago, though, computers were rare and new, and few people had them. Now that they are such a big part of our modern lives, it is more important than ever to understand basic computing concepts.

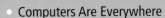
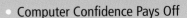

Computers Have Moved Off the Desktop

In almost every environment, computers continue to perform new functions. The smartphone is the primary mobile device for many people, displacing or completely replacing a laptop computer. The tablet computer (the iPad, for instance) is another rising category of personal computer. Cars and trucks increasingly include touch screens and logic systems that control nearly every aspect of a vehicle's performance. In the home, gaming consoles, televisions, and stereo systems also now include powerful computers.

Computers Are Increasingly Interactive Social Devices

Computers are changing more than just the workplace. Increasingly, they enable interactive social functions. The social networking site Facebook, for instance, has more than 500 million active users—more than the population of the United States (in fact, if Facebook were a country, it would be the third most populous country on Earth, after China and India). A much smaller network—a school website—can allow parents to keep track of their children's progress in school or communicate and collaborate with teachers and school administrators. Larger virtual environments, such as Second Life, offer a way to meet and interact with like-minded people all over the world.

Computers have perhaps forever blurred the line between home and work, as well. The same technology that enables you to work from home also allows you to take care of personal and social matters while at work. Professional networking sites such as LinkedIn connect career-minded people with one another, serving as a platform for making recommendations and referrals.

Fundamentally, computers are the platform for both business and personal communication. In the past, a business might print and mail a brochure to explain its products and services to customers. Today, that same business instead can publish a website that can be viewed thousands or even millions of times, with no printing or mailing expense. Think of how difficult it would be to collect brochures and printed publications for every business or organization about which you sought information. The World Wide Web makes all of that information instantly available to anyone who wants it. The amount of communication has increased exponentially, and the future holds even more growth.

Keeping track of all this available information is a challenge—in fact, just keeping track of your *own* information can be a challenge. For example, digital cameras make it easy to take hundreds and even thousands of pictures. This quickly results in a collection so large it becomes almost impossible to find a particular photo. The sheer amount of data can be overwhelming.

When you understand how computers work, however, you can take control of your information life. Learning the concepts presented in this book will equip you to do new things with the pictures you take, the videos you shoot, the audio you record, and the documents you create. Instead of wasting time with an inefficient approach to computers, you can use the power of the computer to your own personal and professional benefit.

COMPUTER CONFIDENCE PAYS OFF

Have you recently applied for a job online? If so, you may have noticed all of the questions about your computer skills. Online job-search services have long lists with check boxes beside each computer skill that an employer desires. How many skills can you list?

The path to acquiring those skills begins with an understanding of basic computer concepts. How do you create a document? Once you create a document, where on the computer do you store it? Once you store the document, how do you retrieve it? After you retrieve it, how do you send the document as an attachment in an e-mail message? These are just a few of the basics that an employee in the modern workforce must know.

Transferable Skills You Can Put on Your Resume

When you dive in and take the time to learn particular skills on the computer, the job-market payoff is sometimes clear and immediate. If you are proficient in

Microsoft Office 2010®, for instance, you can put a check in the "skills" box of any online job application for all of the basic software applications within Office: Microsoft Excel® spreadsheet software, Microsoft Word® word processing software, and Microsoft PowerPoint® presentation software. If you have experience with some of the additional programs that are available in some versions of Microsoft Office, you can list proficiency in those applications, too: Microsoft Access®, Microsoft Visio®, or Microsoft Publisher®. The same is true for a long list of popular programs. What does it take to achieve proficiency? Mostly, it takes persistence and attention, as well as plenty of time working with the programs. The sooner you get busy working on your computer, the sooner you can put into practice the concepts explained in this course.

Applying This Class to Your Life Right Now

Beyond the workplace, the computer enables you to perform useful tasks in many different areas. The skills you learn in this course apply directly to your life, at work and at home. For instance, your church may need someone to make a flier to advertise a pancake breakfast. Your neighborhood association may need a newsletter to get the word out about community events. Your spouse, or a friend, may have a small business that needs to send out professional-looking invoices or correspondence. All of these tasks, and many more, are made easier with computers.

According to the U.S. Bureau of Labor Statistics' presentation *Working in the 21st Century,* 7 of the top 10 fastest-growing occupations (systems analysts, retail salespersons, cashiers, general managers and top executives, office clerks, registered nurses, and computer support specialists) require computer skills. One key use of a computer in today's marketplace is finding a job. More and more employers accept applications exclusively online. You must acquire computer skills, then, to even find most available jobs in the modern job market. The following table outlines various job skills and the software applications that aid workers in mastering them.

JOB SKILL	EXAMPLE SOFTWARE APPLICATIONS
Project management	Microsoft Project®
Word processing	Microsoft Word®
Graphics	Adobe Photoshop Microsoft Publisher® Adobe InDesign Various photo programs
Multimedia	Microsoft PowerPoint®
Spreadsheets	Microsoft Excel®
Databases	Microsoft Access® FileMaker Pro
Internet ability	Microsoft Internet Explorer® (browser) Google Chrome (browser) Mozilla Firefox (browser) Microsoft Outlook® (e-mail)
Website development	Adobe Dreamweaver Adobe Acrobat Professional

Introduction to Computing

THE POWER OF BASIC COMPUTING

The basic principle of computing is the same for every computer you encounter. A computer is a machine that receives input, processes that input, and provides an output. The computer's job is to perform processes for you.

Basic concepts and standard terms are useful across a broad range of computers, from a desktop PC to a smartphone. Knowing these terms ensures that you adapt to technological changes more easily and find help from experts more quickly. Most important, you can use computers of all kinds to do more work in less time, with less effort.

Think of a package delivery serviceperson who rings your doorbell and asks you to sign for a package. In the past, you would have signed a piece of paper. Today, you would sign a portable computer; the moment you do so, the package delivery service instantly receives a confirmation of the delivery. Similarly, a construction estimator today can use a laser device instead of a tape measure to determine a building's dimensions. A nurse can use a digital thermometer to take a patient's temperature. Because of computers, more work is done in less time, with less effort.

KEY CONCEPTS

- The Power of Basic Computing
- A Brief History of Computing
- What Is a Computer?
- Computer Hardware
- Computer Software
- Networks
- Buying a Computer

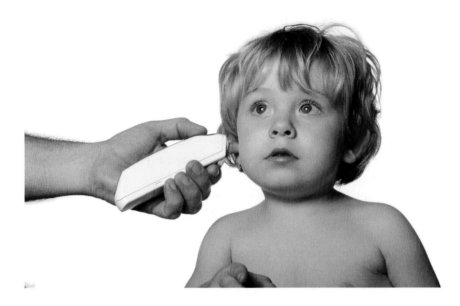

A BRIEF HISTORY OF COMPUTING

Computing machines have been around almost as long as humans have been doing math. From the abacus used in ancient China to the steam-driven contraptions designed by the nineteenth-century English inventor Charles Babbage, the goal has always been to mechanically calculate mathematical tasks faster, without human error.

The modern era of computing began in the 1940s with the creation of the ENIAC, the Electronic Numerical Integrator and Computer, at the University of Pennsylvania. The ENIAC solved computing problems with accuracy and speed never seen before. Continual advances to this technology set the stage for the microcomputer movement starting in the 1970s, culminating in the 1981 introduction of IBM's personal computer. This quickly became the dominant global standard. Soon, thousands of manufacturers were selling computers based on the IBM platform.

MS-DOS An early computer operating system for the IBM PC.

An essential component of the IBM PC was **MS-DOS®**, short for Microsoft Disk Operating System. This operating system eventually evolved into Microsoft Windows® operating system, which is currently the most widely used operating system for personal computers.

In 1984, Apple introduced the Macintosh computer, which now has a long history as the primary alternative to personal computers based on the IBM/Microsoft platform.

Today, smartphones and other small devices compete with personal computers. Continued rapid advances in miniaturization affect both the power and mobility of computers.

WHAT IS A COMPUTER?

Definition

A computer is a device that receives input, which it stores and processes, and then provides a desired output. This easy-to-understand flow—input/process/output—is at the heart of even the most advanced computers. Most computers you encounter today in the work environment are still in the personal computer category, but the landscape is changing rapidly as new, smaller devices are introduced.

Types of Personal Computers

Desktop

The original IBM PC and the first Apple Macintosh were desktop computers, which means that they were installed in a fixed location. A desktop computer, which is also sometimes called a workstation, typically includes a computer case, or chassis, along with a separate monitor, keyboard, and mouse.

Laptop

Sometimes called a notebook or a netbook, a laptop is a personal computer designed for mobile use. A laptop computer typically includes an integrated keyboard and pointing device (usually a touchpad), a fold-out screen, and a rechargeable battery.

Tablet

A rising category of personal computer is the tablet computer, which does not include a separate keyboard and mouse, relying instead on a touch screen for input. An example of a tablet computer is the Apple iPad.

Smartphones and Other Mobile Devices

With the miniaturization of technology, new mobile computing devices continually appear in the marketplace. Perhaps the most significant of these is the smartphone, a term that includes a wide range of mobile telephones that are also computers.

Platforms

Since the 1980s, two **platforms,** Microsoft Windows®-based PC and Apple Macintosh, have dominated the realm of personal computing. In personal computers, a platform is the hardware plus the operating system. In the case of the PC, the hardware is the IBM PC or clones from compatible manufacturers, and the operating system, originally MS-DOS, is now Windows. For the Apple Macintosh, the hardware and the operating system are typically Apple products.

PLATFORM The hardware and operating system of a computer.

The PC and Apple Macintosh personal computer platforms still dominate in the desktop, laptop, and tablet categories. However, smartphones are a new frontier. In recent years, many new operating systems arrived on the market. Smartphone platforms include:

- Apple iPhone
- Google Android
- RIM BlackBerry
- Palm
- Microsoft Windows Phone 7®

The number of smartphone platforms is certain to increase. Many manufacturers and software makers want to compete in the quickly growing global smartphone market.

Basic Operations

Input, Processing, Output, and Storage

As discussed, the fundamental function of all computers is the same: input/process/output. In addition, all computers include some form of data storage. To perform the processes of input/process/output and storage, a computer must have two key elements:

- **Hardware:** This is the machine itself, including computer chassis, monitor, and input devices such as mouse and keyboard. Manufacturers create hardware.
- **Software:** This is the rules and logic that the machine uses to process input, process output, and store data. Programmers create software, which includes both operating systems and applications.

HARDWARE The physical parts of a computer. This includes internal and external parts, such as the hard drive, memory, keyboard, and mouse.

SOFTWARE A program that is not a physical device that directs the computer to perform certain tasks.

COMPUTER HARDWARE

Components in General

Think of computer hardware as the physical computer itself. It includes everything you see with the power off: the computer case (chassis) and all of its contents, the monitor, the keyboard, and the mouse. Unlike software, the logic and calculations performed when the computer is on, computer hardware consists of the physical parts and pieces you can touch.

System Unit

The computer case, or chassis, is also sometimes called the system unit, the console, or simply the main computer box. It contains the guts of the computer, most of which are designed to process and store information. While the shape of the computer case may change and the platform may vary, the essential parts of a computer remain the same. When you open the case, you see a motherboard, processor (CPU), memory (RAM), and a hard disk drive.

Motherboard and Adapter Cards

The **motherboard** (or mainboard) is the large circuit board where you plug in the computer's peripherals. All computers contain a motherboard, whether they are a PC or a Mac, a desktop, or a laptop.

MOTHERBOARD The large circuit board of a computer where peripherals attach.

Motherboards come in many shapes and sizes, but all serve the central function as the mainboard for the computer. A motherboard typically includes a slot for the processor and expansion slots for adapter cards and memory.

An **adapter card** plugs into a mother-board and enables additional functions. To install an adapter card, you must open the computer case.

ADAPTER CARD A card that adds additional functions to a computer by plugging into the motherboard.

Processor (CPU)

The **processor,** or CPU, is the central processing unit of the computer. It is also sometimes called a microprocessor. This is the chip that, when plugged into the motherboard, performs the computing. Usually, the processor has at least one fan attached to dissipate heat generated by the calculations it performs. An example of a popular processor is the Intel Pentium, the heart of many millions of PCs built in the past.

PROCESSOR The computing center of a computer where all information is processed.

Hard Disk Drive

The **hard disk drive,** which is often simply called the hard drive, is where your computer permanently stores data. When your computer is off, the data remains on the hard drive. A large-capacity hard drive might hold 500 gigabytes (GB) to 1 terabyte (TB) of data.

HARD DISK DRIVE The permanent storage on a computer.

Memory (RAM)

In addition to a hard disk drive for permanent storage, a computer has **random access memory (RAM)** chips. These serve as temporary storage for data waiting to be acted on by the processor. When you shut down the computer, the data no longer resides in memory. One of the best ways to improve a computer's performance is to add memory. A typical personal computer today contains at least 1 GB of memory, with more required for newer operating systems, such as the Microsoft Windows 7® operating system.

RANDOM ACCESS MEMORY (RAM) The temporary storage on a computer.

FAQ: WHAT IS A BYTE?

When you work with computers, you will regularly hear about bytes. A **byte** is the basic unit of computer storage and memory. One byte equals approximately one character of text on a computer. Because that is not very much data, you more typically hear the term *byte* used with prefixes that describe a larger amount:

BYTE The basic measurement unit of computer storage and memory, equivalent to one character of text.

- kilobyte (KB): 1,000 bytes
- megabyte (MB): 1 million bytes (or 1,000 KB)
- gigabyte (GB): 1 billion bytes (or 1,000 MB)
- terabyte (TB): 1 trillion bytes (or 1,000 GB)

Peripherals

The computer case contains the core parts of the computer but you need devices that plug into the outside of the box to use the computer. These devices outside the box are **peripheral devices.**

Among the most familiar peripheral devices are the mouse and the keyboard, which are input devices. The most familiar output device is the **monitor** (also sometimes called a display or a screen), which you use to see your work. Other peripherals include storage devices such as a USB flash drive (thumb drive) or an external hard disk drive. Because the modern computer is so powerful and flexible, the category of peripheral devices is vast, including all the various types of devices that can be plugged into a computer case.

PERIPHERAL DEVICE Any device connected to a computer, such as a printer, monitor, keyboard, computer mouse, or WiFi antenna.

MONITOR The screen or display of a computer.

Input Devices

Any device that provides input for the computer to process is an **input device.** Examples include:

INPUT DEVICE A device that provides information for the computer to process.

- Keyboard
- Mouse or touchpad
- Touch screen
- Microphone
- Scanner
- Camera
- Game controller

The category of keyboard includes the traditional standalone keyboard attached to a desktop computer, as well as the integrated keyboard on a laptop, and, increasingly, the tiny keyboards on smartphones.

The category of **pointing device** includes the traditional mouse as well as the touchpad or pointing stick you might see on a laptop computer. The most common pointing device is the mouse, which typically includes a left button for most clicking, a right button for context-clicking (to find out what things are and what options are available), and often a scroll wheel used to move up and down a page.

POINTING DEVICE An input device that moves the computer's cursor around or is used to click to choose a function; examples include the computer's mouse and the pointing stick or touchpad on a laptop.

Output Devices

Any device that accepts output from the computer and does something with it is considered an **output device.** Examples include:

OUTPUT DEVICE A device that accepts information from a computer and does something with it such as a monitor, printer, speaker, or headphones.

- Printer
- Speakers or headphones
- Monitor or projector
- Game controller with feedback. (Yes, this is also an input device, but it is an output device too because of the feedback—typically vibration—that is output from the computer. In fact, many devices, such as touch screens and multifunction all-in-one printer/scanner machines, serve as both input and output devices.)

One essential output device is the monitor you use to view the computer's activity. The images and text you see on the monitor constitute the **graphical user interface (GUI),** which you manipulate with input devices such as a mouse and keyboard. The monitor is either a stand-alone unit, or it is integrated into the computer, as in a laptop or smartphone screen.

Another common output device is the printer, which converts data from the computer to a printed page. The two main types of printer you may encounter as a consumer or in the workplace are laser printer and inkjet printer. Most large office printers are laser printers, which make use of toner (the powdery stuff that copy

machines have long used) instead of liquid ink, typically resulting in lower per-page cost for printing. Inkjet printers are used more in the consumer realm, where color is important and the number of pages printed is typically lower. The color laser printer is now more common, making inroads into traditional inkjet territory.

A printer usually connects directly to the computer via a cable, typically a USB cable. Less common, but increasingly available, are printers with wireless connections to a computer.

Storage Devices

Again, the core functions of every computer are input, processing, and output, plus storage. So far, you have learned about input devices that send data to a computer, as well as output devices that receive data from a computer. The process function is the actual work that the computer does. It is such a big area of discussion that most topics in the rest of this book belong in the process category. This section completes the basics with a discussion of storage devices.

A **storage device** is a piece of equipment that permanently holds a computer's data, even when the computer is turned off. Storage devices include:

- Hard disk drive
- USB flash drive (thumb drive)
- Optical discs, such as CD or DVD
- Shared network storage
- Online storage (cloud storage)
- Backup tape drives

The Hard Disk Drive

The primary storage device on most personal computers is the internal hard disk drive. It is contained within the computer case and is connected directly to the motherboard with a data cable.

Today's hard disk drives store massive amounts of data, and their capacity increases constantly as manufacturers innovate to compete in the marketplace. A typical modern hard disk drive holds 100 GB to 1 TB or more of data. This equates to many thousands of documents, songs, photos, videos, and software programs.

Many computer users desire additional storage that can be moved easily to another location, away from the originating computer. One popular solution for this challenge is the external hard drive, a portable version of the computer's internal hard drive. An external hard drive is typically contained within a plastic or metal housing that protects internal components, and it connects to the computer via a data cable such as USB or FireWire.

FAQ: WHAT DO DRIVE LETTERS MEAN?

If you look at the My Computer page on a PC, you may notice that your primary hard drive is assigned the letter C:, and any additional storage devices have other drive letter assignments. If you know how these drive letter assignments work, you can more easily find the information on your various storage devices, including your hard drives, but also CD/DVD drives, USB flash drives, digital cameras, smartphones, and card readers.

When assigning drive letters, Windows follows these general rules:

- Drive letter A: is assigned to the first floppy disk drive. Because few modern computers have floppy disk drives, you rarely see drive letter A: these days.
- Drive letter B: is assigned to the second floppy disk drive.
- Drive letter C: is assigned to the first hard disk drive. This is usually where Windows is installed, along with My Documents.
- Drive letters D: and later are assigned to (1) any additional internal hard disk drives, (2) any internal CD/DVD (optical) drives, (3) any other internal storage, such as media card readers, and (4) any external storage devices, such as portable hard drives or USB flash drives. See Figure 1.1.

While each computer has its own unique setup, if you understand these general rules about drive letter assignment, you can more easily find the storage device you want, along with the information it has stored.

Name	Type	Total Size	Free Space
▲ Hard Disk Drives (3)			
Local Disk (C:)	Local Disk	73.1 GB	65.0 GB
Local Disk (D:)	Local Disk	107 GB	107 GB
Local Disk (E:)	Local Disk	117 GB	117 GB
▲ Devices with Removable Storage (2)			
Floppy Disk Drive (A:)	Floppy Disk Drive		
KINGSTON (F:)	Removable Disk	3.72 GB	2.63 GB

FIGURE 1.1

Flash Memory Storage

A fast-growing category in today's computer marketplace is flash memory storage, which can include the following:

- **USB flash drive**
- **Memory card,** such as you might find in a digital camera or smartphone
- **ExpressCard**
- **Solid state drive**

EXPRESSCARD A data storage plug-in for PCs.

SOLID STATE DRIVE A storage solution that uses electric charges to read and write data.

USB FLASH DRIVE A small data storage device, also known as a thumb drive, designed to plug into a computer's USB port. Some drives hold more than 32 GB of data.

MEMORY CARD A data storage device used in digital cameras and smartphones.

A flash memory device stores data on a computer chip in a nonvolatile manner, which means the data stays on the device even when the power is turned off.

- *USB flash drive:* Also known as a thumb drive, the USB flash drive is an increasingly common storage device, with capacities of 1 GB to 32 GB and up. Many computer users now use USB flash drives instead of CDs or DVDs to move data from place to place, because USB flash drives can be written and erased an almost unlimited number of times, and they are not as easily damaged as CDs and DVDs. They also are very compact, and are usually compatible with both PCs and Macs.
- *Memory card:* Today's digital cameras store images in the form of data, instead of on film. Digital cameras and their smartphone cousins usually have memory cards as their primary storage device. Popular memory card formats include Compact Flash (CF), Memory Stick, Micro SD, Mini SD, and Secure Digita (SD).
- *ExpressCard:* Not nearly as common as USB flash drives or memory cards, the ExpressCard is a small plug-in card for PCs that is a successor to an older technology called a PC Card.
- *Solid state drive:* The solid state drive, a relatively new technology, uses flash memory storage to replace the traditional hard drive. Initial models are quite expensive, but solid state drives have the attention of many computer users, as they have no moving parts, unlike traditional hard disk drives. Also, solid state drives typically have much faster access times for reading and writing data.

Optical Discs

One of the most common and familiar categories of storage device is the **optical disc,** which includes both CDs and DVDs. This technology is called optical because the read and write functions are based on light. When placed into an optical drive, an optical disc spins rapidly while a laser reads or writes the contents.

OPTICAL DISC A data storage device in the form of a CD or DVD. It is called optical because the reading and writing capabilities rely on light, in the form of a laser, to access or store data on a disc.

The name CD is short for compact disc. The name DVD is short for digital versatile disc or digital video disc. A typical blank CD stores up to 700 MB of data, and a typical blank DVD stores up to 4.7 GB of data. Some less common, and more expensive, optical discs store more data. For instance, the relatively new Blu-Ray format enables storage of 25 GB or more on a single disc.

Optical discs replaced many previous storage media because of their low cost and relatively large amount of data they store. In recent years, however, more and more computer users opt for the reliability, ease of use, and growing storage capacity of USB flash drives instead of optical discs. Still, optical discs remain immensely popular for both home and workplace computer users.

When using optical discs, it is important to be aware of the many variations in optical drives and optical discs. For instance, a very old computer might have a CD reader but not a CD burner, which writes data to the disc. On the other hand, a new computer is much more likely to have an optical drive that reads and writes both CDs and DVDs.

To write data to a CD or DVD, your computer must have a CD or DVD burner and software that enables CD or DVD burning.

Optical drives come in a wide variety of shapes and sizes, depending on the computer or other device. The most common optical drive type is found in a typical desktop computer, where you press a button and a tray slides out. With this type of optical drive, you place the CD or DVD into the tray, shiny side down. Some optical drives, however, do not have a slide-out tray; instead, they have a slot for inserting the CD or DVD. It is critical with these types of optical drives that you insert the CD or DVD with the correct orientation; otherwise the drive cannot read the data from the shiny side of the disc.

Web-Based Cloud Storage

As Internet connections increase in speed, online storage becomes more popular. With this option, data is stored on a server in a data center instead of on your personal computer. This type of storage is certain to grow in coming years, especially as more and more people use mobile devices that are more easily lost; in these cases, online data storage can avert catastrophic data loss.

The marketplace is not yet settled on a single term for this type of storage. It is often referred to as cloud storage, with the cloud consisting of servers on the Internet. When you need to store your data, you connect to the Internet and send data to the cloud. When you need to get your data, you connect to the Internet and retrieve data from the cloud.

An increasing number of free and inexpensive cloud storage options are available. Examples include:

- SkyDrive, Dropbox, and other online data storage services
- Flickr, SmugMug, PicasaWeb, and other online photo storage services
- Carbonite, IDrive, Mozy, and other online data-backup services
- Google Docs (see Figure 1.2), Microsoft Office Live®, Zoho, and other online document creation and storage services

If you have a web-based e-mail account on a service such as Hotmail, Yahoo!, or Gmail, all of your e-mail messages are stored in the cloud. Even the simple act of e-mailing a document to your account so that it is accessible from anywhere with an Internet connection is a form of cloud storage.

FIGURE 1.2

Backing Up Storage Devices

A key task for sophisticated computer users is ensuring that data does not reside in just one location, where an accident can destroy it all. In response to this need, there are now many backup solutions. Options include online backup services, external hard drives, copying data to DVDs and storing them offsite, copying data to tape drives, or installing multiple internal hard disk drives so that if one fails, the others have a copy of the data.

Communications Devices

Our final category of computer hardware is communications devices. These enable a computer to connect to the Internet. No matter which company you use for your Internet service provider, your connection is made possible by a physical device.

Most consumers and small businesses purchase Internet access from their local telephone company or their local cable company. Larger organizations often purchase Internet access from specialty companies that provide massive data transfer capacity. Internet service from a telephone company is usually provided with a technology called **DSL,** the acronym for a digital subscriber line. This service uses the existing traditional phone line, with a DSL modem placed between the phone line and the computer, to carry Internet data. Internet service from a cable company is usually delivered over the same coaxial cable that provides a TV signal, with a cable modem placed between the coaxial cable and the computer.

Smartphones that use the Internet usually have a two-pronged approach to make a connection. If a local wireless network with a fast Internet connection (often called a **WiFi** hotspot) is available, most smartphones use it. If no wireless network is available, a smartphone uses the cellular network to connect; this is often significantly more expensive than the WiFi option.

> **DIGITAL SUBSCRIBER LINE (DSL)** A service providing users Internet access through a phone line or television cable with either a DSL modem or cable modem.
>
> **WIFI (WIRELESS FIDELITY)** A trademark of the nonprofit Wi-Fi Alliance. The term has come to define the ability of certain devices such as computers, multimedia players, and networking devices to connect to the Internet via a wireless interface.

INTERACTION DIVERSITY: GETTING COMFORTABLE—ERGONOMIC ADJUSTMENTS FOR YOUR CONTINUING HEALTH

It is important to arrange your computing workspace so that your body aligns in a comfortable position. This is not just a matter of health and well-being; a person's productivity is significantly diminished by the aches and fatigue that result from a poorly positioned computing setup.

Two crucial components of workspace design are keyboard/mouse height and monitor position. Because body types and sizes vary, it is important that computing furniture allows for adjustments that reduce hand and arm strain while typing and using a mouse. Also, beware of eyestrain from looking at an improperly positioned monitor. For instance, screen glare from a window can cause eyestrain over the course of an entire workday. It is the responsibility of both the individual and the organization to ensure that the configuration of the computing workspace is proper.

COMPUTER SOFTWARE

Definition

Generally speaking, software consists of the rules and logic a computer uses to process input, process output, and store data. Programmers create software, which includes both operating systems and applications, or programs. Unlike computer hardware, which you can touch, software consists of processes and data in digital form.

User Interfaces

When you turn on a computer and view the images and text on the monitor, you see the user interface, sometimes referred to as the graphical user interface (GUI). Using a mouse and keyboard, you interact with the user interface's elements to perform tasks on the computer.

Different computer platforms have their own user interfaces. When you use a PC, the user interface is significantly different from that of an Apple Mac.

Similarly, different applications have their own user interfaces. When you use Microsoft Excel® spreadsheet software to work on a spreadsheet, the user interface is significantly different from that of Intuit Quickbooks, an accounting program.

Installing Software

Preinstalled

Although almost all new computers ship with a great deal of software already on them, at some point it is typically necessary to install additional applications. In fact, the ability of the personal computer to run many different types of software applications is the source of its great power to do many kinds of work.

Installing and Uninstalling

To install software on a computer, you first must transfer, or load, the software program into the computer. This typically occurs in one of two ways:

- Installing from CD or DVD
- Downloading from the Internet and installing (see Figure 1.3)

With today's faster Internet speeds, more and more companies distribute software via the Internet instead of on CD or DVD. No matter which method you use, both accomplish the same result.

FAQ: WHAT IS A DOWNLOAD?

When you transfer a file from the Internet to your computer, you are completing a **download**. A download is the opposite of an upload, in which you transfer a file from your computer to the Internet. How do you remember which is up and which is down? One helpful tip is to remember the idea of the Internet as a cloud. When you receive data from the cloud, you are completing a download. When you send data to the cloud, you are completing an upload.

DOWNLOAD The transfer of a file from the Internet to your computer.

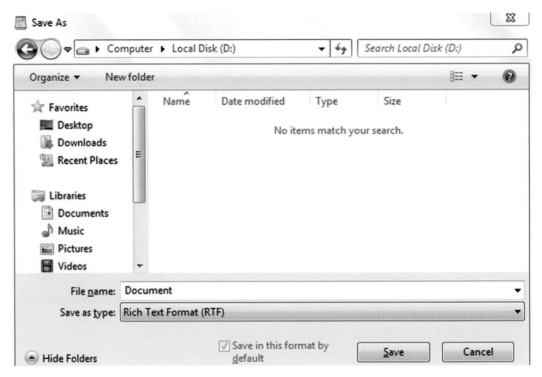

FIGURE 1.3

Access and Use Web Applications

In addition to software programs that run on your personal computer, an increasing number of programs also run on the web. To use such a program, you

normally log on with a user name and password to access the program, which runs on a **server** instead of on your local machine. Some popular free web applications are Facebook, Twitter, and webmail programs such as Hotmail or Gmail. With these web applications, the data resides on the server and not on your own computer. You must have an Internet connection to access the data.

SERVER The host computer that delivers web pages and other applications to your browser.

Software Upgrades

Software developers constantly fine-tune and rebuild their applications. When their new and improved applications are ready, they are released as a **software upgrade.** Upgrades can cost additional money but many software upgrades—especially minor ones—are released at no cost. They keep the applications working properly or add new features that lead to customer satisfaction.

SOFTWARE UPGRADE A change in an application or new feature added to a software program that a developer releases, usually on the Internet, for users to add.

In the past, before fast Internet connections were common, upgrading software was a major endeavor for the software company and for the computer user. It required the mailing of CDs, which were used to install application updates. Because of this expense, software makers often saved up their upgrades until several were ready, then they put them on one CD. Now, software upgrades usually arrive via the Internet, and companies release them much more frequently than in the past.

Software Licensing

The creation of software applications is a major business for many companies. They invest millions and often billions of dollars in their software, which is considered intellectual property, similar to a book, a song, or a patented invention. To protect their software from being used without the creators receiving compensation, software makers often require the purchase of a software license to use their programs. This license is typically granted in the form of an **activation key,** which is usually a unique combination of numbers and letters specific to a single purchaser. When you install such software, you are required to enter the activation key to use the program.

ACTIVATION KEY A combination of letters and numbers a user must enter before using software. These access codes serve as an intellectual property protection for the software developer, granting a license to the user and preventing multiple downloads.

FAQ: WHAT ARE THE CONSEQUENCES OF SOFTWARE PIRACY AND ILLEGAL DOWNLOADING?

Although it might seem easy and inconsequential at the time, software piracy—more formally known as copyright infringement—can have expensive and unpleasant effects on individuals and businesses that are caught in this trap. Both software and music are intellectual property and U.S. and other copyright laws protect them.

Many online file-sharing services make it simple to find and download software and songs you do not own. (Note: These services also make it simple to download files infected with viruses, worms, and malware that can infect your computer.) It is also simple for anyone who knows about such downloads to report the activity to organizations that make it their business to track down and prosecute those who engage in software piracy and illegal downloading. Many of these organizations offer large rewards to individuals who report copyright infringement cases. Individuals who engage in software piracy and illegal downloading can be sued and forced by the court to pay hefty damage awards.

Types of Software

Software comes in three primary categories:

- System software
- Utility programs
- Application software

System Software

System software includes all software that does the job of operating the computer hardware. Example tasks of system software include transferring data between hardware components such as the processor and RAM, as well as preparing output to display on the computer's monitor. System software takes care of these tasks once and for all, making it possible for other types of software to run without having to start over from scratch.

The most well-known system software is the **operating system.** The most common operating system for personal computers is Microsoft Windows, followed by Apple Macintosh OS, which has a much smaller

SYSTEM SOFTWARE Software that operates a computer hardware's most common tasks such as transferring data between components or sending data to display on the computer's monitor.

OPERATING SYSTEM The system software provided to a computer user by the computer manufacturer. Popular operating systems include Microsoft Windows and the Apple Macintosh's OS.

market share. Although other operating systems do exist, they are primarily used to operate servers and not personal computers.

Figure 1.4 shows some examples of popular operating systems from recent years.

OPERATING SYSTEM	PRIMARILY USED BY
Microsoft Windows 7®	Consumers and business users
Microsoft Windows Vista®	Consumers and business users
Microsoft Windows XP®	Consumers and business users
Microsoft Windows NT®	No longer in common use
Mac OS X	Consumers and business users
Mac OS 9	No longer in common use
Linux	Servers (as opposed to personal computers)
Unix	Large corporations and educational institutions

FIGURE 1.4 **Operating Systems**

Utility Programs

A **utility program** is software whose purpose is to maintain, analyze, and configure a computer for optimum performance. For example, a computer's antivirus program is a utility, and so is a program that performs data backup.

There is some gray area between system software and utility programs, as system software makers are constantly offering new utilities as part of their system software.

UTILITY PROGRAM Computer software that maintains the system for maximum performance. Examples of utility programs are a computer's antivirus program or the regular data backup.

INTERACTION DIVERSITY: SETTING SCREEN RESOLUTION

Did you know your computer is almost infinitely adjustable to meet your personal preferences? A great example of this is setting the screen resolution so that text on your monitor is easy for you to read. If you have great eyesight and want to pack a lot of information on the screen, you might set a higher screen resolution that results in smaller text. If you prefer larger text, you can set screen resolution to permanently display fonts and images at a larger size.

On most PCs, you can begin the process of setting screen resolution by right-clicking on the desktop and selecting *Properties* or *Screen resolution*. By experimenting with the different screen resolutions that work with your monitor, you can optimize your computing experience.

Application Software

Application software consists of programs designed to help you do tasks on the computer. An application is also called a program, or simply an app. You spend most of your time on a computer using application software. Although apps have been around for

APPLICATION SOFTWARE These computer programs are designed to help users complete tasks on their computers or smartphones.

years on computers, it is only relatively recently that cellular phones have become powerful enough computers to run applications installed by the user.

The functions of applications are as wide-ranging as the various fields of human endeavor. There are applications for everything from tracking expenses to guiding missiles to managing music on your computer or phone. See Figure 1.5.

Entertainment

Among the more popular applications for computers are entertainment programs. Examples include iTunes or Microsoft Windows Media® Player for music or SimCity or World of Warcraft for games. Developers create new applications every day, and the list of available applications is almost infinite.

SOFTWARE SUITES AND PRODUCTIVITY SOFTWARE

Because certain tasks are common to almost all computer users, especially those who work in an office environment, software makers offer software suites that include more than one program. The most well-known example of this is Microsoft Office 2010®, but others, such as OpenOffice and Google Docs, are available for free and compete with Microsoft Office. Another example of an office suite is Microsoft Works®, a collection of programs for users who do not need all the features of Microsoft Office.

Regardless of the maker, an office suite typically includes applications that perform three fundamental office functions: word processing, spreadsheets, and presentations. A suite will often include other applications, too, such as a database, a contact manager, and an e-mail program.

Word processing applications enable you to create written documents such as letters, reports, brochures, resumes, signs—in short, anything that features words on a page. The most widely known word processor is Microsoft Word® word processing software.

Spreadsheet applications enable you to create a grid with rows and columns of information. When placed in a spreadsheet, information becomes usable in many different ways. For instance, an information technology professional might create a maintenance list of all the company's computers. When this information is placed in a spreadsheet, it can be sorted and viewed as desired. The most widely known spreadsheet program is Microsoft Excel® spreadsheet software.

Presentation applications enable you to create shows for viewing by an audience. In the past, this information was presented with devices that would shine light through the media in order to display it. For instance, many instructors used overhead projectors, which involved physically placing a new sheet on the projector for each page to display. Similarly, photo presentations were often shown with slide projectors. In this case, each picture was on a separate slide in a rotating carousel. Now, however, most presentations are created using a computer. The most widely known presentation program is Microsoft PowerPoint® presentation software.

Database applications enable more sophisticated storage of large amounts of information. Once information is added to a database, you can sort, analyze, and manipulate it in complex ways. Examples of popular database programs are Microsoft Access® and FileMaker Pro.

WORD PROCESSING A computer program that allows a user to create documents with text. One example is Microsoft Word.

SPREADSHEET APPLICATION A computer program that allows a user to create worksheets with data in rows and columns to sort and manipulate as needed. One example is Microsoft Excel.

PRESENTATION APPLICATION A computer program that allows users to create a show to display for an audience with the ability to include media. One example is Microsoft PowerPoint.

DATABASE APPLICATION A computer program that allows users to enter large amounts of data for complex record keeping, sorting, and manipulating as needed.

Graphics

The personal computer enables consumers to perform many functions that once were the exclusive province of specialized professionals. A good example of this trend is the many graphics programs that are available at reasonable cost, or even free. These include applications to organize image collections; create brochures, posters, or fliers; or draw illustrations. Examples of graphics programs include the popular but expensive Adobe Photoshop, Microsoft Publisher®, and Picasa.

NAME	FUNCTION
Microsoft Word®	Word processing
Adobe Reader	Viewing pages with the layout set in place, similar to a printed document
Microsoft Excel®	Spreadsheet
Microsoft Outlook®	E-mail
Norton Antivirus	Protection from viruses, malware
Microsoft PowerPoint®	Presentations
Mozilla Firefox	Web browser
Microsoft Internet Explorer®	Web browser
Apple iTunes	Music library

FIGURE 1.5 **Examples of Popular Applications**

NETWORKS

When two or more computers are connected, the result is a **network.** There are many types of networks. The biggest network of all, which connects networks together worldwide, is the Internet. Once a network is established, it connects additional devices beyond just computers. For instance, a network printer or scanner can serve all computers on a network.

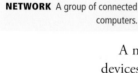
NETWORK A group of connected computers.

A network serves many functions that amplify the power of the computers and devices connected to it. For instance, a server on a network can hold large file libraries that are accessible to all the computers connected in that network. Even more useful, that same server can be set up so that only certain users have access to some files. In large organizations, it is common for one person to access information on many different servers attached to the network.

The network also allows people to access information from remote locations. When you use your home computer to access files at your organization's workplace, you are typically using the Internet to access your workplace's network.

Speaking of the Internet, one of the current primary uses for networking is sharing a single Internet connection among several computers. When a network exists, all of the computers and devices connected to it are easily able to access the Internet using a single device. In most small offices and home offices, this device is a router with one jack plugged into an Internet connection and several additional jacks (usually four or eight) to plug in the various computers and devices on the network. The network can also include wireless connections, also managed by the router. The router divides your Internet connection among the various computers so they have the ability to be online at the same time.

In the days before the Internet was so widely available, networking was the province of large or sophisticated organizations. A computer you bought at the store did not come with any built-in networking capacity as almost all computers do today. Instead, to acquire networking capabilities a computer needed a network card, a device installed by opening the computer case, physically installing the card, and adjusting the computer's settings to ensure the card worked properly. It is now hard to find any computer—whether it is a desktop unit or portable device—that does not have networking capabilities as one of its basic functions.

Types of Networks

In your career and in your personal computing life, you will encounter several different types of networks. Three of the most common types are local area networks, wireless local area networks, and wide area networks.

- The smallest network is a **personal area network,** a PAN, which is the connection formed by all the devices in close proximity to an individual. They may be wired or wireless, consisting of any device from a desktop computer, laptop computer, personal digital assistants, Bluetooth devices, or any other device connected to a network.

- A **local area network,** or LAN, connects computers and devices in a small geographic area. If you have two or more computers connected in your office or home, you most likely have a LAN. The LAN is the most common type of network in the world. You can use a LAN to share not only printers and Internet connections, but to connect computers of different types—for instance, PCs and Macs.

PERSONAL AREA NETWORK (PAN) A very small space that contains all the connected devices in proximity to an individual.

LOCAL AREA NETWORK (LAN) A small group of connected computers.

- A **wireless local area network,** or WLAN, connects computers and devices via a wireless distribution method, typically a radio signal such as those found at a WiFi hotspot.

WIRELESS LOCAL AREA NETWORK (WLAN) A group of connected computers with access to a signal over radio waves, such as WiFi.

- A **wide area network,** or WAN, covers a larger geographic area than a local area network. In fact, a WAN typically connects many local area networks. The Internet can be considered the world's largest WAN. If you look at the blinking lights on the modem that connects your computer to the Internet, often the light indicating an active Internet connection is labeled WAN. In the past, before widespread usage of the Internet, WANs were far more common. A company would, for instance, use a WAN to connect a LAN in its headquarters city with a LAN in another city where it had an office. The connection from city to city was often accomplished using a very expensive dedicated high-speed telephone line. Similarly, a WAN sometimes connects separate buildings on an academic or corporate campus, with each building having its own LAN. Many of these arrangements are no longer in use, as readily available Internet connections make it possible to spend much less money to get the same result—multiple LANs all connected and working together, regardless of distance.

WIDE AREA NETWORK (WAN) A large, often global group of connected computers.

METROPOLITAN AREA NETWORK (MAN) A large group of connected LANs that connect users in a geographical area, such as a city or campus.

- A **metropolitan area network,** or MAN, is a network able to connect a number of LANs to span a large group of buildings, such as a college campus, or a larger metropolitan area.

FAQ: WHAT SHOULD I CONSIDER WHEN BUYING A COMPUTER?

Buying a new computer is an exciting adventure, but it can also be intimidating. There is much to consider. Do you intend to take the computer with you, or will it always reside in the same fixed location? What primary tasks will you perform with the computer? What devices will you attach to the computer? What if you have to service the computer? Will more than one person use the computer? Will you need to upgrade the computer in the future?

If this is your very first computer purchase, the questions must also include those about the various peripherals you need. How will you connect to the Internet? Do you plan to print? If so, is it important to print in color? Will you accumulate a large collection of songs, videos, or images? How will you back up all of this data so that a catastrophic loss does not occur? Perhaps the most important question to be answered is this: What is your budget?

If you are not comfortable answering all of these questions on your own, you can hire a computer consultant to help you shop for the appropriate equipment and set it up for you. It is very useful to have a seasoned veteran help you start. Many computer users accustomed to full-fledged IT support in their workplaces can similarly benefit from an IT specialist in their home office or small business office. This specialist continues as a resource when the inevitable problems arise.

BUYING A COMPUTER

Desktop versus Portable?

Should you purchase a traditional desktop, or workstation, computer? Or should you follow the trend toward increasing mobility of computing devices? In the past, laptop computers were substantially more expensive than desktop computers because of the expense of miniaturization. Now, however, laptop computers are so common that there is little price difference.

Today's newest entrant in the portable computer category is the tablet computer with a portable touch screen. The Apple iPad is the best-known device in this category. Other manufacturers will release sophisticated new competitors in the tablet category. Choices for tablet computers will increase over the next few years.

Consider two key factors when you make the desktop vs. portable decision. First: Will you really, actually take your computer anywhere other than its main location? If not, there is no reason to incur even a little additional expense to purchase a computer with miniaturized components. Second: Do you intend to upgrade your computer much in the future? If so, a desktop computer typically offers much greater expandability, at lower cost.

In general, the trend is toward more portability. If there is a chance at all that you might need to take your computing power on the road, buy a portable computer. Portable computers are now very close to matching the performance of their desktop counterparts.

What About Software?

Often overlooked in the computer purchasing process is the importance of the software you need on your new computer. In many cases, the computer itself is a minor cost compared to the expense of installed software. Software considerations include: Which operating system runs on the computer? Which office programs, if any, do you need? If you work with Microsoft Word documents and Microsoft Excel spreadsheets, for instance, it might make sense to purchase Microsoft Office.

Consider these other software applications: antivirus, e-mail, photo editing, video editing, accounting, and tax programs. Your mix of software should serve you. Always include software purchase expenses in your planning.

Additionally, if your computer use is specialized—if, for example, you edit video—you may need a more powerful processor, more memory, and more storage than the average user. Discuss your computing needs with someone who can help you build your new machine for its intended use.

The Basics

After you answer the desktop/portable and software questions, the basics of your computer purchase narrow to a few key questions:

- Mac or PC?
- What size hard drive?
- How powerful of a processor?
- How much memory?
- Should there be one or more CD/DVD (optical) drives?

Where and How to Purchase?

Many different types of stores sell computers and software. Where should you buy your new computer? Big-box retailers often have a wide selection and a service department. Online retailers usually have a much wider selection and aggressive pricing, but service is often problematic. Smaller specialty stores or consultants usually do not have a large inventory, but they offer personal attention, expertise, and flexibility that their bigger competitors sometimes cannot.

The warranty decision is another part of the purchase process. Typically, the basic warranty on a computer is a year, with an option to extend the term for additional cost. Other warranty options include various levels of service, ranging from ship-in to same-day on-site service.

What Size Laptop Computer?

If you decide to go the portable route and choose a laptop computer, what size computer should you buy? Remember you must carry this device, most likely in a case of some kind. How heavy is the computer? Pick it up and imagine carrying it for hours in a city or through an airport. How large is the computer? Do you have room left in your carrying case for anything else? A large screen is desirable, but not if it makes the laptop computer too difficult to physically manage.

SUMMARY

Today's personal computers provide unprecedented power to accomplish tasks that once were the exclusive province of highly specialized professionals. In one area after another—desktop publishing, video editing, data analysis, and on and on—the barriers are gone. The computer is a powerful, universal tool available to almost everyone.

Alongside this power comes complexity, and with complexity, the need to understand how a computer works. If you take time to master the basics, as explained in this chapter and throughout the remainder of this textbook, you will be more prepared for success than someone who did not make the effort to comprehend these essential modern-day concepts.

Even the most sophisticated computer users often marvel at how much there is to learn in the realm of computing. Many times, an expert user learns a new way to perform a simple everyday task while looking over the shoulder of another user—even a user with very little experience. Because a computer allows individuals to accomplish so many tasks in so many different ways, the learning process is literally endless. If you strive to be a successful computer user, have a desire for lifelong learning. You will encounter occasional frustrations while learning the initial concepts of computing, but there is much joy in discovery.

It is important to remember at all times that the computer is a tool for you. What do you want to do today? With the power of computing behind you, you can probably do it if you are determined and resourceful enough.

KEY TERMS

- activation key
- adapter card
- application software
- byte
- database application
- digital subscriber line (DSL)
- download
- ExpressCard
- graphical user interface (GUI)
- hard disk drive
- hardware
- input device
- local area network (LAN)
- memory card
- metropolitan area network (MAN)
- monitor
- motherboard
- MS-DOS
- network
- operating system
- optical disc
- output device
- peripheral device
- personal area network (PAN)
- platform
- pointing device
- presentation application
- processor
- random access memory (RAM)
- server
- software
- software upgrade
- solid state drive
- spreadsheet application
- storage device
- system software
- USB flash drive
- utility program
- wide area network (WAN)
- WiFi (wireless fidelity)
- wireless local area network (WLAN)
- word processing

THE POWER OF THE INTERNET

The **Internet** has revolutionized much of modern life. Like the invention of the printing press, television, or the telephone, the Internet has made a fundamental difference in how we communicate, socialize, work, and spend our time and money. Virtually all business careers require the ability to use the Internet for accurate research and efficient communication. Education is affected as books and journals move online, and as electronic learning becomes commonplace. As a result, new job areas related to Internet marketing, design, and development continue to appear.

INTERNET The Internet is a digital network of computers spanning the globe.

KEY CONCEPTS

- The Power of the Internet

- A Brief History of the Internet and the World Wide Web

- Accessing the Internet

- The World Wide Web

- Web. 2.0

- Web Research

- Internet Issues

Entertainment

Since before written language was invented, the human race has continuously searched for ways to entertain and be entertained. Over time, entertainment evolved from a simple oral tradition—storytelling—to theater, books, and music. With advancements in technology, our options expanded to radio, television, and movies. Today, we access much of our entertainment through the Internet with a click of a button or the tap of a screen. We are now able to access multimedia in many forms through the Internet. The ability to download and read books online, stream or download music, and watch movies and television shows on demand allows us access to entertainment whenever we want it.

Electronic Commerce

In addition to revolutionizing entertainment, the Internet also brought about electronic commerce, or **e-commerce**). A recent study found that e-commerce sales will continue to grow 10 percent annually through 2014 and will represent 8 percent of all retail sales by then. Today, almost every business needs some sort of online presence to stay viable. Many businesses use the Internet to drive customers to their bricks-and-mortar store or allow them to purchase products online. Increasingly, many businesses exist only online.

E-COMMERCE The buying and selling of goods online.

Electronic Communication

The Internet has also transformed communication. **E-mail** (electronic mail) is a way of transmitting written messages in digital form. Today, it is a key tool in the personal and work lives of most people in industrialized nations. **Social networks** are becoming more prevalent as people conduct more and more of their personal and professional lives online. Popular social networking websites include Facebook, Myspace, and a business-centered site, LinkedIn. **New media** is also flourishing, as music, films, newspapers, and books move into online digital formats.

E-MAIL Electronic mail.

SOCIAL NETWORK An online community.

NEW MEDIA Content not traditionally delivered in digital form that is now found online, such as music, movies, newspapers, or books.

Research and Problem Solving

Scholars and academics, who were among the Internet's first champions, realized early on the power represented by this new technology for research and problem solving across all disciplines. Of course, performing research on the Internet has its dangers, as the Internet is a public forum. Literally anyone with Internet access can publish information to the Internet, and thus there is no guarantee of the accuracy of the content found online.

Therefore, it is important when performing research on the Internet to choose sources carefully. When researching information online, it is best to trust only sites that have trusted print counterparts (e.g., the *New York Times,* the *Wall Street Journal, Encyclopedia Britannica,* and so on), sites hosted by universities (i.e., any site with an address ending in .edu), or sites hosted by the government (i.e., any site with an address ending in .gov).

Another excellent resource is your local public library's website. Many public libraries offer extensive access to online archives of digital versions of published journals, magazines, and books—all from the convenience of your home or office computer.

A BRIEF HISTORY OF THE INTERNET AND WORLD WIDE WEB

Who invented the Internet? A U.S. Defense Department project called the **Advanced Research Projects Agency Network (ARPANET)** was developed in the late 1960s to provide a secure and stable communications system in case of war. ARPANET was used primarily by the U.S. military, scientists, and academics.

In the 1970s, the Internet began to open up to the civilian world. A first e-mail system was established, along with newsgroups, mailing lists, and bulletin board services (thus providing a glimpse of how the Internet could transform communication). **Domain names** came along a decade later. By the early 1990s, the general public had access to the World Wide Web through Mosaic, the first browser. At that time, there were only a handful of web pages, and the Internet looked nothing like it does today. (Contrary to popular usage, "World Wide Web" and "Internet" are not interchangeable terms—this will be covered in more detail later in the chapter.)

ADVANCED RESEARCH PROJECTS AGENCY NETWORK (ARPANET) The first network communications system.

DOMAIN NAME The words or numbers, known as IP addresses, that identify a website.

WEB 2.0 The evolution of the Internet from a place to consume information to a place to participate in content creation such as social networks, blogs, and wikis.

Development continued throughout the 1990s, with the introduction of e-commerce and the proliferation of a wide variety of websites. After 2000, social networking and **Web 2.0** became touchstones for a new generation of Internet users. Technology that began as a link between a handful of university computers now spans the globe.

ACCESSING THE INTERNET

In its simplest terms, the Internet is a series of **networks.** When your computer accesses the Internet, it becomes part of that larger network. Before you can use the Internet, however, you must be able to access it by connecting to a network, usually through a **modem.**

There are two kinds of networks: **local area networks (LANs)** and **wide area networks (WANs).** LANs are small networks of computers, such as the computers linked together in a home or office. WANs are large groups of networked computers that can span across multiple locations—and even across the globe.

NETWORK A group of connected computers.

MODEM A hardware device that allows users to connect to a network.

ONLINE SERVICE PROVIDER (OSP) A company that sells Internet connectivity and services such as e-mail, news feeds, and proprietary content to individuals. Users can access the Internet through the OSP's browser or another provider of their choice.

LOCAL AREA NETWORK (LAN) A small group of connected computers.

WIDE AREA NETWORK (WAN) A large, often global group of connected computers.

INTERNET SERVICE PROVIDER (ISP) A company that sells Internet connectivity to individuals.

When the Internet became available to the general public in the 1980s, technology companies realized that they could sell connection services. A new marketplace was born, selling ways for users to connect to the Internet. Today, these providers include **Internet service providers (ISPs), online service providers (OSPs),** and **wireless Internet service providers.**

WIRELESS INTERNET SERVICE PROVIDER A company that provides Internet connectivity through radio waves.

Internet Service Providers

An ISP is a company that sells Internet connectivity to private individuals, usually requiring a monthly fee. Some ISPs offer e-mail accounts, websites, and home pages. Each ISP can connect to all other ISPs as part of the Internet. Companies offering ISP services include such providers as EarthLink, cable television companies, and telephone companies. ISPs offer either **dial-up service**, which can be quite slow, or **broadband service**, which is any service faster than dial-up service. There is a wide range of speeds available for broadband service.

> **DIAL-UP SERVICE** Slow Internet service, defined as 56 kilobits per second or slower. Dial-up service also ties up the existing land-based phone line in a home or office.

> **BROADBAND SERVICE** Internet service that ranges from 64 kilobits per second to 4.0 megabits per second.

Online Service Providers

OSPs offer the same connection to the Internet as ISPs, but they also provide a wide range of web services, including e-mail, news, and a large amount of proprietary content. OSPs work in a slightly different way than ISPs. Users can access the Internet either through the OSP's proprietary browser or through another browser. You still see the same websites you see when using an ISP—you just access them in a different way. Examples of OSPs include MSN® (Microsoft) and AOL (formerly known as America Online).

> **WIFI** The ability of certain devices such as computers, multimedia players, and networking devices to connect to the Internet via a wireless interface.

Wireless Internet Service

Wireless Internet service is a third option for connecting to the Internet. Wireless (also known as **WiFi** or wireless fidelity) operates on radio waves.

This is particularly useful in rural areas, where it can be challenging for ISPs or OSPs to offer service because of the high cost of laying physical wires or cables.

A device called a **WiFi access point** provides a signal that carries across a certain distance. Anyone with a wireless device, such as a laptop computer or WiFi-enabled smartphone, can then access the Internet. Companies that offer such services include Verizon, Sprint, and T-Mobile. Wireless is available in many businesses and other establishments (such as coffee shops and libraries) as a way of attracting customers. It is the technology of choice in our increasingly mobile society.

THE WORLD WIDE WEB

The terms Internet and **World Wide Web**, also known as the "web," are often used interchangeably, but they do not mean the same thing. The Internet is the backbone of **hardware** and software that allows the applications of the web (e-mail, web browsers, web pages, and social networks) to work. Imagine a drinking glass on a tray: the web is the glass, and the Internet is the tray supporting the glass.

Tim Berners-Lee, a British scientist working for the European Organization for Nuclear Research (CERN), developed the web. In 1989, he proposed using the Internet as a repository for linked documents that could be accessed by researchers through a browser. Users could obtain any document they wanted—whenever they wanted it.

Berners-Lee used a language called hypertext to connect web pages to one another. Hypertext allows the user to move from one page to another; to do this, users click a hypertext link and the link takes them to the next page. (Embedded in text, these links usually appear in blue. On a web page, they often appear as buttons or tabs.) Each web page is created using a markup language called **hypertext markup language (HTML).** This language tells the browser to display graphics, text, and anything else that appears on the page.

Web Pages and Sites

A website is a group of web pages. The **home page,** the first page of the group, usually describes the site's purpose and provides a structure for navigating through the site. There is no limit to the number of pages in a website, and there are websites about every conceivable subject.

HOME PAGE The first page in a group of pages on a website that describes the site's purpose and provides the navigational structure for moving through the website.

Web Servers

Web pages and websites live on a computer known as a **server** (or host). The Internet is set up in a client-server model, which means that the browser on your computer (the client) asks for something (say, a web page or other application) and another computer (the server) delivers it. Once the page is delivered to the browser, the connection is broken between the client and the server.

SERVER The host computer that delivers web pages and other applications to your browser.

Saving data or information to your computer from a website is called "downloading." For example, you might download a new game on your computer or a new system that will help your computer work more efficiently.

Web Browsers

To access websites on the Internet, you must use **software** called a **web browser.** The browser brings up the web page so that the user can see it. The first browser released to the public was Mosaic, in 1993. Throughout the 1990s, many more companies released browsers into what is now a very competitive marketplace.

SOFTWARE A program that is not a physical device that directs the computer to perform certain tasks.

WEB BROWSER The software used to access websites on the Internet.

By 1995, Microsoft had developed its own browser, Internet Explorer®, and had made a business decision to package it with the Microsoft Windows® operating system. The original Mosaic, which had then evolved into a product called Netscape Navigator, rapidly lost market share to Internet Explorer and the **open source** browser Mozilla Firefox. In the 2000s, the search engine company Google also released a browser called Chrome. Figure 2.1 provides a list of pros and cons of the Internet Explorer, Firefox, and Chrome browsers.

OPEN SOURCE Computer code that is free and available for anyone to use.

Standards for Use

Each browser has a home page with **Back** and **Forward** buttons for navigation within a website. Browsers also allow you to **bookmark** frequently visited sites so that typing the web address each time you want to visit it is unnecessary. When you

BOOKMARK An electronic marker for a website.

	MOZILLA FIREFOX 3.1 OR HIGHER	GOOGLE CHROME 12 OR HIGHER	INTERNET EXPLORER 8 OR HIGHER
Pros	• Fast, well organized, and intuitive • Very customizable (over 6,000 options) • Uses fewer system resources than other browsers • Excellent tabs feature (multiple windows can be open at once) • Offers sticky notes option, which allows users to make notes on a web page that remain when the user returns; good for students and researchers (available as an add-on) • Protects against viruses, spyware, malware, phishing, and pop-ups	• Fast, simple interface with innovative design • Many applications available • Private browsing option • Best crash protection of the major browsers • Excellent tab features • Protects against viruses, spyware, malware, and phishing	• Uncluttered interface • Excellent tabs feature (each tab operates independently, so that if there is a crash, only that tab crashes) • Private browsing option • Many applications available • Protects against viruses, spyware, malware, phishing, and pop-ups • Add-ons available for security • Excellent parental controls
Cons	• The 6,000 options available as add-ons might be confusing for users • If one tab crashes, they all crash • Other features require add-ons	• No ad blocking as a standard feature (available as an add-on) • Minimal options available • Uses a lot of system resources	• Slow installation and operation • Uses a lot of memory and system resources • Slower than Firefox and Chrome
Tools	• Web Search • Downloads • Add-ons • Error Console • Page Info • Start Private Browsing • Clear Recent History • Options	• Always Show Bookmarks bar • Extensions • Task Manager • Clear Browsing Data • Encoding • View Source • Developer Tools • JavaScript Console	• Delete Browsing History • InPrivate Browsing • Reopen Last Browsing Session • InPrivate Filtering • InPrivate Settings • Pop-up Blocker • SmartScreen Filter • Manage Add-ons • Compatibility View • Compatibility Settings • Windows Update • Developer Tools • Sun Java Console

FIGURE 2.1 **Browser Comparison**

bookmark a site, the browser captures the website's address and puts the link in a list. You simply scroll down the list, click on the website name, and launch the website.

Browsers also support **add-ons,** such as extra security software (like Norton Antivirus or McAfee Total Protection) and **pop-up blockers.** Many websites have advertisements that pop up in separate windows; pop-up blockers prevent these from cluttering your screen.

Web Addresses

How do you find a specific website? Each website is assigned a unique series of characters known as a **uniform resource locator (URL)** or **web address.** The URL is the means by which the browser and the server communicate. Here is an example of a URL: http://www.yahoo.com.

Each URL has three elements: the **protocol,** the domain name, and the **page name.** The protocol is the set of rules governing how computers talk to one another—this is the http:// part of the address. The domain name is the address of a company or entity on the web (e.g., www.yahoo.com). The page name, if one is used, identifies the particular page you are trying to reach (e.g., /chc/apa/term.html/).

Hypertext transfer protocol is generally shortened to "http" or "https" for secure sites. These letters, followed by a colon and two slashes, appear at the beginning of a URL and indicate the name of the protocol to use when accessing the server. It is not always necessary to type them, however. The "http" is usually assumed, and the requested website will appear even if you leave it out.

To access a particular page, type its URL into the address bar of your browser window and then press the **Enter** key on the keyboard. The browser sends the message to the server where the page is located. The server retrieves the page and sends it back to the browser, where it appears for the user.

FAQ: CAN I CREATE AND PUBLISH A WEBSITE?

Sure! Anyone with access to a computer and the Internet can create and publish a website. A website is published when it is accessible to the public. First, you will need to buy a domain name, which should be relatively inexpensive. (In fact, some web hosting services offer them for free.) In most cases, it is best to find a .com domain name.

Next, arrange for web hosting. Various companies provide hosting, and some do it for free. If it is not free, it is probably relatively inexpensive—as little as $5/month. Each host has different instructions for publishing a website. Many hosts offer free templates for building your web pages. These templates allow users to add content without knowing HTML or any other programming languages.

EXERCISE 2.1: NAVIGATING A WEBSITE

1. To get familiar with moving around a website, launch your browser by double-clicking the browser shortcut icon on your desktop (Internet Explorer, Mozilla Firefox, Google Chrome, etc.).

2. When the window appears, look for the search bar at the top of the page.

3. Suppose you want to search for jobs relevant to your career path. Click in the search bar and type the word "jobs" followed by the name of your career path, such as computer engineering, marketing, culinary arts, and so on. Press the **Enter** key on the keyboard. A page with a list of links to websites will appear.

4. Click on one of the hypertext links to access a site.

5. Once the site appears, find a link on the home page and click on it. Next, find a link on that page and click on it. Now, use the **Back** button to return to the home page. Use the **Forward** button to reverse. (Alternatively, the **Home** button will return you to the home page.)

6. To bookmark the site, go to Bookmark (if you are using Internet Explorer, go to Favorites). Click your mouse to open the drop-down menu and select *Bookmark this page.*

WEB 2.0

The term **Web 2.0** was coined by publisher Tim O'Reilly in 2004. Some consider it to be the next evolutionary phase of the web. As technology has developed, websites and their content have gradually shifted to a more user-generated and participatory style. YouTube is an example of a website that is mainly user-generated content.

Social Networking

As the general public has become more comfortable with digital content, social networking sites have thrived. Sites like Facebook, Twitter, MySpace, and LinkedIn provide users with a place to create a personal profile, link with friends who have profiles, and interact in a digital environment.

Blogs

Blog is the short term for "web log." Blogs have been around since the late 1990s. (A person who blogs is a "blogger.") A blog is an online journal or diary where a person can record his or her thoughts on any given subject. People, corporations, and organizations can have blogs, and many companies consider them to be a vital tool for reaching and interacting with customers. The community created by bloggers is called the "blogosphere." Blogs often enable readers to comment about a blog entry.

BLOG An online journal or diary where an individual records his or her thoughts.

WEB RESEARCH

Procedures

Having the Internet and the web is like having the world's biggest library at your fingertips. It offers a vast collection of information on every conceivable subject. But, unlike a library, materials on the web are not organized in any way—so before you can use all that information, you first have to find it.

Search Engines

If you are looking for a website with movie reviews, you will quickly find that thousands of sites fit that description. Unless you know a specific URL for a site with movie reviews, you will need a **search engine**

SEARCH ENGINE OPTIMIZATION ✔

to find one. Several well-known search engines are Google, Microsoft Bing®, Ask, and Yahoo!

SEARCH ENGINE An automated database that delivers a list of links as a response to a specific keyword request from the user.

Once a user accesses a search engine, the user types a request in the window provided (usually into a search bar near the top of the screen). Search engines use a tool called a **spider** to locate relevant pages and return them to the user in the form of a list of links. Next, the user clicks on one of the links provided to determine if the site is useful or not.

SPIDER The program used by search engines to look for requested content on the web.

Successful Searching

Used properly, search engines can be powerful research tools. Nonetheless, it is impossible for even the best search engine to find what you want if you do not ask the right question. Therefore, the user must be as specific as possible.

Identifying Main Keywords

Keywords are terms you type in a search bar on a search engine site. Using good keywords is vital because your search is only as good as the terms you enter. For example, if you were searching for information about George Washington, you might consider using the following terms:

KEYWORDS A term or group of terms used to find information on the web.

- George Washington
- First President of the United States
- Founding Fathers
- Revolutionary War

Linking keywords with *and, or,* and other qualifiers can help narrow your search parameters if your search results are not what you need. Being specific can help you get the results you want. To help with this, search engines have advanced search options that allow you to be very specific.

Alternate Keywords

If your initial search is not successful, try alternate spellings, synonyms, and other forms of your keywords. This allows the search engine to gather as many related documents as possible. Note: Watch for typos—as with every other situation, when searching the web correct spelling counts and will get you where you want to go quicker. Do not be surprised, however, if the search engine recognizes an incorrect spelling and asks if you really want to search that term.

Browsing

Browsing is another option for finding web pages and websites. However, it is not as efficient as using a search engine because so many documents exist on the web—there is simply no way you can search all of them.

Knowing the difference between searching and browsing will help you narrow your search. When you are searching for something, you are looking for a specific topic or title. Browsing is more like scanning a list of categories to see which ones might apply.

> **BROWSING** The process of performing a search of online categories in order to find a website or web page.

EXERCISE 2.3: USING PROPER KEYWORDS IN SEARCHING

Imagine that you are a student teacher who is preparing for a class field trip to a historic site and need to learn about pipe organs. Go to the search engine of your choice and type the word "organ" in the search bar. As you review the resulting list of links, consider the following inquiry points:

- Look at the top of the page. How many results did you get?

- Count the number of results on the first page. How many are about pipe organs? How many are about body organs or organ donation?

- Type "pipe organ" into the search bar. Did your results improve?

- Next, try the same search using a different search engine. Were your results the same? Were they different?

Sources: Credibility

As described earlier in this chapter, absolutely anyone can create or post to a website—so not all the information you find on the web is accurate. **Credibility** of sources is particularly important to remember when you are using the web for academic or other research. Providing accurate sources is very important. If you are working on a research paper about George Washington, for example, your instructor will expect you to document every source—where you located the information you report in your paper.

> **CREDIBILITY** Whether or not a source provides reliable, accurate information, checked and verified by experts.

Not all sources are the same. For example, Wikipedia is a free, online encyclopedia that offers countless entries on a wide variety of subjects. Anyone can post an article or make changes to an existing article. There are some Wikipedia volunteers who check whether the information posted is correct—but not enough to monitor more than three million Wikipedia pages. If you use Wikipedia to verify George Washington's birth date for your research paper, can you be sure the information is correct?

It is important to find credible sources for the information you report. Always use websites with editorial oversight or other controls in place to make sure that the information they provide is accurate. Reliable sources are written by experts who know their field and provide accurate information. (The best way to use Wikipedia is to first read a Wikipedia article's sources, which are listed at the end of every Wikipedia article.)

How can you tell if a website is credible? One approach is to look at the extension on a website's domain name. Websites with certain extensions, such as .edu or .gov, are more reliable than others. Remember, when looking for information, you should first be looking for experts. Figure 2.2 provides a sample of domain names and an assessment of their reliability as sources.

DOMAIN NAME	RELIABILITY
.edu	Reserved for educational sites; can be good resources, but be alert for materials written by students who are not experts
.gov	Reserved for government; considered to be credible sources
.mil	Reserved for the military; considered to be fairly reliable sources
.museum	Reserved for museums; generally reliable as museum websites often have very good content
.org	Reserved for organizations; can have good information, but may be biased
.com	Reserved for businesses; considered to be somewhat less reliable sources
.info	Available for anyone; considered fairly unreliable

FIGURE 2.2 Table of Domain Names

Citing Sources Found on the Internet

Some content on the web is in the public domain, which means it is not protected by copyright law. Public domain information includes any information from a government website or content written by someone who has been dead for more than 95 years—such as William Shakespeare's plays or the works of Mark Twain. Remember, the vast majority of content found on the web does not fall into that category. If you want to use someone else's content, you must contact that person and ask for permission. In the case of a printed book, contact the book's publisher, who probably retains the copyright to that information.

Once you find a credible website and use information from it in your paper, you need to provide a **citation** for it. A citation is a credit line that gives the source of your information

CITATION A quote from a larger work.

FAQ: INTELLECTUAL PROPERTY CONCERNS

Intellectual property is defined as anything that is created as a result of an intellectual effort. Intellectual property includes ideas, books, music—even processes. If you find an article online, that article belongs to the person who wrote it, and intellectual property laws are in place to protect that person's rights as author. You cannot claim it as your own work simply because you happened to find it online.

(the name of the article, website, etc.) to your readers. Following is an example of how to cite an article from the Encyclopedia Britannica website using APA style. Note the retrieved date in this example. Including this information is helpful for readers to know that information from online sources that may change from time to time is up-to-date and, therefore, relevant.

Aretha Franklin. (2010). In *Encyclopædia Britannica online*. Retrieved December 09, 2010, from http://www.britannica.com/EBchecked/topic/217325/ Aretha-Franklin

See the CEC APA style guide for further examples of APA citation format.

INTERNET ISSUES

Social Issues

Interacting with others on the web can be challenging. When you talk with others in person, you can see their body language and expressions. This is not the case when communicating with others on the Internet. Over time, some informal rules for communicating electronically have evolved. The term **netiquette** ('Net + etiquette) is used to refer to these conventional rules of behavior for Internet-based communication. Following are a few of these general guidelines:

NETIQUETTE Informal rules of behavior for communicating on the web.

- Keep an open mind; do not assume you know anything about the person who wrote it.
- Choose your words carefully; keep your language neutral and professional.
- Do not write messages in all-uppercase letters. On the web, this is interpreted as screaming and turns people off.
- In informal writing, you can use "emoticons," such as a smiley face :), to indicate humor.
- Before joining any discussion, read the website's frequently asked questions (FAQs); the answers to common questions will familiarize you with the website or blog.
- Once you post something on the web, you no longer control who can see it. Do not write anything on a website (or in an email, for that matter) that you would not want to see published on the front page of the *New York Times*.

Anonymity and Bullying

Some people take advantage of the anonymity of the web to treat others badly. These people often hide behind false names and identities when making cruel comments on blogs or other websites with little threat of reprisal (apart from perhaps having their comments removed or being banned from the site). Bullying exists on the web as it does in real life. People who disrupt discussions on purpose are known as **trolls**. They will often post incendiary comments just for the sake of being disruptive.

TROLLS People who intentionally disrupt online discussions.

Privacy

Today, computer users put more personal information on their home computers and on websites than ever before, including financial information (credit card and bank account numbers), medical information (confidential diagnoses), and other

personal information (Social Security numbers). How to keep personal information private is of great concern.

Much of this information exists in databases. **Data mining** is the process of searching large amounts of data to find patterns. Various entities use data mining, including businesses, researchers, and the government. Most data mining looks for general patterns and not specific details. For example, buying patterns such as men buying milk and diapers late at night are collected, but the names and credit card numbers for these transactions are not. Privacy concerns have been raised about the practice, and legislation has been established to protect personal information.

DATA MINING The practice of searching large amounts of electronic data to find patterns.

Security

Online security is a large part of online privacy issues. Because of the interconnected structure of the Internet, the system is not very secure. Users must be aware of the threats that exist and what they can do to protect themselves.

Threats

VIRUS Computer software unknowingly downloaded from what looks like a trusted source that is designed to infect a computer's programs and files by using those programs and files to attack others on the system.

WORM Stand-alone malware that infects a computer after being downloaded from an e-mail, pop-up advertisement, or downloaded software.

Threats include computer **viruses** and **malware**. A virus is software that attacks a computer's programs and files, usually rendering useless the data inside. A virus works by using one program to attack another program, thus creating a domino effect throughout the computer.

Malware (malicious software) includes such viruses as **worms, Trojan horses,** and **rootkits** that work as independent programs. They usually infect a computer by being downloaded from an e-mail, a pop-up ad, or software users download onto their computers. Trojan horses look like normal programs or files but are actually viruses. The particularly devastating rootkit virus attacks a computer's internal storage system.

MALWARE Computer software that works as an independent program that infects a computer's files and programs after being downloaded from what looks like a trusted source.

TROJAN HORSE A computer virus disguised as a normal program that infects a computer after being downloaded from an e-mail, pop-up advertisement, or downloaded software.

ROOTKIT A computer virus that attacks a computer's internal storage system.

Social Engineering

Cybercriminals often trick people into handing over important information, such as passwords or bank account numbers, through a practice known as **social engineering.** One method is to include a misleading link in an e-mail that looks to be from the user's bank or other financial institution that asks users to log onto their accounts to verify information. Users click on the link and find there a copy of the financial institution's website that looks legitimate, but is not. If the user provides any information there, it is then stolen.

Often these links arrive in **spam** e-mails. Much like the junk mail you receive in your mailbox each day, spam arrives in your e-mail inbox. This is known as **phishing**, a practice that can be very lucrative for cybercriminals trying to access personal information such as credit card and Social Security numbers. Some spam is harmless and just annoying—nonetheless, you should never open an e-mail that looks suspicious.

SOCIAL ENGINEERING The usually criminal practice of manipulating a person into providing sensitive information online.

SPAM Unsolicited mass-produced e-mail.

PHISHING The practice of using spam e-mail to elicit a response and obtain a computer user's private information.

Protection: Surfing Securely

You can take precautions to protect yourself and your computer. Your browser is the first line of defense to identify unsecure websites. Each browser window features an image of a padlock, which is known as a **lock** icon. (Note that different browsers place this icon in different places on the page.) Click this icon to check the security of a website. You can also set your browser to block unsecure sites. Installing a pop-up ad blocker is also a good idea, as some viruses are transmitted by clicking these ads.

Virus Protection Programs

Various **virus protection programs** exist that can protect your computer from outside threats. They run regular checks of your computer's system for viruses that may lurk in your programs or files. Examples of such programs include Norton Internet Security and McAfee Total Protection.

VIRUS PROTECTION PROGRAM Software installed on a computer that runs regular checks of programs and files, alerting the computer's owner of any viruses.

SUMMARY

The Internet has transformed the world. It has come a long way from its early days as a military project limited to a few specialized users, and today it affects almost every element of human existence in industrialized nations. The Internet has changed how people socialize, shop, pay bills, choose a doctor, or get an education, and it is one of the most powerful tools available to you. If you have a computer and an Internet connection, the world is at your fingertips. After reading this chapter, you should now have a good idea about *how* the Internet works, and how you can make it work better for you.

- You should recognize the difference between the Internet and the World Wide Web.
- You should be able to distinguish between a web page, a website, and a web browser.
- You should be able to choose a browser, launch it, type a URL to find a website, and navigate that site confidently.
- When researching online, you should know how to evaluate your sources critically and provide correct citations.
- You should know that because of Web 2.0, you can now produce content, and not just consume it.
- When navigating the web, you should know how to follow accepted conventions for behavior.
- You should be aware of threats like viruses and malware and should know how to protect your computer and your data from cybercriminals.

KEY TERMS

- add-ons
- ARPANET
- blog
- bookmarks
- broadband service
- browsing
- citation
- credibility
- data mining
- dial-up service
- domain name
- e-commerce
- e-mail
- hardware
- home page
- hypertext markup language (HTML)
- hypertext transfer protocol (HTTP)
- Internet

- Internet service provider (ISP)
- keyword
- local area network (LAN)
- malware
- modem
- netiquette
- network
- new media
- online service provider (OSP)
- open source
- page name
- phishing
- pop-up blocker
- protocol
- rootkit
- search engine
- server
- social engineering
- social networks

- software
- spam
- spider
- Trojan horse
- trolls
- uniform resource locator (URL)
- virus
- virus protection programs
- wide area network (WAN)
- Web 2.0
- web browser
- web page
- web server
- website
- WiFi
- WiFi access point
- wireless Internet service
- World Wide Web
- worm

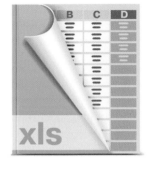

Productivity Software: Navigation

THE POWER OF SOFTWARE

What Is Software?

All computers have two main parts: the **hardware** and the **software.** The hardware represents the physical components of the computer such as the monitor, **central processing unit (CPU),** and keyboard. By contrast, the software represents the intangible workings of a computer. In short, computer software is a collection of programs and data that tells the computer what to do and how to do it.

HARDWARE The physical parts of a computer. This includes internal and external parts, such as the hard drive, monitor, memory, keyboard, and mouse.

SOFTWARE A program that is not a physical device that directs the computer to perform certain tasks.

CENTRAL PROCESSING UNIT (CPU) The main system of a computer that controls and carries out its functions.

Over the years, computer software evolved to become more sophisticated and powerful to meet the needs of a diverse user audience operating in the information age. Robust and useful software must adhere to specific standards and thorough testing before release to the end user. Software compatibility and the ability to function with other types of computer operating systems are very important characteristics in today's computing environment. Computer software is classified into the following three main categories:

- System software
- Programming software
- Application software

Knowledge and use of different software programs are essential for effective computer use. Equally important is upgrading to the latest versions of software programs and learning the new features. Fortunately, many software programs retain their basic functionality from version to version, eliminating steep learning curves once the user upgrades.

The Operating System

The **operating system** is the most important software component of a computer. Without an operating system, the computer cannot function properly. In short, the operating system is the software responsible for managing and controlling the hardware and software components. It also enables communication between the two components.

OPERATING SYSTEM The system software provided to a computer user by the computer manufacturer. Popular operating systems include Microsoft Windows® and the Apple Macintosh's OS.

A computer operating system functions much like the gears inside a clock. Each gear is necessary and dependent on other gears to advance the hour and minute hands while synchronizing to the cadence of a ticking second hand. The computer operating system controls the computer's memory needed for processes and manages your disk space and peripheral devices (such as a printer or scanner). Most importantly, the operating system allows you to communicate with your computer without your having to completely understand how it functions.

KEY CONCEPTS

- The Power of Software
- Starting and Operating the Computer
- Starting Windows 7
- Starting a Program with the Start Menu
- Working with Windows 7
- Working with Files and Folders
- Using Application Software

Today's personal computer users have a few main operating systems to choose from. The most popular are Microsoft Windows® operating system and Mac OS; some server computing systems use the Unix/Linux platform. Learning the basic functionality and features of the operating system increases a user's productivity and comfort level with computers.

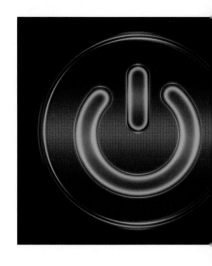

STARTING AND OPERATING THE COMPUTER

Turning on the Computer

Press the power button located on the front panel of the central processing unit (CPU) (for desktop computers) or above the keyboard (for laptop computers) to turn on your computer. The power switch is identified by the universal power switch symbol.

Shutting Down the Computer

To properly shut down a Microsoft Windows 7®–based computer, use the following steps:

1. Click the Windows **Start** icon located in the bottom left corner of the Windows screen. See Figure 3.1.
2. Click the **Shut down** button at the bottom of the *Start* menu.

Using the Mouse

The computer mouse is a pointing device that allows a user to easily access and manipulate menus, programs, icons, and other types of **graphical user interfaces (GUIs)** displayed on a computer screen.

> **GRAPHICAL USER INTERFACE (GUI)** A way to manipulate a computer system by interacting with graphics (icons, buttons, menus, and so on) instead of by typing in commands.

FIGURE 3.1

FAQ: SHOULD I TURN MY COMPUTER OFF AT NIGHT?

Computers have moving parts called hard disk drives that operate at high rates of speed for hours at a time. In order to prevent wear and tear on computer hard disk drives, it is best if computers are powered down at the end of the day or when not in use for long periods of time. Powering down computers also conserves electricity.

You operate the mouse by resting your hand over the top of the device, covering the left mouse button with your index finger and the right mouse button with your middle or ring finger (for right-handed users). (See inset photo at right.)

Clicking and holding mouse buttons achieve different outcomes. Double clicking a mouse button involves a rapid press and release motion and is typically used to open a program or application. Holding a mouse button involves pressing down the mouse button without releasing and is used to move or resize windows or move icons. Figure 3.2 describes some basic mouse button functions.

BUTTON ACTION	MOUSE BUTTON	PURPOSE
Single click	Left mouse button	To select an image or icon To navigate the cursor through a word processing program
Double click	Left mouse button	To execute an action such as opening a program
Single click	Right mouse button	To expose shortcuts in a variety of programs
Hold	Left mouse button	To move items around the computer's desktop To resize a window

FIGURE 3.2 **Mouse Button Functions**

Keyboard Alternatives to Using the Mouse

Instead of using the mouse device, the Windows 7 operating system offers a variety of keyboard alternatives. For example, if you want to copy a selected item, you press and hold down the **Ctrl** key while you press the **C** key. If you want to paste the copied item, you press and hold down the **Ctrl** key while you press the **V** key. In summary, any time you see a **Ctrl+C** or **Ctrl+V** command, or any other **key+key** or **key+key+key** sequence, it indicates that you must first hold down the first key while you press the second key and so on. Figure 3.3 describes some common keyboard shortcuts for Windows-based computers.

The Function Keys

The **function keys** are a row of keys labeled F1 through F12 located above the main keyboard. These keys are used as keyboard alternatives to the mouse device. Each key is pressed and released once and not used in

> **FUNCTION KEY** One of the 12 keys located at the top of the computer keyboard, labeled F1 through F12. They are used to perform shortcut functions.

PRESS THIS KEY(S)	TO ACCOMPLISH THIS RESULT
Ctrl+C	Copy the selected item.
Ctrl+X	Cut the selected item.
Ctrl+V	Paste the selected item.
Ctrl+Z	Undo the last action.
Ctrl+Y	Redo the last action.
Delete	Delete the selected item and move it to recycle bin.
Shift+Delete	Delete the selected item without moving to recycle bin.
Ctrl+Right Arrow	Move the cursor to the beginning of the next word.
Ctrl+Left Arrow	Move the cursor to the beginning of the previous word.
Ctrl+Down Arrow	Move the cursor to the beginning of the next paragraph.
Ctrl+Up Arrow	Move the cursor to the beginning of the previous paragraph.
Ctrl+Shift with arrow key	Select a block of text.
Shift with any arrow key	Select more than one item in a window or on the desktop or select text within a document.
Ctrl with any arrow key+spacebar	Select multiple individual items in a window or on the desktop.
Ctrl+A	Select all items in a document or window.
Alt+Enter	Display properties for the selected item.
Alt+spacebar	Open the shortcut menu for the active window.
Alt+Tab	Switch between open items.
Ctrl+Alt+Tab	Use the arrow keys to switch between open items.
Ctrl+mouse scroll wheel	Change the size of icons on the desktop.
Alt+Esc	Cycle through items in the order in which they were opened.
Ctrl+Esc	Open the *Start* menu.
Alt+Up Arrow	View the folder one level up in Windows Explorer.
Esc	Cancel the current task.
Ctrl+Shift+Esc	Open the Task Manager.
Ctrl+Shift	Switch the keyboard layout when multiple keyboard layouts are enabled.

FIGURE 3.3 Keyboard Shortcuts

combination with other keys (unless specified). Figure 3.4 provides examples of the uses of each function key.

STARTING WINDOWS 7

The Windows 7 Welcome Screen

After you press the power button on the computer, the computer begins its power-up sequence. During this time, the screen displays a startup screen followed by a Starting Windows screen with an animated Windows logo. After these screens disappear, the Windows 7 Welcome screen appears.

Depending on the system setup, the Windows 7 Welcome screen displays two to four image icons with names below them. These icons are user accounts. To begin a Windows 7

PRESS THIS FUNCTION KEY	TO ACCOMPLISH THIS RESULT
F1	Opens the Help screen.
F2	Renames a highlighted icon or file.
F3	Opens a search feature for programs.
F4	Opens a find window.
F5	Refreshes or reloads a page or document window.
F6	Moves the cursor to the Address bar in Microsoft Internet Explorer® and Mozilla Firefox.
F7	Launches spell and grammar check in Microsoft Office® programs.
F8	Enters Windows startup menu. Commonly used to access Windows Safe Mode.
F9	Opens the Measurements toolbar in Quark 5.0.
F10	Activates the menu bar of an open application in Microsoft Windows.
F11	Activates full-screen mode in all browsers.
F12	Opens the Save As window in Microsoft Word® program.

FIGURE 3.4 Function Keys

session, simply click on a named user account or click **Guest.** If a user account is password protected, the user must enter a system password to enable a Windows 7 session.

Shut Down, Sleep, and Restart Options

Windows 7 offers the user several options to manage the computer while not in use. You access all of these options from the **Start** button located in the lower left corner of the Windows screen. After you click the **Start** button (see Figure 3.5), click the arrow next to the **Shut down** button to select an option. See Figure 3.6.

FIGURE 3.5

FIGURE 3.6

The following is a brief description of three common shut-down options:

- **Restart:** The restart option is used to briefly shut down the computer and immediately start it again. This is commonly referred to as a "reboot" and is typically done to refresh the system after installing a new program or after a system update has occurred.
- **Sleep:** The sleep option places the computer in a paused power saving state without shutting the computer completely off. In sleep mode, the computer resumes full-power operation (usually in a matter of seconds) once the user presses a key or moves the mouse.
- **Shut Down:** The shut-down option completely powers down the computer and is recommended as the proper way of powering down a Windows 7 computer. Always use this method instead of pressing the power button.

INTERACTION DIVERSITY: THE EASE OF ACCESS BUTTON IN WINDOWS 7

The **Ease of Access** button appears in the lower left-hand corner of the Windows 7 Welcome screen. The *Ease of Access* menu contains six options designed to accommodate users with a disability. See Figure 3.7 for a complete list of its options.

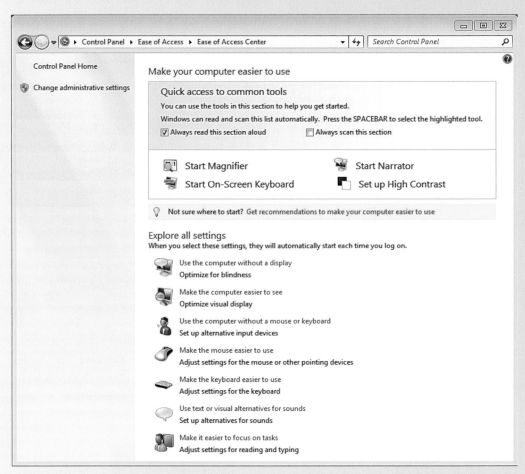

FIGURE 3.7

Optional Log-in to Windows 7

If you do not have a user account set up on a computer with the Windows 7 operating system or the computer does not belong to you, you can log in to a Windows system as a Guest. Using a Guest account on a computer requires the computer owner to enable the Guest account before the guest attempts to log in. Using the Guest account allows a user to log in to a Windows 7 system and enjoy most of the benefits of Windows 7 software. However, the Guest user does not have access to any password protected files or programs. The Guest account is a great way to share a computer with friends or a visiting relative without the worries of important files being accidentally accessed or modified while in use.

To enable the Guest account on a computer, use the following steps:

1. Click **Start** and then click **Control Panel.** See Figure 3.8.
2. Click **Add or remove user accounts**. See Figure 3.9.

FIGURE 3.8

FIGURE 3.9

3. Click the **Guest Account** icon. See Figure 3.10.
4. Click **Turn On** to enable the Guest account. See Figure 3.11.

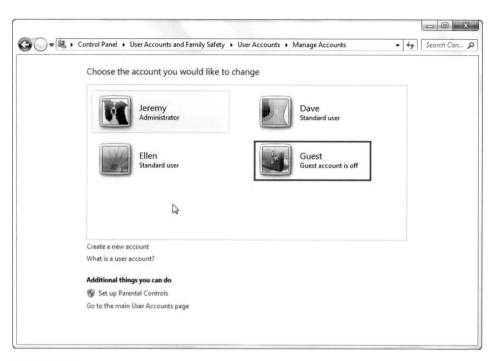

FIGURE 3.10

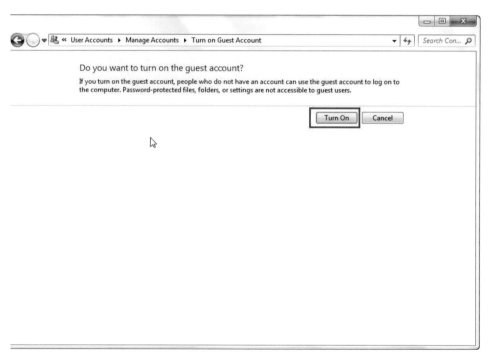

FIGURE 3.11

Overview of the Windows 7 Desktop

The Windows 7 desktop is the main Windows screen that displays after you power up a Windows computer. Much like a traditional desktop in an office, the Windows desktop contains access to all essential office tools in one space. You can customize and organize your Windows 7 desktop to meet your individual needs. You can also display pleasing background images or photographs of family members, a favorite vacation spot, or a hobby. Like a physical desktop, the Windows 7 desktop can even display a calendar or a clock. In short, all Windows 7 desktops have five main parts. Each of these parts is briefly described below (see Figure 3.12).

- **Start Button:** The **Start** button is located in the lower left corner of the screen and accesses the main control panel for the Windows 7 system. The **Start** button is used to start programs, adjust computer settings, or shut down the computer.
- **Task Bar:** The task bar is located at the bottom of the screen and contains all running programs, frequently used programs, computer system diagnostics, and the date and time.
- **Recycle Bin:** The Recycle Bin is a wastebasket-shaped icon located in the upper left corner of the screen. The Recycle Bin contains discarded files you can retrieve if you accidentally delete a file. If the contents are no longer needed, you can permanently empty the Recycle Bin by right-clicking and choosing Empty Recycle Bin from your options.
- **Gadgets:** Gadgets are small programs with a specific purpose such as a clock, calendar, or weather icon. These are usually located in the upper right corner of the screen.
- **Shortcuts:** Shortcuts are graphical representations of programs you access in a direct manner instead of using a longer path through the *Start* menu.

TASK BAR Appears at the bottom of the computer desktop screen and displays all running programs, frequently used programs, diagnostics, and the date and time.

RECYCLE BIN A location on the desktop, represented by a wastebasket icon, where files appear after you delete them. In this location, you can retrieve deleted files or permanently delete them.

GADGET Standard specific programs on the computer's desktop such as the clock, calendar, or weather.

SHORTCUT The graphical icons on your desktop for programs you access frequently or those you choose to access directly from your desktop.

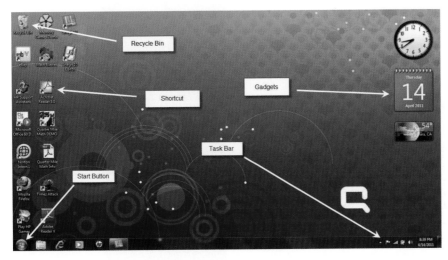

FIGURE 3.12

FAQ: WHY DOES MY SCREEN LOOK DIFFERENT? CUSTOMIZATION AND INSTALLED PROGRAMS

You can personalize your Windows 7 desktop in many ways. Change the theme or background to a photograph of a favorite vacation spot or an image of your family, or move icons and gadgets to different locations on the screen. When you install new programs on your computer, you can set them as shortcuts that appear as icons on the desktop.

STARTING A PROGRAM WITH THE *START* MENU

Launch the *Start* menu from the **Start** button located in the lower left corner of the Windows 7 screen. The *Start* menu contains access to all programs, applications, computer settings, and computer diagnostics. Launch programs from the *Start* menu by clicking on the program in the shortcut list in the left column or clicking **All Programs** at the bottom left and then clicking the program to launch. Access files, computer settings, or computer diagnostics by clicking on one of the categories in the right column. Place your cursor over the right arrow symbol to access the program buttons in the left column for additional features, files, or programs. Figure 3.13 shows the *Start* menu's sections—recently used program buttons are enclosed in the upper left-hand red box; access to files, computer diagnostics, and computer settings are shown in the right-hand red box; and the button to access all other programs is pictured in the lower left-hand red box.

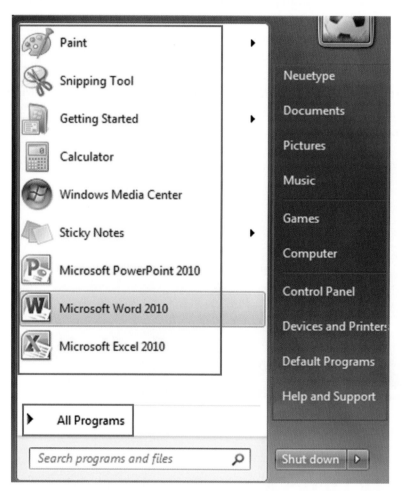

FIGURE 3.13

Menus, Commands, and Dialog Boxes

You direct programs and applications on a computer through menus, commands, and dialog boxes. Each of these is briefly described below.

- *Menus:* A **menu** is a graphical collection of options and commands a user chooses from to direct a program or application to perform a specific function.

MENU A graphical collection of options that appears on your desktop so you can perform a function on your computer.

- *Commands:* A **command** is an instruction or directive that tells a program or application what to do. Commands are the language computers understand and respond to.
- *Dialog boxes:* A **dialog box** is a small window that appears during the use of a program or application to ask the user a brief question or confirm an instruction or command. The dialog box establishes a "dialog" between the user and computer.

COMMAND A command is the language of the computer, telling the program or application what function to perform.

DIALOG BOX A window that appears during the use of a computer application. The window contains a question or requests confirmation of an action the user must reply to before continuing.

Using Windows 7 Help

Click the **Help and Support** button located at the bottom right column of the *Start* menu to access Windows 7 Help topics. Additional information and support is found on the Microsoft website at http://support.microsoft.com. See Figure 3.14.

FIGURE 3.14

If you purchase a new printer and need to know how to add the printer to your printer list, access the Help and Support feature of Windows 7 in the steps below:

1. Click **Help and Support** in the *Start* menu.
2. In the search field at the top of the window, type the keywords "adding a printer" or "installing a printer" and then click the magnifying glass at the right. See Figure 3.15.

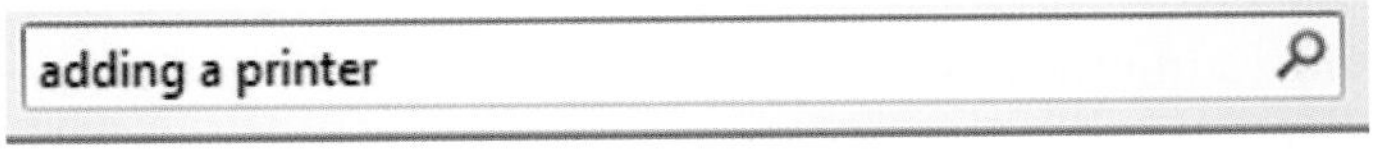

adding a printer

FIGURE 3.15

3. From the list of search results, click the link that is closest to the keyword used. See Figure 3.16.

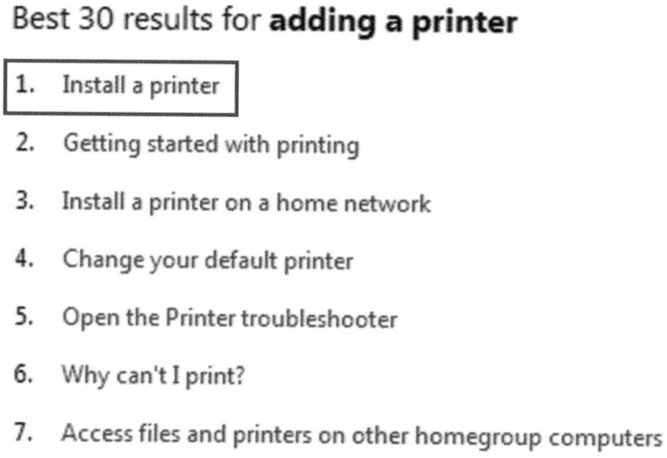

Best 30 results for **adding a printer**

1. Install a printer

2. Getting started with printing

3. Install a printer on a home network

4. Change your default printer

5. Open the Printer troubleshooter

6. Why can't I print?

7. Access files and printers on other homegroup computers

FIGURE 3.16

4. Follow the instructions and links to add the printer. See Figure 3.17.

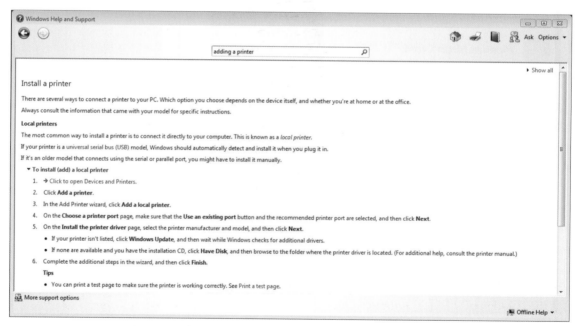

FIGURE 3.17

WORKING WITH WINDOWS 7

Opening, Closing, Maximizing, Minimizing, and Restoring Windows

- Double-click the **folder** icon to open a window.
- Click the red X button located in the upper right corner of the window to close a window completely.
- Maximizing a window automatically increases the size of a window on all four sides and allows the window to occupy the entire screen. Click the rectangular button located in the upper right corner of the window to maximize it.

- Minimizing a window collapses a window back into an icon symbol and moves the icon away from the center of the desktop area. Click the dash button located in the upper right corner of the window to minimize it.
- Restoring a window from a maximized state resizes a window back into the shape it was prior to maximizing it. Click the double square button located in the upper right of the window to restore it. See Figures 3.18A, B, C, and D.

FIGURE 3.18A Closing a Window

FIGURE 3.18B Maximizing a Window

FIGURE 3.18C Minimizing a Window

FIGURE 3.18D Restoring a Window

Moving and Resizing Windows

Place the cursor inside the top margin of the window and drag the window while holding down the left mouse button to move a window. Position the cursor at any edge of the window until the cursor changes to a double arrow symbol and then drag the edge while holding down the left mouse button to resize a window.

For example, imagine that you need to include some important financial information from a Microsoft Excel® spreadsheet in the body of an e-mail to a coworker. If you resize both the Excel spreadsheet and e-mail windows to fit side by side, you can cut and paste numbers directly from the spreadsheet into your e-mail's compose window. Similarly, if you review and respond to a Microsoft Word® document over e-mail, you could resize the document under review next to your e-mail window and scroll the contents of the document while you add comments into the e-mail message. Again, you can cut and paste critical sections of the Word document directly into the e-mail message.

Switching Between Windows

Switch between windows by clicking once on a window, thus making it active. The active window moves to the top of the window stack. Another way to switch between windows is to collapse all windows into the task bar located at the bottom of the Windows 7 desktop and then select and click the windows as needed. Another advantage of using the task bar option is the preview feature. You can display a thumbnail-sized preview of the file, program, application, or image by placing your cursor over the icon.

Using Scroll Bars

Scroll bars are sliding control tools located on the bottom and right side of windows. Use the scroll bars to move the contents of windows up and down and left to right. Scroll bars are manipulated in a number of ways. One method to control the scroll bar is to place the pointer on the slider and drag it while you hold down the left mouse button. You can also click the up/down/left/right arrow buttons. This method provides a steady, slow movement of the page. Finally, for a more rapid scroll action, click above or below the slider control. See Figure 3.19.

SCROLL BAR Sliding control tools on the bottom and side of the computer window that allow you to navigate within your document.

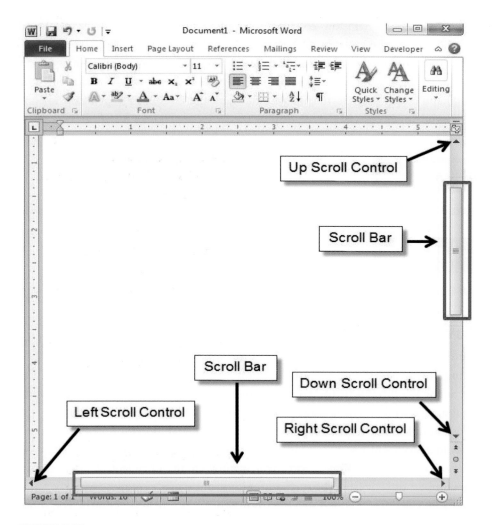

FIGURE 3.19

Status Bars

The **status bar** is located at the bottom margin of an application window and contains document information, tools, and short-cuts. In Microsoft Office 2010®, place the pointer inside the bar and click the right mouse button to customize the status bar. See Figure 3.20.

STATUS BAR A row of information about the current application that appears at the bottom of the document window.

Using Windows Explorer

Windows Explorer is the main file manager for Windows 7 systems. Think of a file as the most basic information unit in a computer system. Windows Explorer allows the user to quickly locate document files, photo files, music files, video files, and other Windows programs and applications anywhere on the system. The **Windows Explorer** icon for Windows 7 is located in the bottom left corner of the screen. Click once on the **Windows Explorer** icon to open it.

WINDOWS EXPLORER The main file manager for Windows 7 systems, providing the graphical user interface.

The Windows Explorer Window

Once opened, the Windows Explorer main window (see Figure 3.21) displays the categories where you store files, programs, and applications. Clicking on any category displays its contents. The main default categories for file libraries fall within

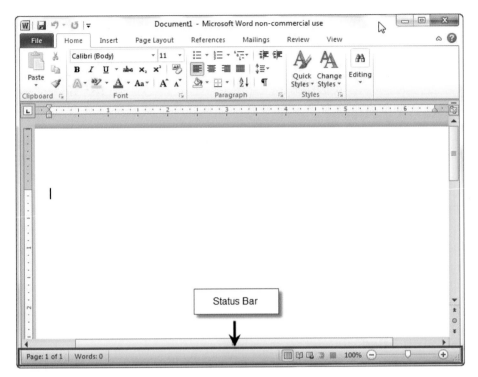

FIGURE 3.20

FIGURE 3.21

these four categories: document files, music files, picture files, and video files. Each category is briefly explained below:

- **Document Files:** These are saved as Microsoft Word, Microsoft Excel, or Microsoft PowerPoint® files generated from Microsoft Office 2010.
- **Music Files:** These are MP3 format music files or other audio files downloaded from iTunes.

- **Picture Files:** These are JPEG format image files or other image files downloaded from a digital still camera.
- **Video Files:** These are MPEG format video files downloaded from a digital video camera.

Renaming Files

To rename a file, click the filename from the Windows Explorer list to select it and then select *Rename* from the *Organize* pull-down menu located in the top left corner of the Windows Explorer window. As you type in the new name of the file, the characters appear inside the highlighted box around the file name. Press **Enter** or click outside of the filename when you finish. See Figure 3.22.

Remember to only rename files that belong to you or files that you are familiar with. Never attempt to rename a program or application, especially if it contains a file extension (a filename followed by a period and additional characters). Doing so could disable or corrupt an important program the computer needs to run properly.

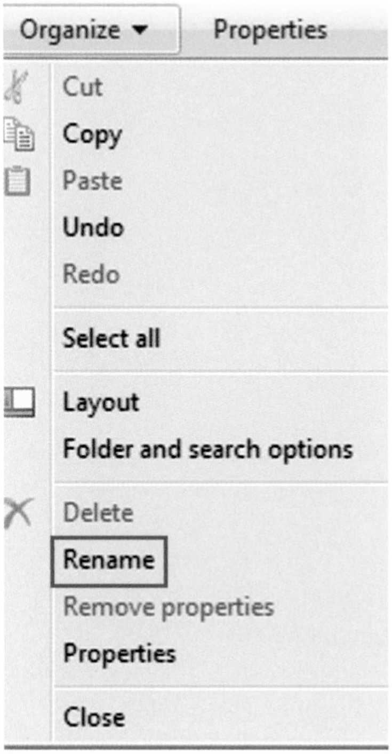

Moving Files

To move a file, find and select the file from the Windows Explorer list and drag it while you hold down the left mouse button. Position the file over a destination folder or space and release the left mouse button. The file is moved to the new destination.

Copying Files

To copy a file, find and select the file from the Windows Explorer list and then click the *Organize* pull-down menu located at the top left corner of the Windows Explorer window and select *Copy.* Locate and click a destination folder to open it and then select *Paste* from the *Organize* menu. The file is now copied to the new destination. See Figure 3.23.

Deleting Files

To delete a file, find and select the file from the Windows Explorer list and then click the *Organize* pull-down menu located in the top left corner of the Windows Explorer and select *Delete.* The file is moved from the folder or space to the Recycle Bin.

For example, imagine that you have several versions of a document you created for an important project at work. As the project is wrapping up, you determine that one of the document versions is obsolete and proceed to delete the file. Later on, you realize that an important section from the deleted file is needed for the other versions. You panic because you believe that you permanently deleted the document forever from the computer's hard drive. Not to worry. When you deleted the file, it went to the Recycle Bin, where you can retrieve it and use it again. When you discover this, you immediately move the file from the Recycle Bin back into your project folder. See Figure 3.24.

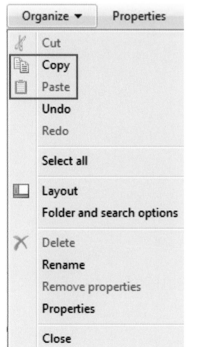

FIGURE 3.22

FIGURE 3.23

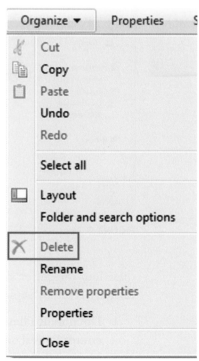

FIGURE 3.24

INTERACTION DIVERSITY: CHANGING SCREEN RESOLUTION

One necessary feature in Windows 7 is the ability to change the screen resolution to accommodate persons with visual impairments such as glaucoma, cataracts, myopia, or presbyopia. According to the 1995 U.S. National Survey on Vision Loss, one in six Americans (17 percent) 45 years or older and one in four Americans (26 percent) 75 years or older reported some form of vision impairment.

To adjust screen resolution, use the following steps:

1. Position the cursor anywhere within the desktop and click the right mouse button.

2. Select *Screen resolution*.

3. Click the **Resolution** button and adjust the slider up and down to a desired resolution. See Figure 3.25.

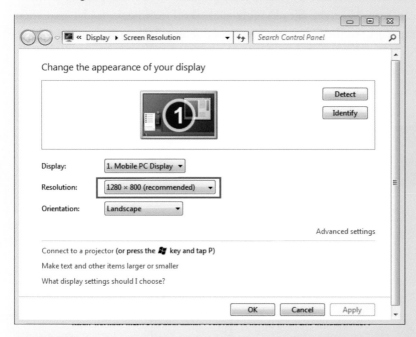

FIGURE 3.25

4. Click outside the slider and then click **Apply** to see how you like the changes.

5. A dialog box appears to ask if you want to **Keep changes** or **Revert**. Keeping the changes locks in the new resolution. Revert defaults back to your previous resolution settings. (Note: You must make a decision within 15 seconds or the system discards the new setting.)

6. If you select **Keep changes,** click **OK** to apply the new setting.

WORKING WITH FILES AND FOLDERS

Organizing Files within Folders

Imagine working in an office environment without an organized filing system. Papers and file folders are spread out over desks and tables. Frantic employees spend hours looking for important documents that cannot be found in a timely manner.

Computer systems are no different and require organization as well. A user could have files and folders spread out over many locations. Much like the office scenario, the user could also spend hours searching for forgotten or missing file or folder names. Taking the time to organize files and folders early on when using computers pays huge dividends down the road.

For example, imagine that you want to send an important e-mail to a coworker and need to include a file attachment that describes a new product introduction. As you finish composing the e-mail, you conclude the message with the statement, "Please see attached for more details about the product we are about to launch in two weeks." You organized your documentation up front prior to taking on this new project, and created several project folders. You named one of these folders "New Product Introductions." Under this folder are several subfolders with the following names:

- Data Sheet for Product A
- Data Sheet for Product B
- Data Sheet for Product C

Click the attach file feature in your e-mail program to access a pop-up window where you can search for the file. Double-click the Documents folder and then immediately navigate to the "New Product Introductions" folder and open it. Next, select Data Sheet for Product A and attach this file to your e-mail. Figure 3.26 illustrates a simple and organized folder structure.

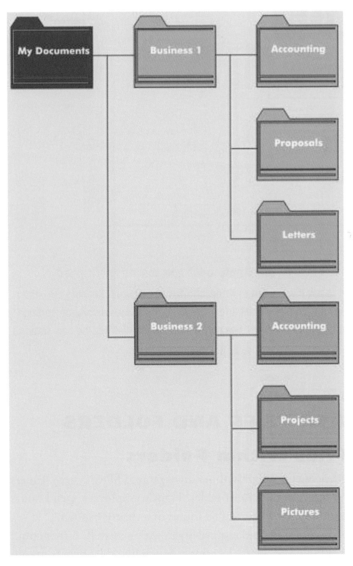

FIGURE 3.26

Creating a Folder

Double-click in one of the libraries located in the Windows Explorer main window and then click the **New folder** button at the top to create a new folder. See Figure 3.27.

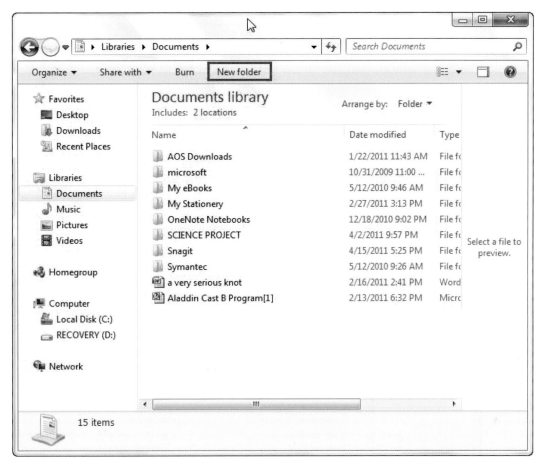

FIGURE 3.27

After you click the **New folder** button, a new folder icon appears in the file listing with highlighted text that reads "New folder." To rename the folder, type the new folder name and click outside the folder.

When you name folders, consider a name that best represents what the folder contains. For example, if the folder contains tax information for the year 2009, consider naming it "Taxes 2009." Avoid long names and special characters, such as these: [ ] / \ ? & *.

As an example, imagine that you are an accountant specializing in personal income taxes. One of your clients is John Doe and you have done his personal income taxes from the years 2000 through 2010. You could organize his tax information using the following steps:

1. Click the **Windows Explorer** icon.
2. Double-click the **Documents** icon.
3. Under the Documents library, click the **New folder** button at the top of the window.
4. Inside the highlighted folder space, type "John Doe." Press the **Enter** key or click outside the highlighted box.

5. Double-click inside the folder *John Doe.*
6. Repeat steps 3 and 4. This time, however, name each folder *Taxes 2000, Taxes 2001, Taxes 2002,* and so on.

Once you create this file framework, you can move and store all the tax files into the appropriate folders for each tax year.

Parts of a Folder Window

The folder window has four main parts. Each of these parts is briefly explained below (See Figure 3.28):

- *Navigation Pane:* The Navigation Pane is the top hierarchy listing where all files, programs, and applications reside on the computer.
- *Address Bar:* The address bar displays the horizontal path to locate files, programs, and applications.
- *Refresh Button:* The **refresh** button updates the listing of content.
- *Search Window:* The search window searches the current location and lists all findings based on a specific keyword.

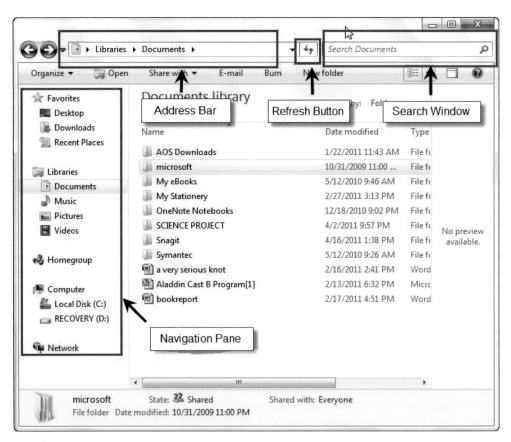

FIGURE 3.28

Expanding and Collapsing a Folder

There are eight different ways you can resize and list folders. To resize or change the listing of the folder and file list, click the **change view** button on the top right side of the folder window and then adjust the slider tool to the desired viewing preference. See Figures 3.29 amd 3.30.

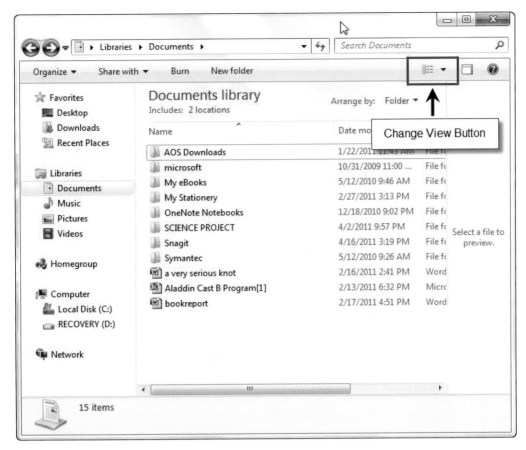

FIGURE 3.29

FIGURE 3.30

Click the diagonal arrowhead to expand and collapse folders. This allows the user to quickly view the contents of the main folder. See Figure 3.31.

As an example, imagine that you need to find a specific file (whose exact filename escapes you) that is in one of two different folders. If you use the folder expansion feature of Windows Explorer, you can create a hierarchical snapshot within seconds without using the Windows Explorer search window. From this view, you can quickly scan each folder hierarchy and identify the filename.

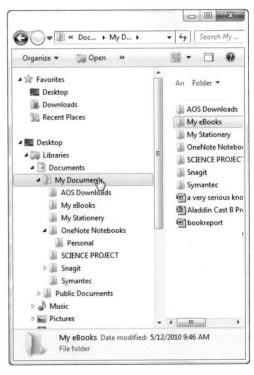

FIGURE 3.31

SAVING A FILE INTO A FOLDER

As you type a letter to a coworker using Microsoft Word, you know that, at some point, you will save this document in a place where you can easily locate it for future reference. Instead of saving the letter to the default Documents library, you will save it to a specific folder. Once you save a new file to a new folder, you can open and save it back into that same folder.

To save a new file (such as a Word or Excel document) to a regular folder, use the following steps:

1. Click **Save** under the *File* tab.
2. In the **File name** section, type in a new filename.
3. Click on categories in the Navigation Pane or click on the individual folders listed in the main window to locate a folder destination.
4. Once a destination folder is selected, click **Save.** See Figure 3.32.

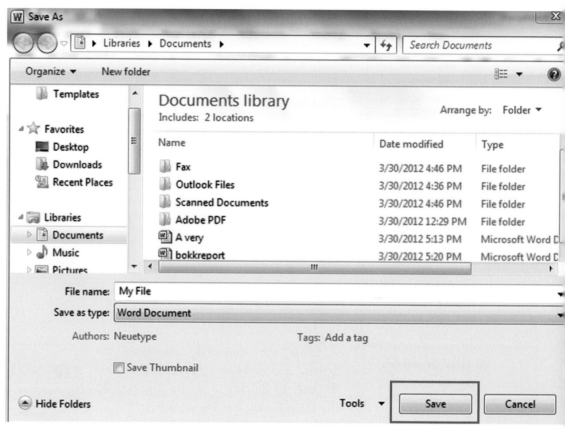

FIGURE 3.32

When you name files, follow the same guidelines you learned to name folders. Remember to pick a name that best represents the contents of the file, keep the name brief, and avoid special characters.

Example Procedures

Saving a File to a Shared Folder

Windows systems have a feature that allows a user to save a file to a shared folder, enabled through a **network drive.** The advantage of the network drive is that other computer users have access to a shared folder's files over a network connection.

To save a file to a shared folder, you must map a network drive (or, as in most businesses, have access to the network drive). To map a network drive, use the following steps:

NETWORK DRIVE A location on a server where networked users can access shared files by mapping to the specific location where they reside.

1. From the *Start* menu, select *Computer*.
2. Click the **Map network drive** button at the top of the window. See Figure 3.33.

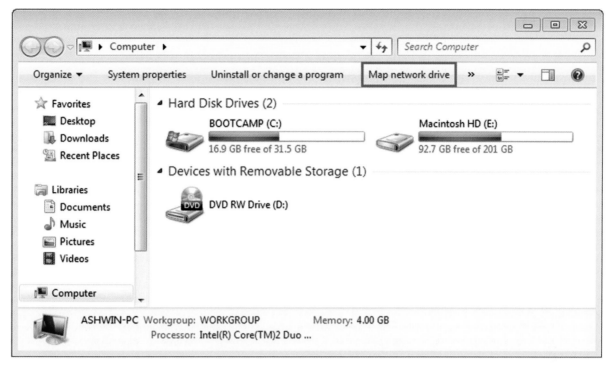

FIGURE 3.33

3. In the Map Network Drive window, click the **Drive** button to select a drive letter and then click the **Browse** button to select a shared folder. When complete, click **Finish.** See Figure 3.34.

4. The **Network Drive** icon appears under the **Computer** icon in the Navigation Pane.

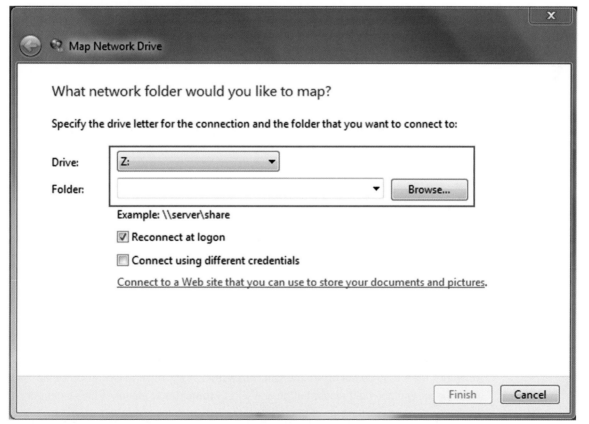

FIGURE 3.34

To save a file to a shared folder, use the following steps:

1. Click **Save** under the *File* tab.
2. In the **File name** section, type a new filename.
3. Click the **network drive** icon located under Computer in the Navigation Pane. See Figure 3.35.

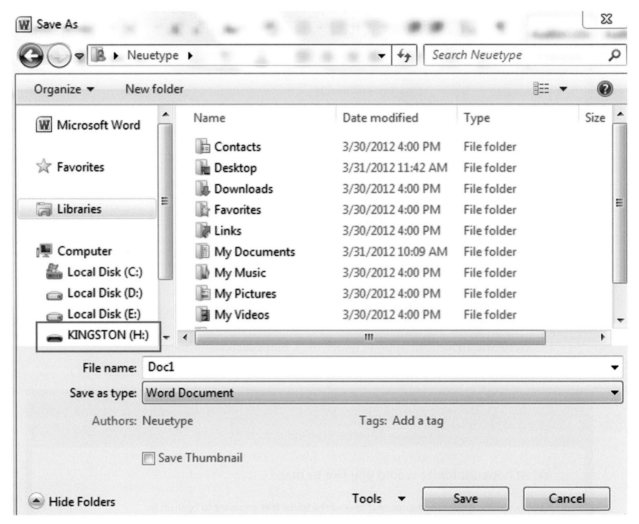

FIGURE 3.35

4. Locate and double-click the folder where you want to save the document.
5. Click **Save.**

FAQ: WHY DOES THIS FILE REFUSE TO OPEN?

Different applications (such as Microsoft Word, Excel, and PowerPoint) produce files with different formats. These formats are usually identified by an extension at the end of the file. For example, if you tried to open a Word file without Microsoft Word installed on your computer, the file would not open. The same holds true for any other Microsoft Office file. Click the file with the right mouse button and select **Properties** to identify a file's extension. Under the *General* tab, the type of file and its extension are defined.

Figure 3.36 lists some common extensions for Microsoft Office 2010 files.

Microsoft Office Product	Icon Image	File Extension
Microsoft Word®		.docx
Microsoft Excel®		.xlsx
Microsoft PowerPoint®		.pptx
Microsoft Access®		.accdb
Microsoft Publisher®		.pub
Microsoft OneNote®		.one

FIGURE 3.36

The Difference Between Save and Save As

There are two distinct ways to save a file. The differences between the two are described below:

- **Save:** The **Save** command saves a new file to a folder or updates the data within an existing file.
- **Save As:** The **Save As** command allows you to save the contents of an existing file under a different name.

As an example, you apply for a specific job opening and need to write a cover letter. You write your letter in a generic manner with the intention of saving this version as a template to create a more targeted and specific letter in the future. After saving this letter as *Generic Cover Letter*, you reopen the file and make modifications to address the specific job requirements for this position. This time, you save the letter with the **Save As** option and name the letter *Cover Letter for Cisco Job Number 16834*. Your folder now contains two documents: *Generic Cover Letter* and *Cover Letter for Cisco Job Number 16834*.

Version Control

Windows contains an automatic backup program to track and restore previous versions of files. To view previous versions of a file, right-click the file and then click **Properties.** Click the *Previous Versions* tab on the Properties pop-up window to view the previous versions of the file.

To restore a previous version, right-click the file and select **Restore previous versions.** Select the version to restore and then click **OK** to preview the restored file.

Compressing and Zipping Files

Many e-mail programs cannot manage large file attachments. A large file is typically defined as a file larger than 5 megabytes (5 MB). In Windows, you can compress or

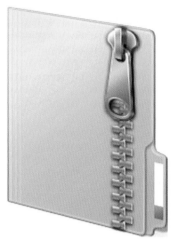

"zip" a file into a manageable size and then successfully send it as an e-mail attachment. To compress a file, right-click with the mouse over a filename and place the pointer over **Send to.** Next, click **Compressed (zipped) folder.** A zipped folder icon appears with the same name as the file. You can now send the zipped folder as an e-mail attachment.

For example, imagine that you just returned from an exotic vacation in the Bahamas. You cannot wait to e-mail family and friends to summarize your adventures and share some breathtaking photographs. As you complete your e-mail message, attach 30 photographs, and press send, your e-mail program informs you that you have exceeded the maximum file size for attachments. Instead of diminishing your exciting trip story by reducing your photo count, you can instead compress the photos into a zipped folder and send them all.

FIGURE 3.37

USING APPLICATION SOFTWARE

In addition to producing the Windows operating system, Microsoft Corporation produces an office productivity suite called **Microsoft Office 2010.** Microsoft Office 2010 contains applications to produce a wide variety of documents, including word processing files, spreadsheet files, and presentation files. All Microsoft applications have standardized window and Ribbon layouts and share similar menu systems and buttons. Once you learn one application, it is not difficult to learn another. The following table lists the different Microsoft Office 2010 suite editions with applications included.

MICROSOFT OFFICE 2010 A suite of computer programs created and distributed by Microsoft that includes word processing, spreadsheet, presentation, and database software.

MICROSOFT OFFICE EDITION	INCLUDED APPLICATIONS
Microsoft Office 2010 Professional	Word Excel PowerPoint OneNote Outlook Publisher Access
Microsoft Office 2010 Home and Student	Word Excel PowerPoint OneNote

FIGURE 3.38 Microsoft Office 2010 Edition Packages

The following list briefly describes each application:

- **Microsoft Word** is a general word processing program.
- **Microsoft Excel** is a spreadsheet program.
- **Microsoft PowerPoint** is a presentation program.
- **Microsoft Outlook®** personal data management software is a program for e-mail, tasks, contacts, and calendar.
- **Microsoft Publisher** is a desktop publishing program.

MICROSOFT WORD The word processing program in the Microsoft Office suite.

MICROSOFT EXCEL The spreadsheet program in the Microsoft Office suite.

MICROSOFT POWERPOINT Presentation software in the Microsoft Office suite of products. The software provides the user the ability to create professional-looking presentations with graphics, sound, animation, and movie clips.

- **Microsoft Access** is a database management program.
- **Microsoft OneNote** allows multiuser collaboration.

Managing Office Files

Microsoft Office 2010 applications offer many features to produce and print documents. The following sections briefly describe some of these features.

Creating a New Office File

After you start the Office 2010 application, click the *File* tab at the top left corner of the window and then click **New.** Depending on the application, Microsoft Office 2010 offers several template options. Figures 3.39A, 3.39B, and 3.39C display template options for Word, Excel, and PowerPoint.

MICROSOFT OUTLOOK A personal information manager and e-mail client that is offered as a part of the Microsoft Office software package, Microsoft Exchange Server®, and as a standalone product.

MICROSOFT PUBLISHER The desktop publishing program in the Microsoft Office suite.

MICROSOFT ACCESS The database creation and management program in the Microsoft Office suite.

MICROSOFT ONENOTE The multiuser collaboration program in the Microsoft Office suite.

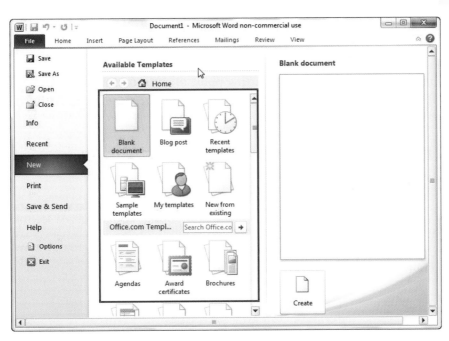

FIGURE 3.39A

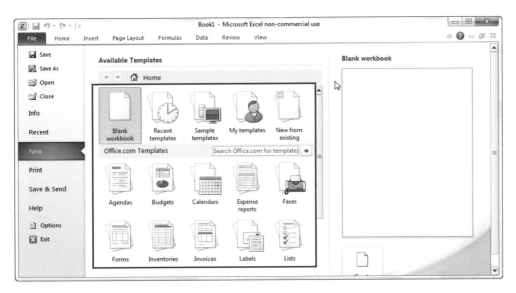

FIGURE 3.39B

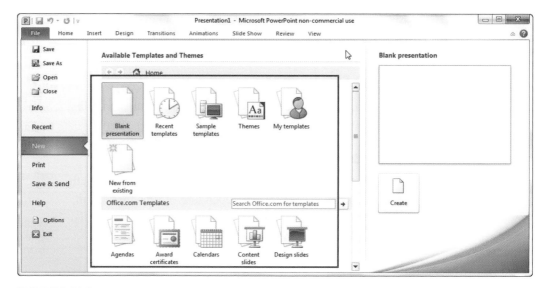

FIGURE 3.39C

A template provides an excellent starting point to create a new file, giving you a convenient predesigned framework to compose effective documents. Template offerings range from fax cover sheets to expense reports.

Using Backstage View to Create a File

One of the many enhancements included with Microsoft Office 2010 is a feature called **Backstage View.** Click the *File* tab at the upper left corner of the window to display this view. Backstage View allows the user to manage files in an application, set options, adjust data within files, and print and e-mail documents all within one space. See Figure 3.40.

BACKSTAGE VIEW A new feature in Microsoft Office 2010 that allows users to manage files, set options, adjust data, print, and e-mail documents from one location.

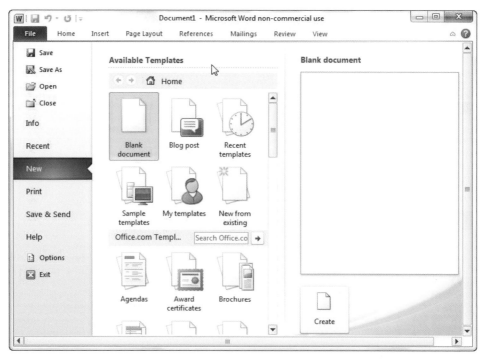

FIGURE 3.40

To create a new file using Backstage View, use the following steps:

1. Click the *File* tab at the upper left corner of the window.
2. Click the *New* tab in the far left column.
3. Double-click on a desired template.
4. When you complete your document, click **Save** under the *File* tab.
5. Type in the new filename and then click **Save.** Notice at the top of the window that the generic name of the file is replaced by the new filename.

To open an existing file using Backstage View, use the following steps:

1. Click the *File* tab at the upper left corner of the window.
2. Click **Open.**
3. Search for and select a file from the Documents library inside the pop-up window and then click **Open.**

To open existing files recently created or edited using Backstage View, use the following steps:

1. Click the *File* tab at the upper left corner of the window.
2. Click the *Recent* tab in the far left column.
3. Locate the file under the Recent Documents listing and then double-click the file. See Figure 3.41.

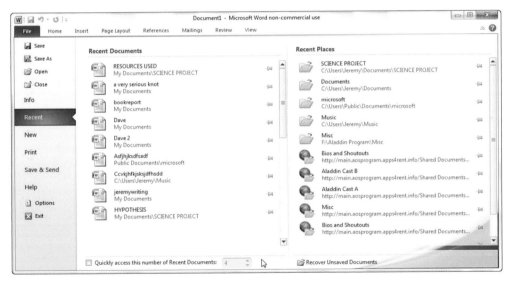

FIGURE 3.41

FAQ: WHEN SHOULD I USE ACCESS INSTEAD OF EXCEL?

In general, Access has the following two advantages over Excel:

- In Access, you can manage large quantities of complex data and can generate reports from the data.
- In Access, you can create custom reports quickly.

Opening a File from Windows Explorer

As an alternative to opening files using Backstage View, you can open files with Windows Explorer. Using Windows Explorer to open files provides the advantage of opening files without first launching an application. Instead, you double-click the file to launch the application that created it. Another advantage of using Windows Explorer to navigate and open files is that you can view all files on the computer system under one space.

To open an existing file using Windows Explorer, use the following steps:

1. Click the **Windows Explorer** icon located in the bottom left corner of the screen.
2. Double-click in the Documents library to search for a file. See Figure 3.42.
3. Double-click the filename to open a file.

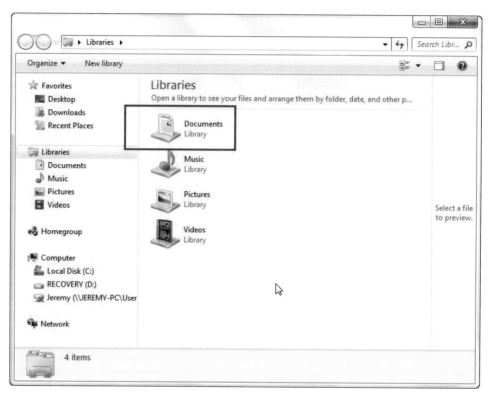

FIGURE 3.42

FAQ: WHAT DOES A BROWSE BUTTON DO?

The **Browse** button is a navigation feature that allows a user to search for a file and then select and place that file into a search field. Clicking a **Browse** button typically launches a dialog box with a path to selected files on the user's computer.

For example, imagine you are in the market for a job and you need to post your resume on a resume-posting website, such as *www.dice.com.* After you complete your online profile, the site asks you to copy your resume (written using Microsoft Word) into the site's resume repository. Use the **Browse** button to temporarily link your computer to the website and allow transfer of a document.

To use the browse feature in this situation, a job seeker would follow these steps:

1. Click the **Browse** button on the website. A pop-up window appears.

2. Search for and select the resume file from the Documents library in the pop-up window and then click **Open.** See Figure 3.43.

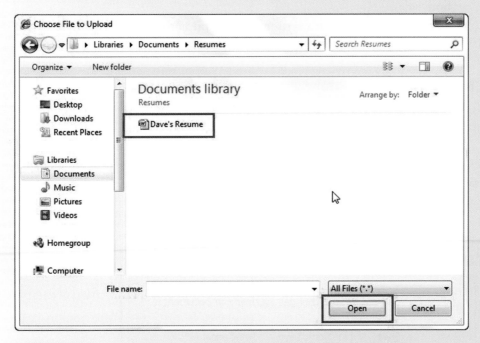

FIGURE 3.43

The file loads into the browse field and is ready for transfer to the website.

Printing an Office File

To print an existing file, use the following steps:

1. Click the *File* tab in the upper left corner of the window.
2. Click **Print** in the far left column. See Figure 3.44.
3. Select a Printer device and then select printer **Settings.** When finished, click the **Print** button.

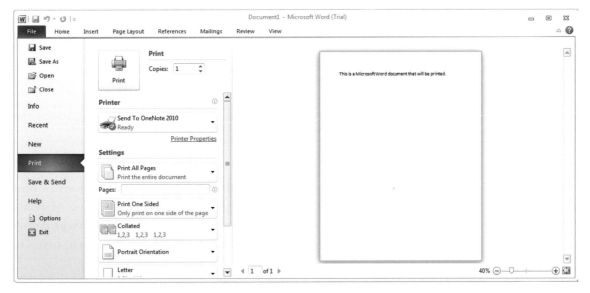

FIGURE 3.44

The following is a brief description of frequently used printer settings:

- *Print All Pages:* This setting tells the printer how many pages to print. You can instruct the printer to print all pages, one page only, or a range of pages.
- *Print One Sided:* This setting instructs the printer to print pages on one or both sides.
- *Portrait Orientation:* This setting tells the printer to print pages in a vertical (portrait) or horizontal (landscape) orientation.

Closing an Office File

To close a Microsoft Word file using the Backstage View, click the *File* tab at the upper left corner and then click **Close** on the upper left column.

To close Microsoft Word, click the red X located at the upper right corner of the window. If an open file has unsaved changes prior to closing the program, a dialog box appears to query the user about saving the changes. See Figure 3.45.

FIGURE 3.45

The Application Interface

Using the Ribbon

The main user interface for Microsoft Office 2010 applications is called the Ribbon. The Ribbon appears across the top of the window above the workspace and contains tabs, buttons, and pull-down menu shortcuts.

FIGURE 3.46

Click the individual tabs above the Ribbon to display a different set of buttons. Each tab is categorized into groups by function, such as inserting, viewing, page layout, and reviewing. Click the up arrow button in the upper right corner of the window to minimize the Ribbon (retract it). Click the down arrow to restore the Ribbon.

Within the Ribbon there is a feature called Galleries. Galleries are small thumbnail images of what a setting looks like in a document. See Figure 3.47.

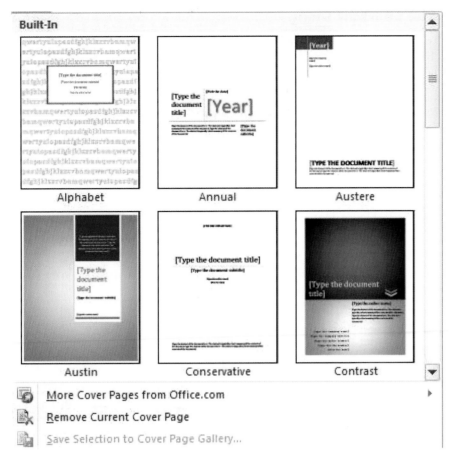

FIGURE 3.47

FIGURE 3.48

The Ribbon interface also contains a small group of frequently used commands on the **Quick Access Toolbar.** The Quick Access Toolbar is in the top left corner of the window. See Figure 3.48.

Click the customization pull-down menu (see Figure 3.49) to customize the Quick Access Toolbar. The customization menu allows you to add or subtract command buttons. To add or subtract command buttons from the Quick Access Toolbar, place the pointer over the button, right-click once with the mouse, and select *Remove from Quick Access Toolbar* or *Add to Quick Access Toolbar*.

Finally, the Ribbon has a feature called **Key Tips** that allows you to use keyboard keys instead of a mouse to switch tabs or activate commands from the Quick Access Toolbar. To display the Key Tips, place the cursor inside the Ribbon and press the **Alt** key. Each tab or icon is labeled with a bubbled letter or number. To execute a command, press the **Alt** key and the letter or number together to execute the specific command. The Key Tips feature also works hierarchically and displays more bubbled letters within each tab category. To remove the bubbled letters, press the **Alt** key again.

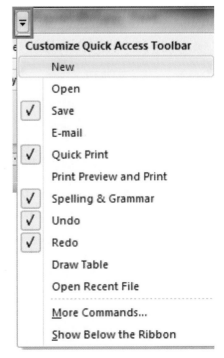

FIGURE 3.49

Using the Shortcut Menu

Windows has a shortcut menu system called **context-sensitive menus.** Right-click the mouse anywhere on your screen to activate context-sensitive menus. The menu choices vary depending where you right-click. Selecting any context-sensitive command or option executes the command directly.

CONTEXT-SENSITIVE MENUS
These menus offer shortcut choices that appear as a user right-clicks on the computer screen.

You want to know how much disk space is left on your computer. The following steps are a shortcut way to find out:

1. Click **Start** and select **Computer.**
2. Under **Hard Disk Drives**, right-click with the mouse over the image marked **Local Disk (C:)** and then select **Properties.** See Figure 3.50.
3. From the *General* tab, you can view the disk space on your computer. See Figure 3.51.

FIGURE 3.50

Conventions for Entering and Editing Text

Text entered into a document is always generated to the left of the flashing vertical line or insertion point. You can press and release the **Shift** key for mixed case typing (upper and lower cases together). Use the **Caps Lock** key for all uppercase typing. Use the **Enter** key to begin a new line or continually type to the right margin and allow the application to automatically begin a new line. This method is the recommended way to begin a new line instead of using the **Enter** key. Only use the **Enter** key when you begin a new paragraph.

Correct typing errors in any of the following ways:

- The **Backspace** key removes letters to the left.
- Select text and press the **Delete** key to remove words and sentences to the right.
- Press **Ctrl+Z** keys to undo typing commands.
- Press **Ctrl+Y** keys to restore typing commands.

Use the **undo** and **redo** commands on the Quick Access Toolbar as an alternative.

Conventions for Selecting Text

Before a specific action is applied to text, you must select the text. Selecting text prepares the text for many purposes, such as deleting, formatting, or renaming. For example, to quickly delete text without using the **Backspace** key, select the text and then press the **Delete** key. To replace incorrect text, select the text to modify and then type over the selected text. There is no need to delete the selected text before entering new text; the new text will automatically fill the space that is selected.

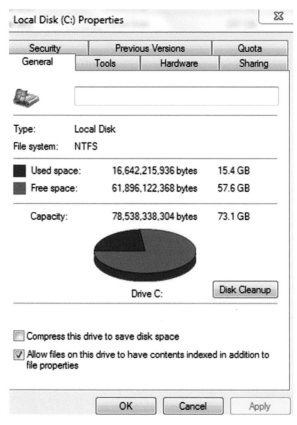

FIGURE 3.51

To cut and move text to another location, select the text and then press the **Ctrl+X** keys to cut it. Place the cursor at a new location and then press the **Ctrl+V** keys to paste the text. To copy and move text to another location, select the text and then press the **Ctrl+C** keys. Place the cursor at a new location and then press the **Ctrl+V** keys to paste the text.

As an example, you wrote a large Word document and then saved it in your files. You discover that the filename you originally assigned to the document is wrong. To fix this issue, you can rename the file using the following steps:

1. Locate and select the filename.
2. Click **Organize** and select **Rename.** The selected filename becomes highlighted in a box.
3. Type the corrected filename into the highlighted box and press **Enter.** The filename is now corrected.

Formatting Text

To format text, select the text you want to format and use the font formatting options in the Ribbon toolbar under the *Home* tab (see Figure 3.52). To select an entire word, double-click on the word. To select large amounts of text in a single click, hold down the **Shift** key while you click. For example, if you wanted to select text in an entire paragraph, you position your cursor at the beginning of the paragraph, press the **Shift** key, and click once with the left mouse button.

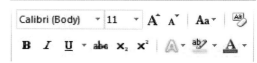

FIGURE 3.52

FAQ: HOW CAN I SELECT ITEMS IN A LIST?

There are two ways to select items in a list. You can use the **Ctrl** key or the **Shift** key. Each method is briefly described below:

- **The Ctrl key:** Hold down the **Ctrl** key to click and select specific items in a list.
- **The Shift key:** Hold down the **Shift** key to click the first item and select everything in the list. For example, you have a bulleted list of 50 items and want to select all 50 items. Press the **Shift** key and click the left mouse button once at the beginning of the list. All 50 items are now selected.

Conventions for Working with Dialog Boxes

The dialog box is a small window that appears during use of an application or program to ask the user a brief question or confirm a command. The following are some basic conventions for working with dialog boxes in Windows 7:

- *Confirming or Canceling Queries:* When a dialog box appears, the user has an opportunity to confirm or "opt out" of a change. For example, if an unsaved document exists before exiting Microsoft Word, a dialog box appears to ask the user to save, not save, or cancel the changes.
- *Using Enter to Confirm a Selected Button:* In addition to the mouse, the **Enter** key also activates the highlighted button in a dialog box. In the example above, you can press the **Enter** key to choose the Save commands without using the mouse.
- *Using the Tab Key to Move Among Options:* Using the **Tab** key cycles through and highlights the different option buttons in a dialog box. For example, if your mouse is disabled or not connected, you can tab through the different options and press **Enter** to confirm your choice.
- *Using the Esc Key to Cancel:* The **Esc** key removes the dialog box completely from the screen.

Commonly Used Office Commands

Microsoft Office 2010 has hundreds of commands, options, and features to choose from when creating a document. The following are some common Microsoft Office commands.

Cut, Copy, Paste, and Paste Special

For text editing, cut, copy, and paste are probably three of the most commonly used commands in Microsoft Office. The user has two choices to perform these commands: keyboard keys or the Ribbon. For keyboard keys, the following keys are used:

- To cut, use the **Ctrl+X** keys.
- To copy, use the **Ctrl+C** keys.
- To paste, use the **Ctrl+V** keys.

On the Ribbon, the **Cut, Copy,** and **Paste** buttons are located under the *Home* tab in the upper left corner of the window. If you paste items from the web or from another document source, click the down arrow under the **Paste** button to use the Paste Special feature. The Paste Special feature allows you to control the formatting attributes of the data prior to pasting it into a document. Formatting issues such as text and graphics size are corrected before the data is pasted, thus eliminating any later clean-up work.

Changing Views

Microsoft Office 2010 offers many options to view your documents. Click the *View* tab in the Ribbon to display all your viewing options. For example, in Microsoft Word, you could view the document in Full Screen Reading and the pages appear like the open pages of a book. In Microsoft PowerPoint, you can preview the slides all on one screen in numerical order (Slide Sorter) or set up a slide notebook combination to add notes about each slide (Notes Page). See Figure 3.53.

FIGURE 3.53

Using the Format Painter

The **Format Painter** allows you to apply formatting styles to other text with the click of a button. Click the text with the desired style, click the **Format Painter** button, and then click the text to change the style. The **Format Painter** button is under the *Home* tab Ribbon in the upper left corner.

> **FORMAT PAINTER** A command on the *Home* tab that provides access to document formatting styles.

Using Find and Replace

The Find and Replace feature allows you to quickly search for keywords and replace them. The **Find and Replace** button is located under the *Home* tab Ribbon in the upper right corner of the window. See Figure 3.54.

FIGURE 3.54

Using Go To

The Go To feature allows the user to navigate anywhere in the current document. Access the *Go To* menu through the *Find* pull-down menu under the *Home* tab Ribbon in the upper right corner of the window. Click the **Find** button pull-down arrow and then select **Go To.**

Inserting Graphics and Symbols

Microsoft Office 2010 offers the user hundreds of graphical options to enhance documents. Under the *Insert* tab Ribbon are several categories of graphics and symbols under the *Illustrations* group. See Figure 3.55.

FIGURE 3.55

Using the Thesaurus

Microsoft Office 2010 contains a thesaurus in the *Review* tab Ribbon. Click the **Thesaurus** button and enter a word into the pane on the far right of the window to generate suggestions for similar words. See Figure 3.56.

FIGURE 3.56

Spell Checking, Grammar Checking, and AutoCorrect

Microsoft Office 2010 has features to check spelling and grammar, and to automatically correct both. The spelling and grammar check feature is located under the *Review* tab of the Ribbon. Each of the checking modes is briefly described below.

- *Spell Checking:* Microsoft Office 2010 checks the spelling of words against a preloaded dictionary within the application. Once the application identifies a misspelled word, you receive several suggestions for correcting the word or you can ignore the error. For example, if you misspelled the word "telephone" by spelling it "telefon," the checker would highlight "telefon" and present several substitute words. The first word in the list represents the closest match to the misspelled word and is, in fact, the word "telephone." To correct the word, click **Change.**

- *Grammar Checking:* Microsoft Office 2010 also checks grammatical errors within sentences and offers you suggestions for rephrasing or lets you ignore the error. For example, if you type a sentence as a fragment, the grammar checker highlights the fragment and suggests ways to rephrase the sentence. After you choose the most appropriate sentence, click **Change.**

- *AutoCorrecting:* The AutoCorrect feature accepts the first highlighted item under the Suggestions window and applies that correction automatically to the word or phrase in the future. For example, if you misspelled the same word 30 times, you correct all 30 errors by accepting the first correction and applying it 29 more times by clicking **AutoCorrect.**

Using the Document Information Panel

The Document Information Panel provides information and statistics about a given document and allows you to change properties of a document in one centralized location. Click the *File* tab and then **Info** on the far left to open the Document Information Panel. Click the three buttons on the left side of the window to change settings and properties.

If you want to know some basic information about a Word file such as how many pages the document contains, who the author is, or when the file was last modified or printed, you use the Document Information Panel. See Figure 3.57. Here you can determine the following basic information:

- File size
- Number of pages
- Number of words
- Total editing time
- Date last modified
- Date created
- Date last printed
- Document author

FIGURE 3.57

FIGURE 3.58

Using Office Help

You can click on the **question mark** icon (see Figure 3.58) in the upper right-hand corner of the window to access help information for any Microsoft Office application. As an alternate, press the F1 function key.

EXPANSION

Other software applications on the market perform the same tasks as Microsoft Office, including the OpenOffice suite of products. The OpenOffice suite is a free, open-source software offering with similar applications for word processing, presentations, and spreadsheets. Once you learn how to use Microsoft Office, you can apply this knowledge to OpenOffice. More information on OpenOffice can be found at www.openoffice.org.

SUMMARY

Few will argue that computer skills are one of the most important requirements in today's competitive jobs marketplace. Over the years, computers have become smaller, more powerful, faster, and capable of handling more information than ever before. Knowing how to harness and use these advanced features creates limitless possibilities for the average computer user.

Computers are now more user-friendly and engage the user with simple menu systems and clearly labeled buttons. Tasks that once took hours are now accomplished in minutes using advanced software and programs. Imagine for a moment all of the organizing, writing, communicating, printing, entertainment, and educating that is accomplished from one machine. Let the journey begin.

KEY TERMS

- Backstage View
- central processing unit (CPU)
- command
- context-sensitive menus
- dialog box
- Format Painter
- function key
- gadget
- graphical user interface (GUI)
- hardware

- Key Tips
- menu
- Microsoft Access
- Microsoft Excel
- Microsoft Office 2010
- Microsoft OneNote
- Microsoft Outlook
- Microsoft PowerPoint
- Microsoft Publisher
- Microsoft Word

- network drive
- operating system
- Quick Access Toolbar
- Recycle Bin
- scroll bar
- shortcut
- software
- status bar
- task bar
- Windows Explorer

Productivity Software: Word Processing

THE POWER OF WORD PROCESSING

Perhaps you have caught yourself saying, "I have to go—I have a paper to type." You might think of using a word processor as typing, but consider the differences between typewritten sheets of paper and documents created by a word processing application. When a document is created and saved electronically, it can be retrieved for **editing**. Corrections can be made and the document can be resaved for future reference or reuse. Spelling Check catches words that might be misspelled and suggests possible corrections; AutoCorrect even fixes common mistakes as you type.

With a typewriter, the only way to emphasize a word is by underlining it. With word processing, you can design pages that direct your reader's eyes through the content by adding elements of **formatting**; such as changing the text's color, **point** size, or **font**; aligning text; or adding **bullet points**. Headers and footers can add information automatically to the top and/or bottom of each page, including page numbers.

A finished document can be distributed to others by e-mailing it as an attachment to a message, copying it to a CD-ROM, or saving it as a web page for posting to the web. Or you can simply print a **hard copy**—just like a typewritten page.

EDITING Correcting text by inserting, replacing, or deleting.

FORMATTING Changing the appearance of text by changing its size, color, typeface, and so on.

POINT A unit of measurement for sizing text in word processing programs.

FONT A typeface design, such as Times New Roman or Verdana.

BULLET POINTS Content that is indented and begins with a large dot; frequently used to set off lists.

HARD COPY A printed copy of a document.

KEY CONCEPTS

- The Power of Word Processing

- Common Business Tasks That Use Word

- A Brief History of Word Processing Applications

- Word Processing Basics

- Advanced Topics in Word

COMMON BUSINESS TASKS THAT USE WORD PROCESSING

Microsoft Word 2010® word processing software, which is better known as just "Word," is the most popular word processing application worldwide. It is used in every type of business and in every type of industry. For instance, in the health care industry, medical transcriptionists might use Word to finalize doctors' notes from daily patient visits, which are then uploaded to an electronic medical record (EMR) system for use by other staff. Hospital personnel might use Word to print instructions for patients, write referrals, and prepare administrative reports for executives and owners.

Legal assistants might use Word to create and save multiple versions of a lease as a real estate transaction is negotiated, or they may use it to draft legal briefs for use in court. Draft briefs are saved and edited many times before being submitted to court for approval by a judge. The American Association for Paralegal Education lists word processing skills as a core competency for all paralegal graduates. Law enforcement officers might use Word to type police reports and investigative reports from crime scenes and arrests. The documents are then saved into large record management systems that can be searched at a later date. Virtually every worker today uses a word processing application at some point. Learning to use one efficiently is an essential skill.

A BRIEF HISTORY OF WORD PROCESSING

The earliest word processors developed from the simple text editors running on large mainframe computers and from semiautomated typewriters, such as the IBM Selectric, which became popular in the late 1960s and 1970s. Most were standalone office machines. In order to see what a page actually looked like, you had to print it. Word processors took a giant step forward with the introduction of **graphical user interfaces** that could show a document's pages on the screen in their

GRAPHICAL USER INTERFACE
A way to manipulate a computer system by interacting with graphics (icons, buttons, menus, and so on) instead of by typing in commands.

final format. This **WYSIWYG** (what-you-see-is-what-you-get) ability made word processing significantly faster and easier. Apple's MacWrite software popularized WYSIWYG word processors for the general public in 1984, when it was released as a companion to the original Apple Macintosh computer.

WordPerfect was the most popular word processor for IBM personal computers in the late 1980s and 1990s; subsequently, Microsoft Word took the lead. WordPerfect was especially popular in the legal industry, and a small number of law firms continue to use it today. Free alternatives to Microsoft Word include the downloadable application OpenOffice.org Writer and Google Docs, a web-based word processor.

Microsoft Word has been revised a number of times since its introduction in 1989. Word 2002 was included with the Microsoft Office XP® operating system software package and is still used by some individuals and small businesses. Word 2003 showed only minor improvements, but Word 2007 provided a redesigned interface with a ribbon toolbar instead of menus and commands. Word 2010 improves on that design and is the application used in this chapter to illustrate word processing concepts.

There are often several ways to accomplish the same task in Word. You will discover alternatives to the methods described in this chapter as you gain more experience in word processing. Reading, experimenting, and talking to other users will help you learn shortcuts and will help keep your work interesting.

WORD PROCESSING BASICS

Creating a New Document

You already know how to launch Microsoft Windows® applications. When Microsoft Word is launched, it opens with a new blank document on the screen. See Figure 4.1. If you close that document, you can create a new one at any time.

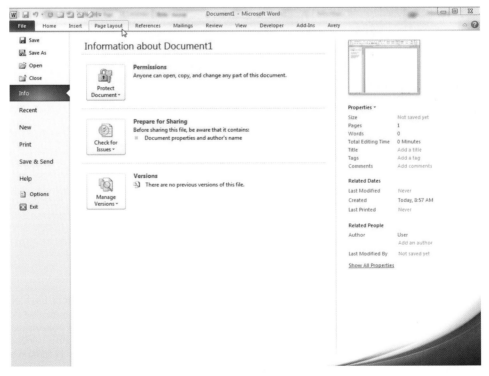

FIGURE 4.1

To create a new document in Word:

1. Click the *File* tab.
2. Click **New**.
3. Under **Available Templates**, click a document icon.
4. Click **Create**.

Fundamentally, all new documents created in Word are based on a template. In addition to the blank document template, Word offers dozens more to help you create documents such as resumes and cover letters, newsletters, and reports. Some are included with the application; others can be downloaded from office.microsoft.com if you are connected to the Internet. See Figure 4.2.

If you choose one of these templates to create a new document, you can add your own text and make modifications as needed. The template itself will not be altered, and you can use it again. When you click on a document template icon, a template preview window allows you to see what the template formatting looks like.

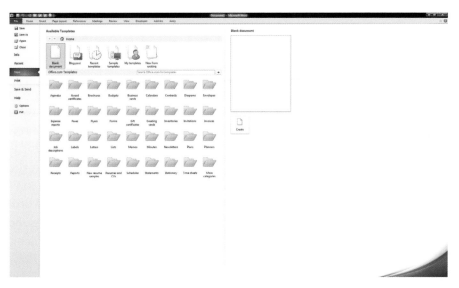

FIGURE 4.2

The Word Window

The onscreen document is displayed in a document window within the Word application window. See Figure 4.3.

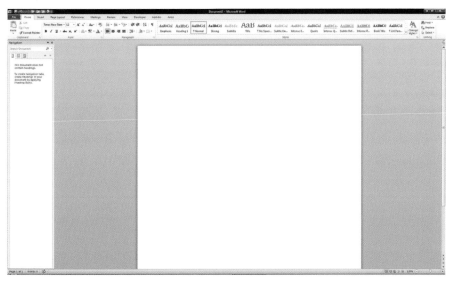

FIGURE 4.3

The Ribbon at the top of the screen contains the set of commands for working in a document. It is organized into tabs, which are labeled *File, Home, Insert, Page Layout, References, Mailings, Review, View, Developer, Add-Ins*, and *Avery*. Other tabs appear as you need them. For example, it is possible to add tables to a document. When you click in a table, *Design* and *Layout Table Tool* tabs automatically appear.

Click a tab to display buttons for features organized by groups. For example, under the *Home* tab, the *Clipboard* group contains buttons for **Cut**, **Copy**, **Paste**, and the **Format Painter**. See Figure 4.4. Some groups have a small arrow at the bottom right called the dialog box launcher. Click the dialog box launcher to find settings for additional features related to the group.

FIGURE 4.4

Click the *File* tab to access the Backstage View. The Backstage View is where you manage documents. As you have seen, you can click **New** to create a new document. **Open** lets you retrieve an existing document. You also save, send, and print documents from the Backstage View. To return to your document from the Backstage View, click the *Home* tab or press the **Esc** key on the keyboard.

FIGURE 4.5

The *Home* tab contains commands for basic tasks in Word. The *Font* group, for example, contains buttons for changing the appearance of characters (letters and numbers) in the document, such as the size of the text, boldfacing, and italicizing. The *Paragraph* group buttons change paragraph features such as the space between lines, the alignment of text, and shading. Refer again to Figure 4.4. The *Editing* group includes buttons to find and replace words in your document. See Figure 4.5.

The *Insert* tab is used to insert items such as tables, pictures, diagrams, and headers/footers into your document. See Figure 4.6.

FIGURE 4.6

The *Page Layout* tab has commands for page-level formatting, such as setting the size of the margins and changing the page orientation and paper size. See Figure 4.7.

FIGURE 4.7

The *References* tab is useful for academic papers. Use it to add footnotes and citations, and to create a table of contents automatically. See Figure 4.8.

FIGURE 4.8

The *Mailings* tab is used for creating envelopes and labels, and for mail merges, such as creating form letters. You can create a data document for the parts of the letter that change, such as the recipients' names and addresses, and a main document with the remaining parts of the letter that do not change, and merge them together to create personalized letters. See Figure 4.9.

FIGURE 4.9

The *Review* tab includes commands to check the accuracy of your document, such as checking spelling and grammar, and the Track Changes feature that lets you manage the changes made to a document. See Figure 4.10; in this image, Track Changes is turned on (note the yellow shading on the option).

FIGURE 4.10

The *View* tab lets you customize the way your document appears on the screen. You can zoom in and out, see your document as it will print, and display a ruler on the screen for precise measurements. See Figure 4.11.

FIGURE 4.11

As with most other applications, scroll bars on the right side of the screen allow you to move up or down in the document window. If the view is very large, the screen may not accommodate the entire width of the document; if this is the case, scroll bars will also be available at the bottom of the screen to help you move to the left or right and see all of the document.

How to Use the Help Feature in Word

On the top right of the document window is a question mark icon. Click it to look for help on a topic using the Word Help function (or press the F1 function key on your keyboard as a shortcut). See Figure 4.12.

FIGURE 4.12

A list of Help topics appears in a pop-up window. If your computer is connected to the Internet, topics from microsoft.office.com are listed (note the lower right-hand corner of Figure 4.12). If your computer is not connected to the Internet, topics from the Word built-in Help are displayed. To find out more about a Word feature, click in the search box at the top of the Help dialog box, enter a keyword to identify what you are searching for, and then press the **Enter** key. If you do not know what the feature you are interested in is called, click on the topics listed to browse through them.

When you are finished with the Help feature, click the close button in its top right corner to close the window and return to your document. If the Help feature in Word does not answer your question, consider asking it with a general web search tool, such as Google or Microsoft Bing®, including the keywords Word 2010 in your search. Usually, someone else has already asked your question and at least some assistance has been posted online.

Status Bar Options

The status bar is the strip along the bottom of the Word window. It displays useful information such as the current page and the total number of pages in the document, the number of words in the document, available document views, and a zoom feature.

The area that displays the current page and total number of pages in the document is actually a button. Click it to display the Find and Replace dialog box. You can also jump to a certain page number by entering the page number and clicking **Go To**. See Figure 4.13.

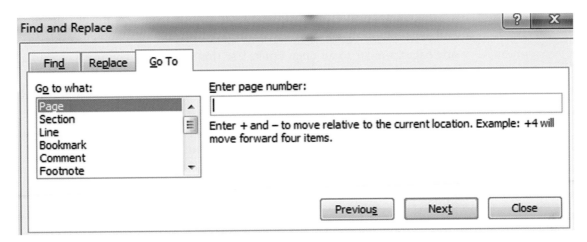

FIGURE 4.13

Have you ever needed to know how many words are in your document? If you are writing for publication, or have an assignment due, you might be required to produce a certain number of words and pages. Click **Word Count** on the status bar to display a dialog box with the number of pages, words, characters, paragraphs, and lines. See Figure 4.14.

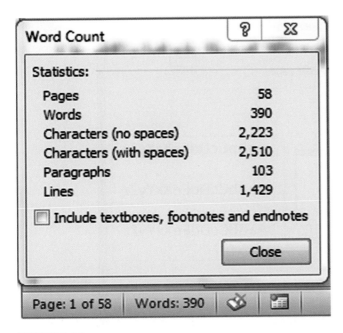

FIGURE 4.14

FIGURE 4.15

Word allows you to view your document in a variety of ways while entering and editing text. The **View** button on the status bar contains icons that allow you to change the display in the document window. These buttons are also available from the *View* tab on the Ribbon. To change from one view to the other, click on the view's button. When you close a document in a view and reopen it, the same view will be active. See Figure 4.15.

- Print Layout view, which is the first option on the left, shows you the page as it will look when printed. This is the typical working view of the document.
- Full Screen Reading view, the next option, displays the document in side-by-side pages, similar to an open book. Use this view when you want to read a document instead of working on it.
- Web Layout view, the third option, displays the document window as it would appear if it were saved in Word as a web page and then displayed in a web browser.
- Outline view, the fourth option, is used with the Word outlining feature that uses styles and numbering to organize the layout.
- Draft view, the fifth option, is a very simple view that displays only the text from the document, without graphics or margins, and can be helpful while editing a document.

The sliding zoom bar on the right of the status bar is used to make the screen display of the document larger or smaller. Point to the sliding zoom bar, hold down the mouse button, and drag. As you zoom in to make the text display larger, only one page of the document is shown. As you zoom out and make the text display smaller, you will see more pages of your document. Click **Zoom In** (plus sign) or **Zoom Out** (minus sign) to expand or shrink the display 10 percent at a time. See Figure 4.16.

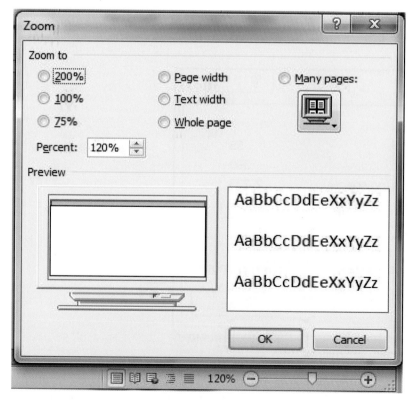

FIGURE 4.16

A more detailed Print Preview is available from the Backstage View. Click the *File* tab on the Ribbon and click **Print**. Print options are available on the left side of the screen and a preview of the document is on the right. Below the document are a left arrow followed by a page number, total pages, and a right arrow. Click the left arrow to view the previous page in the document and the right arrow to view the next page. See Figure 4.17.

FIGURE 4.17

EXERCISE 4.1: CREATING A NEW DOCUMENT AND USING THE HELP FEATURE IN WORD

You are the president and founder of the new Student Technology Association (STA) AT your college. The group is holding its first meeting on campus in two weeks. Before then you need to get the new organization approved, publicize the meeting, and prepare for the event. With work, family responsibilities, and a demanding class load, your free time is limited. Your goal is to create the documents needed for the STA as quickly and efficiently as possible. You begin by creating a new document in Word 2010 and reviewing the screen layout and Help feature.

1. Launch Microsoft Word.

2. Review the Word window by clicking the tabs and pointing to the buttons (without clicking) to read the Help information that is displayed.

3. Access the Word Help feature.

4. Search for help on saving, closing, and opening files if you need a review.

5. Browse the Help feature. Write a brief summary of the most interesting Word fact you learn.

6. Save the document to the location specified by your instructor. Name it "Draft STA Letter." Close it, or leave it open for the next exercise.

Entering Text

Before you begin to type, make sure you are in Print Layout view and that the non-printing formatting marks are turned on. What are formatting marks? They represent the keys you press while typing that do not appear in the printed document, such as the spaces that are created when you press the spacebar, and the blank lines that are created when you press the **Enter** key.

Word has a toggle button to turn on or off the display of formatting marks. When they are displayed, you see a dot on the screen each time you press the space-bar, a ¶ (paragraph mark) each time you press the **Enter** key, and an arrow each time you press the **Tab** key. It is a good idea to display them while working on a document. You can more easily see why text appears where it does on the page, and they are easy to delete if needed. See Figure 4.18A for a document without formatting marks and Figure 4.18B for the same document with formatting marks.

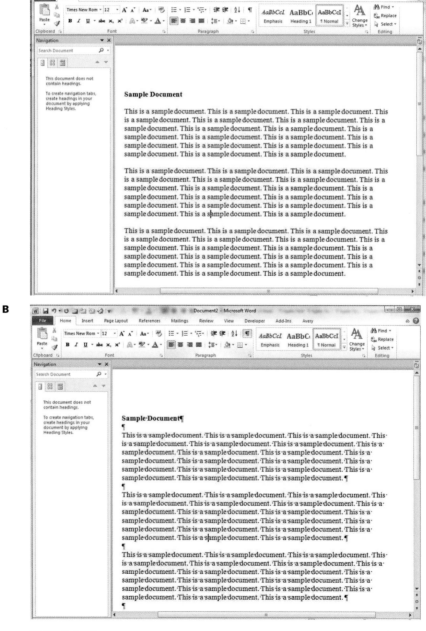

FIGURE 4.18

To show or hide formatting marks:

1. Click the *Home* tab.
2. In the *Paragraph* group, locate the **Show/Hide Paragraph** button.
3. If the button is gold, formatting marks are set to be displayed. If the button is not gold, click it to display them.

Positioning and Inserting Text

The document window contains an insertion point that appears as a blinking, black vertical line. A blinking insertion point signals where the text will appear when you start to type.

Your mouse pointer also communicates information. As you move it around the document window, the pointer shape is what is called an i-beam. The i-beam shape signals that you are in an area of the screen where text can be typed. Moving the mouse pointer over the Ribbon, for example, changes the shape of the pointer to an arrow. The arrow is a signal that you can make a choice by clicking. As you type, the insertion point moves to the right. To reposition it, for example, to insert a word into a paragraph written previously, use the mouse to position the i-beam pointer (see Figure 4.19) where you want to insert and click to place the insertion point. You can also use the keyboard to position the insertion point.

FIGURE 4.19

Word offers a number of ways to navigate through the text of a document on the screen using the keyboard. See Figure 4.20.

PRESSING THIS...	MOVES THE INSERTION POINT HERE...
Home	the beginning of the current line
End	the end of the current line
Page Up	up one full screen
Page Down	down one full screen
Up Arrow	up to the previous line
Down Arrow	down to the next line
Right Arrow	one character to the right
Left Arrow	one character to the left
Ctrl+Home	the beginning of the document
Ctrl+End	the end of the document

FIGURE 4.20   *Navigating Through Document Text on the Keyboard*

Remember, using the keyboard moves the insertion point. If you use the mouse to move through the document, you must then click to place the insertion point where you want to begin typing.

As you type a paragraph, notice that as one line is filled, the insertion point moves on to a new line automatically. You do not need to press the **Enter** key until a paragraph is completed. When you do, the insertion point moves to the next line. If you are typing a short line, such as a title, press the **Enter** key at the end of the line. Word considers everything that ends with a paragraph return mark to be a paragraph, even if it is shorter than one line.

Typists using typewriters pressed the spacebar two times between sentences. In word processing, as with typesetting, the standard is to enter only one space between sentences.

If you make a mistake while typing, press the **Backspace** key to remove one character to the left of the insertion point each time you press it. If the insertion point is positioned in existing text, you can use the **Delete** key to remove one character to the right each time you press it.

As you type enough to fill a page, the insertion point moves on to a new page automatically. If you want to start a new page before the one you are on is filled, for instance, in order to start a new chapter, you can insert a manual page break.

EXERCISE 4.2: ENTERING TEXT

The dean of student affairs must approve all new student organizations. You need to write a letter to the dean to request permission to launch the association as an official campus organization.

1. Check to make sure your view is set to Print Layout.

2. Check to make sure your formatting marks are displayed.

3. Open the Draft STA Letter.docx file you created in the last exercise, if necessary.

4. Enter the following text:

   Dean Juanita Alvarez
   Room 100, E Building
   College Campus, IL 60060

   Dear Dean Alvarez:

   I am the president of a new student group called the Student Technology Academic Association (STAA). I am writing to request that the STAA be granted official recognition as a campus organization.

   We have recently developed our website and, if granted official recognition, we would like it to be displayed on your office's home page. I look forward to hearing from you.

   Our mission is to share with our 30 members the latest use of communication tools and to encourage our members to pursue careers in the technology field. We plan to invite a leader from a local technology firm to speak to our group at a monthly meeting we would like to hold in the Student Center. The STAA will help raise our campus's visibility in the local technology community. Professor Margaret Lee of Computer Science is our faculty advisor.

   Sincerely,

   [enter your name here]
   President, Student Technology Academic Association

5. Save the changes to your document. Close it, or leave it open for the next exercise.

WHAT'S THE SQUIGGLY RED LINE? AUTOMATIC SPELLING AND GRAMMAR CHECKING IN WORD

Have you ever typed a sentence and noticed a squiggly line underneath your text? This is actually a friendly warning from Word that something may need correction. A red line below a word signals that it does not match any of the entries in the Word internal dictionary and may be spelled incorrectly. A green line means a phrase or sentence appears to be grammatically incorrect.

In either case, right click on the underlined text to find suggestions for corrections. Click on a correction to make the change in your document, but beware—an automated system like this is not always accurate. As a human writer, it is your job to determine whether the word or phrase is correct as written or not.

To enter a manual page break:

1. Click where you want to start a new page.
2. Click the *Insert* tab.
3. In the *Pages* group, click **Page Break**. (Or press **Ctrl+Enter**.)

Selecting Text

In Word, as with other Windows-based applications, you must select (highlight) text before you act on it. Selecting indicates what you want a command to act on. For example, if you have several words, a large paragraph, or several paragraphs to delete, it would be time-consuming to press the **Delete** key over and over to delete it one character at a time. By first selecting the entire text you want to delete (by holding down and not releasing the **Shift** key as you first click on the first word you wish to delete and then click on the last word you want to delete), you can press the **Delete** key to act on, and remove, the entire block at once. If you want to emphasize one word in a sentence, you can select that word before clicking **Bold** on the Ribbon. Or, if you want to copy an address from one part of your document to another, you can select the address and then choose the **Copy** command.

Selected text appears highlighted in a black background with white lettering. You can select text using the mouse, the keyboard, or a combination of both.

To select text by dragging with the mouse:

1. Position the insertion point at the beginning of the text you want to select.
2. Hold down the mouse button and drag the i-beam pointer to the end of the text you want to select.
3. Release the mouse button.

To deselect the text, click anywhere in the document or press any navigation key.

When trying this for the first time, you may "lose the highlight." Do not worry. Just start over and keep practicing to get it right, or try the following mouse/keyboard combination method, which is especially useful for selecting text across multiple pages.

To select text with **Shift+Click**:

1. Click to place the insertion point at the beginning of the text you want to select.
2. Hold down the **Shift** key on the keyboard.
3. Without dragging, click again at the end of the text you want to select.

Word offers several additional mouse or mouse/keyboard shortcuts. See Figure 4.21.

TO SELECT THIS...	DO THIS...
Word	double-click anywhere on the word
Paragraph	triple-click anywhere on the paragraph
Paragraph	move your pointer into the left margin of the document so that it takes the shape of a right-slanting arrow and double-click
Sentence	hold down the **Ctrl** key and click anywhere in the sentence
Document	move your pointer into the left margin of the document so that it takes the shape of a right-slanting arrow and triple-click

FIGURE 4.21 **Mouse and Keyboard Shortcuts**

To select text using the keyboard, hold down the **Shift** key on the keyboard while following any of the navigation methods in the table above. For example, hold down **Shift** and press the **End** key to select everything from the insertion point to the end of the current line. Holding down **Shift** and pressing **Ctrl+End** selects everything from the insertion point to the end of the document. To select the entire document using the keyboard, press **Ctrl +A**.

As you select text, you will notice a small, faint, floating toolbar above and to the right of the selected text. This is the Mini-Toolbar. Rest your pointer on it to make it stronger, or continue with your work to make it disappear. The Mini-Toolbar is a quick way to access some common formatting commands that are also available from the Ribbon. See Figure 4.22.

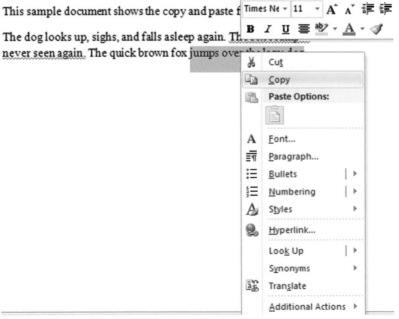

FIGURE 4.22

Editing Text

Editing text refers to making changes by inserting, deleting, or replacing text. To insert text, click to place the insertion point where you want to begin typing. Keep in mind that the i-beam pointer is necessary only to position the insertion point. After you have clicked to put the insertion point where you want it, you can begin to type without any concern about the i-beam pointer's location.

To delete text, click to place the insertion point to the left of the text to be deleted and press the **Delete** key. Or click to place the insertion point to the right of the text to be deleted and press the **Backspace** key. If you select text and then press either **Delete** or **Backspace,** the entire selection is deleted. See Figures 4.23A and 4.23B.

To replace text, select it and begin typing. You do not need to delete the text before typing. If text is selected and you begin to type, whatever you type replaces the selected text.

A

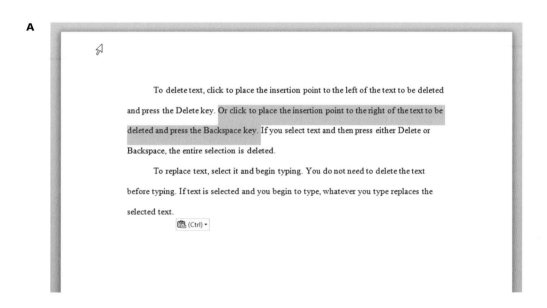

B

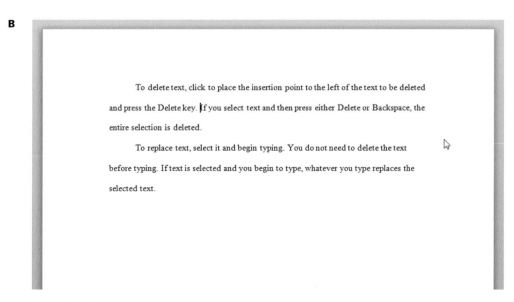

FIGURE 4.23

Cut, Copy, and Paste

If something is already typed in your document or in another location, you do not need to retype it to use it again. You can select text and copy it from one location, then paste it where you want to use it. See Figure 4.24.

FIGURE 4.24

To copy and paste text:

1. Select the text to be copied.
2. Click the *Home* tab.
3. In the *Clipboard* group, click **Copy**.
4. Click to place the insertion point where you want to insert the copied text.
5. From the *Clipboard* group, click **Paste**.

Cut and paste is used to move text from one location to another. To move text using cut and paste:

1. Select the text to be moved.
2. Click the *Home* tab on the Ribbon.
3. In the *Clipboard* group, click **Cut**.
4. Click to place the insertion point where you want to insert the copied text.
5. In the *Clipboard* group, click **Paste**.

Look closely at the **Paste** button and you will notice that it has two parts. The top part has the **Paste** icon. The bottom part has a small triangular arrow pointing down. Clicking the top part of the button pastes according to the default paste settings in Word. Clicking the drop-down arrow gives you a choice of three ways to paste. The *Keep Source Formatting* choice will paste what you cut or copied with its formatting intact. The *Keep Text Only* choice is often used to paste material from other documents or web pages, because it can be used to leave any source formatting codes behind, keeping your document more stable.

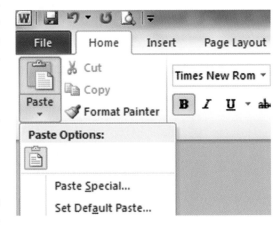

FIGURE 4.25

To paste unformatted text (see Figure 4.25):

1. Cut or copy text and position the insertion point as described above.
2. Click the lower half of the **Paste** button.
3. Click *Keep Text Only*.

Or if you prefer, you can use the **Paste Options** button to control exactly what is pasted. Immediately after a paste, a small icon appears at the bottom right of the pasted text. This **Paste Options** button looks like a small clipboard, because Microsoft's term for the holding area of cut or copied text is the Clipboard. Click its drop-down arrow to choose how the information is pasted into your document.

Default paste settings—the settings that are followed when you click the top half of the **Paste** button—are set in Word Options, along with many other Word customizations.

To set Word Options for pasting:

1. Click the *File* tab.
2. Click **Options.**
3. Click **Advanced** on the left.
4. In the *Cut, Copy, and Paste* group, use the drop-down arrow to set the Pasting from Other Programs option to *Keep Text Only* to be sure that you are only bringing "clean" text into your document no matter what you paste into it, without having to expand the **Paste** button.

Keyboard shortcuts are popular for cut, copy, and paste. Use **Ctrl+X** to cut, **Ctrl+C** to copy, and **Ctrl+V** to paste. Or try using the right-click shortcut. Right-click on selected text and click **Cut** or **Copy**. Right-click where you want to paste and click the appropriate **Paste** icon. See Figure 4.26.

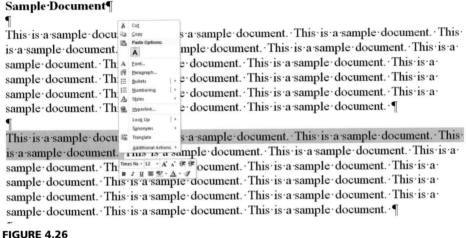

FIGURE 4.26

Global Find and Replace

Word allows you to edit text by automatically replacing it with other text. This can be done one word at a time or throughout the entire document, globally. As an example, imagine that Tanya Smith, a paralegal, just finished typing the final draft of a legal brief she has prepared. The 10-page brief is about the famous *Brown v. Board of Education* landmark case and thus uses the name in several places throughout the document—but she has just realized that she misspelled the name Brown as Browne.

In this case, the name does not have to be deleted from 10 pages worth of text. Instead, Tanya can use the global Find and Replace function in Word to make all of the substitutions.

To find each occurrence of a word or phrase and replace it with another:

1. Click the *Home* tab.
2. In the *Editing* group, click **Replace.**
3. In the *Find what* box, type the text that you want to search for and replace.
4. In the *Replace with* box, type the replacement text.
5. Click **Find Next**, and then select one of the following:

   - Click **Replace** to replace the highlighted text and find the next time it occurs in the document.
   - Click **Replace All** to replace all instances of the text in your document.
   - Click **Find Next** to skip this instance of the text and proceed to the next time it appears in the document.

EXERCISE 4.3: EDITING TEXT

Your draft letter to the dean requesting official status for the STA has been reviewed by the other founding members, and you need to make a few changes.

1. Check to make sure your view is set to Print Layout.

2. Check to make sure your formatting marks are displayed.

3. Open the Draft STA Letter.docx file you created in the last exercise, if necessary.

4. Insert today's date and four blank lines at the top of the letter, above the paragraph that reads "Dear Dean Alvarez." (Tip: Type the date or experiment with the *Insert* tab | *Text* group | **Date & Time** feature.)

5. Replace "Sincerely" with "Yours truly." (Tip: After you type "Your," notice the AutoCorrect option that appears on the screen. Press **Enter** to choose it.)

6. Delete the word "Academic" from the two places it appears in the document. (Tip: Experiment with the *Home* tab | *Editing* group | Find command.)

7. Change every instance of the word STAA in the document to STA, without correcting each instance individually.

8. Move the second paragraph (that starts with "We have recently...") after the third paragraph (that starts with "Our mission is...").

9. Save the changes as a new document to the location specified by your instructor. Name it "Revised STA Letter."

10. Copy your name and title to a new Word document. Save it to the location specified by your instructor. Name it "STA Flyer." Close Revised STA Letter.docx. Close STA Flyer.docx, or leave it open for the next exercise.

Formatting Text

As described earlier, formatting refers to changing the appearance of the letters, numbers, and layout of your document to make it more visually appealing and readable. It may be easier to understand the hundreds of formatting choices available by thinking of them at the character, paragraph, and page level.

Character Formatting

Character formatting in Word includes everything that can change the appearance of individual letters and numbers. As with other formatting choices, it can be applied to selected text, or turned on before typing and turned off after typing the formatted text. For example, to make the word "success" appear bolded and italicized, you can type "success," select it, and then click the **Bold** and **Italic** buttons on the Ribbon. Or you can click the **Bold** and **Italic** buttons first, then type "success," then click the **Bold** and **Italic** buttons again to stop using them before you continue typing. The former technique provides a useful preview of the effect of the change on the selected text. The latter technique is especially useful if you use keyboard shortcuts to turn the formatting commands on and off.

To change the appearance of existing characters:

1. Select the text you want to change.
2. Click the *Home* tab.
3. In the *Font* group, click the button for the desired effect.

To choose character formatting before typing text:

1. Click the *Home* tab.
2. In the *Font* group, click the button for the desired effect.
3. When you start to type, the text will appear with the formatting you have preset.
4. Click the formatting button again to turn it off before continuing.

Remember that the small arrow in the bottom right of the *Font* group is a dialog box launcher. Click it to access even more character formatting choices. See Figure 4.27.

FIGURE 4.27

Paragraph Formatting

Paragraph formatting in Word includes all the commands that can change the appearance of text ending in a paragraph return mark, whether the text is one line or many. As with character formatting, you can type text first and then select it and apply paragraph formatting, or present paragraph formatting before you begin typing and change or turn the options off when you are finished. See Figure 4.28.

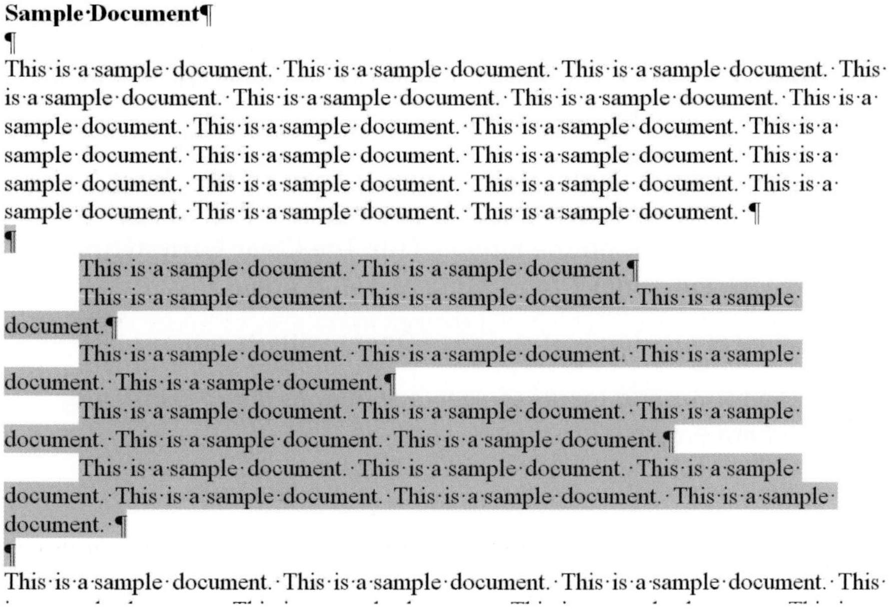

Sample·Document¶
¶
This·is·a·sample·document.·This·is·a·sample·document.·This·is·a·sample·document.·This· is·a·sample·document.·This·is·a·sample·document.·This·is·a·sample·document.·This·is·a· sample·document.·This·is·a·sample·document.·This·is·a·sample·document.·This·is·a· sample·document.·This·is·a·sample·document.·This·is·a·sample·document.·This·is·a· sample·document.·This·is·a·sample·document.·This·is·a·sample·document.·This·is·a· sample·document.·This·is·a·sample·document.·This·is·a·sample·document.·¶
¶
   This·is·a·sample·document.·This·is·a·sample·document.¶
   This·is·a·sample·document.·This·is·a·sample·document.·This·is·a·sample· document.¶
   This·is·a·sample·document.·This·is·a·sample·document.·This·is·a·sample· document.·This·is·a·sample·document.¶
   This·is·a·sample·document.·This·is·a·sample·document.·This·is·a·sample· document.·This·is·a·sample·document.·This·is·a·sample·document.¶
   This·is·a·sample·document.·This·is·a·sample·document.·This·is·a·sample· document.·This·is·a·sample·document.·This·is·a·sample·document.·This·is·a·sample· document.·¶
¶
This·is·a·sample·document.·This·is·a·sample·document.·This·is·a·sample·document.·This·

FIGURE 4.28

EXERCISE 4.4: CHARACTER FORMATTING

To promote your first STA meeting, you want to prepare an eye-catching flyer to post around campus.

1. Check to make sure your view is set to Print Layout.

2. Check to make sure your formatting marks are displayed.

3. Open the STA Flyer.docx file you created in the last exercise, if necessary.

4. Select and delete everything in the document (your name and title).

5. Enter the following text:

   What: Inaugural Meeting of the Student Technology Association (STA)

   Where: Student Center Room 220

   When: September 30 from 7 to 8 p.m.

   Who: Darlene Thomas, vice president of Allied Health Technology Corporation, is the guest speaker. A 20-year veteran in the communication and technology field, Ms. Thomas will describe career opportunities in the high-tech health care field.

   Other details: Admission is free. All students, faculty, and staff are welcome. You do not need to be a member of the STA, although new members are welcome. Refreshments will be served. This will be a great opportunity to network with other students who plan to enter the technology or health care fields.

   For more information, call Ext. 1212 or visit the STA website at www.pretend.edu/sta.

   (Tip: Did you notice the hyperlink formatting applied to the website after you typed it? Right-click on www.pretend.edu/sta to investigate the hyperlink options.)

6. Use the *Home* tab | *Font* group buttons to apply character formatting to give the flyer a clear and appealing look. Experiment with each of the options on the Ribbon. (Tip: The **Clear Formatting** button lets you remove formatting and start again.)

7. Open the Font dialog box and experiment with its options.

8. Hide the formatting marks to see your flyer as it will print, and view a Print Preview.

9. Save the document and close it, or leave it open for the next exercise.

There is a *Paragraph* group on the *Home* tab and also on the *Page Layout* tab. The *Paragraph* group on the *Page Layout* tab includes settings that have more impact on the overall page appearance.

To change the appearance of existing paragraphs:

1. Select one or more paragraphs that you want to change.
2. Click the *Home* tab or the *Page Layout* tab.
3. In the *Paragraph* group, click the button(s) for the desired effect(s).

To choose paragraph formatting before typing text (see Figures 4.29A and B for the Home and Page Layout paragraph formatting groups):

1. Click the *Home* or *Page Layout* tab.
2. In the *Paragraph* group, click the button for the desired effect.
3. When you start to type, the text will appear with the formatting you have preset.
4. In the *Paragraph* group, click the button again to turn it off before continuing.

A
B

FIGURE 4.29

Remember that the small arrow in the bottom right of each *Paragraph* group is a dialog box launcher. Click it to access even more paragraph formatting choices. See Figure 4.30.

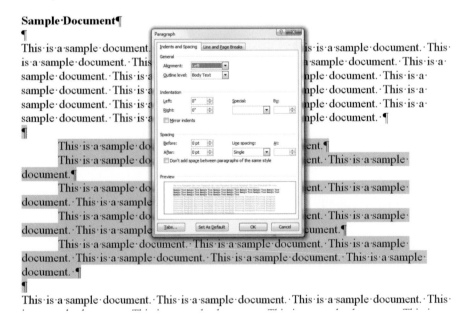

FIGURE 4.30

Alignment

The *Paragraph* group on the *Home* tab includes options for changing the alignment of paragraph text between the left and right margins of the page. By default, paragraphs have a straight left margin, but you can choose to center text, align text with a straight right margin (right-aligned), or spread the text to keep both left and right margins straight (justified). Following are examples of each type:

Left-aligned text

This is just a sample paragraph. This is just a sample paragraph. This is just a sample paragraph. This is just a sample paragraph. This is just a sample paragraph. This is just a sample paragraph. This is just a sample paragraph. This is just a sample paragraph. This is just a sample paragraph. This is just a sample paragraph.

Centered text

This is just a sample paragraph. This is just a sample paragraph. This is just a sample paragraph. This is just a sample paragraph. This is just a sample paragraph. This is just a sample paragraph. This is just a sample paragraph. This is just a sample paragraph. This is just a sample paragraph.

Right-aligned text

This is just a sample paragraph. This is just a sample paragraph. This is just a sample paragraph. This is just a sample paragraph. This is just a sample paragraph. This is just a sample paragraph. This is just a sample paragraph. This is just a sample paragraph. This is just a sample paragraph.

Justified text

This is just a sample paragraph. This is just a sample paragraph. This is just a sample paragraph. This is just a sample paragraph. This is just a sample paragraph. This is just a sample paragraph. This is just a sample paragraph. This is just a sample paragraph. This is just a sample paragraph.

Line and Paragraph Spacing

Line spacing refers to the amount of space between the lines of text in a paragraph. Paragraph spacing refers to the space above or below a paragraph. In Word 2010, the default line spacing in most cases is 1.15. The default paragraph spacing puts a blank line between paragraphs. This was designed to give a more open and readable look to online documents, but can be changed to suit your preferences.

To change the line spacing for selected paragraphs:

1. Select the paragraph or paragraphs you want to change.
2. Click the *Home* tab.
3. In the *Paragraph* group, click **Line and Paragraph Spacing**.
4. Then do one of the following:

   - Click the number of line spaces that you want. For example, click 2.0 to double-space, and click 1.0 to single-space precisely; click 1.15 to single-space with a more open appearance.
   - Click **Line Spacing Options,** and then select the options that you want. See Figure 4.31.

You may be accustomed to adding space between paragraphs by pressing **Enter** to create a blank line. This is a less than ideal method because it requires extra keystrokes and prevents the use of some advanced paragraph formatting options. You can add space before or after paragraphs from the Line and Paragraphs Spacing options, but a more direct method is on the *Page Layout* tab.

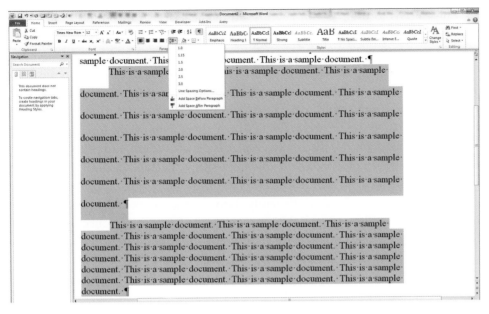

FIGURE 4.31

To change the paragraph spacing for selected paragraphs:

1. Select the paragraph or paragraphs you want to change.
2. Click the *Page Layout* tab.
3. In the *Paragraph* group, click an arrow next to *Spacing Before* or *Spacing After* to enter the amount of space that you want. See Figure 4.32.

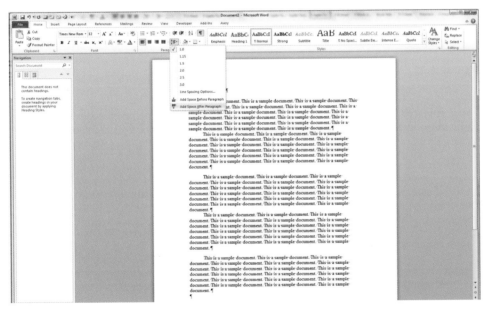

FIGURE 4.32

Tabs

Tanya Smith, the paralegal, is typing a list of clients and their e-mail addresses. She types a client's name, presses the spacebar repeatedly until the insertion point is a couple of inches to the right, types the e-mail address, and presses **Enter**. She types the next client's name, presses the spacebar until it looks to her like the insertion point is lined up with the previous e-mail address, then types again. After repeating this for several more lines, Tanya prints her list, only to find to her frustration that none of the e-mail addresses line up neatly.

Tanya needs to use the **Tab** key instead of the spacebar to position the e-mail addresses. With the exception of a few mono-spaced fonts, such as Courier, spaces can vary in width and are not a good choice for aligning text within paragraphs.

By default, left-aligned tab stops are set at every horizontal half-inch on the page. That means that each time you press the **Tab** key on the keyboard, the insertion point is positioned one-half inch to the right of its previous location. Tanya could type a client's name and press the **Tab** key a few times to move the insertion point to the two-inch mark on the Ruler, then type the e-mail address and press **Enter**. On the next line, she can type the client's name and press the **Tab** key until the insertion point is again at the two-inch mark.

If she wishes to work more efficiently, Tanya can set a new tab stop at the two-inch mark. That will remove all the tab stops to the left of two inches, and she will only need to press the **Tab** key once after typing the name. Tabs can be set directly on the Ruler, or by using the Tab dialog box. See Figure 4.33.

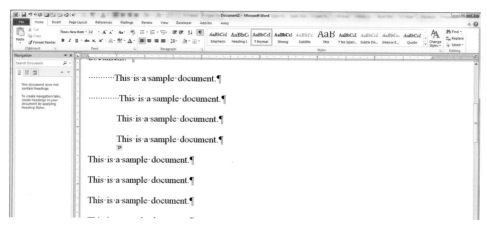

FIGURE 4.33

In addition to the left-aligned tabs described above, Word can set center tabs, right-aligned tabs, decimal tabs, and even a tab that inserts a vertical bar. Consult the Help feature for more information.

To set a new left-aligned tab on the Ruler:

1. If the Ruler is not displayed on your screen, click the *View* tab and in the *Show* group, click a checkmark next to Ruler.
2. Select the paragraph or paragraphs of text for which you want new tab settings, if they have already been typed.
3. Verify that the icon on the far left of the Ruler looks like the letter L for left-aligned. (If you need to change it, click the icon repeatedly to cycle through various tab options.)
4. Point to the Ruler where you would like to set the tab and click to place the tab stop. If you don't get it positioned precisely where you want it, point to the tab stop, hold down the mouse button, and drag to reposition it on the Ruler. To delete the tab stop, point to it, hold down the mouse button, and drag it off the Ruler.

To set a new tab in the Tab dialog box (see Figure 4.34):

1. Select the paragraph or paragraphs of text for which you want new tab settings, if they have already been typed.
2. Click the *Home* tab.

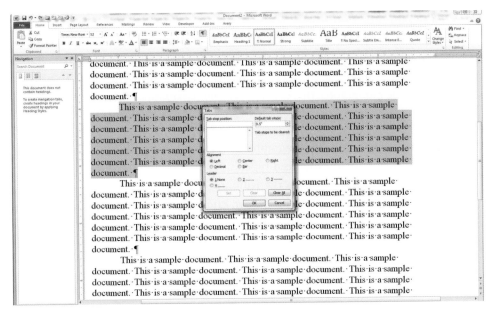

FIGURE 4.34

3. In the *Paragraph* group, click the dialog box launcher.
4. In the Paragraph dialog box, click **Tabs**.
5. Choose from the available settings and click **OK**.

Indents

Indented paragraphs do not extend all the way to the left margin, the right margin, or both margins. Left indents position text away from the left margin while right indents position text away from the right margin. Paragraphs with hanging indents have a first line that begins at the left margin, but subsequent lines are positioned away from it. Indenting is helpful to call attention to certain paragraphs, present poetry, and display quotes and citations. Set a first-line indent to indent the first line of each paragraph as you type, without having to press the **Tab** key. Following are examples of each type:

Left indented, one-half inch

> This is just a sample paragraph. This is just a sample paragraph. This is just a sample paragraph. This is just a sample paragraph. This is just a sample paragraph. This is just a sample paragraph. This is just a sample paragraph. This is just a sample paragraph. This is just a sample paragraph.

Left and right indented, one inch

> This is just a sample paragraph. This is just a sample paragraph. This is just a sample paragraph. This is just a sample paragraph. This is just a sample paragraph. This is just a sample paragraph. This is just a sample paragraph. This is just a sample paragraph. This is just a sample paragraph. This is just a sample paragraph. This is just a sample paragraph.

First-line indent, one-half inch

> This is just a sample paragraph. This is just a sample paragraph. This is just a sample paragraph. This is just a sample paragraph. This is just a sample paragraph. This is just a sample paragraph. This is just a sample paragraph. This is just a sample paragraph. This is just a sample paragraph. This is just a sample paragraph.

Hanging indent, one-half inch

This is just a sample paragraph. This is just a sample paragraph. This is just a sample paragraph. This is just a sample paragraph. This is just a sample paragraph. This is just a sample paragraph. This is just a sample paragraph. This is just a sample paragraph. This is just a sample paragraph.

To indent paragraphs from the Ribbon (see Figure 4.35):

1. Select the paragraph or paragraphs of text for which you want new tab settings, if they have already been typed.
2. Click the *Page Layout* tab on the Ribbon.
3. In the *Paragraph* group, under *Indent,* click the arrows next to Left or Right as needed.

FIGURE 4.35

To set a first-line or hanging indent from the Paragraph dialog box (see Figure 4.36):

1. Click at the beginning of the line to be indented.
2. Click the *Home* tab.
3. Click the Paragraph dialog box launcher.
4. Click **Indents and Spacing**.
5. Under Special in the *Indentation* group, use the drop-down arrow to choose **First line** or **Hanging**, and in the By box, set the amount of space that you want for the first-line or hanging indent.

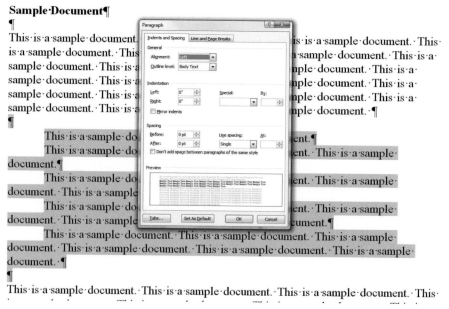

FIGURE 4.36

Bulleted and Numbered Lists

Word sets hanging indents automatically when you create a bulleted or numbered list. That way, the bullets or numbers line up neatly next to left indented text. Bullets can be dots, dashes, checkmarks, or other symbols that set off a list from

surrounding text. Numbered lists are typically used to show sequential information. Word can create simple or multilevel lists. Consult the Help feature for more
information about multilevel lists.

To type a simple bulleted or numbered list (see Figures 4.37A and B):

1. Click the *Home* tab.
2. In the *Paragraph* group, click **Bullets** or **Numbering**.
3. Type the first entry in your list, then press the **Enter** key. Word automatically
   inserts the next bullet or number.
4. Type the next entry, press **Enter**, and repeat as needed.
5. To finish the list, press **Enter** twice.

To apply simple bullets or numbering to existing text:

1. Select the paragraph or paragraphs you want to add bullets or numbering to.
2. Click the *Home* tab.
3. In the *Paragraph* group, click **Bullets** or **Numbering**.
4. Click the arrow next to Bullets or Numbering to choose from a bullet or
   numbering library of styles.

A
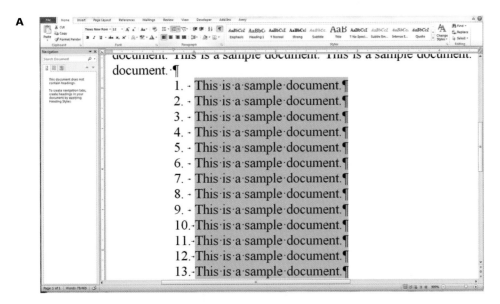

B
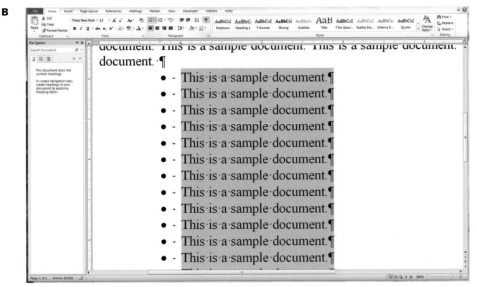

FIGURE 4.37

FAQ: SAVING FORMATTING AS A STYLE

All of the formatting discussed so far is more accurately called direct formatting. The desired formats were applied directly to the text. A more powerful way of working with formatting in Word involves styles. A style in Word allows you to save and reapply formatting so that it is consistent within a document and easy to update.

Word comes with many predefined styles, which are presented in the Style Gallery of the *Home* tab. See Figure 4.38. To apply a style:

1. Select the text you want to change.

2. Click on the *Home* tab.

3. In the *Styles* group, point to any style to see a live preview of the effect of the style on your text. (Remember that you can scroll through a gallery or expand it by clicking the More button in the bottom right.)

4. Click a style you like and apply it to the selected text.

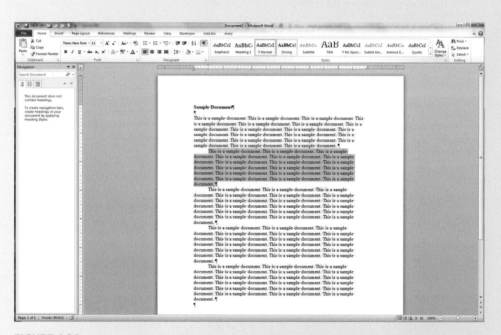

FIGURE 4.38

To create a style from your own formatting:

1. Type some text and format it to your preferences.

2. Select the text, point to it, and right-click.

3. Click **Styles**.

4. Click **Save Selection as a New Quick Style**.

5. Type a descriptive name for the new style.

6. Click **OK**. Your new style can be applied from the Style Gallery as described above.

By default, the text you enter into a document is in Normal style. If you want to make a global change to the text in your document, modifying Normal style is much more efficient than using direct formatting to change every paragraph in it. For example, if you want the text of your document to be Verdana 10 point instead of Times New Roman 12 point, modify Normal style once and everything you type will be Verdana 10 point.

To modify a style:

1. Point to the style in the Style Gallery and right-click.

2. Click **Modify Style**.

3. Choose your preferred formatting from the dialog box. (To make more detailed formatting choices, click the **Format** button in the lower left.)

4. Click **OK**.

EXERCISE 4.5: PARAGRAPH FORMATTING

Now that you have reviewed paragraph formatting possibilities, you want to improve your flyer's layout.

1. **Check to make sure your view is set to Print Layout.**

2. **Check to make sure your formatting marks are displayed.**

3. **Open the STA Flyer.docx file you created in the last exercise, if necessary.**

4. **Set a tab for the What, Where, and When lines of the flyer, and add a tab after the colon on each line, so that the words "Inaugural," "Student," and "September" line up.**

5. **Change the alignment of the Who paragraph as you see fit.**

6. **Experiment with line spacing, paragraph spacing, and indenting to arrange the text to your preferences.**

7. **Revise the last paragraph so that the telephone number and website address appear as bulleted list items.**

8. **Hide the formatting marks to see your flyer as it will print, and view a Print Preview.**

9. **Save the document and close it.**

Page and Document Formatting

We have discussed character and paragraph formatting. The third level of formatting is at the page level. You can change the appearance of document pages in Word by using the commands in the *Page Setup* group of the *Page Layout* tab. Page Setup options include settings such as margins, page orientation, and headers and footers.

The dialog box launcher for the *Page Setup* group displays the Page Setup dialog box. It has three tabs: *Margins*, *Paper*, and *Layout*. The most common page formatting choices can be made from the Ribbon; launch the Page Setup dialog box for a more comprehensive set of page formatting options. See Figure 4.39.

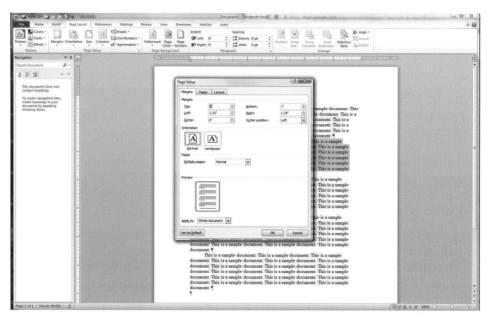

FIGURE 4.39

Margins

When you create a new document, the default margins are one inch each for top, bottom, left, and right. This means that the text will be positioned one inch from each edge of the paper.

To change the margins for a document:

1. Click the *Page Layout* tab.
2. In the *Page Setup* group, click **Margins.**
3. Click the margin setting you prefer.

If none of the predefined margin combinations meet your needs, you can set custom margins.

To set custom margins for a document:

1. Click the *Page Layout* tab.
2. In the *Page Setup* group, click **Margins**.
3. Click **Custom Margins**.
4. In the Page Setup dialog box, enter the margin settings you want by typing them or by clicking the blue up and down arrows to increase or decrease the setting.
5. Click **OK**.

Paper Orientation

Text can be arranged on a page in Portrait (vertical or long format) or Landscape (horizontal or wide format). See Figures 4.40A and 4.40B. The default page orientation for Word documents is Portrait.

To change the page orientation:

1. Click the *Page Layout* tab.
2. In the *Page Setup* group, click **Orientation**.
3. Click **Landscape**.

A

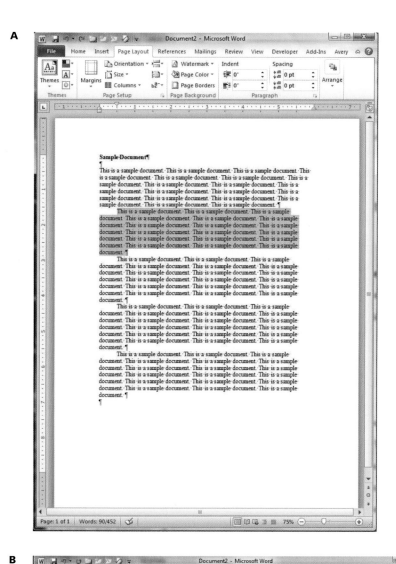

B

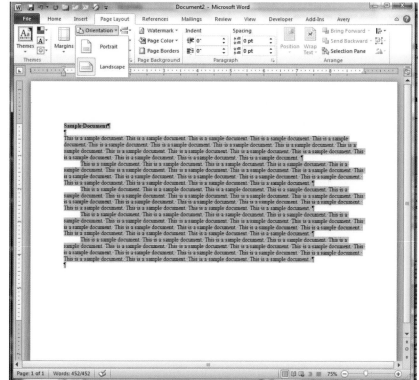

FIGURE 4.40

Headers and Footers

Headers and footers are areas set aside in the top and bottom margins for information that needs to be repeated on every page of the document. Whatever you enter into a header is automatically repeated at the top of each page. In a report, for example, you might want the title of the report or a company logo at the top right of each page. Whatever you enter into a footer is automatically repeated at the bottom of each page. Footers are often used to add page numbers to a document. Page numbers added in a footer (or header) are actually field codes. They will always be correct for each page of the document without any editing on your part. Headers and footers are often smaller or italicized to stand out on the page from the rest of the document.

Word includes easy, predefined header and footer choices, or you can create your own custom header or footer. Consult the Word Help feature to learn more about headers and footers in Word.

To insert an easy header or footer (see Figure 4.41):

1. Click the *Insert* tab.
2. In the *Header & Footer* group, click **Header** or **Footer**.
3. Click one of the predefined choices.
4. The decorative elements of your choice are added to the document.
5. The insertion point is positioned within the bottom margin.
6. The *Header/Footer Design* tab appears on the Ribbon with additional options.
7. Select any placeholder text that says [Type text] and replace it with your own text.
8. To return to your document, click **Close Header and Footer** on the *Header/Footer Design* tab, or double-click anywhere on the document outside of the footer area.

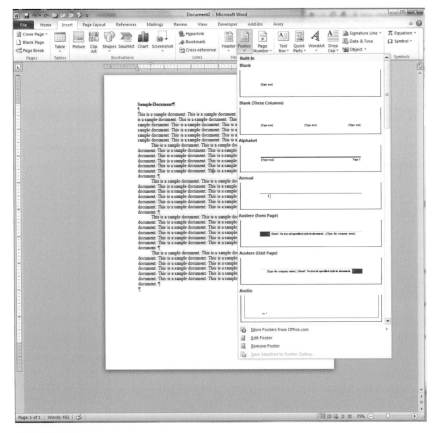

FIGURE 4.41

For more control over the items included in your header or footer, you can edit them directly using the *Header/Footer Design* tab.

To create a custom header or footer:

1. Click the *Insert* tab.
2. In the *Header & Footer* group, click **Header** or **Footer**.
3. To create a custom header, click **Edit Header**. Or to create a custom footer, click **Edit Footer**.
4. The insertion point is positioned within the bottom margin.
5. The *Header/Footer Design* tab appears on the Ribbon with additional options.
6. Choose from the options on the *Header/Footer Design* tab.
7. For example, to date-stamp your document, click **Date & Time** and then click a date format.
8. To return to your document, click **Close Header and Footer** on the *Header/ Footer Design* tab, or double-click anywhere on the document outside of the footer area.

Page numbers can be added from the *Header/Footer Design* tab, or from the *Page Layout* tab of the Ribbon.

To add page numbers to your document from the Ribbon:

1. Click the *Insert* tab.
2. In the *Header & Footer* group, click **Page Number**.
3. Choose the position of your page number by clicking **Top of Page**, **Bottom of Page**, **Page Margins**, or **Current Position** (to insert the page number at the current position of the insertion point).
4. Click one of the predefined choices.
5. To return to your document, click **Close Header and Footer** on the *Header/ Footer Design* tab, or double-click anywhere on the document outside of the footer area.

To change the appearance of the page number:

1. Click the *Insert* tab.
2. In the *Header & Footer* group, click **Page Number**.
3. Click **Format Page Numbers**.
4. Select options such as the number format.
5. Click **OK**.

Footnotes

A footnote in a document is a superscripted (small, raised) number attached to the end of a word, sentence, or paragraph. It is used to make a reference, explain, or comment on the text in the document. Footnote numbers in a document are presented in sequence throughout the document. The footnote's text is printed at the bottom of the page on which the footnote appears. Endnotes are very similar, except they print at the end of the document instead of at the bottom of the page.

Footnotes display differently in Print Layout view and Draft view. The instructions below assume that the document is displayed in Print Layout view. See Figure 4.42.

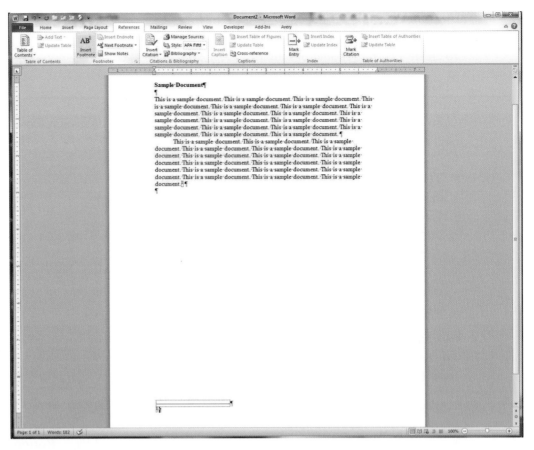

FIGURE 4.42

To insert a footnote:

1. Place the insertion point where you want the footnote number to appear, typically at the end of a word or sentence.
2. Click the *References* tab.
3. In the *Footnotes* group, click **Insert Footnote**.
4. A small superscripted footnote number appears in the text.
5. The insertion point is positioned at the bottom of the page, just after a corresponding footnote number, so that you can type the footnote text.
6. A divider bar separates the footnote text from the rest of the document.
7. After you type the footnote, click in the document to continue typing or editing.

To edit an existing footnote's text, click the text at the bottom of the screen and make changes to it directly. To delete a footnote, delete its number from the document. Deleting the number in the document removes the footnote number and the footnote text from the bottom of the page. Any remaining footnotes in the document will renumber accurately.

To change footnote options:

1. Click the *References* tab.
2. Click the dialog box launcher in the *Footnotes* group.
3. Choose desired options for the document's footnotes such as selecting endnotes instead of footnotes, changing numbers to Roman numerals, or using a custom mark—such as an asterisk—instead of numbers.
4. Click **OK**.

Using Spelling and Grammar Check

One of the best features of word processing software is the ability to check your document's spelling, grammar, or both with just a few keystrokes. Avoiding spelling and grammar errors is essential to producing quality documents.

The Spelling Check feature in Word allows you to check a word, sentence, paragraph(s), or the entire document. It works on specific portions of text if you select the text before accessing the Spelling Check dialog box. The Spelling Check feature works by comparing each word in your document to a built-in dictionary. When a word that does not match any in the dictionary is encountered, Word presents it to you so that you can decide if it is actually spelled correctly or not.

Why do you have to decide? In many cases, words will be flagged even though they are spelled correctly. For example, acronyms, such as ASPCA, or proper nouns, such as a person's last name, will not be in the Word dictionary. You have the option to add the acronym or name to the Word dictionary so that it will flag it as a possible misspelling again, or just tell Word to ignore it.

Keep in mind that some words may not be flagged by the Spelling Check even if they are misspelled. For example, in the sentence "Everyone forgot there suitcases," the word *there* should be spelled *their*. The Spelling Check does not flag *there* because it is a word that is in the dictionary. Always proofread a document, even if it has been spell checked, to catch these usage errors. See Figure 4.43.

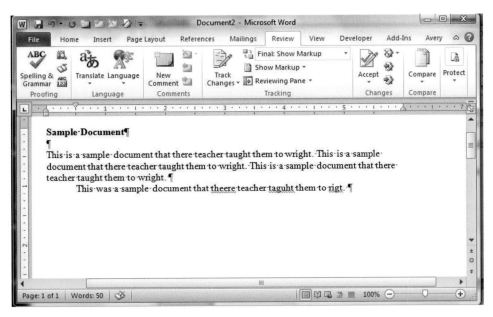

FIGURE 4.43

To check spelling in a document (see Figure 4.44):

1. Click the *Review* tab.
2. In the *Proofing* group, click **Spelling & Grammar**.
3. The Spelling & Grammar dialog box opens, with the first word that does not match the dictionary displayed and, if possible, a list of suggested correct spellings. Click an appropriate action.
4. **Ignore Once, Ignore All**: Word will ignore this occurrence or ignore all of the same occurrences of the error.

5. **Add to Dictionary**: This action allows you to add the word in question to the Word dictionary so that the spell checker will not stop on it in the future.

6. **Change, Change All**: Word will change just this occurrence or all occurrences of the word in question to the selected suggestion.

7. **AutoCorrect**: Choose this if you would like Word to correct future incorrect spelling of this word to the selected suggestion without prompting you.

8. After your click, Word advances to the next potential error in the document for you to decide upon an action for it.

If you place a checkmark next to the option to check grammar, Word will also review the document's grammar you spell check. Upon discovering possible grammatical errors, Word presents actions for you to choose from.

1. **Ignore Once**: Word will not make a correction but instead will move on to the next sentence.

2. **Ignore Rule**: Word will not make a correction but instead will ignore any occurrence of errors with that grammatical rule.

3. **Next Sentence**: Word will skip to the next sentence.

4. **Change**: Word will change the text.

You can customize the spelling and grammar check features in Word by clicking the **Options** button in the Spelling & Grammar dialog box. The options allow you to choose specifically how Word checks for spelling and grammar. The Options window also allows you to choose the writing style—standard, technical, formal, or your own custom choices.

Be aware that this automated grammar checking is not always correct. The English language is complex and requires your judgment to decide if a grammatical error is present or not. However, if you are not confident about your ability to recognize possible errors, the Word grammar check can help draw your attention to possible problems.

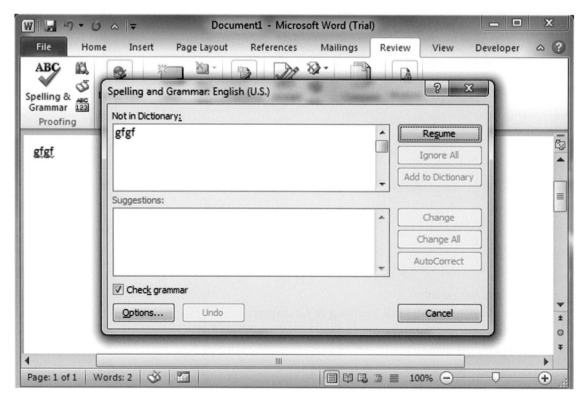

FIGURE 4.44

Clearly, you should not depend entirely on a word processing program for accuracy. Purchase a good book on the use of proper English when writing documents. Those who work in technical, legal, and medical fields often use industry-specific language books that contain common terms and phrases used by professionals in the field. As you spell check documents with industry-specific content, it is helpful to continually add changes to the Word dictionary to make it more accurate and easier to use each time.

EXERCISE 4.6: PAGE FORMATTING, FOOTNOTES, AND SPELLING CHECK

You are looking forward to the first meeting of the STA, where you plan to distribute a report you have written on the new features of Office 2010. Your goal is to produce a double-spaced hard copy of the document so that the association members can write in their own comments and changes.

1. Create a new blank document and save it to the location specified by your instructor, naming it "Office Report."

2. Check to make sure your view is set to Print Layout.

3. Check to make sure your formatting marks are displayed.

4. Instead of typing an actual report for this exercise, enter the following: type =rand(10,10) and press **Enter**. (The =rand feature is provided in Word to generate sample text.)

5. Change the margins to one inch top and bottom and three-quarters inch left and right.

6. Change the font, font size, and line/paragraph spacing to what is typically requested by your professors, or to your preferences. (Tip: Select the document and apply direct formatting, or select the document and apply Body Text style, then modify Body Text style as needed.)

7. Add "New Features of Office 2010" as the title of your document, and format it to your preferences.

8. Add the page number to the bottom right of each page, without typing it on each page.

9. Add the report title to the top right of each page, using a header.

10. Add this footnote to the end of one of the paragraphs: Microsoft Word Users Group, n.d.

11. Add this footnote to the end of another paragraph: Gates, Jobs, Zuckerberg, 2009, p. 2.

12. Cut and paste the second footnote number in the document in order to move it before the previous footnote; notice the

renumbering. (Tip: Try double-clicking on a footnote number in the body of the document, and in the footnote at the bottom of the page, to see how your insertion point moves.)

13. Insert a page break, and center the title "References" on this page. (We will not add actual references for this example.)

14. Edit some words of the document so that they are misspelled and grammatically incorrect, then experiment with the Spelling Check feature.

15. Hide the formatting marks to see your report as it will print, view a Print Preview, and print a hard copy if possible.

16. Save the document and close it.

INTERACTION DIVERSITY: SETTING POINTER SPEED AND KEY REPEAT RATE

Operating systems, such as Windows and MacOS, allow you to change the speed of your mouse pointer. In most WYSIWYG software such as Microsoft Office, the basic interaction involves pointing to a command using a mouse or touch pad device. The pointer speed determines how fast the symbol for the pointing device moves on the computer screen. For example, setting the mouse pointer speed to fast will cause the mouse cursor to move very quickly when you move the mouse device. Setting it to a slower rate will cause the mouse cursor to react more slowly when you move the mouse. Users who are new to computers and users with disabilities may find they can control the pointer more comfortably with a slower pointer speed.

You can also customize the key repeat rate, that is, how quickly a character displays on the screen after a key is pressed. Lowering the key repeat rate means that the screen will display characters more slowly while typing text. This is helpful for users with limited finger mobility. This limitation causes them to press more heavily on the keys, leading to repeated characters on the screen.

There are many ways that devices can be adjusted to meet the needs of a diverse group of users. An area of research and practice known variously as interaction design, human factors, or usability trains professionals to design more usable computer systems and devices. To learn more about the field, try a web search on any of these terms. To learn more about changing your operating system settings, see the Windows Help feature.

ADVANCED TOPICS

Graphics

Graphics—pictures, figures, drawings, or other images—are an important part of many word-processed documents. They help make the final product more attractive, easier to understand, and fun to read. Microsoft Office also contains a graphics presentation program called PowerPoint.

Inserting Graphics

There are quite a few graphics options available for use in Word on the *Insert* tab, as well as the *Illustrations* group, the *Text* group, and the *Symbols* group, as described below. When you have inserted a graphic into your document, clicking on it automatically displays one or more additional Ribbon tabs with additional design and layout options.

To insert a graphic into your document (see Figure 4.45):

1. Click the *Insert* tab.
2. In the *Illustrations* group, click one of the following options:
3. **Picture**—Use this option to choose an image file from the computer's hard drive, a network drive, or a CD. Word accepts many different graphic file formats such as JPEG, PNG, bitmap, and GIF.
4. **Clip Art**—This option allows you to choose from small images created for electronic documents. Search for Clip Art graphics by content or keyword in the Clip Art Task Pane that appears on the right side of the document window. When you type a word or phrase in the Search for: text box and click **Go**, relevant clip art appears in the bottom half of the window. Word has an extensive library of additional images, figures, graphs, illustrations, videos, and audio files included with the software and available for free at office.com.
5. **Shapes**—Use this option to add graphic shapes such as lines, rectangles, and arrows to your document. Click the shape, move the pointer to your document, hold down the mouse button, and drag to draw the shape on the page.
6. **SmartArt**®—Use this option to insert a variety of sophisticated diagrams into your Word document, such as organization charts, flowcharts, pyramids, or arrangements of pictures with labels.
7. **Chart**—This option inserts a default columnar chart along with a data table for the chart's values. You can replace the values in the default data table with your own values, change the chart type, and make other modifications. Charts and other types of data graphs will be discussed in further detail in the chapter on spreadsheets.
8. **Screenshot**—Click this option to capture a snapshot of any of the application windows currently open on your computer.
9. **WordArt** (in the *Text* group)—Use WordArt to insert text with special decorative effects into your Word document. You can click any WordArt style, type, and then alter the effects from the *Drawing Tools Format* tab that appears.
10. **Symbols** (in the *Symbols* group)—Click this option to insert a commonly used symbol such as π (mathematical Pi), € (Euro sign), or © (copyright). Click on **More Symbols** in the window for a more extensive choice of symbols and special characters.

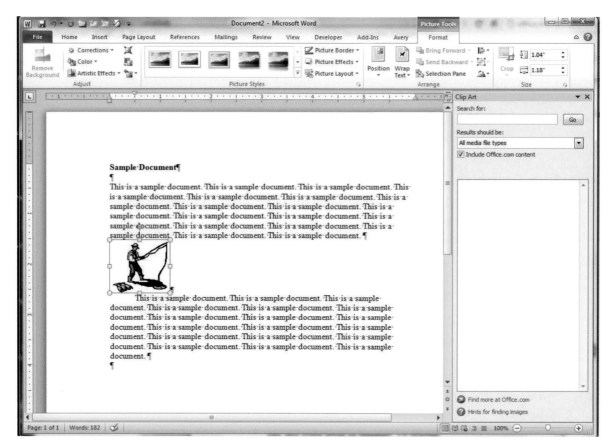

FIGURE 4.45

You also may need to delete a graphic. Symbols are characters and can be deleted like any other letter or number. To delete a graphic object, click it to select it and then press the **Delete** key on the keyboard. You know a graphic is selected when small dots or squares known as handles appear on its edges. If you have trouble selecting a graphic, click elsewhere on the page and then click the graphic again.

Resizing Graphics

When you move the pointer over the handles of a selected graphic, the pointer shape changes to a two-headed arrow. Two-headed arrow pointers always indicate that you can drag to change the size of something. Drag the corner handles to re-size a graphic in proportion. This means that if you shrink the picture on the right corner then it will automatically shrink by the same amount on the opposite corner, and the proportions of the image overall will not change. If you want to adjust the picture disproportionately, drag the handles on the sides of the graphic object.

Commands to resize a graphic with more precision are available from the design tabs that appear when a graphic is selected. Or, right-click the graphic and look at the bottom of the right-click menu for the exact height and width of the graphic. Type in the precise measurements you prefer, or click the arrows to change the dimensions.

Graphics can also be formatted from the tabs that appear when they are selected, or from a right-click. The right-click menu will include the word "Format" followed by the type of graphic that you clicked, such as **Format Picture** or **Format Shape**. For example, if you right-click a picture graphic and choose **Format Picture**, you can add special artistic effects and adjustments to the picture, including cropping, another more specific way to size a graphic. See Figure 4.46.

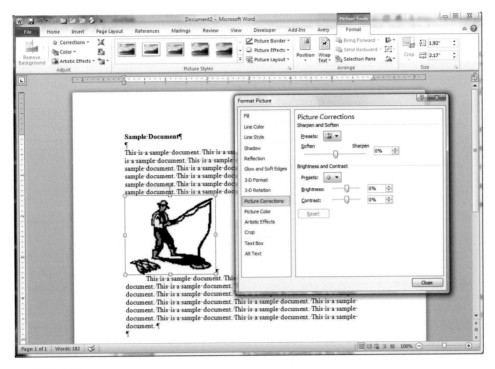

FIGURE 4.46

Wrapping Text around Graphics

Word lets you control how text wraps around a graphic in a variety of ways to suit the paragraph. The Position and Wrap Text commands are available on the tabs that appear when a graphic is selected, and on the *Page Layout* tab.

To position a graphic on the page:

1. Click the graphic to select it, if it is not selected.
2. Click the *Page Layout* tab.
3. In the *Arrange* group, click **Position**.
4. Point to **In Line with Text** and various Position options for a live preview of where your graphic will appear on the page, then click the one you prefer.

To wrap text around a graphic:

1. Click the graphic to select it, if it is not selected.
2. Click the *Page Layout* tab.
3. In the *Arrange* group, click **Wrap Text**.
4. Point to the various text wrapping options for a live preview of how your graphic will appear on the page, then click the one you prefer.
5. **In line with the text** keeps the graphic on the same line as the text.
6. **Square** flows the text around the graphic on all sides, forming a square pattern.
7. **Tight** aligns text closely around the graphic on all sides.
8. **Through** flows text around the graphic as closely as possible and is similar to the Tight option.
9. **Top and bottom** stops text above the graphic and continues it below the graphic.
10. **Behind text** runs text over the graphic; the graphic floats behind it.
11. **In front of the text** runs text behind the graphic; the graphic floats on top of it.

Tables

Tables are structures used to arrange text on a page in rows and columns. They are a popular format because they make it easy to enter text in an organized, side-by-side layout. There are various ways to insert a table into your document. Dragging over a grid of rows and columns is perhaps the most accessible.

To insert a table by dragging:

1. Click the *Insert* tab.
2. In the *Tables* group, click **Tables**.
3. Hold down the mouse button and drag across the number of columns and down the number of rows to indicate the size of the table you want. For example, to create a table that has three columns and four rows, drag your mouse across three columns and then down four rows in the grid.
4. Release the mouse button to insert the table in your document.

Click anywhere inside of the table to display the *Table Tools Layout* and *Table Tools Design* tabs. If you click in the document outside the table, the tabs disappear. Options on the *Table Tools Layout* tab have to do with the structure of the table, and options on the *Table Tools Design* tab have to do with its appearance. See Figure 4.47.

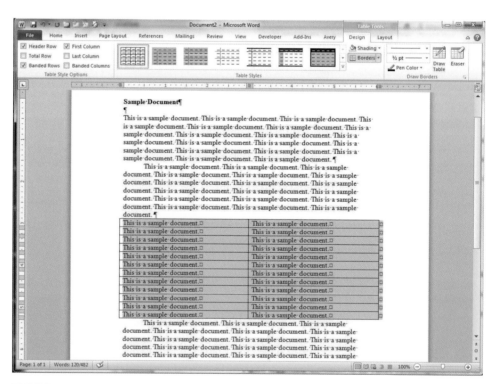

FIGURE 4.47

Entering Text into a Table

Once you insert a table into your Word document, you can type in the cells. Use the mouse to position the insertion point in any table cell (the box formed by the intersection of a row and a column), click, and enter text. If your insertion point is already in a cell of the table, you can use the keyboard to move through the table as you type. Press the **Tab** key to move to the next cell to the right. To move to the next cell to the left, hold down the **Shift** key and press the **Tab** key. See Figure 4.48.

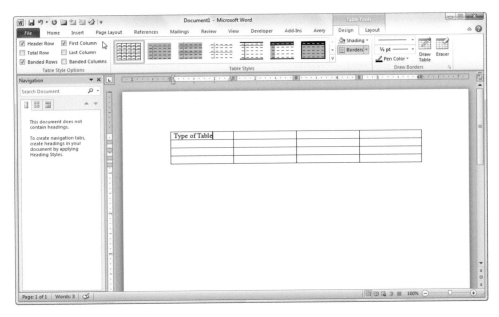

FIGURE 4.48

Inserting, Deleting, and Resizing Rows and Columns

Paralegal Tanya Smith created a three-column, five-row table to keep track of her firm's expert witnesses' contact information. As she types text into her table, she presses the **Tab** key as needed to advance to the next cell. When she reaches the last cell of the bottom row of the table, Tanya realizes that she has three more expert witnesses to add. By pressing the **Tab** key again, she creates a new row. Pressing the **Tab** key from the bottom right cell of a table is an easy way to create a new row.

To insert columns and rows that are not at the bottom of the table, use the *Table Tools Layout* tab. The *Rows & Columns* group includes buttons that allow you to click in a table cell and insert rows and columns to the left, right, above, or below the cell that holds the insertion point. See Figure 4.49.

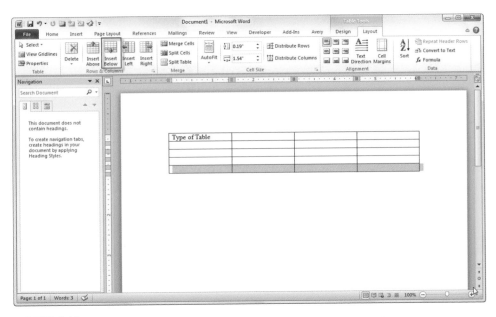

FIGURE 4.49

To insert rows and columns into a table:

1. Click in a cell of your table that is adjacent to where the new row or column should be inserted.
2. Click the *Table Tools Layout* tab.
3. In the *Rows & Columns* group, click on the desired Insert option.
4. **Insert Above** inserts a row above the cell the insertion point is in.
5. **Insert Below** inserts a row below the cell the insertion point is in.
6. **Insert Left** inserts a column to the left of the cell the insertion point is in.
7. **Insert Right** inserts a column to the right of the cell the insertion point is in.

To delete some or all of a table:

1. Click in a cell of your table that is relevant to what will be deleted.
2. Click the *Table Tools Layout* tab.
3. In the *Rows & Columns* group, click **Delete** and click the desired Delete option.
4. **Delete Cells** displays a dialog box where you can choose how to handle the cells surrounding the deleted cell, shifting them to the left or up. Or, you can choose to delete the entire row or the entire column of the cell the insertion point is in.
5. **Delete Column** deletes the column of the cell the insertion point is in.
6. **Delete Row** deletes the row of the cell the insertion point is in.
7. **Delete Table** deletes the entire table.

You can also add or delete table cells, columns, and rows from the right-click menu. Right-click on a table element to see the options available. See Figure 4.50.

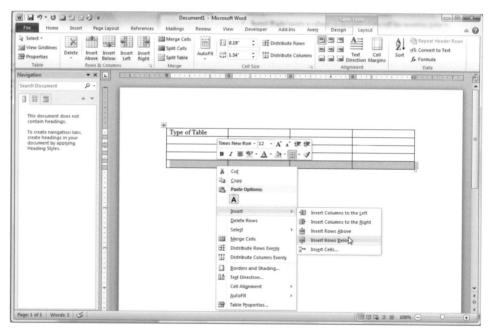

FIGURE 4.50

You can adjust the width of table columns and the height of table rows using the mouse or using the Ribbon.

To resize a column or row using the mouse:

1. Position the mouse pointer on the vertical line between two columns, or the horizontal line between two rows, so that the pointer appears as a double-headed arrow.

2. Hold down the mouse button and drag the arrow to the left or right to narrow or widen the column, or drag up and down to make the row taller or shorter. (Double-click with the two-headed arrow pointer to automatically make the column to the left or the row below just wide enough to contain the text typed within it.)

To resize a column or row using the Ribbon:

1. Click in a row or column to be resized.
2. Click the *Table Tool Layout* tab.
3. In the *Cell Size* group, type in a new height or width, or click the arrows to choose it.

Table Design Options

Making formatting changes to a table requires that you first select the table element you want to change—cells, rows, columns, or the entire table. Use the **Select** button on the *Table* group of the *Table Tools Layout* tab to select elements as needed, or drag to select them.

One common table formatting decision has to do with the lines, or borders, around table cells. By default, each cell in a table is surrounded by printed borders. You may want to remove the side borders so that each row of your table has only a line separating it from the rows above and below. Or you may want to remove the borders completely, so that you can arrange text in a side-by-side layout on the page without showing the underlying grid at all.

To remove table borders (see Figure 4.51):

1. Click in a cell of the table.
2. Click the *Table Tools Layout* tab.
3. In the *Table* group, click **Select**.
4. Click **Select Table**.
5. Click the *Table Tools Design* tab.
6. In the *Table Styles* group, click **Borders**. (Click the drop-down arrow to see all the Borders options.)

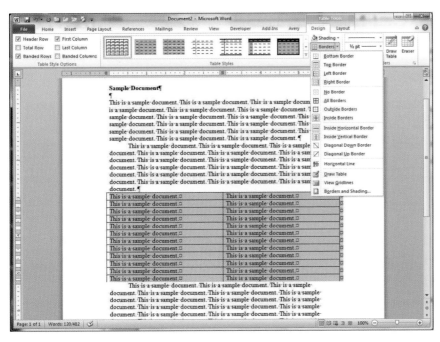

FIGURE 4.51

To quickly format your table overall, you can apply preset Table Styles to your table from the *Table Tools Design* tab. For example, click to position the insertion point within a table, and point to various options on the Table Style Gallery to preview the changes. Click to apply a style that you prefer.

To save time formatting, Word 2010 offers nine built-in, preformatted tables called Quick Tables. There are Quick Tables for calendars and lists, with and without subheadings. You can insert a Quick Table and then replace the contents of its cells with your own data. This is faster than creating a table from scratch, even if you need to make a few changes. Right-click on table elements to make changes.

To add a Quick Table:

1. Click the *Insert* tab.
2. In the *Tables* group, click **Table**.
3. Click **Quick Tables**.
4. Click the Quick Tables design that you prefer.

Columns

In Word, columns and tables are used to structure the appearance of text on a page. Both are easy to create and are useful for laying out large amounts of text such as in a newsletter or brochure. Columns differ from tables in that columns flow down the page and then begin again at the top—just like the columns in a newspaper or magazine.

The columns feature of Word is a page formatting command. By default, it applies to all the pages of your document.

To arrange an entire document in columns:
1. Click the *Page Layout* tab.
2. In the *Page Setup* group, click **Columns** for a drop-down list of column choices.
3. Click to choose a one-column, two-column, left-column, or right-column layout.

To arrange only part of a document's text in columns:

1. Select the text that you want to appear in columns.
2. Click the *Page Layout* tab.
3. In the *Page Setup* group, click **Columns** for a drop-down list of column choices. See Figures 4.52A and 4.52B.
4. Click to choose a one-column, two-column, left-column, or right-column layout.

FIGURE 4.52A

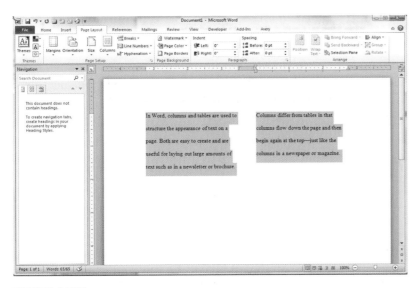

FIGURE 4.52B

How does Word apply a page formatting command—one that is designed for all the pages of the document—to only a portion of the text? It inserts section breaks above and below that portion. Section breaks allow page formatting to change within your document. That means you can use section breaks to change other types of page formatting, not just columns, within a document. You can change margins, paper size or orientation, headers and footers, and page numbering formats for individual sections.

To better understand how sections work, consider again the paralegal, Tanya Smith, who is working on a legal document for court. Her new legal brief is about 10 pages, with the following parts:

1. Cover sheet (1 page)
2. Table of Contents and Table of Authorities (3 pages)
3. Statements and Arguments (6 pages)

Tanya wants no page number on the cover sheet, small Roman numerals as page numbers on the Table of Contents and Table of Authorities sections, and standard numbering in the Statements and Arguments section of the document. By adding a next page section break after each, Tanya can vary the page numbering for each part.

To insert a section break:

1. Position the insertion point where the section break should be inserted.
2. Click the *Page Layout* tab.
3. In the *Page Setup* group, click **Breaks**.
4. Click a section break option.
5. **Next Page** inserts a section break and starts the new section on the next page.
6. **Continuous** inserts a section break and starts the new section on the same page.
7. **Even Page** or **Odd Page** inserts a section break and starts the new section on the next even-numbered or odd-numbered page.

Once the section breaks are in place, headers and footers are numbered consecutively on the screen. Tanya clicks within a section and adds page numbering as described previously, using the Format Page Number options to change the appearance and control whether the numbering continues from the previous section or starts anew.

Track Changes

Teamwork is an essential part of the business world. Often more than one person will make editing and formatting changes to a document. As multiple parties make changes, it becomes hard to know what changes have been made and whether or not those changes are acceptable to the team overall.

The Track Changes feature in Word meets this need to work collaboratively on a document. It is a system for marking changes made to a document as you make them, for accepting or rejecting those changes as a reviewer, and for adding comments that, by default, are visible on the screen but not printed.

Imagine that the paralegal Tanya is assisting with lease negotiations. After a meeting to review the current lease, Tanya saves a new copy of it and makes revisions to it with Track Changes turned on. (See Figure 4.53.) With Track Changes on, any text she inserts is underlined and color-coded. Text she deletes is marked as strikethrough, with a line through the middle of the text, and color-coded. She e-mails a copy of the original lease and the modified lease to the client, Marcus. Marcus can review the document and make Tanya's changes permanent (by accepting the changes) or remove them (by rejecting the changes). If Marcus has a question as he reviews the document, he can add a comment that Tanya will see on the screen when the document is returned to her. His comment will appear color-coded and contains his initials, easily identifying him as the person making the comment.

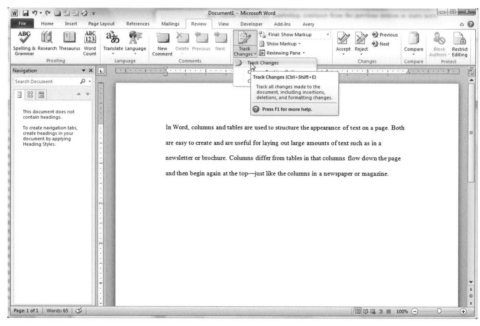

FIGURE 4.53

To edit a document with Track Changes:

1. Click the *Review* tab.
2. In the *Tracking* group, click **Track Changes**. The button appears gold when the feature is on.
3. Edit the document. Revisions are marked automatically. If you make a mistake, undo it and the change will not be recorded.
4. When you are finished editing, click **Track Changes** again. When the feature is turned off, the button is not gold.

You can turn Track Changes on and off as you work. If you notice a minor correction that does not need to be tracked, you can turn Track Changes off, make the change, and then turn it back on to continue marking revisions.

To review a document that has tracked changes (see Figure 4.54):

1. Click the *Review* tab.
2. In the *Tracking* group, verify that the view is set to **Final: Show Markup**. (If it is not, use the drop-down arrow to select it.)
3. In the *Changes* group, click **Next**. The insertion point moves to the next revision in the document.
4. To make the revision permanent, in the *Changes* group, click **Accept**. To remove the revision and return to the original text, in the *Changes* group, click **Reject**. (Click the drop-down arrow in the bottom half of the button to choose **Accept All Changes in Document** or **Reject All Changes in Document**, without stepping through the changes one by one.)
5. The insertion point moves to the next revision in the document. When there are no more revisions, a notification box appears to let you know.

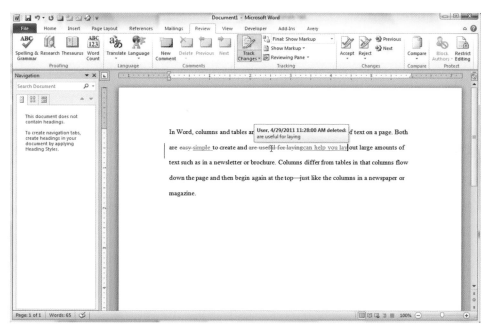

FIGURE 4.54

To add a comment:

1. Click to place the insertion point where you want the comment to appear, or select text to relate the comment to all of it.
2. Click the *Review* tab.
3. In the *Comments* group, click **New Comment**.
4. Type the comment text.
5. To return to working on your document, click in the document.

To delete a comment:

1. Click the comment or the text the comment is associated with in the document.
2. Click the *Review* tab.
3. In the *Comments* group, click **Delete**.

Envelopes and Labels

Word has features for printing envelopes. It can also be used to print label sheets for packages, file folders, CD-ROMs, and other uses.

To create an envelope (see Figure 4.55):

1. Select the recipient's name and address information in your letter.
2. Click the *Mailings* tab.
3. In the *Create* group, click **Envelopes**. The Envelopes and Labels dialog box appears, with the *Envelopes* tab selected. Choose from the following options from the dialog box as needed.
4. **Delivery address.** This will be filled in from the Clipboard—either the information you selected in the first step or the last text you copied or cut. You can replace this with the recipient's name and address if necessary, or click the small address book icon to copy it from your Outlook contacts.
5. **Return address.** Enter a return address or choose to leave it out by checking Omit.
6. **Feed.** The dialog box shows the recommended way to feed envelopes into your printer, based on the installed printer.
7. **Options.** If you are not printing to a standard size 10 business envelope, click the **Options** button to choose a different size from the drop down. Click **OK**.
8. Click **Print** to print the envelope directly, or click **Add to Document** to add the envelope in a new section of the document and print the envelope when you print the document.

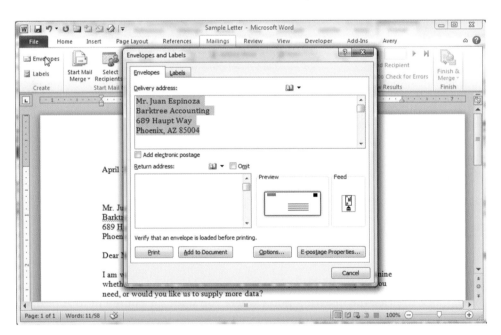

FIGURE 4.55

To create one or more labels (see Figures 4.56A and 4.56B):

1. Select the recipient's name and address information in your letter.
2. Click the *Mailings* tab.
3. In the *Create* group, click **Labels**. The Envelopes and Labels dialog box appears, with the *Labels* tab selected. Choose options from the dialog box as needed.

A

B

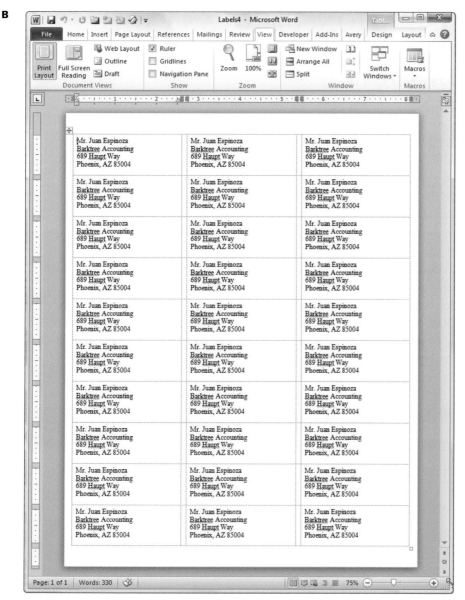

FIGURE 4.56

4. **Address.** This will be filled in from the Clipboard—either the information you selected in the first step or the last text you copied or cut. You can replace this with the recipient's name and address if necessary, or click the small address book icon to copy it from your Outlook contacts.

5. **Print.** Click to choose **Full Page** or **Single Label.** Word can create entire label sheets or just one label in a specific row or column of a premade blank label sheet. This is helpful when you need to use preprinted shipping or message label sheets.

6. Click the **Options** button. Use the drop-down list next to Label Vendors to choose the manufacturer of the labels you are using. Scroll through the Product Number list to choose a label type. Click **OK.**

7. Insert the sheet of labels into your printer's manual feeder according to the printer manufacturer's directions.

8. Click **Print** to print the labels directly, or click **New Document** to review your label sheet in a new Word document before printing.

INTEGRATION: USING AN EXCEL WORKBOOK AS A MAIL MERGE DATA SOURCE

Word's Mail Merge feature lets you create a set of documents that use much of the same content, but with personalization. For example, you could create form letters with "boilerplate" text—the date, the word *Dear*, the body of the letter, and your closing signature—but with different names and addresses. Or you could create attendance certificates for a conference. The name and date of the conference, decorative graphics, and so on would stay the same; the attendees' names would be different on each certificate.

The Mail Merge feature is available from the *Mailings* tab, in the *Start Mail Merge* group, and requires two documents. The Main Document contains the "boilerplate" text along with merge fields that act as placeholders for the personalized information. The Source Document contains the actual names, addresses, and so on that will change for each document created. You merge these two documents together to create the set of customized documents.

The Source Document can be a Word table. However, to take full advantage of the integrated nature of the Office applications, always look for ways to combine them. For example, if you already have a list of names and addresses saved as an Excel workbook, you can use it as your Source Document for Mail Merge in Word.

EXERCISE 4.7: ADVANCED FEATURES

The first STA meeting is fast approaching. You want to jazz up your flyer, create an attendance sheet, polish your report, and send the letter to the dean.

1. **Check to make sure your view is set to Print Layout.**

2. **Check to make sure your formatting marks are displayed.**

3. **Open the STA Flyer.docx file you created previously.**

4. Choose a graphic element that you think will enhance the flyer. Insert it, resizing it and adjusting the placement and text wrapping as needed.

5. Print a copy of the flyer if possible, then save and close it.

6. Create and save a new document to the location specified by your instructor. Name it "Attendance Sheet."

7. Center the title "STA Meeting Attendance" at the top of the page. Add the meeting date on the second line.

8. Skip two lines, and then create a two-column table with enough rows to fill the rest of the page.

9. Center "Printed Name" at the top of the first column and "Signature" at the top of the second column.

10. Format the table so that it makes an attractive sign-in sheet.

11. Save and close the document.

12. Open the Office Report.docx file you created previously.

13. Change the report formatting to single-spaced, two columns.

14. Turn on Track Changes, and make several editing changes to the report. Be sure to insert, delete, replace, and move text.

15. Turn off Track Changes and reject all the changes in the document.

16. Save and close the document.

17. Open the Revised STA Letter.docx file you created previously.

18. Create an envelope addressed to the dean, adding it to the document.

19. Save and close the document.

BONUS EXERCISE: FAST-TRACK PROJECT

Create a two-page newsletter for your school or workplace. The newsletter should present the content in an attractive, readable form with appropriate character, paragraph, and page formatting. Spell check all work before printing. Save the document to the location specified by your instructor. Name it "Newsletter." It must contain the following items:

- Name, date (month, year), and version of the newsletter

- Newsletter graphic logo (use clip art, a shape with text, WordArt, or other artwork)

- **Table of contents (list of headlines for the newsletter in a table, not the Word table of contents feature)**

- **A two- or three-column layout for all or part of the newsletter**

- **Main story and figure**

- **At least two other stories**

- **One or two advertisements**

- **One story must include a footnote with an asterisk instead of a number.**

- **A Word comment added to one story, reminding yourself to double-check the source**

- **A footer with relevant information, such as a slogan or the newsletter's first publication date**

- **In a separate document, create a sheet of labels for the newsletter recipients. You can use fictional addresses.**

SUMMARY

The differences between typewritten sheets of paper and documents created by a word processing application are striking. With word processing, you can create and edit documents, format them for readability, and save them for future reference, reuse, or electronic distribution.

Microsoft Word is the most widely used word processing application for personal and business use. Employees and business owners in virtually every field benefit from the ability to create written documents quickly and efficiently, with a minimum of trial and error.

The history of word processing can be traced back to the 1960s and 1970s, when people used semiautomated typewriters to enter text and print documents, and mainframe computers provided simple text editors. The introduction of PCs with graphical user interfaces that allowed WYSIWYG editing and formatting dramatically improved the ease of using word processing applications. Word 2010 is the result of years of adding features and refining the user interface. There are often many ways of accomplishing tasks in Word. After you master the basics, you can continue to acquire advanced skills and shortcuts to speed up your work.

Some basic features of Word are creating documents; entering text; editing; formatting at the character, paragraph, and page level; footnotes; and spell checking. Advanced features include graphics, tables and columns, tracking changes, and envelopes and labels.

KEY TERMS

- bullet points
- editing
- font
- formatting

- graphical user interface
- hard copy
- point
- WYSIWYG

Productivity Software: Spreadsheets

THE POWER OF SPREADSHEETS

Spreadsheets make math easier for everyone. If you have an aptitude for math, you may be immediately drawn to spreadsheets' ability to perform mathematical operations and statistical analysis. If you are intimidated by math, you may still find that you like spreadsheets—because once they have been created, they will do mathematical calculations for you.

The term *spreadsheet* comes from the onscreen layout of rows and columns that intersect to form cells. You enter numbers into some cells, supply labels to identify them, and configure formulas to perform calculations. When different numbers are entered, the formulas recalculate and new results are provided. Businesses use this ability to do a **what-if analysis** to forecast future conditions, as in "What if our annual advertising costs decline by 20 percent?" or "What if sales increase by $20,000 in November?"

Of course, spreadsheets are also useful in your personal life, making budgeting, tax preparation, and other tasks easier and more efficient. Even if you do not prepare spreadsheets yourself, an understanding of spreadsheet concepts is critical for interpreting and verifying financial work done by accountants and financial planners. Given their prevalence in the workplace and at home, an ability to create and manipulate spreadsheets is a key skill for adults today.

WHAT-IF ANALYSIS Testing various scenarios by re-entering spreadsheet data in order to recalculate formulas and thus gauge the impact of proposed changes.

KEY CONCEPTS

- The Power of Spreadsheets
- Common Business Tasks That Use Excel
- A Brief History of Spreadsheets
- The Basics of Excel
- Advanced Topics in Excel

COMMON BUSINESS TASKS THAT USE EXCEL

Microsoft Excel 2010® spreadsheet software is the most popular spreadsheet application available today. It is universally used in corporations for recording data, forecasting, analysis, and planning. Excel is indispensable for small businesses, too. Small businesses often fail because their owners do not know how to manage money or other core business activities. Excel can help them keep track of how their business is doing, identify what areas are not reaching their potential, and study what can be done to improve.

Excel can also be used in areas such as education, general business, computer science, information technology, health care, law, and criminal justice. For instance, in the health care field, Excel can help nurse managers create nursing schedules for staff during the week. Many factors go into creating a schedule for nursing in a unit, such as how many patients are on a ward, how many nurses with appropriate skills are available, and the amount of time needed on a ward. Law firm project assistants and paralegals can use Excel to maintain a trial docket or prepare charts in support of litigation. Criminal justice professionals can use Excel to analyze data downloaded from national or international law enforcement databases. Teachers use Excel for a variety of applications, including grading. Excel is versatile and agile, and applicable to almost every field imaginable.

A BRIEF HISTORY OF SPREADSHEETS

Can you picture the dusty ledger books used by bookkeepers years ago? Entries were made in ink and all calculations were done by hand. Spreadsheet applications arose from a need to combine the organization of ledger books with the calculating power of early computers.

The first spreadsheet applications developed from the work of several researchers. Professor Richard Mattessich conceived many of the principles behind spreadsheet applications in a paper for the *Accounting Review* in 1961 and two later books. Dan Bricklin, a student at the Harvard School of Business, built on Mattessich's ideas to program the first visual, interactive, electronic calculator. Bricklin later teamed with Bob Frankston, an MIT student, to co-create VisiCalc. The goal of VisiCalc was to allow users to see and visualize the spreadsheet that they were creating—a visible calculator.

VisiCalc was released for the Apple II in 1979 and for IBM PCs in 1981, at a time when affordable personal computer hardware was just becoming available to the general public. Lotus 1-2-3, which refined and promoted VisiCalc's concepts, was extremely successful in the 1980s. In fact, many observers credit spreadsheets with the success of personal computers in general—once businesses saw spreadsheet applications in action, they purchased PCs in order to run them.

Microsoft Excel was introduced in the mid-1980s as an easier-to-use alternative to Lotus 1-2-3 and has been the market leader since the early 1990s. Excel 2010 is the version used to illustrate spreadsheet concepts in this chapter. Understanding concepts is key, as procedures can vary. In other words, there are often several ways to accomplish the same task in Excel. You will pick up shortcuts as you gain more experience working with spreadsheets.

THE BASICS OF EXCEL

When you launch Microsoft Excel, a new blank workbook appears on the screen. (While *spreadsheet* is the general term for the kind of application you will be using, files in Excel are called workbooks, composed of multiple worksheets.) If you close a workbook, you can create a new one at any time.

To create a new workbook in Excel:

1. Click the *File* tab.
2. Click **New.**
3. Under *Available Templates,* click a workbook icon.
4. Click **Create.**

In addition to the **Blank Workbook** icon, you will see icons to create workbooks for specific purposes. Some are included with the application; others are downloaded from Office.com if your PC is connected to the Internet. There are templates to create budgets, calendars, reports—even meal planners and expense trackers. If you choose one of these templates to create a new workbook, you can save the workbook and make modifications as needed. The template itself will not be altered, and you can use it again.

When you click on a workbook template icon, a template preview window allows you to see what the workbook based on the template will look like. See Figure 5.1.

FIGURE 5.1

How to Use the Help Feature in Excel

On the top right of the Excel window is a question mark icon. Click it to look for help on a topic using the Excel Help function (or press the **F1** function key on your keyboard as a shortcut). A list of Help topics appears in a pop-up window. If your computer is connected to the Internet, topics from Office.com are listed. If your computer is not connected to the Internet, topics from the Excel built-in Help are displayed.

To find out more about an Excel feature, click in the search box at the top of the Help dialog box, enter a keyword to identify what you are searching for, and then press the **Enter** key. If you do not know what the feature you are interested in is called, click on the topics listed to browse available Help topics. When you finish with the Help feature, click the close button in its top right corner to close the window and return to your workbook.

If the Help feature in Excel does not answer your question, consider asking the question with a general web search tool, such as Google or Microsoft Bing®, and including the keywords "Excel 2010" in your search. The chances are good that someone else has already asked your question and at least some assistance has been posted online. See Figure 5.2.

FIGURE 5.2

The Excel Window

The onscreen workbook appears in a workbook window within the Excel application window. See Figure 5.3.

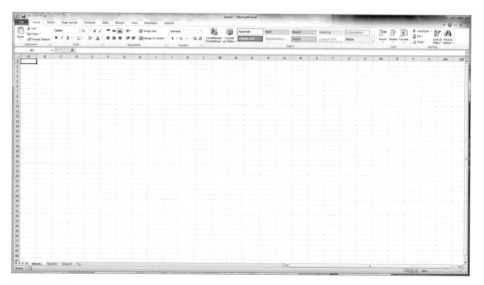

FIGURE 5.3

The Ribbon

The Ribbon at the top of the screen contains the set of commands for working in a workbook. It is organized into tabs labeled *File, Home, Insert, Page Layout, Formulas,*

Data, Review, and *View.* Other tabs appear as you need them. For example, it is possible to create charts in Excel. When you click in a chart, *Design, Format,* and *Layout Chart Tool* tabs automatically appear. See Figure 5.4.

FIGURE 5.4

Click a tab to display buttons for features organized by groups. For example, under the *Home* tab, the *Clipboard* group contains buttons for **Cut, Copy, Paste,** and the **Format Painter.** Some groups have a small arrow at the bottom right called the dialog box launcher. Click the dialog box launcher to find settings for additional features related to the group.

Click the *File* tab to access the Backstage View. The Backstage View is where you manage workbooks. As you have seen, you can click **New** to create a new workbook. **Open** lets you retrieve an existing workbook. You also save, send, and print workbooks or individual worksheets from the Backstage View. To return to your workbook from the Backstage View, click the *Home* tab or press the **Esc** key on the keyboard.

Tabs in the Excel window include (refer to Figure 5.4):

- The *Home* tab contains commands for basic tasks in Excel. The *Font, Alignment, Number,* and *Styles* groups, for example, contain buttons for changing the appearance of characters (letters and numbers) in the worksheet. The *Cells* group buttons allow you to enter or delete cells of the worksheet. The *Editing* group includes buttons to find and select data in the worksheet and to sort data (change its order) or filter it (extract data based on criteria you enter).
- The *Insert* tab is used to insert items such as Pivot Tables (a data analysis tool), pictures, clip art, charts, and headers/footers into your worksheet.
- The *Page Layout* tab has commands for page setup, such as setting the size of the margins, changing the page orientation and paper size, and controlling print options.
- The *Formulas* tab is essential for Excel calculations. Use it to add preset formulas called functions, give names to groups of cells, and troubleshoot formulas.
- The *Data* tab is used to connect the data in an Excel workbook to other applications, such as Microsoft Access, and to manipulate lists of information. List features, for example, can be used to organize workbooks of employee data such as names, home addresses, Social Security numbers, hire dates, and so on.
- The *Review* tab includes commands to proofread your workbook, such as checking spelling and grammar; to set security; and to add comments.
- The *View* tab lets you customize the way workbooks are displayed on the screen. You can change views, zoom in and out, and freeze cells that contain labels on the screen to make scrolling easier.

The Formula Bar

Underneath the Ribbon is the Formula bar. On the far left is the Name box that identifies the active cell—the cell that is currently selected. The Formula bar buttons are next, and are used for data entry with the mouse and to insert functions. The remainder of the Formula bar shows the contents of the active cell. When you click a cell to select it, you see what was actually typed into the cell on this area of the Formula bar. See Figure 5.5.

FIGURE 5.5

The Worksheet Area

Most of the Excel window is composed of cells, which are formed by the intersections of rows and columns. Rows run horizontally (left and right) and columns run vertically (up and down). Each worksheet in an Excel workbook contains more than 16,000 columns and more than 1,000,000 rows.

Rows are identified with numbers along the left of the window. Columns are identified with letters along the top of the window. Each cell name refers to the intersection of the row and column that create it. For instance, cell A1 is in column A and row number 1. After the letters A through Z are all used to identify the columns, they are repeated as AA, AB, AC, and so on, ending with XFD.

When you create a new workbook, it includes three worksheets. Tabs that can be clicked to move between the worksheets are displayed in the bottom left of the worksheet area, labeled Sheet1 through Sheet3. You can add new worksheets, rename them, or delete them from this area too. Think of worksheets as individual ledger pages, and think of workbooks as binders to contain them.

A scroll bar on the right side of the screen allows you to move up or down in the workbook window, and a scroll bar along the bottom of the screen is used to move left and right. See Figure 5.6.

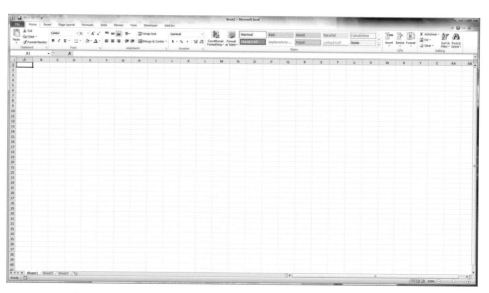

FIGURE 5.6

Navigating the Excel Worksheet

You can navigate Excel—move around a worksheet while changing the active cell—with the mouse or the keyboard. For example:

1. Scroll through the worksheet and click on any cell to move to that cell.
2. Press an arrow key on the keyboard to move to the next cell to the right, left, above, or below the current cell.
3. Press the **Enter** key to move down one cell or the **Tab** key to move one cell to the right. **Shift+Tab** moves one cell to the left.

4. Type a cell address in the Formula bar's Name box and press **Enter.**

5. Press **Ctrl+Home** to move to cell A1.

6. Press **Ctrl+End** to move to the lower-right cell of the worksheet.

Selecting in Excel

In Excel, as with other Windows applications, you must select (highlight) something before you act on it. Selecting indicates in which cells you want a command to perform an action. For example, if you want the numbers in several cells to appear as currency, with two decimal places and a dollar sign, it would be time-consuming to format the cells one by one. By selecting all the cells, you can apply the currency format to them all at once. If you want to add together the contents of a group of cells, such as all numbers in a column, you can select the cells as you build the formula.

A block of cells is called a **range.** A range is referenced by the cell in its top left corner, followed by a colon, then by the cell in its bottom right corner. For example, C3:H12 refers to all the cells in columns C through H that are in rows 3 through 12. See Figure 5.7.

RANGE A block of cells in Excel.

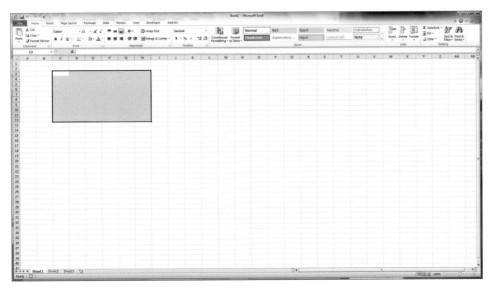

FIGURE 5.7

You can use select in Excel in several ways, depending on what you want to do:

- To select a single cell, click on it.
- To select an entire column or row, click its letter heading or row number.
- To select multiple columns or rows, drag across multiple letter headings or row numbers.
- To select an adjoining range of cells, click the cell in the top left corner of the range, hold down the **Shift** key, and click the bottom right cell of the range you want. Or, hold down the mouse button and drag over a group of cells to select the range.
- To select nonadjoining cells, click a cell, hold down the **Ctrl** key, and click each additional cell you want to select.
- To select an entire worksheet, click just to the left of column A and above row 1, or press **Ctrl+A.**

Click anywhere on the worksheet to deselect a range of cells.

The Status Bar

The status bar at the bottom of the Excel window includes a mode indicator on the far left. Ready displays when Excel is ready for you to type data into a cell, for example, and Edit displays when you edit the contents of a cell. See Figure 5.8. The AutoCalculate indicator automatically displays the average and sum of the selected cells that contain numbers, and a count of all the selected cells.

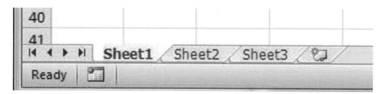

FIGURE 5.8

The **View** buttons on the status bar allow you to change the display in the workbook window. These buttons are also available from the *View* tab on the Ribbon. To change from one view to the other, click on the view's button. When you close a workbook in a view and reopen it, the same view will be active. See Figure 5.9.

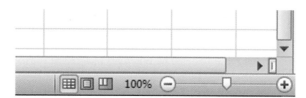

FIGURE 5.9

The **View** buttons in the Excel window are, from left to right:

- Normal view shows you the worksheet with its cells, and row and column headings. This is the typical working view.
- Page Layout view shows the page margins, headers/footers, and page breaks of the worksheet.
- Page Break Preview lets you adjust the pages before printing.

The sliding zoom bar on the right of the status bar is used to make the screen display of the worksheet larger or smaller. Point to the sliding zoom bar, hold down the mouse button, and drag to zoom in or out on the cells in the worksheet. Click **Zoom In** (plus sign) or **Zoom Out** (minus sign) to expand or shrink the display 10 percent at a time.

EXERCISE 5.1: CREATING A NEW WORKBOOK AND USING THE HELP FEATURE IN EXCEL

You are the president and founder of the new Student Technology Association (STA) at your college. The group's first meeting was a great success and you feel inspired by the networking opportunities it provides. Still, you need to draft a budget for the association. Your experience with math classes has not always been positive, but your

friends and coworkers assure you that Excel is different, and well worth mastering. Your goal is to create the STA budget as quickly and efficiently as possible. You begin by creating a new workbook in Excel 2010 and reviewing the screen layout and the Help feature.

1. Launch Microsoft Excel.

2. Review the Excel window by clicking the tabs and pointing to the buttons (without clicking) to read the Help information that is displayed.

3. Practice navigating the worksheet and selecting cells in it.

4. Select cell Z100.

5. Select the range C3:H12.

6. Select the ranges C3:H12 and H15:J17 at the same time.

7. Select all the cells in a worksheet.

8. Deselect and move the mouse pointer to cell A1 without using the mouse.

9. Click the sheet tabs to move through the workbook.

10. Access the Excel Help feature.

11. Search for help on saving, closing, and opening files if you need a review.

12. Search the Help feature for information on entering data in a worksheet. Write a brief summary of the procedure.

13. Save the workbook to the location specified by your instructor. Name it "STA Budget." Close it, or leave it open for the next exercise.

Worksheet Design Considerations

When you first start using Excel, it can be helpful to sketch out the worksheet you want to create on a piece of paper before creating it in Excel. Picture your worksheet as the grid of a traditional ledger sheet, and sketch out an idea of the numbers (values) that will be included, and how they will be labeled (text). Consider the following:

- Should there be a title at the top of the worksheet? If so, what will it be?
- How will the numbers be arranged? For example, if you are creating a monthly budget, would you like the months to be arranged in columns and the budget categories arranged in rows, or the reverse?
- Will you need more than one worksheet? In other words, will a full year of your monthly budget fit on one worksheet, or should you make a new worksheet for each month?
- Will you print it as a report for others to read, or is it just for your use? A printed report will benefit from formatting to improve readability.

While you can always modify a workbook later to make it suit your purposes, starting with a clear idea of what you need can save time in the long run.

Labels are particularly important. Even if a worksheet is just for your own use, and you know what the numbers represent when you first enter them, it is possible that you will forget if you have to set the workbook aside for a while. You can enter text into cells to label the numbers in adjacent cells, and you can label worksheet tabs by renaming them. See Figure 5.10.

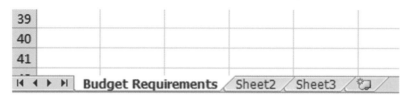

FIGURE 5.10

To rename worksheet tabs:

1. Double-click the worksheet tab you want to rename. (Or, right-click the worksheet tab and click **Rename.**)
2. The current name of the worksheet is selected. Replace it by typing a new name.
3. Press **Enter.**

Entering and Editing Data in Excel

To enter data in Excel:

1. Click in a cell.
2. Type the data.
3. Press **Enter** to enter the data and move one cell down. (Or press any navigation key, such as the **Tab** key to enter the data and move one cell to the right, or the up arrow to enter the data and move up one cell. If you prefer to use the mouse, click the green checkmark on the Formula bar to enter the data.)

To cancel what you have typed before you press **Enter,** press the **Esc** key or click the red **X** on the Formula bar. To erase one character at a time before you press **Enter,** press the **Backspace** key.

You can enter three types of data in Excel: numbers (also called values), text (labels), and formulas (instructions for performing calculations). Excel recognizes the type of data you enter and acts accordingly. For example, numbers are automatically right-aligned in the cell and trailing zeros are removed. If you enter 5.00, 5 appears on the right side of the cell. Numbers that constitute dates are changed to the Excel default date format. For instance, if you enter 3/1/2012, Excel displays 1-Mar by default. You can change the appearance of numbers using the formatting commands described below. Text is automatically left-aligned in the cell, but can also be realigned with formatting.

Editing Cell Contents

To delete the contents of a cell or cells:

1. Select the cell or cells.
2. Press the **Delete** key.

To replace the contents of a cell:

1. Select the cell.
2. Type over it with new data.
3. Press **Enter.**

To modify the contents of a cell:

1. Select the cell.
2. Click in the Formula bar and make editing changes. (Or double-click the cell. The mode indicator at the bottom left of the screen displays Edit, and you can make editing changes directly in the cell.)

FAQ: WHAT HAPPENS IF A LABEL OR VALUE IS TOO WIDE FOR A CELL?

What happens if you enter text, perhaps the title of a column, that is wider than the cell width? If there is nothing in the next cell to the right, the text that you entered overlaps it and looks fine. But if there is anything entered in the cell to the right, the text you entered will not be displayed. It is not deleted—you can still see it if you select the cell and look at the Formula bar—it is just hidden behind the other text. To display it, either widen the column (described below) or rearrange your worksheet so that there is nothing in the cell to the right of the label. See Figure 5.11.

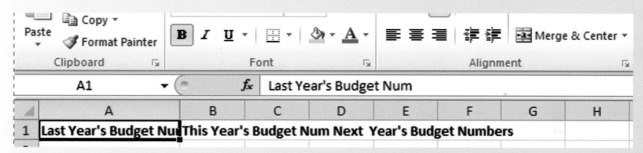

FIGURE 5.11

What happens if a value is too wide for the cell—if, for example, you increase the font size of the numbers so that they no longer fit the cell? Instantly, a series of # (pound) signs are displayed instead of the value. This can be alarming, but it makes sense—it would be misleading for Excel to display only part of a number, so it doesn't display it at all until the column is widened or the formatting is changed to make the font size smaller.

Inserting and Deleting Rows and Columns

To add more data to an existing Excel worksheet, you may need to insert new cells, columns, or rows. You can also delete cells, rows, or columns. (This is different from pressing the **Delete** key with cells selected, which in effect clears the contents of the cells.)

To insert or delete new cells:

1. Select the cells where you want the new, blank cells to appear or be deleted. (Select the cells you want to move. For example, if you need to insert four new cells, select the four cells to be shifted. Or select the cells to be removed.)

2. Click the *Home* tab.
3. In the *Cells* group, click the drop-down arrow on the **Insert** button or on the **Delete** button.
4. Click to choose the direction to shift the surrounding cells.

To insert or delete entire rows or columns:

1. To insert a single row or column above an existing row or column, select the whole row or column that you want to shift down by clicking its row number or column label. To insert multiple rows or columns, select the same number of rows or columns as you want to insert by shifting the selected cells down.
2. Click the *Home* tab.
3. In the *Cells* group, click the drop-down arrow on the **Insert** button or on the **Delete** button.
4. Click *Insert Sheet Rows* or *Insert Sheet Columns*, or *Delete Sheet Rows* or *Delete Sheet Columns*.

If you have not yet experimented with the right-click options in Excel, this is a good opportunity to do so. Select the cells, rows, or columns to move or delete, point to them, and right-click to see the choices available. See Figure 5.12.

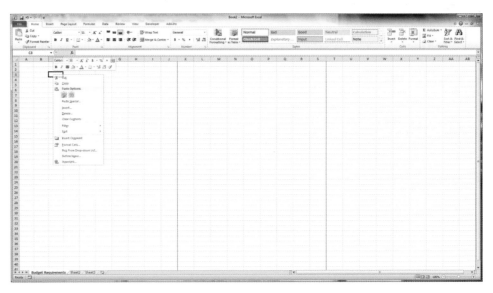

FIGURE 5.12

EXERCISE 5.2: ENTERING AND EDITING DATA

You promised the other officers of the STA that you would draft a budget for the association to monitor expenses for promotion, refreshments, and other items for the group.

1. Open the STA Budget.xlsx file you created in the last exercise, if necessary.

2. Delete any text or numbers you may have entered while experimenting with features in the previous exercise.

3. Enter the data shown in Figure 5.13, widening the columns as needed.

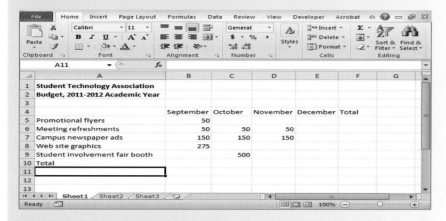

FIGURE 5.13

When preparing the budget, you forget to include a service project the STA intends to conduct at a local elementary school in November. The association members will donate their time as tutors, and contribute $1,000 for computer lab updates.

1. Add a row above the existing row 8 labeled "Charitable Donations." (Tip: Enter the value as 1000; the dollar sign and comma will be added later with formatting.)

2. Capitalize "involvement fair" in what is now cell A10.

3. You realize there will be no meeting in December. Delete the cost of refreshments and ads from cells E6:E7.

4. Rename Sheet1 to read "Fall Qtr."

5. Save the changes to your workbook. Close it, or leave it open for the next exercise.

Formatting

Excel allows you to format the appearance of a cell's contents, such as changing the font size; adding bold, italics, or underlining; and shading with color. Formatting labels and important values such as subtotals and grand totals makes it easier to comprehend results from the worksheet. For businesses, formatted text and values can help make a worksheet more presentable and understandable for an audience. Great formatting can actually be used to sell an audience on an idea or business concept.

To format a cell's font and alignment attributes (see Figure 5.14):

1. Select a cell or a range of cells.
2. Click the *Home* tab.
3. In the *Font* and *Alignment* groups, click on the desired button, including those to:
   - Apply cell borders and shading
   - Change the font and font size
   - Make text bold, italic, or underlined
   - Change the text color and alignment

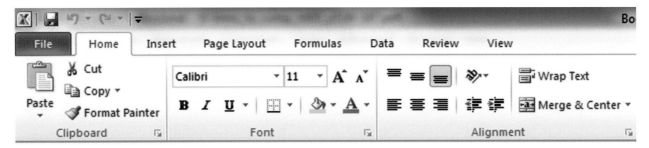

FIGURE 5.14

The **Merge & Center** button is especially useful for centering titles of worksheets. Imagine that paralegal Tanya Smith, working in the International Trade Practice Group of her firm, prepared a worksheet of export data for a client. The labels and values are in the range B1:H25. She typed a title for the worksheet—Export Details, 2002-2010—in cell A1, but would prefer it centered above the worksheet cells. Tanya selects A1:H1 and clicks **Merge & Center** to merge the cells in the range and center her title within it.

Aligning and Rotating Text

Another formatting option involves repositioning data within a cell by changing its alignment or rotating it. Alignment choices include centering, left-aligning, and right-aligning data vertically, horizontally, or both. Rotating data (usually text) refers to changing its orientation so that it slants up or down within the cell.

To change the alignment of text in a cell (see Figure 5.15):

1. Select a cell or a range of cells to realign.
2. Click the *Home* tab.
3. In the *Alignment* group, click the desired **Alignment** button or click the **Orientation** button and the desired choice of layout.

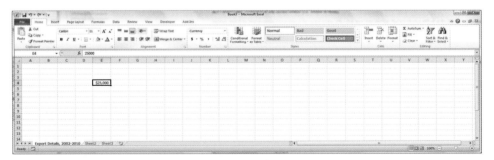

FIGURE 5.15

Formatting Numbers

Excel worksheets usually include lots of numbers. Often, you want them to appear in specific ways such as currency, or to display only a certain number of decimal places, or to add commas every three digits. You can format numbers in a variety of ways.

Formatting affects how the number is displayed in its cell and how the number is printed. It does not change the number entered into the cell. For example, if you enter 15.6876 into a cell and format it to display two decimal places, 15.69 will display and print, but any calculations that use the cell will use 15.6876 to compute results.

To format numbers (see Figure 5.16):

1. Select a cell or a range of cells with the numbers to be formatted.
2. Click the *Home* tab.
3. In the *Number* group, click on the desired dialog box launcher.
4. Choose from the options described below.
5. Click **OK.**

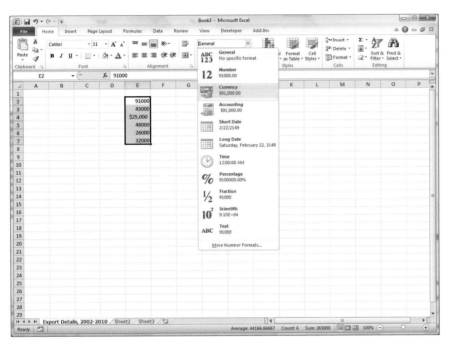

FIGURE 5.16

Popular number formats include:

- The General format displays the number as it is entered.
- The Number format shows the number with the desired number of decimal places and adds a comma as a separator for numbers over 999. You can also choose to display a negative number starting with a — (minus) sign, in red, in parentheses, or both.
- An Accounting format displays the currency symbol (such as a dollar sign or euro) on the left edge of the cell, lines up the decimal places in a column, and shows negative values in parentheses.
- The Currency format uses the same formatting as accounting but places the currency symbol right next to the number and gives you a choice of negative number displays.
- A Date format shows the number as a calendar date in many formats based on type and location. For instance, the date 10/1/2000 can be formatted as 10/20/2000, 10/20/00, 10/20, 20-Oct-00, October 10, 2000, and so on.
- The Percentage format calculates the percentage by multiplying the decimal number entered into the cell by 100, and then displaying the number with a percent symbol. You can also display percents with decimal precision.

If you understand the effect of applying various number formats, you can also select cells and choose the formatting directly from the Number group of the Ribbon. (The **Comma** button applies the Number format, with two decimal places.)

Adjusting Row Height and Column Width

Modifications made to the row height and column width can greatly improve the readability of your worksheet. You can modify the height of a row, or more commonly, the width of a column by using the Ribbon commands or by dragging.

To adjust row height and column width precisely, using the Ribbon (see Figure 5.17):

1. Select the row or column you want to change.
2. Click the *Home* tab.
3. In the *Cells* group, click the drop-down on the **Format** button.
4. Click *Row Height* or *Column Width*.
5. Type a size for the selected row in points. (Or choose *Auto Row Height* or *Auto Column Width* to have Excel automatically adjust it to fit the contents of the cells.)

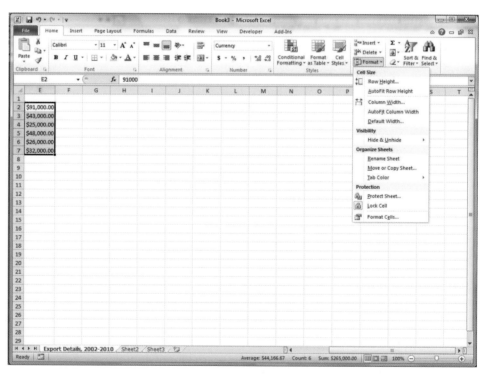

FIGURE 5.17

To adjust row height and column width manually, using the mouse:

1. Working only within the column letters and the row numbers, point to the border to the right of the column you want to change, or to the top of the row you want to change.
2. Make sure your pointer shape is a two-headed arrow.
3. Hold down the mouse button and drag left or right (for columns) and up or down (for rows). (Or double-click to automatically adjust the width or height to fit the contents of the cells.)

Formatting Borders

A border in Excel is a printed line traced around the edges of a cell or cells. To divide your worksheet visually, or call attention to a particular section, you can add borders of various sizes and styles. These borders are not the same as the gridlines that separate cells on the screen. You can choose to view or print gridlines by checking options on the *Page Layout* tab. Borders are always printed.

To add a border (see Figure 5.18):

1. Select the cells that you would like to be bordered.
2. Click the *Home* tab.
3. In the *Font* group, click on the **Border** button's drop-down list.
4. Click the desired border choice.

The *No Border* option removes any borders applied to the selected cells.

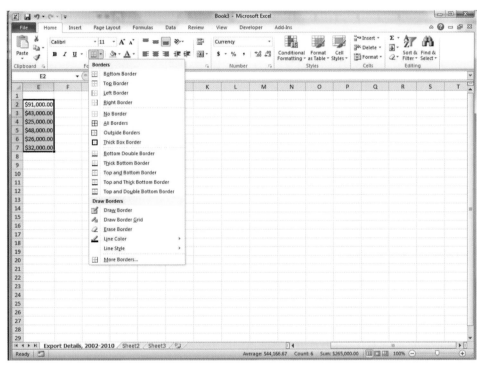

FIGURE 5.18

Using Workbook Themes

To help you format worksheets more efficiently, Excel allows you to apply a workbook design theme. Themes are professionally designed compilations of color, fonts, and artistic effects, such as shading. When you choose a theme, all the choices are applied to the cells of your worksheet at once. Using themes gives a consistent presentation of your workbook for your audience. You can also create your own themes; consult the Excel Help feature for more information.

To apply themes to your workbook (see Figure 5.19):

1. Click the *Page Layout* tab.
2. In the *Themes* group, click *Themes.*
3. Under *Built-In*, click the theme that you want to use. You can hover over it first to see a Live Preview applied to your current worksheet.

FIGURE 5.19

INTERACTION DIVERSITY: BEST PRACTICES FOR FORMATTING WITH COLOR AND CONTRAST TO CONVEY INFORMATION

Formatting in Excel is essential to presenting key information to an audience because worksheets often contain many numbers that can easily get lost. When creating a worksheet, think about what the most important information on that worksheet is and how you want to format it to be noticeable.

Once you have figured out what is important in the worksheet, emphasize it with color, bolding, borders, font size, and so on.

Keep in mind, however, that some color combinations may be hard to read by people with color blindness. And, if you rely on color to convey information, limit it to no more than five categories or so—any more than that can lead to a complicated design that loses your audience. If a hard copy is needed, will you be able to print the worksheet to a color printer? If not, the design may be too dark printed in black, white, and shades of gray.

Avoid background colors that are too close to text colors in their hue or shading. A lack of contrast makes text difficult to read for people with impaired vision or anyone reading in low light conditions.

EXERCISE 5.3: FORMATTING DATA

The other officers of the STA have approved the draft of your budget. Now you want to format it to give it a more readable and appealing look. See Figure 5.20.

1. Open the STA Budget.xlsx file you created in the last exercise, if necessary.

2. Merge and center each of the two titles across the top of the worksheet.

3. Format the main title in Arial, Bold, 14 point.

4. Bold the subtitle.

5. Apply Currency style to the values in B5:F11.

6. Center the column headings—the months and the word "Total."

7. Bold the word "Total" both times it appears.

8. Add a bottom border to B4:F4 and to B10:F10.

9. Add a double bottom border to B11:F11.

10. Save the changes to your workbook. Close it, or leave it open for the next exercise.

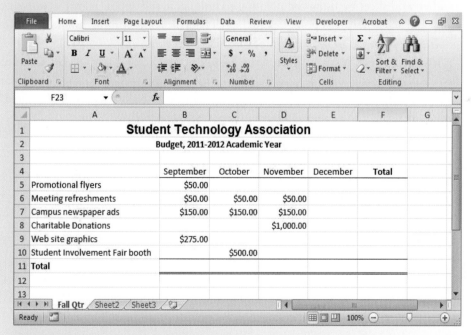

FIGURE 5.20

(Note: Be sure to save this sample file, as you will be asked to apply additional formatting in an upcoming exercise.)

Formulas

The real power of Excel comes from formulas. Understanding how to work with formulas is the most important part of understanding Excel. Formulas perform calculations. When you use a pocket calculator to add, subtract, multiply, or divide, you are really entering a formula. If you want to subtract 14 from 25, for example, you press 25, then the minus sign, then 14, and then the equal sign. Creating a formula in Excel is similar, except that you enter the formula into a cell. You must follow the rules in Excel for entering the formula, so that the result is calculated as you intended.

And, often you refer to cells rather than numbers. For example, if the number 25 is in cell A2 and the number 14 is in cell A3, your formula will subtract A3 from A2. That way, if you need to change the numbers in the cells, Excel automatically recalculates the formula. Your results are always accurate and up-to-date.

Formula Building

When you enter a formula, you first type an equal sign (=). That tells Excel that you plan to enter a formula rather than just a series of numbers. The equal sign is followed by cell references, numbers, and operators as needed: the plus sign (+) to add, the minus sign (−) to subtract, the asterisk (*) to multiply, and the slash (/) to divide.

POINTING Clicking on a cell or dragging over a range of cells for use in a formula.

To include a cell reference in a formula, type it or click on it with your mouse. Clicking on a cell or dragging over a range of cells for use in a formula is called **pointing.** The cell references included in a formula do not all have to be on the same page of the worksheet. If you include a cell reference from another worksheet by using the pointing technique, it will appear with the worksheet name and an exclamation point before the cell reference, for example, as Sheet1!A22.

The following is an illustration of formulas in action:

Jerome Knight is learning to write formulas in Excel as part of his Criminal Justice degree program. He used Excel while in the military, but only to add data to worksheets that someone else created. He had never built his own. He created a simple worksheet to experiment with, shown below in Figure 5.21A.

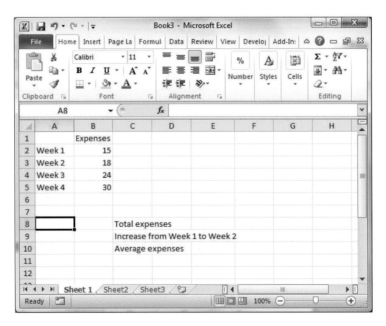

FIGURE 5.21A

Example 1. Jerome wants to calculate the total expenses and display the result in cell B8. He clicks in cell B8 and types:

=B2+B3+B4+B5

Then, Jerome presses **Enter** to enter the formula into the cell. On the Formula bar, he sees the formula he typed. In cell B8, he sees the correct total, 87.

Instead of typing each cell that he included in the formula, Jerome could have clicked on them. He would still need to type the equal sign and plus signs, however. See Figure 5.21B.

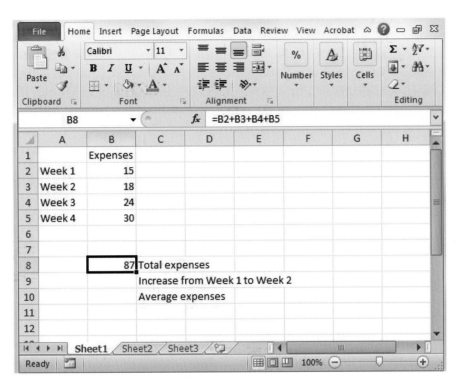

FIGURE 5.21B

To test his formula, Jerome changes the amount in cell B2 to 115. His total in cell B8 recalculates correctly to 187—the formula works. He clicks the **Undo** button to return to the original figure.

Example 2. In cell B9, Jerome wants to calculate the difference between his expenses in Week 1 and Week 2. He clicks in cell B9 and enters:

=B3−B2

Once the formula is entered, B9 correctly displays the result, 3. The Formula bar displays the formula as it was typed.

Example 3. Jerome wants to figure his average expenses for the four weeks in cell B10. He knows that to calculate an average, or mean, he can add a series of numbers and divide that figure by how many numbers are in the series. He clicks in cell B10 and enters:

=B2+B3+B4+B5/4

However, when Jerome checks the result, 64.5, he realizes it is incorrect. This number is too high to be the average of his four expenses. What happened? The answer has to do with the mathematical order of operations that Excel follows when calculating the results of formulas that contain multiple operators. (You may have learned to use Please Excuse My Dear Aunt Sally [PEMDAS] as a mnemonic, or memory aid, for this order of operations.)

Working from left to right, Excel first solves any numerical expressions inside of parentheses (P), then performs any exponentiation (E), then performs any multiplication and division from left to right (MD), and finally any addition and subtraction from left to right (AS). Following the order of operations in Jerome's formula, he realizes that because multiplication and division are performed before addition and subtraction, Excel divided B5 by 4, then added the numbers from the rest of the cells—not at all what he intended.

In order to force Excel to first add all four expenses and then divide by 4, he must use parentheses. Remember that working from left to right, Excel first solves numerical expressions that are inside of parentheses. By enclosing part of his formula with parentheses, he can ensure that the numbers are totaled first, before that total is divided. He enters the formula this way:

=(B2+B3+B4+B5)/4

The result is 21.75, which is correct. Jerome reminds himself to always test any formulas he writes, and to remember the order of operations when troubleshooting incorrect results.

Functions

Functions are predesigned formulas that come with Excel. They were written by Microsoft's software developers to help users save time writing formulas, or to provide the ability to do complex calculations that might not be possible with formulas.

FUNCTIONS Predesigned formulas created by Microsoft for Excel.

Functions do not replace formulas completely—there are still many situations that require a formula to perform the calculation you need—but they expand your mathematical options considerably.

Functions are formulas, so you begin entering them with an equal sign (=). After the equal sign, enter the name of the function, followed by parentheses. Inside the parentheses are the arguments, which are the data that the function requires in order to work. As you might imagine, identifying a function by name and providing the correct arguments for it to work can be challenging.

To assist you with these challenges, Excel organizes functions into categories on the *Fromulas* tab, in a dialog box displayed by clicking the **Insert Function** button on the *Fromulas* tab or the *fx* button on the Formula bar. The dialog box guides you through adding the bits of information that make up the arguments. The function is built for you as you complete the choices in the dialog box.

To enter a function (see Figure 5.22):

1. Click in the cell where the result of the calculation should appear.
2. Click the *fx* button on the Formula bar, or *Insert Function* on the *Formulas* tab in the *Function Library* group.
3. Click the desired function in the *Select a Function* list box. (Click **All** to display all Excel functions.)
4. Review the description of the selected function in the bottom of the dialog box. If it is the one you would like to use, click **OK.** If not, select another function.

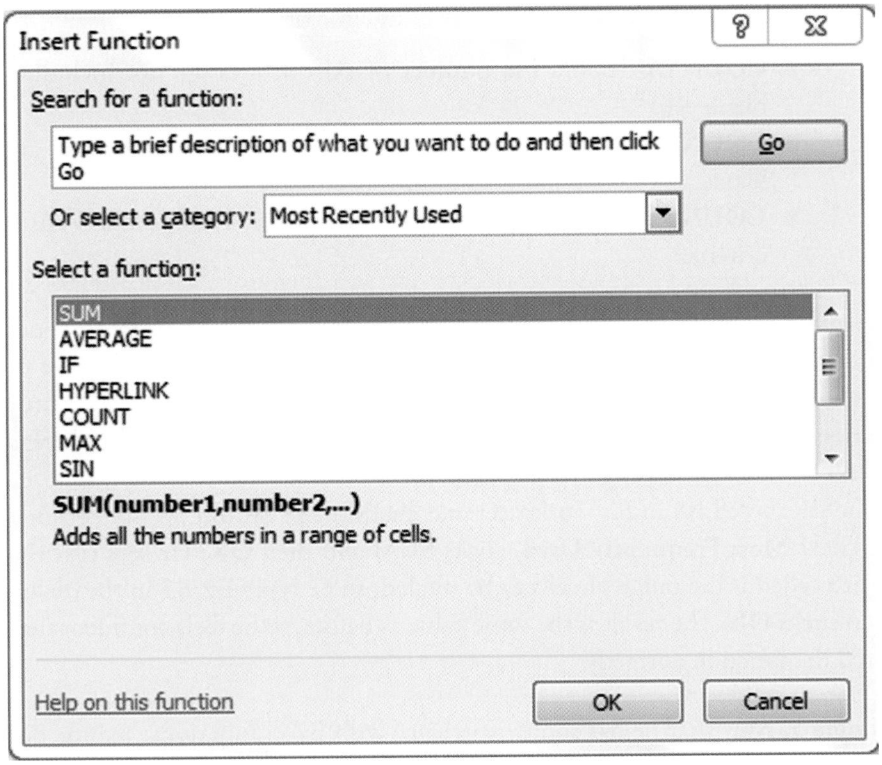

FIGURE 5.22

5. Read the instructions and enter the arguments as prompted. Arguments in bold are required; those not bold are optional. The arguments you add may be cell references, text, numbers, or other formulas. (If you need help understanding the prompts for the arguments, consult the Excel Help feature or other resources, including those at www.office.com.)

6. Click **OK.**

When entering arguments using Insert Function, you will notice buttons with red arrows at the end of each argument box. Click the red arrow button to temporarily collapse the dialog box, so you can select a cell or a range of cells with your mouse, instead of typing it in. Click the red arrow button again to expand the dialog box and return to your work.

If you know what a function should look like, you do not have to create it using Insert Function. You can type the function into a cell directly. Just be sure that you do not press the spacebar in the function and that you remember to type the closing parenthesis.

Basic Excel functions include:

- **SUM**—totals values or the contents of a range of cells
- **AVERAGE**—averages values or the contents of a range of cells
- **MIN**—returns the smallest number in a range of cells
- **MAX**—returns the largest number in a range of cells
- **COUNT**—tallies (counts) the number of cells in a range

There are over 350 functions in Excel, and many are not so basic. UPPER, for example, converts lowercase letters to uppercase letters. If cell A1 contains the word *summer*, you could click a cell and enter =UPPER(A1) to enter SUMMER.

SUM An Excel function that totals values or the contents of a range of cells.

AVERAGE An Excel function that averages values or the contents of a range of cells.

MIN An Excel function that returns the smallest number in a range of cells.

MAX An Excel function that returns the largest number in a range of cells.

COUNT An Excel function that tallies (counts) the number of cells in a range.

COUNTA An Excel function that tallies the number of cells in a range not including blank cells.
COUNTBLANK An Excel function that tallies the number of cells in a range that are blank.
COUNTIF An Excel function that tallies the number of cells in a range that satisfy criteria.

Some variations on the COUNT function are:

- **COUNTA**—tallies the number of cells in a range not including blank cells
- **COUNTBLANK**—tallies the number of cells in a range that are blank
- **COUNTIF**—tallies the number of cells in a range that satisfy criteria

Example 4. Another student has mentioned the SUM function to Jerome, describing it as the easiest way to total a range of numbers. (Although his short list of expenses was not hard to total with a formula, imagine if he had several years' worth of expenses to total. Setting up the formula by entering each cell followed by a plus sign would be time-consuming and impractical.)

Jerome selects cell B8 in his worksheet and clicks the *fx* button on the Formula bar. He clicks **Most Frequently Used,** clicks **SUM** and then **OK.** He sees that the argument needed is the range of cells to be totaled, so he types B2:B5 in the dialog box, then clicks **OK.** The result is the same value as before, so he feels confident that he created the function correctly.

Example 5. Now that he has some experience with Excel functions, Jerome decides to try the AVERAGE function. He has looked up the function on the Help feature, and knows that it also requires a range of cells as its argument.

Jerome selects cell B10 in his worksheet. Knowing that formulas and functions are not case sensitive (uppercase and lowercase letters have the same effect), he enters:

=average(b2:b5)

The result is the same value as before—the correct average of his expenses—but with less effort than writing the correct formula.

The AutoSum Feature

The SUM function is used so frequently that Excel has a button just to add it to a worksheet, called **AutoSum.** When you click in a cell and then click the **AutoSum** button, Excel creates the SUM function in the cell, choosing a likely range of cells as the argument, that is, the numbers to be totaled.

AUTOSUM A button in Excel that allows quick access to the SUM function.

How does Excel know what range to choose? Think of where totals generally are used in a worksheet with its rows and columns. Most often, the total is at the bottom of a column or the right end of a row. Excel chooses the range of cells based on this pattern. If the range Excel selects happens to be wrong, you can change it.

To use the AutoSum feature:

1. Click the cell where you want the total to appear. Typically this is below or to the right of the numbers you want to sum.
2. Click the *Home* tab.
3. In the *Editing* group, click the **AutoSum** button.
4. The suggested range is displayed. If it is not correct, use your mouse to select the correct range in the worksheet, replacing what is displayed.
5. Press **Enter.**

Figure 5.23 shows an example involving a worksheet Mary Rutherford, a paralegal intern, created as a timesheet for her work.

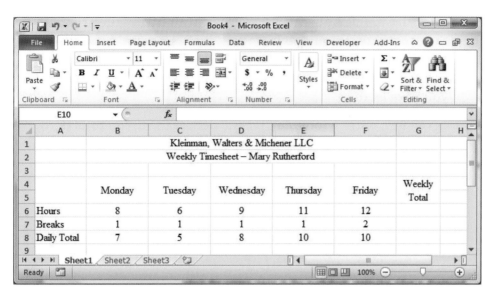

FIGURE 5.23

Could Mary have used the AutoSum feature to calculate her Daily Total hours in row 8? No, a simple formula is needed for that calculation. Here is what Mary entered:

B8=B6−B7
C8=C6−C7
D8=D6−D7
E8=E6−E7
F8=F6−F7

However, Mary sees an opportunity to use the AutoSum feature to calculate her Weekly Total hours. She clicks in cell G6 and clicks **AutoSum** in the *Editing* group on the *Home* tab. The range to the left, B6:F6, is selected as the argument for the function. It is correct, so she presses **Enter,** and the task is done.

EXERCISE 5.4: FORMULAS

You want your STA budget to calculate the total expenses per month so you can report back to the other officers. In addition, you need to see how much money you can expect to have left after expenses are paid from the members' dues. At this point, only $500 has been collected in dues—any remaining expenses will have to be paid for with a fundraiser.

1. Open the STA Budget.xlsx file you created in the last exercise, if necessary.

2. In cell G2, enter the label "Dues:".

3. In cell H2, enter 500.

4. In cell A13, enter the label "Balance:" Right-align it.

5. Add SUM functions in row 11 and in column F as needed to total the expenses by month, by category, and as a grand total. (Do not type in the numbers that are shown below; use functions to calculate them.) Enter the SUM functions using any of the techniques you have learned.

6. In cell B13, enter a formula that will deduct the grand total (F11) from the dues collected (H2).

7. Format cells H2 and B13 as currency. Adjust column widths as needed. See Figure 5.24.

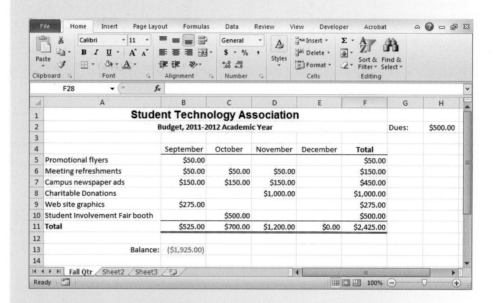

FIGURE 5.24

As it is, the STA needs to raise a lot of money with a fundraiser to meet its expenses. Try some what-if analysis. Change the amounts allocated for charitable donations, meeting refreshments, and so on, until you think the budget is reasonable.

Save the changes to your workbook. Close it, or leave it open for the next exercise.

Copying and Pasting in Excel

Often, when creating a new worksheet, you will want to reuse the contents of some cells to save the time of having to type contents over and over again. In Excel, there are different ways to accomplish this copy and paste technique, depending on the type of data you are copying and the location of the cells you are pasting to. One way to reuse the contents of cells is to use the copy and paste commands. Another is to use your mouse and drag the fill handle of a cell.

Using the Ribbon or Keyboard to Cut, Copy, and Paste

Do you know how to copy and paste text in a Microsoft Word® word processing software document? The technique is very much the same in Excel, and in any Office application, for that matter.

To copy and paste in Excel:

1. Select the cells you want to copy.
2. Click the *Home* tab.
3. In the *Clipboard* group, click **Copy.** (Or press **Ctrl+C.**) Excel indicates the selection that has been copied with a blinking marquee.
4. Click the cell in the upper-left corner of the range you want to paste to.
5. Click **Paste.** (Or press **Ctrl+V.**)

If you choose **Cut** instead of **Copy** in the procedure described above, the contents of the cells will be moved to the new location instead of copied.

Notice the **Paste Options** button that displays at the end of the pasted range. Click its drop-down arrow to display a range of choices for pasting, including options that restrict the type of content being pasted and options to control the formatting. See Figure 5.25.

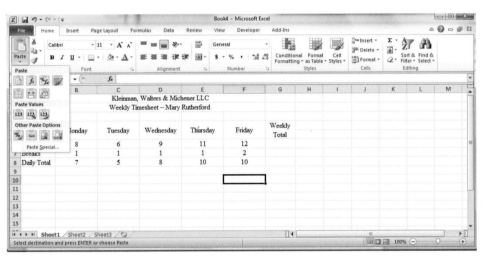

FIGURE 5.25

Imagine that Mary Rutherford is working on a weekly timesheet summary for all the paralegal interns at Kleinman, Walters, & Michener LLC. She entered the time for Week 1 and wants to reuse it as a start on Week 2, because for all the interns except Zach Michaels, the numbers are the same. See Figure 5.26.

Mary selects B4:B8 and clicks **Copy** on the *Home* tab. She clicks C4 and then clicks **Paste.** Now Mary edits C4 to Week 2, and changes Zach Michaels's Week 2 hours to 30.

Note that when pasting, Excel pastes over any existing information in the destination cells. Make sure that the destination cells match the starting cells in number of rows or columns.

Relative and Absolute Addressing

What happens if Mary copies and pastes a formula, rather than labels and values? If she adds a SUM function to cell B9 that totals the results of Week 1 and copies it to cell C9 for Week 2, won't it show the wrong total—the sum of Week 1 instead of

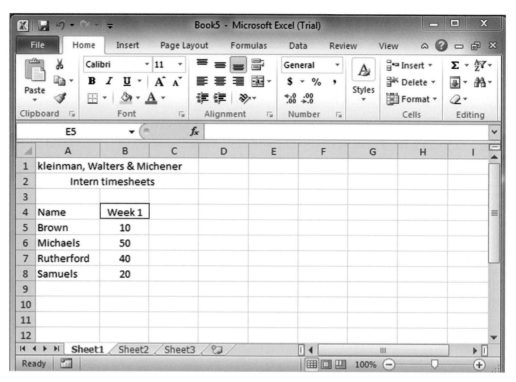

FIGURE 5.26

Week 2? No, because of a concept called **relative addressing.** When you copy or move a formula, Excel does not duplicate it exactly. It actually copies the cell references relative to the location of the formula. In this case, the formula being copied sums up the four cells above the function. So if B9 contains =SUM(B5:B8) and is copied to C9, the result will be =SUM(C5:C8).

This is the most desired result when you move or copy a formula, so you might not notice it happening, at first. Yet eventually you may run into a situation where you do not want the cell references to change as they are copied or moved. In that case, it is possible to create an **absolute cell address** in a formula.

Absolute cell references or addresses have dollar signs in them. The dollar signs have nothing to do with currency in this case—they are a code that spreadsheet applications have used for many years to indicate a cell address that should not be altered. If a cell in a formula or dialog box appears as A25, for example, both the column and the row are "locked in" and will not change no matter how the cell is referenced in a worksheet.

If you encounter unexpected results when copying and pasting formulas, analyze the situation to decide if an absolute cell address is called for. Consult the Excel Help function or tutorials on www.office.com for more information on relative and absolute addressing.

Using the Fill Handle to Copy and Paste, and to Create Series

Another way to copy information into cells is to use the **fill handle** of the cell to be copied. The fill handle is the small box that appears on the bottom right of a cell when you select it. The fill handle works well when you need to copy information from one cell to cells that are adjacent to it, either in the same row or in the same column. You can select a range of cells and drag the fill handle to copy all the cells at once.

To copy using the fill handle (see Figure 5.27):

1. Select the cell or cells to be copied to adjacent cells.
2. Move your pointer over the fill handle so that the pointer takes the shape of a small plus sign.
3. Hold down the mouse button and drag over the cells to paste into.
4. Release the mouse button.
5. The **AutoFill Options** button appears. Click it if you want to change how the selection is filled, such as with or without formatting.

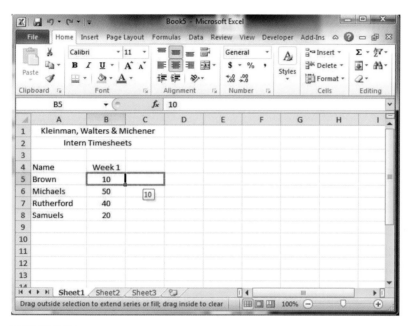

FIGURE 5.27

You can also drag the fill handle to create a **fill series.** A fill series is created when the data that is being copied suggests that it is part of a sequence, such as the name of a month, a day of the week, or a commonly used label such as Quarter. You can enter an entire word, such as Monday, or its abbreviation, such as Mon.

FILL SERIES Created in Excel when data being copied suggests that it is part of a sequence, such as the name of a month or day of the week.

For example, if you type "Wednesday" in a cell, select the cell, and drag its fill handle, the cells will contain Thursday, Friday, Saturday, and so on, continuing the days of the week for as long as you drag the fill handle. If the original cell contains Qtr 1, dragging the fill handle will fill cells with Qtr 2, Qtr 3, Qtr 4, and back to Qtr 1 for as long as you drag the fill handle.

To create a fill series that is a sequence of numbers, you must type the first two numbers in the series and select them before dragging the fill handle. This tells Excel what unit to increase the series by when dragging. For instance, if you enter 1990 in one cell and 1995 in another, select both cells, and drag the fill handle, the series will continue as 2000, 2005, 2010, and so on.

If Mary had known about the fill handle method of copying when she set up her weekly timesheet, she could have avoided some tedious work. Once she entered Monday in B4 she could select it, find the fill handle, and drag over C4:F4 to continue the series for the column headings. Once she entered the formula to calculate her daily total in B7 she could select it and drag the fill handle over C7:F7 to copy it. (Thanks to relative cell addressing, her formulas will be accurate for the columns she copies to.) And the SUM function entered in G5 could be copied, using the fill handle, to G6:G7. See Figure 5.28.

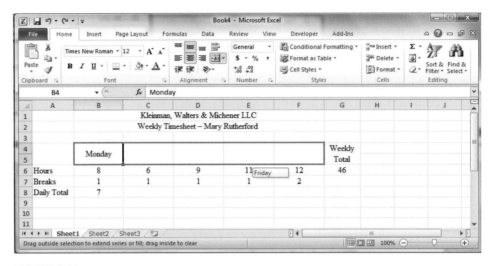

FIGURE 5.28

EXERCISE 5.5: COPY AND PASTE

Now that you know some methods for copying, pasting, and filling series in Excel, you want to try them out as you prepare for the next quarter's budget. See Figure 5.29.

1. Open the STA Budget.xlsx file you created in the last exercise, if necessary.

2. Delete the contents of C4:E4, C11:E11, and F6:F11.

3. Use the fill handle to copy B4, B11, and F5 as needed to recreate the content.

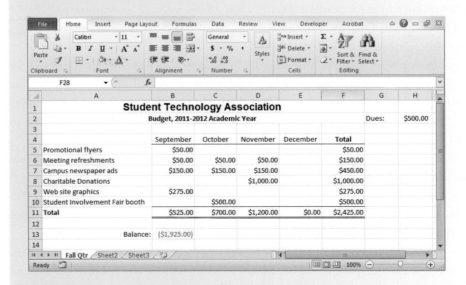

FIGURE 5.29

4. Copy and paste the entire worksheet, A1:H13, to Sheet2 of your workbook.

5. Rename Sheet2 to Spring Qtr.

6. Change the column labels to January, February, March, and April.

7. Clear the contents of H2 and B5:E10 in preparation for the next quarter's budget data.

8. Save the changes to your workbook. Close it, or leave it open for the next exercise.

Printing Worksheets

Many Excel users have been frustrated by the same experience—they create a worksheet that is functional and looks great on the screen, but the printout is a mess. The worksheet data spreads over multiple sheets in an awkward way, or is not labeled properly, or does not include the data they need. Understanding how to control print features can help you design a worksheet that functions as a report when printed.

Orientation

Text can be arranged on a page in Portrait (vertical or long format) or Landscape (horizontal or wide format). The default page orientation for Excel worksheets is Portrait. If your worksheet is wider than it is tall, consider changing its orientation to Landscape to fit more columns on the page when printed. See Figure 5.30.

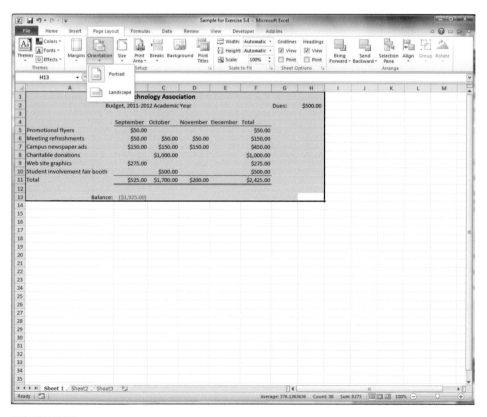

FIGURE 5.30

To change the page orientation:

1. Click the *Page Layout* tab.
2. In the *Page Setup* group, click **Orientation.**
3. Click **Landscape.**

Margins

Margins indicate how far the worksheet data will print from the edge of the page. When you create a new workbook, the default margins are .75 inch for the top and bottom, and .7 inch for the left and right. Reducing the left and right margins might fit more columns on a page, and reducing the top and bottom margins might fit more rows on a page.

To change the margins using the Ribbon (see Figure 5.31):

1. Click the *Page Layout* tab.
2. In the *Page Setup* group, click **Margins** to display:
   - **Normal**—0.75″ (top, bottom); 0.7″ (left, right); 0.3″ (headers/footers)
   - **Narrow**—0.75″ (top, bottom); 0.25″ (left, right); 0.3″ (headers/footers)
   - **Wide**—1″ (top, bottom, left, right); 0.5″ (headers/footers)
   - **Custom**—used to set your preferred measurements. (If you set a custom margin, the next time you choose **Margins** the option **Last Custom Setting** will be offered.)
3. Click the margin setting you prefer.

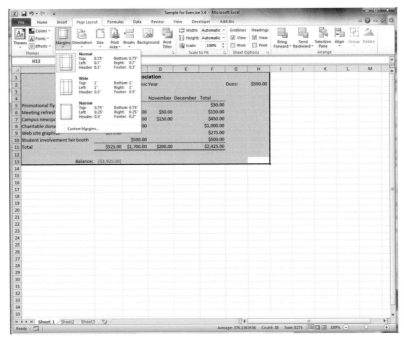

FIGURE 5.31

Scale to Fit

SCALE TO FIT A feature in Micro-soft Office® that allows users to shrink the font size in a document so that it prints on a single page.

If your worksheet is a bit too large to print on a single page, or on the number of pages you want, the **Scale to Fit** feature may be able to shrink the font size just enough to fit. There are scaling features on the *Page Layout* tab and also in the Page Setup dialog box. Click the *Page Layout* tab and adjust the settings in the *Scale to Fit* group, or follow the directions below for more precise control.

To scale a worksheet to fit a page or pages:

1. Click the *Page Layout* tab.
2. In the *Scale to Fit* group, click the dialog box launcher.
3. In the Scaling section of the Page Setup dialog box, click **Select the Fit To** option and specify the number of pages for your printout.
4. Click **OK.**

Headers and Footers

Headers and footers are areas set aside in the top and bottom margins for information that needs to be repeated on every page of the printout. What you enter into a header is automatically repeated at the top of each page, and what you enter into a footer is automatically repeated at the bottom of each page. Footers are often used to add page numbers to a printout. Page numbers added in a footer (or header) are actually field codes. They will always be correct for each page of the printout without any editing on your part. Headers and footers are often smaller or italicized to stand out on the page from the rest of the document.

Worksheets are often printed with headers and footers to include information such as:

- Worksheet title
- Author name
- Date written
- Current page numbers
- Total page numbers

To insert a header or footer:

1. Click the *View* tab.
2. In the *Workbook Views* group, click *Page Layout*.
3. Locate the Click to add header section at the top and the Click to add footer section at the bottom.
4. Click to place the insertion point in the left, center, or right section of the header or footer area.
5. Click the *Header Footer Design* tab.
6. In the *Header & Footer* group, click either *Header* or *Footer*, depending on which you are adding.
7. Click one of the predefined choices.
8. Repeat from step 6 if you would like additional header or footer information to be included.

Click the *View* tab and in the *Workbook Views* group, click *Normal* if you prefer to work in that view.

Printing

The Excel Print feature allows you to print a worksheet, a selection of cells, or an entire workbook file. You can access the Excel printing feature from the Backstage View. When you click the *File* tab on the Ribbon and then click **Print,** you will notice commands on the left pane and a right pane displaying the open workbook file and active worksheet. Always preview your document before printing.

To print a worksheet (see Figure 5.32):

1. Click the *File* tab.
2. Click *Print.*
3. Change any print settings as needed.
4. Click the **Print** button.

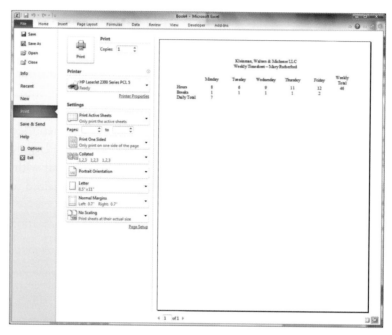

FIGURE 5.32

As a shortcut, consider adding the **Quick Print** button to your Quick Access Toolbar in Excel. (Click the Customize Quick Access Toolbar drop-down and then click to display the **Quick Print** button.) Clicking **Quick Print** sends the current Excel worksheet to the printer using the default print settings.

EXERCISE 5.6: COMPLETING THE WORKSHEET

Your budget is complete. Now you just need to polish it and print it before you meet with the other officers for coffee later this afternoon.

1. **Open the STA Budget.xlsx file you created in the last exercise, if necessary.**

2. **Add formatting that makes the worksheet as clear, readable, and professional in appearance as possible.**

3. **Add a descriptive header to the worksheet, with your choice of content.**

4. **Save the changes to your workbook.**

5. **Print the worksheet.**

6. **Close the workbook or leave it open for the next exercise.**

ADVANCED TOPICS IN EXCEL

Working with Lists

Sometimes Excel is useful not just because of its ability to do calculations, but because of its ability to organize data. While not a true relational database application, Excel has great capabilities for sorting and filtering cells in worksheet lists (more properly called tables in Excel 2010).

A list or table is a consistently formatted range of cells, with column headings in a single row at the top and the data below. No rows or columns are left entirely blank in a table or list. For example, paralegal intern Mary Rutherford has now begun preparing a client contact list. See Figure 5.33.

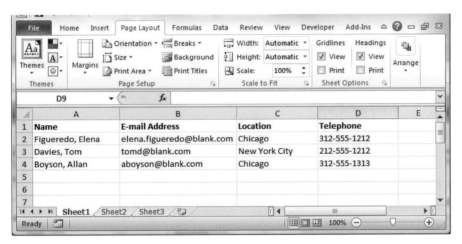

FIGURE 5.33

Sorting

Imagine that after adding 50 additional clients in 50 more rows, she realizes that it would be much easier to locate information in the list if it were in alphabetical order. Ordering by some criterion, such as putting text in alphabetical order or putting numbers in sequence, is called sorting. Mary can sort by column A to reorder the list. The information in each row will stay together as the list is sorted. An ascending sort puts text in order from A to Z, numbers in order from the lowest number to the highest number, and dates in order from the oldest date to the newest. A descending sort is the opposite.

To perform a quick sort (see Figure 5.34):

1. Click a cell of the column you want to sort by. (Do not select the entire column.)
2. Click the *Data* tab.
3. In the *Sort & Filter* group, click the **Sort A to Z** button for an ascending sort or the **Sort Z to A** button for a descending sort.

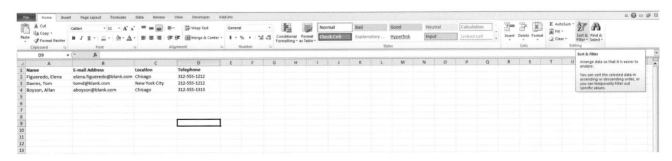

FIGURE 5.34

Filtering with the AutoFilter Feature

As Mary's table grows, there may be times when she wants to see only a subset of it. The AutoFilter feature in Excel was designed to accomplish this kind of filtering. To filter a table (list):

1. Click any cell inside your table (list).
2. Click the *Data* tab.
3. In the *Sort & Filter* group, click *Filter* (or press **Ctrl+Shift+L**). Filter arrows will be displayed in each of your column headings.
4. Click the filter arrow for the column you want to filter by. Excel displays a list of each item that has been entered into that column.
5. Click to uncheck *Select All.*
6. Click to check the items you want to match when the filter is applied.
7. Click **OK.**

For example, imagine Mary wants to limit the display to only the clients in Chicago. She clicks in a cell of her list, turns on the *AutoFilter* from the *Data* tab, and clicks the filter arrow next to Location. She can then uncheck *Select All*, check *Chicago*, and click **OK.** To remove the filter arrows, return to the *Data* tab and in the *Sort & Filter* group, click *Filter* again.

Charting and Graphing

Charting in Excel allows you to easily insert a chart based on data from a worksheet, and is easier than you might think. Charts come in various types that are appropriate for different situations. Some commonly used chart types in Excel are shown in Figure 5.35.

Pie chart	Pie	Used to show a part of a total.
Bar chart (horizontal)	 Bar	Used to show comparisons of multiple items.
Column chart (vertical)	 Column	Used to show comparisons across categories.
Line chart	 Line	Used to show trends in multiple sets of data over time.

FIGURE 5.35

Create a worksheet based on the following data from the Internet Movie Database (IMDB; www.imdb.com) regarding the highest grossing movies worldwide. The data appears in the table of information given in Figure 5.36, which is taken from IMDB and contains each movie's name, its revenue (in billions of dollars), and the year in which it was released.

1. Create a new workbook in Excel.
2. Enter the labels and values in the cells as shown.
3. Format the worksheet with bolding, font size, and colors as shown.
4. For cell B14, use an AutoSum command and add currency formatting for the dollar sign.

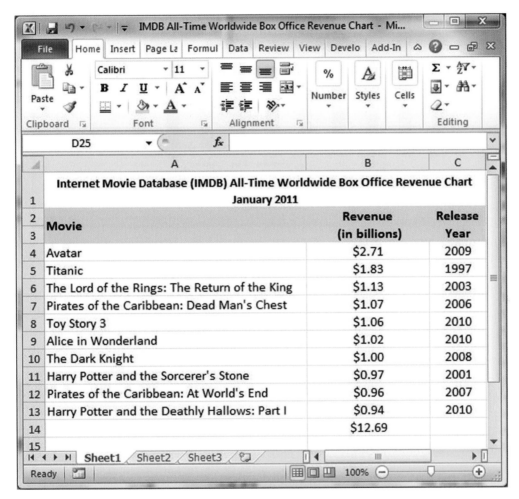

FIGURE 5.36

To create a Quick Chart on a separate sheet using F11 to visually compare the movies' revenue:

1. Select A2:B13, the cells that have the values you want to chart, and the labels that identify them.
2. Press the **F11** function key on your computer's keyboard. Notice that the *Chart Tools* tab appears on the Ribbon.

The resulting column chart appears on a separate worksheet labeled Chart1. See Figure 5.37.

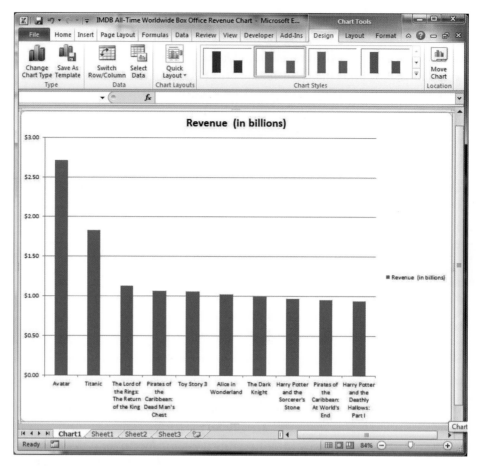

FIGURE 5.37

Embedded Charts and Graphs

You can also create an embedded chart, rather than a separate chart sheet. Embedded charts appear on the same worksheet as the data and values. See Figure 5.38.

FIGURE 5.38

To embed a column chart into the worksheet you just created:

1. Select A3:B13.
2. Click the *Insert* tab.
3. In the *Charts* group, click the **Column Chart** button
4. Choose the 2-D chart option from the drop-down list. You'll notice that the chart below will appear inside of the same worksheet.

To move an embedded chart, position your pointer on the border of the chart. You will notice that the pointer will take the shape of a four-directional arrow. Hold down the mouse button and drag the entire chart to reposition it.

To resize an embedded chart, position your pointer over any corner of the chart. You'll notice that the pointer will take the shape of a two-headed arrow. Click and drag the mouse pointer inward or outward to adjust the overall size of the chart.

Modifying a Chart or Graph

To make changes to any existing chart, click anywhere inside of the chart. You will notice that the *Chart Tools* tab appears on the Ribbon at the top of the screen. Additional chart options are offered in three tabs that appear under the *Chart Tools* tab—*Design, Layout,* and *Format.*

The Design Tab

- In the *Type* group, click on the **Change Chart Type** button to switch to a different chart.
- In the *Data* group, click on the **Select Data** button to reselect a cell range for the chart.
- In the *Chart Layout* group, click on the desired button to change the look of features within the chart itself. For example, in the IMDB column chart, you can change it to appear with values in the columns themselves and along the horizontal x-axis.
- In the *Chart Styles* group, click on the desired button to change the colors of the chart.

The Layout Tab

In the *Current Selection* group, click on the *Chart Elements* drop-down list to select parts of the chart to change. From the list, you can choose the chart's title, legend, x-axis label, y-axis labels, values, and so on. *Tip:* You can also right-click on the part of the chart that you want to change.

Once a chart area is selected, click on the **Format Selection** button to change the bordering, shadowing, and alignment (left, right, center, vertical) options.

To slant the x-axis labels (movie names) on the IMDB chart (see Figure 5.39):

1. Click on the chart to reveal the *Chart Tools* tab at the top of the screen.
2. Click the *Layout* tab. In the *Current Selection* group, choose *Horizontal Category* (x-axis) from the list to select the movie names.
3. Click **Format Selection.**
4. In the Format Axis dialog box, click **Alignment.**
5. Under the Custom Angle textbox, type "−15°" to slant the movie names.

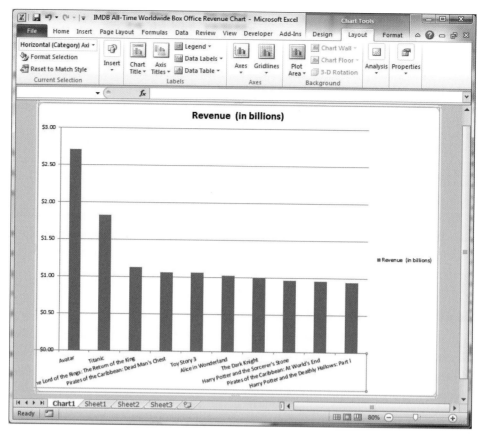

FIGURE 5.39

In the *Labels* group, click on buttons such as **Chart Title, X-axis label, Y-axis,** and **Legend** to choose a preset layout for different chart labels. This controls how the labels appear in the chart.

To make the title of the chart appear above the chart:

1. Click on the chart to reveal the *Chart Tools* tab at the top of the screen.
2. Click the *Layout* tab.
3. In the *Labels* group, click the **Chart Title** button to change the title "Revenue (in billions)." You'll notice that the title will appear with a border around the text.
4. Choose *Above Chart.*

To make the chart's labels appear outside of the column bars:

1. Click on the chart to reveal the *Chart Tools* tab at the top of the screen.
2. Click on the *Layout* tab.
3. Under the *Labels* group, click on the **Data Labels** button and choose *Outside End* from the drop-down list.

In the *Axis* group, you can add gridlines to a chart that make it easier for users to read.

To add gridlines to a chart:

1. Click the chart to reveal the *Chart Tools* tab at the top of the screen.
2. Click the *Layout* tab.
3. In the *Axis* group, click the **Gridlines** button. Choose *Primary Horizontal Gridlines* and then *Major Gridlines* from the drop-down list.

The Format Tab

From the *Format* tab, you can change the look of any part of your chart by selecting it and then choosing the appropriate formatting.

To change the look of the chart's title:

1. Click the chart to reveal the *Chart Tools* tab at the top of the screen.
2. Click the *Format* tab.
3. In the *Current Selection* group, click *Chart Title* to select or click directly on the chart's title.
4. Click the desired effects from the *Shape Styles* group and the *WordArt Styles* group. Be sure to choose effects that enhance readability. For example, the title in the chart shown in Figure 5.40 has been modified with a WordArt style called Fill-White Drop Shadow. As a result, it is very difficult to read.

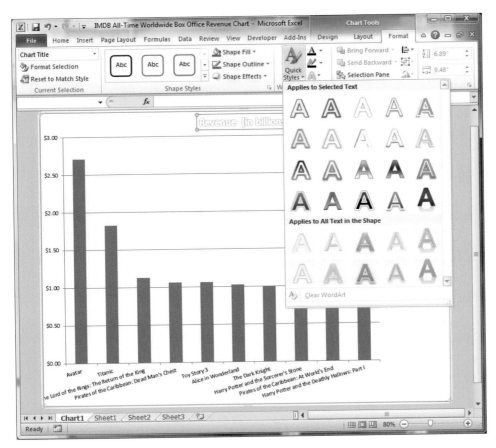

FIGURE 5.40

Tip: To make changes to the font family/size and color, click on the chart element (chart title, data labels, etc.) to select. Next, click on the *Home* tab on the Ribbon and choose the desired formatting.

Conditional Formatting

The Excel **Conditional Formatting** feature allows you to format values and text based on criteria you specify. Formatting options include colors, bolding, font changes, and adding shapes to highlight the data from other values on the worksheet.

CONDITIONAL FORMATTING
A feature in Excel that allows users to format values and text based on chosen criteria. Options include colors, bolding, font changes, and adding shapes to highlight the data so that it stands out from the other values on the worksheet.

To apply conditional formatting:

1. Select the range of cells to check.
2. Click the *Home* tab.
3. In the *Styles* group, click *Conditional Formatting.*
4. Point to *Highlight Cells Rules* and then select the criterion to use.
5. Enter the values or cell references as needed.
6. Click the format options drop-down arrow and select the formatting you want.
7. Click **OK.**

If the numbers in the selected range change, the formatting will update automatically.

Consider the Internet Movie Database (IMDB) worksheet from the previous example. See Figure 5.41.

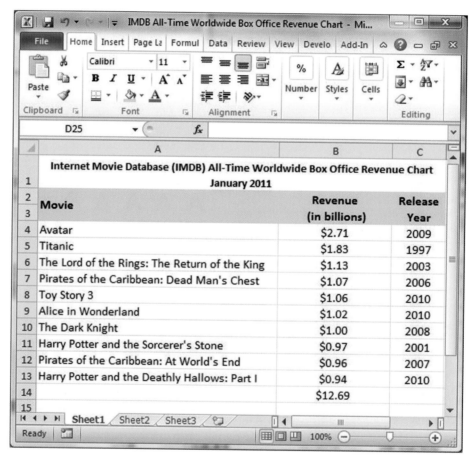

FIGURE 5.41

Imagine you are interested in movies that grossed less than $1 billion in box office sales. You can highlight any cells with revenue below that amount in red by following these steps:

1. Select B4:B13.
2. Click the *Home* tab.
3. In the *Styles* group, choose *Conditional Formatting* and *Highlight Cells Rules.* Choose the *Less Than* option from the list.
4. In the **Less Than** dialog box, type "1.0" in the text box and choose *Light Red Fill* with *Dark Red Text* from the drop-down list. Click **OK.** See Figure 5.42.

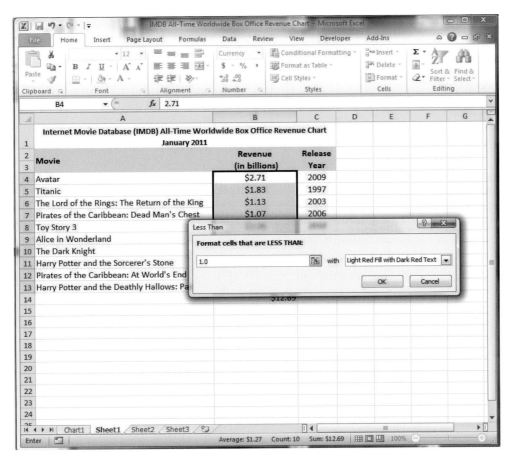

FIGURE 5.42

Other ways to apply conditional formatting to this example might be to format:

- All movies that were made after 2008
- All movies that were made between 2003 and 2010
- All movies that grossed between $1.5 and $1.7 billion

To clear conditional formatting:

1. Click the *Home* tab.
2. In the *Styles* group, click *Conditional Formatting*.
3. Click the *Clear Rules* option and then *Clear Rules* from the entire worksheet.

Using IF/THEN Functions to Control for Conditions

Imagine that you are creating a worksheet to track parole data. If a parolee was released prior to 2000, he or she will be reviewed on September 1. If a parolee was released in 2001 or after, he or she will be reviewed on December 1. You would like to add a column to your worksheet with the review date. Do you have to go through your worksheet row by row, checking the parolee's release date and entering in the review date by typing it in? Because of the **IF function** in Excel, this is not necessary. The IF function was designed to check the data in a cell, compare it to some criterion you have set, and then return a value (or text) based on whether the data meets or fails to meet the criterion.

IF FUNCTION A function in Excel that checks the data in a cell, compares it to some set criterion, and returns a value (or text) based on whether the data meets or fails to meet the criterion.

While a detailed look at the IF function is beyond the scope of this book, it helps to have a general idea of its use so that you can investigate it further as needed.

The IF function's arguments are:

- The **condition argument** is the value that you want to test. In the example, that would be the release date. If the release dates are in column C, this argument would look something like C1<1/1/2001.
- The **value_if_true argument** is what you want to happen if the condition is met. For the example, if the condition is true, you want the September 1 release date to appear in the cell, so this argument would look something like "September 1" (quotation marks are required if the argument is text rather than a value).
- The **value_if_false argument** is what you want to happen if the condition is not met. For the example, if the release date is not earlier than 1/1/2001, you want something like "December 1" to appear in the cell.

For more information about the IF function and its variants, consult the Help feature in Excel or the online tutorials at www.office.com.

Working with Dates in Excel

In everyday life, you cannot do arithmetic with dates. For example, if you want to figure out the date that is two weeks from April 28, 2001, you cannot simply add 14 to 4/28/2001. Yet Excel can do this calculation. How is this possible?

Excel stores dates as serial numbers. The numbers are serial in the sense that they are created by counting a series. They actually represent the number of days since the beginning of the year 1900. For example, the date 7/8/2008 is represented by the serial number 39637. If you enter a date into a cell, then click the *Home* tab and click *Clear*, then *Clear Formats*, you will see the serial number for that date in the cell. (The serial numbers are not typically displayed on the screen but instead work behind the scenes as numerical representations.) Date formatting, such as the formats you saw earlier in the Format Cells dialog box, allows the serial number to appear in a way you can interpret. It is because of these serial numbers that dates can be used in calculations and in date-related functions that provide meaningful date information in a worksheet.

Given this handling of dates, it is important to enter dates that are recognized by Excel. In other words, if you enter a date in an unusual style, such as Sept 13 2012, Excel will not recognize it as a date and will treat it as text. You cannot use text in calculations. It is best to enter dates with numbers and slashes, such as 9/13/2012. If you use abbreviations, use three characters, and if you include the year, use a comma, such as Sept. 13, 2012.

Named Ranges

Named ranges are another useful feature in Excel that can be used to label ranges of data. Naming cell ranges is particularly useful when you are sharing your worksheet with others who may not be familiar with how your formulas are calculated. When creating named ranges, you can make them active for the entire workbook file or just for a particular worksheet. It is a good idea to make them active for the entire workbook file for greater power and flexibility in using your formulas.

To create a named range:

1. Select the range of cells you want to name.
2. Click the *Formulas* tab.
3. In the *Defined Names* group, click *Define Name*.
4. In the Name text box, type a descriptive name for the range.

To use the defined name to navigate the worksheet, click the drop-down arrow in the Name box at the far left of the Formula bar. Click the name of the range in the list to select the range.

To create named cell ranges for the monthly revenue columns that represent January, February, and March revenues in the small-business worksheet shown in Figure 5.43:

1. Select the January expenses, C11:C15.
2. Click the *Formulas* tab.
3. In the *Defined Names* group, click *Define Name*.
4. In the *New Name* dialog box, type `JanuaryExpenses`. Click **OK.**

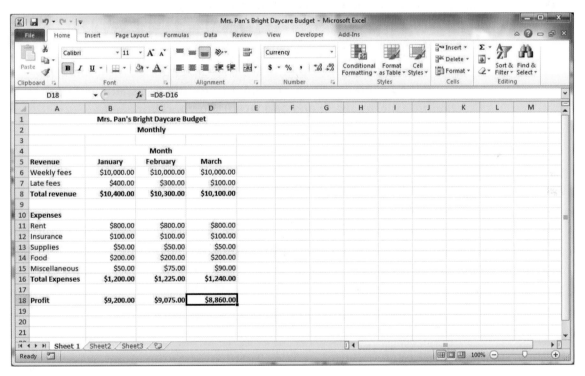

FIGURE 5.43

Having named the range, you could build the formula for the total January expense in cell C16 by entering =SUM(JanuaryExpenses). This format is much more meaningful to someone looking at the calculations on the worksheet.

If you do not remember the name for a range, you can choose it from a list. When typing your function, begin with the equal (=) sign. Then click the *Formulas* tab, and in the *Defined Names* group, click the **Use in Formula** button. Choose the desired named range from the drop-down list.

INTEGRATION: COPYING AND PASTING FROM EXCEL TO WORD

You may need to move data from an Excel worksheet to a Word document. Excel worksheets are similar to tables in Word in that entries are stored in rows and columns. Because both applications are part of the Office suite, copying and pasting from Excel to Word is easy. The data from the Excel worksheet becomes part of the Word document and can be edited and formatted in Word.

To begin, select the cells in the Excel worksheet that you would like to copy and choose the Copy command you learned previously. Open an existing Word document or create a new one. Click the bottom of the **Paste** button in Word, so that you can then click *Paste Special*. The Paste Special dialog box lists options for pasting whatever was last copied or cut. In this case, you can paste your selection as a spreadsheet, table, picture, or text.

Also experiment with copying text from a Word table into Excel. Keeping the integration between the Office applications in mind will make your work more fluid and efficient.

EXERCISE 5.7: ADVANCED FEATURES

Your meeting with the other officers was postponed until tomorrow morning. Having a little extra time, you decide to experiment with conditional formatting and add a chart to your worksheet.

1. Open the STA Budget.xlsx file you created in the last exercise, if necessary.

2. Add conditional formatting that makes monthly expenditures in excess of $50 appear formatted in red.

3. Create a chart that represents some aspect of your data that you think should be communicated visually. It could be a pie chart of the category totals, a line graph of the monthly totals—whatever you decide to highlight. Format the chart appropriately.

4. Save the changes to your workbook and close it.

FAST TRACK PROJECT: MONTHLY BILLING REPORT

Ellis and Associates, LLC is an architectural firm that plans and builds health care facilities throughout the southeastern United States. You need to create a monthly billing report that summarizes the client projects for the month, number of hours billed, and employee rate. Create a professional-looking spreadsheet using the information in Figure 5.44 somewhere in the worksheet.

Contact information for the firm	Ellis and Associates, LLC 7801 Summit Way Lane (Suite #603) Plano, Texas 75025
Title of report, prepared by, current date (use a page header or footer)	Monthly Billing Report Prepared by M. Smith Date: <current>

Monthly billing data:
   Client projects for the current month
   Department
   Type of work
   Billable hours
   Pay rate
   Comments
	Southeastern Regional Medical
	Architectural Studio 1
	Planning
	56.0 hours
	$75/hour
	architectural planning – phase 1
	Gastroenterology Sciences Corporation
	Mechanical Engineering
	Design/Build
	100.5 hours
	$125/hour
	mechanical/HVAC planning, design – phase 1,2
	Mayo Facility
	Interior Design
	Design board, sampling
	35.0 hours
	$65.00/hour
	interior design – phase 3
	Sloan Regional Hospital
	Medical Equipment Planning
	Client review, planning
	90.75 hours
	$90/hour
	equipment planning – phase 3
	Sloan Regional Hospital
	Medical Equipment Planning
	Procurement
	30.0 hours
	$65/hour
	equipment procurement – final phase

Total billable amount per client	Number of hours * pay rate
Total billable amount per month	Sum of all billable amounts per client

FIGURE 5.44

The workbook should include:

- Headers and footers
- Appropriate formatting with at least two different fonts and sizes
- Appropriate borders, shading, and colors
- Some example of conditional formatting
- A pie chart for the month, with each client's billable amount as a slice of the pie

Save the file to a location specified by your instructor. Name it "Ellis Monthly Billable Report." Preview and then print a hard copy of the worksheet.

SUMMARY

Spreadsheet applications are used to organize data and perform calculations. The data is organized in rows and columns in a layout derived from the sheets of ledger paper formerly used for bookkeeping and accounting. The calculations are performed by formulas that are entered into cells, the intersection of the spreadsheet's rows and columns. The real power of spreadsheets comes from their ability to recalculate automatically when the numbers the formulas use are changed. What-if analyses are based on this ability.

Spreadsheets are widely used in business. In fact, some observers see spreadsheets as the reason so many people use PCs today. Their influence on the business world was immediate following their introduction in the early 1980s. Today, some expertise in a spreadsheet application is a valuable skill both in the workplace and for personal use. Businesspeople who do not need to create and manipulate spreadsheets themselves still benefit from knowledge of the concepts in order to communicate with financial professionals.

Microsoft Excel is the most widely used spreadsheet application today. The most recent version, and the one used to illustrate procedures in this book, is Excel 2010. Creating worksheets in workbook files involves entering numbers (values), text (labels), and formulas. Once a worksheet is created it can be modified as needed. Formatting is added to change the appearance of the worksheet for best viewing onscreen or as a printout.

Functions are predesigned formulas built into Excel. More than 350 functions are available, grouped by categories such as financial, logical, and engineering. Once data and formulas are created, they can be copied and pasted to other cells. Shortcuts for copying and entering new data are available, such as continuing a series.

More advanced features of Excel include charting and graphing, conditional formatting, and named ranges.

KEY TERMS

- absolute cell address
- AutoSum
- AVERAGE
- condition argument
- Conditional Formatting
- COUNT
- COUNTA
- COUNTBLANK

- COUNTIF
- fill handle
- fill series
- functions
- IF function
- MAX
- MIN
- pointing

- range
- relative addressing
- Scale to Fit
- SUM
- value_if_false argument
- value_if_true argument
- what-if analysis

Productivity Software: Presentations

THE POWER OF PRESENTATIONS

Business professionals use presentation software to communicate data and information to an audience. Presentation software applications such as **Microsoft PowerPoint** 2010® presentation software create attractive electronic slide shows of text, charts, and graphics.

An onscreen presentation visually echoes spoken information to clarify and reinforce concepts for an audience. That does not mean, of course, that the screen should be used as a teleprompter for the presenter to read aloud. Effective presentations capture an audience's attention and highlight important information. Effective presenters often use color, sound, video, and animation to do so.

PowerPoint slide shows are also popular because they can be shared electronically with those who cannot attend a presentation in person. In addition, PowerPoint includes features that allow the presentation to be printed and distributed as handouts. This way, the audience can follow along as the presenter talks about each section, including making their notes on the handouts and asking questions at the appropriate time.

Presentations can be timed to run automatically—for example, each time a CD is launched. They can be advanced with a remote control so that a presenter can move around during the presentation. They can even be set to repeat automatically on a continuous loop in a booth or kiosk location.

MICROSOFT POWERPOINT
Presentation software in the Microsoft Office® suite of products. The software provides the user the ability to create professional-looking presentations with graphics, sound, animation, and movie clips.

KEY CONCEPTS

- The Power of Presentations
- Common Business Tasks That Use PowerPoint
- A Brief History of Presentation Application Software
- PowerPoint Basics
- Advanced Topics in PowerPoint

COMMON BUSINESS TASKS THAT USE POWERPOINT

PowerPoint is used in a variety of businesses where professionals need to present and share information. It is rare to attend a conference or a large meeting that does not include a presentation as an electronic representation of the speaker's main points.

PowerPoint is an important component of courtroom technology used by attorneys to present evidence to jurors during trials. Presentations help communicate technical evidence with charts and graphs in a format that is easy for jurors to understand. Law enforcement professionals might use PowerPoint for community programs, public safety education, or security training.

Health care providers might use PowerPoint for compliance training or for patient health education. Fashion designers might use PowerPoint to present their project plans to potential investors. IT professionals use PowerPoint to present training sessions to staff members usually intimidated by learning new software and concepts.

Business professionals use PowerPoint in many areas. Sales representatives and marketing and advertising professionals can present new product information to customers, company management can share company data and information with employees, and financial professionals use PowerPoint to present numerical data in meetings with company shareholders or clients.

PowerPoint is also popular outside the business world. For example, churches use it to present the music and lyrics of hymns to congregations. Videographers use it to add captions and music to picture slide shows.

As the saying goes, "A picture is worth a thousand words." The ability to reinforce a spoken presentation with appropriate, engaging visuals is a valuable skill anywhere your work takes you.

A BRIEF HISTORY OF PRESENTATION APPLICATION SOFTWARE

Before presentation software, pictures used in business presentations were often displayed with a slide projector or an overhead projector. Slide projectors held individual slides, each photographically developed and then manually sorted, arranged, and slotted into the projector. Typed or handwritten text and hand-drawn images were often projected with clear plastic sheets, called transparencies, laid on the lighted glass of an overhead projector.

The earliest presentation software was used by large graphics service companies to automate the production of slides—quite an expensive process. As PCs became more common and the popularity of PowerPoint grew, users began to develop their own presentations. Nonetheless, they still often relied on service companies for output, sending their PowerPoint files to be converted and returned as high-quality slides for a slide projector. Users with overhead projectors and access to laser printers printed their presentations directly to overhead transparency sheets.

As video delivery technology evolved, slide and overhead projectors gave way to flat, LCD-based screens that were placed on overhead projectors as a replacement for transparency sheets. PowerPoint slide shows could then run directly from the application. These screens were eventually replaced by the sharper, more vivid display of video projectors, which were originally very expensive but gradually became more affordable.

The PowerPoint application as it exists today evolved from a software package called Presenter, which was developed in the mid-1980s, acquired by Microsoft in the late 1980s, and renamed and released for Windows in 1990. PowerPoint 2010, the most recent version of PowerPoint, was used to illustrate the concepts of presentation software in this chapter.

POWERPOINT BASICS

Planning a Presentation

Before creating a presentation in PowerPoint, consider the purpose of the presentation and the intended audience. Being clear about your target audience sets the tone and feel of the presentation and makes it easier to decide what visual elements and effects (sound, graphics, **animation, transitions,** and so on) to use. Next, identify the key points of the presentation and outline those on a sheet of paper. For example, if a college student named Marisa Abrogar makes a speech about becoming a lawyer, her information outline of this presentation might look something like Figure 6.1.

ANIMATION Movement of graphics, images, or words used in a PowerPoint presentation.

TRANSITION An option in PowerPoint that allows you to choose different effects when you move to another slide during a presentation. These effects include a slow fade, a spiral effect, or a wipe from top to bottom.

Title of speech: How to Become a Lawyer

Audience: College students who are interested in a law career

Main points:

Types of lawyers

- corporate
- entertainment
- matrimonial (marriage)
- criminal

What qualifications do you need to be a lawyer?

- law degree
- good research skills
- good analytical skills
- good communication skills
- personal traits (determination, persistence)

What is the process of becoming a lawyer?

- get into law school (make good grades, take the LSAT)
- get through law school (study hard, make good grades)
- pass the bar exam
- find a job

FIGURE 6.1 Information Outline

When you design a presentation, often called a **slide deck,** in PowerPoint, you must break up the information into manageable chunks for your audience. In the previous example, Marisa could choose to break up her outline so that each section appears as a page, or slide, to display for the audience. See Figure 6.2; the title slide is shown in the main frame, and on the left side, you can clearly see the other three slides that make up Marisa's presentation.

SLIDE DECK A common term used for a collection of PowerPoint slides that form a working or finished presentation.

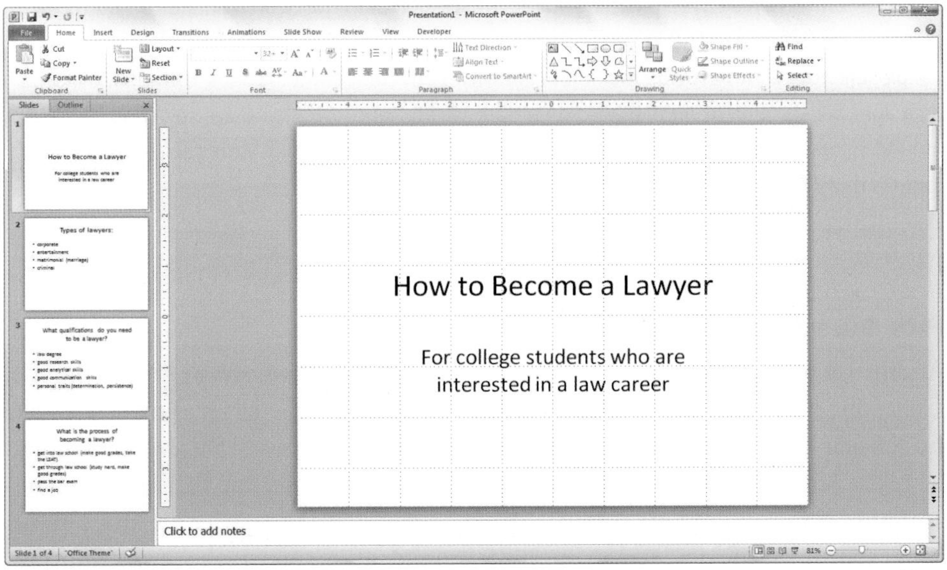

FIGURE 6.2

Design Guidelines

When you design visual presentations for an audience, certain design considerations will help you create successful presentations every time. The goal is to create a consistent, organized, and attractive presentation that audiences find pleasing and informative. The following are some conventional tips for designing visual presentations:

- **Minimize the number of different fonts used.** Typical presentations have one or two different fonts—a font for headings and a font for the body text. Use text enhancements, such as bold and italics, to emphasize other text.
- **Avoid font sizes smaller than 30 points.** Your audience members will not all sit in the front row. Smaller fonts are hard to see from a distance.
- **Use fewer than six bullets on each slide.** If you include more than six bullets on a slide, it will be too long and dense, and you may risk losing the audience. Pages are wider than they are long, so more than six bullets also makes the slide crowded and unappealing.
- **Avoid using paragraphs and long sentences.** Break information into a numbered or bulleted list, a few short phrases, or lists of key words. This is the best way to highlight important information for your audience without losing their attention while they try to read a slide.

INTERACTION DIVERSITY: IMPROVING READABILITY

One of the most significant benefits of PowerPoint is its ability to supplement the spoken word. One estimate suggests that one of every nine people in the U.S. workforce has some degree of hearing loss. By providing information in written form as well as the spoken word, you can help ensure that hearing-impaired listeners will not misunderstand or miss your point completely.

To improve the readability of a presentation for all members of your audience, make sure the font is large enough for even those with less-than-perfect eyesight to see from the farthest corner of the room. Choose simple and clear fonts, and avoid novelty fonts with excessive ornamentation.

Reserve the use of uppercase letters for short lines of just a few words, as research has shown a connection between reading speed and recognizing the overall shapes of words that contain both uppercase and lowercase letters used together.

Be sure your slides provide maximum contrast with color combinations, using dark shades on a light background or light shades on a dark background. When you are selecting background colors, be sure to consider the room lighting—light on dark is only successful if the room is dark as well.

File Size Considerations

Another consideration for an electronic presentation is the overall size of the file. Generally, the more slides included in the presentation, the larger the file size. The use of graphics, sound, and animation substantially increases file size and should be taken into account. It is especially important to consider the file size if the presentation is transmitted via e-mail, as many e-mail systems restrict file attachments larger than a specified size as a security feature. And, if you plan to show your presentation directly from a web location, larger files are slower to load and display.

Creating a New Presentation

You already know how to launch Windows applications. When you launch Microsoft PowerPoint, it opens with a new blank presentation on the screen. The blank presentation includes one slide with two centered text boxes—one for a title and one for a subtitle. See Figure 6.3.

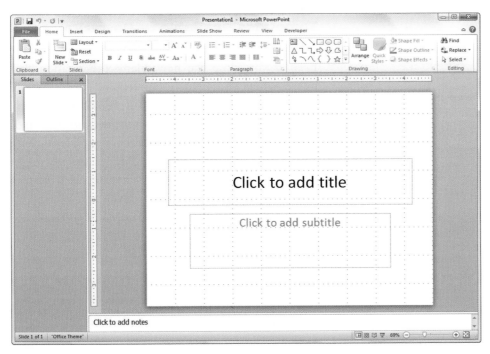

FIGURE 6.3

How to Use Help in PowerPoint

Chances are that you will have questions about working in PowerPoint that will not be covered in this book. Doing some of your own research to find the answers to your questions, using either the Help feature in PowerPoint or general web research, is an important component of success with PowerPoint.

On the top right of the PowerPoint window is a question mark icon. Click here to look for help on a topic using the PowerPoint Help function (or press the **F1** function key on your keyboard as a shortcut). See Figure 6.4.

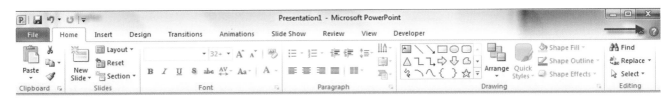

FIGURE 6.4

A list of Help topics appears in a pop-up window. If your computer is connected to the Internet, topics from Office.com are listed. If your computer is not connected to the Internet, topics from the PowerPoint built-in Help are displayed. To find out more about a PowerPoint feature, click in the search box at the top of the Help dialog box, enter a keyword to identify what you are searching for, and

FIGURE 6.5

then press the **Enter** key. If you do not know what the feature you are interested in is called, click on the topics listed to browse them. When you finish with the Help feature, click the **close** button in its top right corner to close the window and return to your slides. See Figure 6.5.

Templates Available in PowerPoint and on Microsoft Online

Even if you close the new, blank presentation that opens when you launch PowerPoint, you can still create a new one at any time. PowerPoint has a variety of preset templates available within the program itself and in the Microsoft online library. Templates include suggestions for slide content and design, so you might choose to close the blank presentation and create a new one based on a template to save time.

To create a new presentation based on a template:

1. Click the *File* tab.
2. Click *New* (see Figure 6.6).
3. Under Available Templates and Themes, click a presentation icon (see Figure 6.7).
4. Click **Create.**

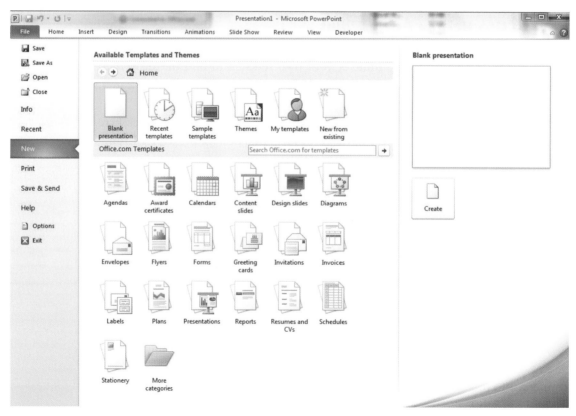

FIGURE 6.6

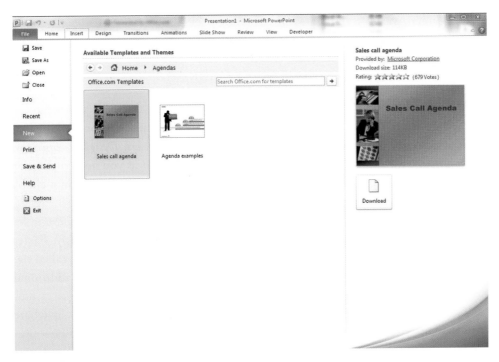

FIGURE 6.7

Choosing a Document Theme

Themes in PowerPoint are preset combinations of colors and fonts designed to produce professional, consistent presentations. PowerPoint 2010 has 40 built-in themes. You might choose to create a new presentation based on a theme, although you will see later in this chapter that you can apply a theme at any time.

To create a new presentation based on a theme (see Figure 6.8):

1. Click the *File* tab.
2. Click *New*.

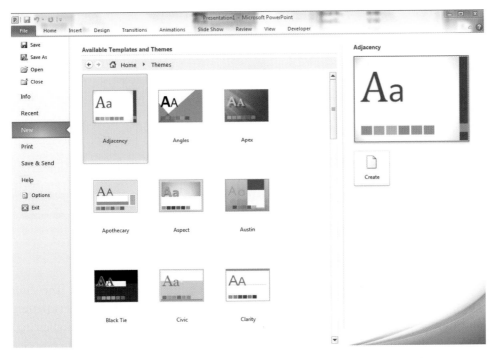

FIGURE 6.8

3. Under Available Templates and Themes, click a theme icon.
4. Click **Create.** You will notice that your slide(s) will all change to the theme background, font, and color choices.

The PowerPoint Window

The Ribbon at the top of the window contains the set of commands for working in a presentation. It is organized into tabs labeled *File, Home, Insert, Design, Transitions, Animations, Slide Show, Review,* and *View.* Other tabs appear as you need them. For example, it is possible to add charts to a presentation. When you click in a chart, *Design, Layout,* and *Format Chart Tool* tabs automatically appear.

Click a tab to display buttons for features organized by groups. For example, under the *Home* tab, the *Clipboard* group contains buttons for **Cut, Copy, Paste,** and **Format Painter.** Some groups have a small arrow at the bottom right called the dialog box launcher. Click the dialog box launcher to find settings for additional features related to the group.

Click the *File* tab to access the Backstage View. The Backstage View is where you manage your presentation. As you know, you click *New* to create a new presentation. *Open* lets you retrieve an existing presentation. You also save, send, and print documents from the Backstage View. To return to your presentation from the Backstage View, click the *Home* tab or press the **Esc** (escape) key on the keyboard. See Figure 6.9.

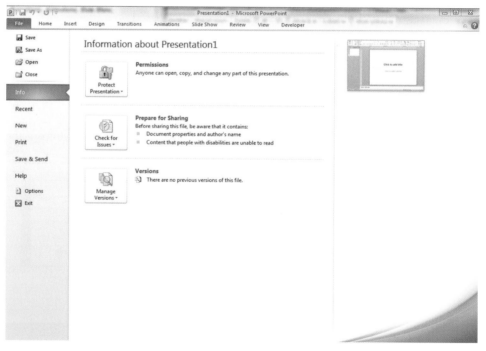

FIGURE 6.9

Create new slides and change their appearance from the *Home* tab. The *Font* group, for example, contains buttons to change the appearance of characters (letters and numbers) in the slides, such as the size of the text, boldfacing, and italicizing. You can also group and arrange graphic objects on your slide from this tab. See Figure 6.10.

FIGURE 6.10

Use the *Insert* tab to insert items such as tables, shapes, charts, and headers/footers into your document. See Figure 6.11.

FIGURE 6.11

Customize the background of your presentation from the *Design* tab. You can also change the theme design and colors, and modify the page setup of your presentation. See Figure 6.12.

FIGURE 6.12

The *Transitions* tab allows you to control what happens on the screen when a presenter moves to the next slide. For example, you can use a slow fade, a spiral effect, or a wipe from top to bottom. Sounds played during the presentation and settings to advance from slide to slide are also set here. See Figure 6.13.

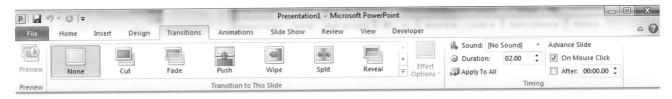

FIGURE 6.13

Use the *Animations* tab to create movement on the screen when the slide is displayed. You can apply, change, or remove animations to objects on this tab. See Figure 6.14.

FIGURE 6.14

To control the presentation of your slide show, use the *Slide Show* tab. From here, you can set up a repeating slide show and hide slides for a given presentation. See Figure 6.15.

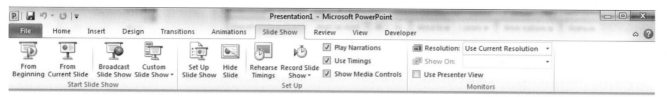

FIGURE 6.15

The *Review* tab includes commands to check the accuracy of your presentation, such as a spelling and grammar check and the Compare feature that lets you compare one presentation to another, marking any changes. See Figure 6.16.

FIGURE 6.16

Make global changes to the appearance of your presentation using the Slide Master in the *View* tab. Zoom in and out, display rulers, display gridlines, and show drawing guidelines on the screen for precise measurements. See Figure 6.17.

FIGURE 6.17

As with most other applications, scroll bars on the right side of the screen allow you to move up or down in the window.

Views in PowerPoint

When you open PowerPoint, the presentation displays in Normal view. Normal view is the typical working view of a presentation. A pane on the left of the window includes a *Slides* tab and an *Outline* tab. The *Slides* tab displays thumbnails of the existing slides. Click on the desired slide to quickly navigate through a presentation.

When you click on a slide, it displays in the larger Slide Pane to the right. This is where you create or edit each slide. The *Outline* tab displays only the text of the presentation arranged in an outline layout, and is useful when you want to focus on writing and editing text content. See Figure 6.18.

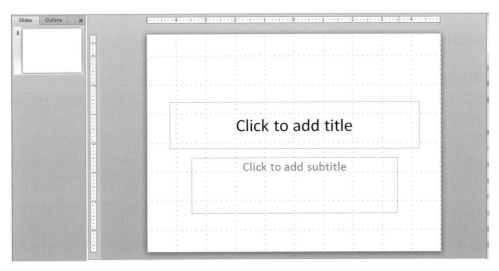

FIGURE 6.18

Use the Slide Pane to enter and edit text, graphics, and other objects in your presentation. Notice it includes areas outlined with dotted lines, which are called **placeholders.** Placeholders are areas set aside to make it easy to enter text or insert objects, such as charts, tables, or clip art graphics. The two placeholders on the default title slide created with a new blank presentation are labeled **Click to add title** and **Click to add subtitle.** As you will see shortly, you will do exactly that to add content to this slide.

PLACEHOLDER A space on a PowerPoint slide designated by a dotted outline for text insertion.

In addition to the *Slides* tab, *Outline* tab, and Slide Pane, Normal view includes a Notes Pane below the Slide Pane. You can type notes for yourself for prompts or a script when you present the slide show. You can also type notes to print for your audience's reference. Initially, the Notes Pane is very shallow (see Figure 6.19). To make it larger, position your pointer over the top of the Notes Pane, so that your pointer changes to a two-headed arrow shape. Hold down the mouse button and drag up to allow more space for notes.

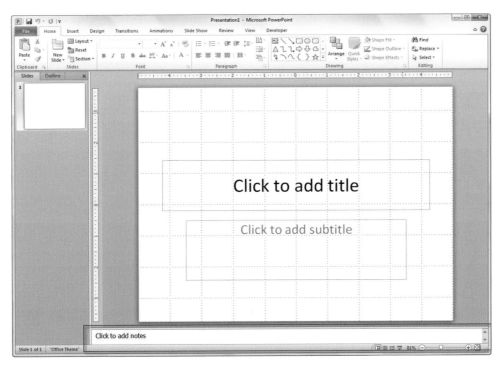

FIGURE 6.19

Status Bar Options

The left side of the status bar in PowerPoint tells you the slide number of the selected slide along with the total number of slides in the presentation and the name of the currently applied document theme. On the right of the status bar are buttons used to switch between the following views:

- *Normal view*—The default edit view for working with slide content. See Figure 6.20A.
- *Slide Sorter view*—A view that allows you access to all slides on the same screen. In Slide Sorter view, you can drag slides to change their order, copy, and delete slides. See Figure 6.20B.
- *Reading view*—A presentation view that lets you run the presentation as a slide show on a PC, rather than on a projector in front of an audience. It includes navigation arrow keys on the status bar to navigate through the slide presentation. This view makes it easy to switch back to Normal or Slide Sorter view for editing. See Figure 6.20C.
- *Slideshow view*—This view runs the slide presentation as a slide show, using your full screen and advancing as you click the mouse, press the **Page Down** or **Enter** key, or click a remote controller. Press the **Esc** key to return to Normal view. See Figure 6.20D.

These views, along with others that allow more specific control of the slide show and set global choices for formatting, are also available from the *View* tab. The status bar also includes a zoom slider at the bottom right for you to zoom in or out on slide content, making it larger or smaller by moving the slider bar.

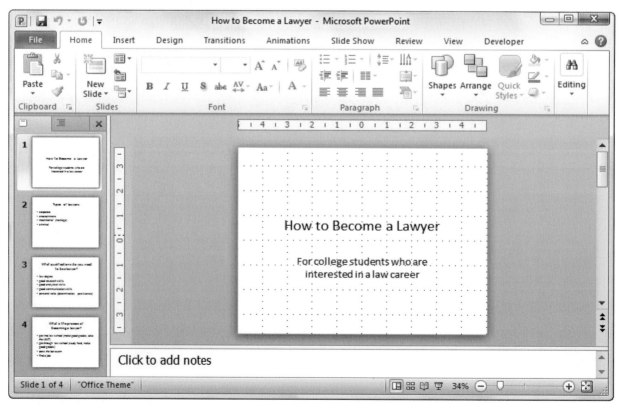

FIGURE 6.20A

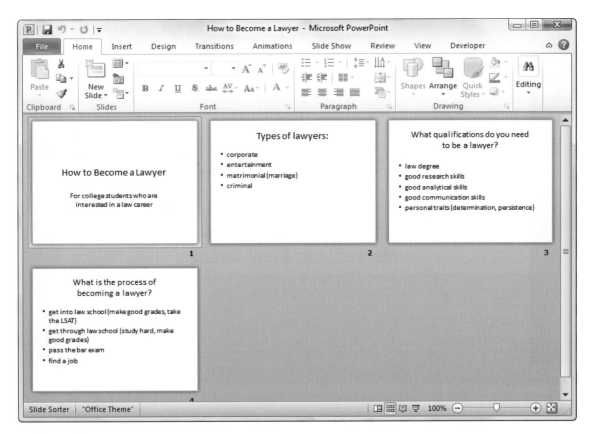

FIGURE 6.20B

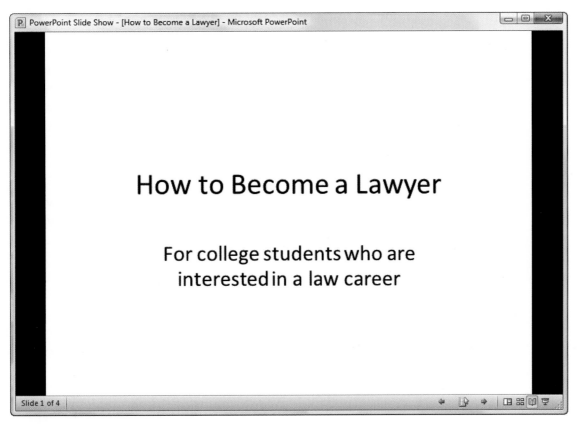

FIGURE 6.20C

How to Become a Lawyer

For college students who are
interested in a law career

FIGURE 6.20D

EXERCISE 6.1: CREATING A NEW PRESENTATION AND USING THE HELP FEATURE IN POWERPOINT

As president and founder of the new Student Technology Association (STA), you have volunteered to create a PowerPoint presentation for the upcoming Technology Fair at your college. Not only will this promote the STA to potential members, it will also provide you with a chance to experiment with PowerPoint and improve your presentation software skills.

1. Launch Microsoft PowerPoint.

2. Click the tabs and point to the buttons (without clicking) to review the PowerPoint window and read the Help information displayed.

3. Access the PowerPoint Help feature.

4. Search for help on how to save, close, and open files if you need a review.

5. Browse the Help feature.

6. Write a brief summary of a PowerPoint feature you want to learn how to use.

7. Save the presentation to the location specified by your instructor. Name it "STA Presentation." Close it or leave it open for the next exercise.

Entering Text in PowerPoint

When you create a new default presentation in PowerPoint, the Title Slide layout is the first thing you see on the screen. As you add more slides to the presentation, you can choose from eight additional slide layouts that define the general structure of the slide by the placeholders they include and their placement on a slide. For example, there are placeholders to add bulleted text, tables, graphics, or movies to a slide, accessed by a click of your mouse. Most slides also contain a title slide placeholder at the top of the slide.

To enter text on a slide, click inside of the placeholder and type your desired text. For example, imagine that small business owner Lee Schuster needs to prepare a presentation for the new staging component of his interior design business. After creating a new presentation, Lee clicks on the **Click to add title** placeholder. The placeholder changes to contain a blinking insertion point to show Lee that he can enter text. Selection handles also appear around the placeholder object. Lee types "Home Staging Presentation" and notices that the text is centered automatically within the placeholder and the slide. He clicks the **Click to add subtitle** placeholder and types the name of his company, "Interior Furnishings, Inc." See Figure 6.21.

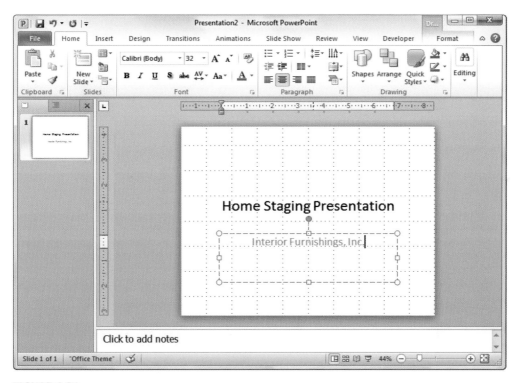

FIGURE 6.21

Selecting in PowerPoint

You select text and objects on a PowerPoint slide for the same reason you select them in other applications—to mark them as the relevant content for the action or command you choose next, such as deletion, copy and paste, or reformat.

Hold the mouse button down and drag over the text to select it. You can also click to place the insertion point at the beginning of the text to select, then hold down the **Shift** key and click at the end of the text to select. Many of the shortcuts you learned using Microsoft Word work in PowerPoint too, such as double-clicking on a word to select it and triple-clicking a paragraph to select the paragraph.

Click an object on a PowerPoint slide to select it. When you click a placeholder object, a dashed borderline and small selection handles appear around the object. To select multiple objects (i.e., text boxes, graphics) on a slide, hold down the **Shift** key as you click on each object in turn.

PowerPoint also allows you to select objects using the Selection and Visibility task pane from the Ribbon, which is helpful when you have many objects on a slide, possibly overlapping. The Selection and Visibility task pane is also available in Microsoft Excel 2010® spreadsheet software.

To select objects using the Ribbon:

1. Click the *Home* tab.
2. In the *Editing* group, click **Select.**
3. Click **Selection Pane.** See Figure 6.22.
4. From the Selection and Visibility task pane, click the item or items you want to select.

FIGURE 6.22

Editing Text in PowerPoint

Editing text in PowerPoint is similar to editing in Microsoft Word® word processing software. For instance, to insert a word into an existing sentence, click to place the insertion point where the word should appear. To delete letters or numbers one at a time on a slide, click to place the insertion point at the beginning of the text to delete and press the **Delete** key, or click to place the insertion point at the end of the text to delete and press the **Backspace** key. Pressing **Delete** or **Backspace** with text selected will delete all the selected text. Typing with text selected will replace the selected text with any text you type.

The procedure for moving or copying text within a presentation is also consistent with the procedure in Word. To cut or copy and paste text:

1. Select the text.
2. Click the *Home* tab.
3. In the *Clipboard* group, click **Copy** to copy the text, or click **Cut** to remove the text and place it on the internal clipboard for the next step. (Or use the keyboard shortcuts **Ctrl+C** to copy and **Ctrl+X** to cut.)
4. Click to place the insertion point where the copied or cut text should appear, and then in the *Clipboard* group, click **Paste.**

Global Find and Replace

You can also edit text in PowerPoint by automatically replacing it with other text. This can be done one word at a time or throughout the entire presentation, globally. For example, imagine that legal assistant Marisa Abrogar has completed her 25-slide presentation, "How to Become a Lawyer"—and then she decides that she would rather use the word "attorney" instead of "lawyer." Marisa can use the global Find and Replace function in PowerPoint to make all of the substitutions at once, instead of searching each slide of the presentation for the word "lawyer."

To find each occurrence of a word or phrase and replace it with another:

1. Click the *Home* tab.
2. In the *Editing* group, click **Replace** (see Figure 6.23).
3. In the Find what box, type the text that you want to search for and replace.
4. In the Replace with box, type the replacement text.
5. Click **Find Next,** and then one of the following:

   - Click **Replace** to replace the highlighted text and find the next time it occurs in the document.
   - Click **Replace All** to replace all instances of the text in your document.
   - Click **Find Next** to skip this instance of the text and proceed to the next time it appears in the document.

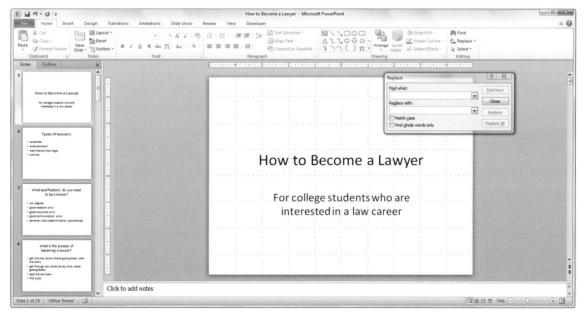

FIGURE 6.23

EXERCISE 6.2: ENTERING TEXT ON A SLIDE

The dean of students asks you to speak at the upcoming Technology Fair about the variety of technology resources available to students on campus. Your goal is to create a lively, interesting slide show to accompany your 20-minute lecture. It will also post to the campus website, so accuracy and a professional appearance are very important.

1. On paper, outline the points you will cover in your presentation. Consider topics such as the campus computer lab(s), WiFi locations on campus, the college's elearning portal, student discounts on hardware and software, and so on. Collaborate with your classmates and consult with your instructors as needed.

2. Divide your outline into the content for your presentation's slides. Draft an introductory slide to follow the title slide and a summary slide to end the presentation. You need approximately 10 slides for the 20-minute lecture.

3. Think of an engaging title for your presentation, one that explains its purpose in an intriguing way.

4. Open the STA Presentation.pptx file you created in the last exercise, if necessary.

5. Enter your title in the title placeholder and enter your name in the subtitle placeholder.

6. Save the changes to your presentation.

7. Close it, or leave it open for the next exercise.

Formatting in PowerPoint

Recall that you can use document themes in a PowerPoint presentation, and that the theme imposes consistent colors, fonts, sizes, background art, and so on. You can choose a document theme when you create a new presentation, or apply it to an existing presentation. The default theme is Office Theme.

To change the document theme:

1. Click the *Design* tab.
2. In the *Themes* group, point to various document theme buttons to preview the changes that choosing them will make. If you click the **More** button in the bottom right of the *Themes* group, the expanded Gallery view gives you more themes to preview. See Figure 6.24.
3. Click the theme you like best and apply it to all the slides of your presentation. Next, set it as the default for new slides you add.

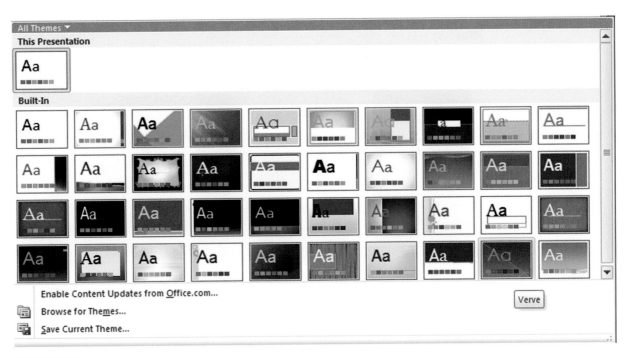

FIGURE 6.24

For example, interior designer Lee Schuster wants to make his "Home Staging Presentation" more visually appealing. He expands the Themes gallery of the *Design* tab, and after previewing several options, selects the Aspect theme. See Figure 6.25.

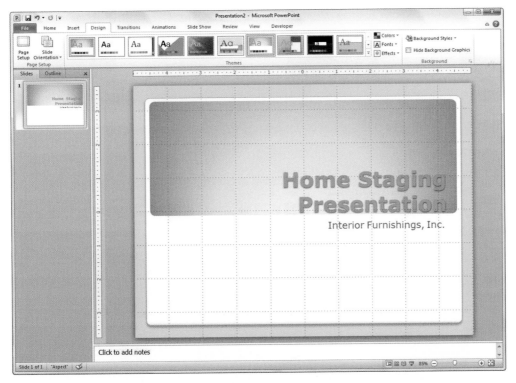

FIGURE 6.25

Here are some examples of Marisa's "How to Become a Lawyer" title slide with various themes applied. Notice that the text does not change; instead, only the arrangement of the placeholder text, the fonts and font formatting, and the colors used are changed. See Figures 6.26A–C.

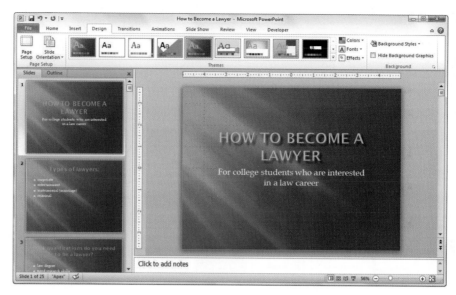

FIGURE 6.26A

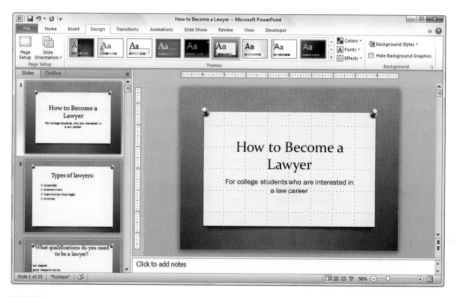

FIGURE 6.26B

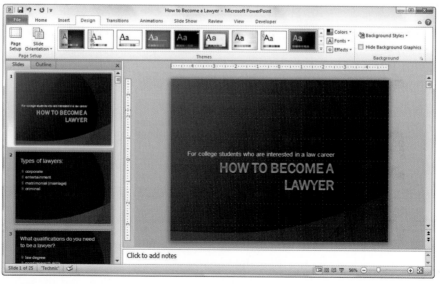

FIGURE 6.26C

Marisa and Lee can reformat slides based on their own preferences, of course. If Lee wants to experiment to draw more attention to his company name, he can select Interior Furnishings, Inc. and click the **Increase Font Size** button from the *Font* group on the *Home* tab a few times to see if he likes it larger. If he decides that he does not, he can click the **Decrease Font Size** button, or he can click the **Bold** button with the company name selected to see if he prefers to put emphasis on the words.

To change the appearance of existing characters:

1. Select the text you want to change.
2. Click the *Home* tab.
3. In the *Font* group, click the button for the desired effect.

Remember that the small arrow in the bottom right of the *Font* group is a dialog box launcher. Click it for more character formatting choices.

Paragraph Formatting

Paragraph formatting in PowerPoint includes commands to change the line spacing, indentation, text direction, and alignment.

To change the appearance of existing paragraphs:

1. Select one or more paragraphs you want to change.
2. Click the *Home* tab.
3. In the *Paragraph* group (see Figure 6.27), click the button(s) for the desired effect(s).

FIGURE 6.27

Background Formatting

You can reformat many elements of the slide's appearance, including the slide background. You can use backgrounds made of solid color, textured patterns, and pictures. See Figures 6.28A (solid color) and 6.28B (pattern fill) slide backgrounds for the slide presentation on home staging. Changing background styles affects all slides in a presentation.

To modify background styles:

1. Click the *Design* tab.
2. In the *Background* group, click the *Background Styles* drop-down arrow.
3. Choose from the available preset background styles. Notice the color and pattern choices are limited to those that combine well with the theme already chosen for the presentation.
4. For more options, click the *Format Background* from the drop-down. The *Fill* tab on the left lets you choose a solid or gradient (shaded) fill, or a picture or texture to use as a fill.
5. Click **Apply to All.**

The button choice makes it clear that changes made to the background are applied to all the slides in a presentation, but what about other formatting changes, such

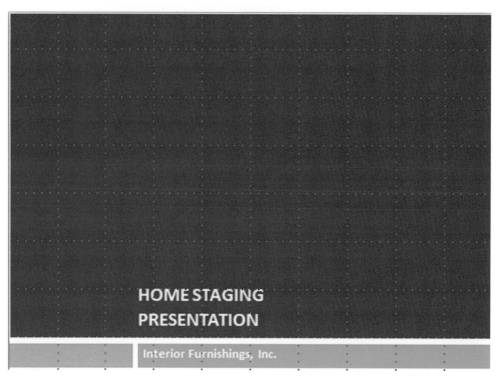

FIGURE 6.28A

FIGURE 6.28B

as making all the title placeholders on all slides of a presentation italic, or increasing the line spacing of bulleted lists on each slide? You might assume that you must make these changes on each and every slide. However, you can make the changes on a "behind-the-scenes" slide called the Slide Master and ensure changes will be made globally throughout the presentation and help keep the look of your slides consistent.

To use the Slide Master:

1. Click the *View* tab.
2. In the *Master Views* group, click **Slide Master.**
3. The Slide Master thumbnail appears, along with thumbnails of individual masters for various slide layouts. The *Slide Master* tab also displays (see Figure 6.29).
4. To make global changes, click the top thumbnail and make necessary font, color, and layout changes in the master slide to the right, using the options on the *Slide Master* tab.
5. When you finish, click **Close Master View** in the *Close* group.

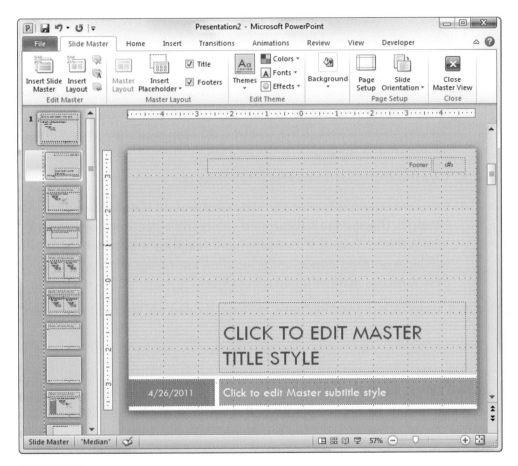

FIGURE 6.29

If you have already made some formatting changes by hand on individual slides of your presentation, changes made in the Slide Master do not override your previous choices.

Using action buttons within a presentation makes navigation easy as you can click a button directly on the slide to move within a presentation. To insert action buttons using the Slide Master:

1. Click the *View* tab.
2. In the *Master Views* group, click **Slide Master.**
3. The Slide Master thumbnail appears, along with thumbnails of individual masters for various slide layouts.
4. On the *Slide Show* tab, select **Action Buttons.**

5. Choose the navigation you want to apply to your presentation: *Home, Back* or *Previous Slide*, and so on.

6. Save your presentation.

EXERCISE 6.3: FORMATTING A PRESENTATION

You are ready to select an eye-catching combination of fonts, colors, and placeholder arrangements for your presentation. These must be highly visible when you make your presentation at the Technology Fair and also look good on screen when it is downloaded from the campus website.

1. Open the STA Presentation.pptx file from the last exercise, if necessary.

2. Apply a document theme of your choice. Feel free to click More Themes on Microsoft Office Online if you have Internet access and can download themes.

3. Save the changes to STA Presentation.pptx.

4. Experiment and reformat the slide background if necessary; for example, change the background colors to better represent your school colors. Save the changes if you feel they are successful. (You will have another opportunity to refine your color scheme in the next exercise, after you add more slides.)

5. Close STA Presentation.pptx, or leave it open for the next exercise.

Adding New Slides

As noted, new blank presentations typically begin with a title slide. You add slides for the remaining presentation content. As you show the presentation, a new slide displays each time you click the mouse or press the **Enter** key to advance through the slide show.

Changing the Slide Layout

When you add a slide to a presentation, you choose from one of nine built-in Power-Point slide layouts. The slide layout you choose depends on the intended purpose of the slide. See Figure 6.30.

To insert a slide:

1. In Normal view, click the thumbnail of the slide preceding the slide you will insert.
2. Click the *Home* tab.
3. In the *Slides* group, click the drop-down arrow in the bottom half of the **New Slide** button.
4. Click a slide layout (see Figure 6.31).

SLIDE LAYOUT	PURPOSE
Title Slide	Contains a title and subtitle placeholder, used to begin a presentation
Title and Content	Contains a title placeholder and a content placeholder, used to enter bulleted text or to insert a table, chart, or picture
Section Header	Used as an optional divider slide to begin a new section of the presentation
Two Content	Similar to Title and Content, but with two content or bulleted text areas
Comparison	Similar to Two Content, but with extra text placeholders for explanatory text describing the differences between the content
Title Only	Contains a title placeholder; the rest of the slide used to draw graphics or paste content
Blank	Adds a completely blank slide to draw graphics, paste content, or create your own custom slide layout
Content with Caption	Similar to Comparison, but with only one title placeholder, content area, and text placeholder for explanatory text
Picture with Caption	Similar to Content with Caption but specifically for picture content

FIGURE 6.30 Slide Layouts and Their Purpose

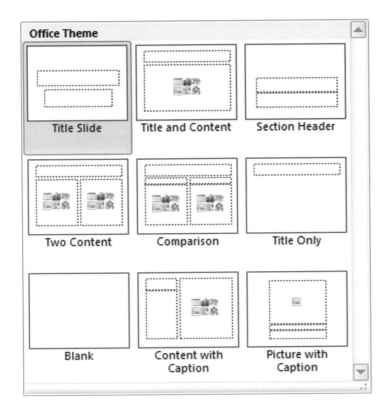

FIGURE 6.31

You can change a slide's layout at any time. For example, if Lee Schuster adds a Blank slide as the second slide of his presentation and later realizes that a Title and Content slide is more helpful for adding bulleted text, he can change the Blank slide to a Title and Content layout. If he adds a slide and then changes his mind, he can always delete it.

To change a slide layout:

1. In Normal view, click the thumbnail of the slide you want to change.
2. Click the *Home* tab.
3. In the *Slides* group, click the drop-down arrow next to the **Layout** button.
4. Click a slide layout.

To delete a slide:

1. In Normal view, click the thumbnail of the slide you want to delete.
2. Press the **Delete** key on the keyboard.

The Title and Content slide layout is the most commonly used layout; a title followed by bulleted text is a popular arrangement for on-screen information. Its content placeholder includes a bullet followed by the instruction **Click to add text.** After you click and type the first line of the slide, press the **Enter** key to create a new line with a bullet. If you prefer, you can click the *Outline* tab in the pane to the left, and type the content there.

EXERCISE 6.4: ADDING SLIDES

Now that you have a theme in place and a draft of the content of your presentation, you are ready to build the rest of the presentation by adding slides with bulleted text.

1. Open your STA Presentation.pptx file from the last exercise, if necessary.

2. Add slides for the text content of your presentation. Choose from the slide layouts as needed to best present your information. (Slides with graphics will be added in another exercise.)

3. Type your bulleted text on each slide.

4. Save the presentation.

5. Experiment with new document themes and reformatting. Note the effect on each slide of the presentation.

6. Save the changes if you feel they are successful.

7. Close STA Presentation.pptx, or leave it open for the next exercise.

Graphics in PowerPoint

"A picture is worth a thousand words." That is even true when creating PowerPoint slides. Combining images and text on a slide makes for a much more interesting presentation for your audience.

Images

You have learned that you can use content placeholders to add bulleted text to a slide. You can also use content placeholders to add images. Just click their icons in the center of the placeholder. Click the icon with the green arrow to add a Microsoft SmartArt® diagram. Click the icon with a landscape to insert a picture from a file, or click the icon with small images to insert a clip art image. See Figure 6.32.

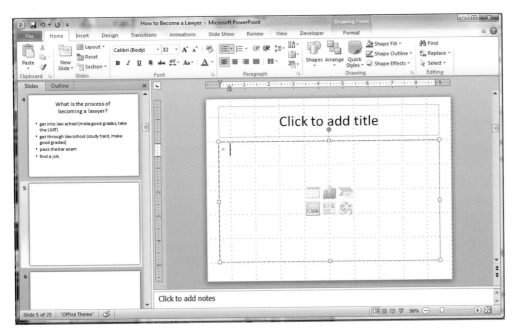

FIGURE 6.32

Click the **Clip Art** icon, for example, to open a task pane on the right where you can type in a keyword for the type of image you want and search for it from clip art images saved on your computer or found on the Internet. See Figure 6.33.

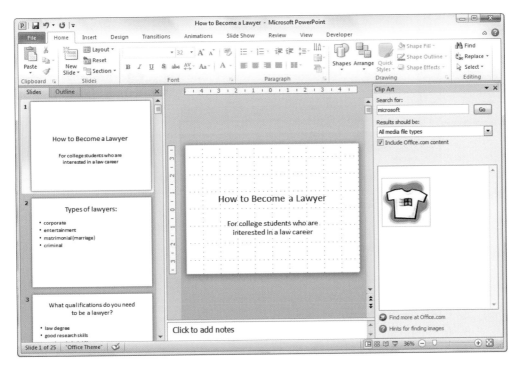

FIGURE 6.33

To insert images using a placeholder:

1. Add a slide with a content area layout, such as the Title and Content or Two Content layout.
2. Click the **Clip Art** icon in the center of the content area.

3. In the Clip Art task pane, type a keyword or phrase that describes the image that you are looking for.
4. Click the drop-down arrow next to *Search in* to specify the source of the images.
5. Click the drop-down arrow next to *Results should be,* and click to check the media types you would like to use.
6. Click **Go.**
7. Click a clip art image to insert it.

You are not limited to adding images based solely on the arrangement of content areas on the slide layout. The content of the second slide in Marisa's presentation could be laid out with images rather than text, and would look something like Figure 6.34.

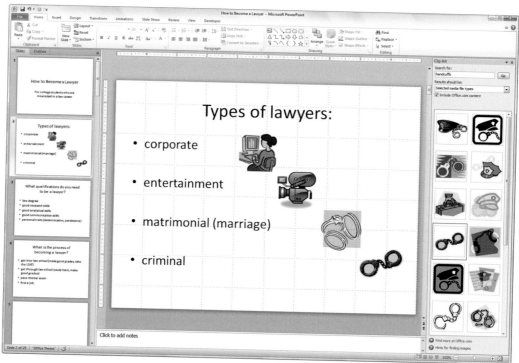

FIGURE 6.34

To insert images without a placeholder:

1. Add a slide without a content area layout, such as a Title Only or Blank Slide layout.
2. Click the *Insert* tab.
3. In the Images group, click **Clip Art.**
4. In the Clip Art task pane, type a keyword or phrase that describes the image that you are looking for.
5. Click the drop-down arrow next to *Search in* to specify the source of the images.
6. Click the drop-down arrow next to *Results should be,* and click to check the media types you would like to use.
7. Click **Go.**
8. Click a clip art image to insert it.

After you add the image, you will most likely need to resize and position it on the slide.

- To resize an image, click to select it and then position the pointer over one of the small selection handles that appear. Your pointer will take the shape of a two-headed arrow. Hold down the mouse button and drag to resize the image. Dragging a selection handle on the corner of the image will resize it while keeping the proportions intact.
- To move an image, place your pointer directly on top of the image, so that it takes the shape of a four-headed arrow. Hold down the mouse button and drag to move it to a new location on the slide. See Figure 6.35.

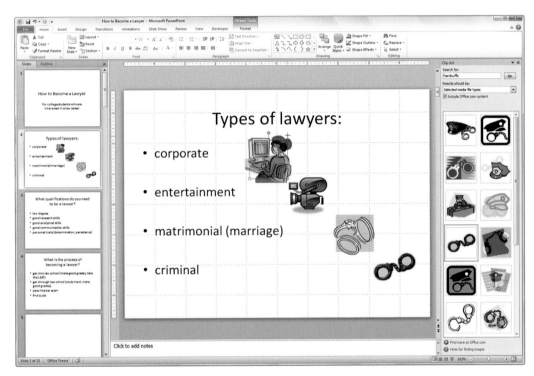

FIGURE 6.35

Inserting Movie Clips and Sound

Use movies and sound files in slide presentations to give them life and make them exciting to view.

Inserting Movie Clips

Movie clips (video files) consist of a few seconds to several minutes of video. Supported video file formats include Adobe Flash Media (with the extension .swf), Microsoft Windows Media® file (.asf), Windows Video file (.avi), Movie file (.mpg or .mpeg), and Windows Media Video file (.wmv). Videos in the .mp4, .mov, and .qt formats are compatible if the Apple QuickTime player is installed.

Click the **Insert Media Clip** icon in the center of a content area to insert a movie clip into your presentation, or follow the steps below.

To insert a movie clip into a slide presentation (see Figure 6.36):

1. Click on the slide where you want to insert the video.
2. Click the *Insert* tab.

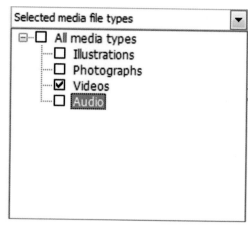

FIGURE 6.36

3. In the *Media* group, click **Video** to reveal a drop-down list. From the drop-down list, choose:

- *Video from file*—use this option to pick a movie file from your computer.
- *Video from website*—choose this option to link to an uploaded movie on a video sharing website such as YouTube.
- *Clip Art Video*—this option allows you to choose a video file from the PowerPoint built-in library displayed in the task pane on the right side of the document window. In the task pane, you can search for a sample video by keyword, choose the type of video, and search the Office.com website for more samples.

A video inserted on a slide has controls displayed beneath it. Use the controls to play the video, pause it, and stop it.

Inserting Sound

In addition to inserting movie files, you can use sound and music clips in your slide presentations. Compatible formats for sound and music files include AIFF Audio (.aiff), AU Audio (.au), MIDI (.mid or .midi), MP3 Audio (.mp3), Windows Audio (.wav), and Windows Media Audio (.wma).

To insert sound and music clips into a presentation:

1. Click the slide where you want to insert the sound and music clip.
2. Click the *Insert* tab.
3. In the *Media* group, click the **Audio** button to reveal a drop-down list.
4. From the drop-down list, choose:

- *Audio from file*—Use this option to choose an audio file from your computer. In the Insert Audio dialog box that appears, choose the desired location and name of the file.
- *Clip Art Audio*—This option is used to open the PowerPoint built-in music and sound library.
- *Record Audio*—This option allows you to record and use sound and music that you record on your computer. Your computer must have a microphone to create the file. In the Record Audio dialog box that appears, click on the red button (RECORD) to record the sound. Once the recorder is on, speak or play music into your computer's built-in or plug-in microphone. While recording, you will see a "total sound length" message. When you are finished recording, click on the blue square button to stop recording.

PowerPoint inserts an icon on the slide for the sound. Click the icon to display controls for audio settings.

Inserting Pictures

You can insert pictures from files on your computer with the *Insert* tab on the Ribbon or click the **Insert Picture from File** icon in the center of a content area.

To insert a picture into a slide presentation:

1. Click the slide where the picture will appear.
2. Click the *Insert* tab and the **Picture** button. Or, click the **Insert Picture from File** icon in the center of a content area.
3. In the Insert Picture dialog box, navigate to the folder location of the image you want to use.
4. Click on the desired picture and then click **Insert**.

FAQ: COPYRIGHT IMAGES

A copyright is a legal right given to an author to share and make copies of created work. Copyrights are provided for books, writings, images, movies, fine art, and any created work. When you work with images in PowerPoint, it is important to note whether that image has a copyright that protects it from unauthorized use or if the image is *public domain* and available for free use.

If an image is copyrighted, you must obtain permission from the creator of the image or pay a fee (sometimes called a license) to copy and use the image in your PowerPoint presentation. There are many places to find copyright-free images and images in the public domain. In fact, the U.S. government manages one of the most comprehensive websites of this material.

If you have a budget to pay for copyrighted images, you could use one of many stock image companies. Most of these companies require a per image fee to be paid for a one-time use of the image. These companies will also allow you to pay a set fee to download multiple copyrighted images when needed. Veer, Corbis Images, and Getty Images are a few of the many stock photo companies that offer copyrighted images for a fee.

Correcting Images: Brightness and Contrast

In general, you will resize and move pictures following the procedures described above for images. You can adjust their brightness and contrast with the *Picture Tools* tab.

To adjust picture images:

1. Click on the picture to select it. A *Format Picture Tools* tab appears (see Figure 6.37).
2. In the *Adjust* group, click **Corrections.**
3. Point to the various images to preview the corrections available and then click on the picture that shows the desired levels of sharpness, brightness, and contrast for the image on your slide.

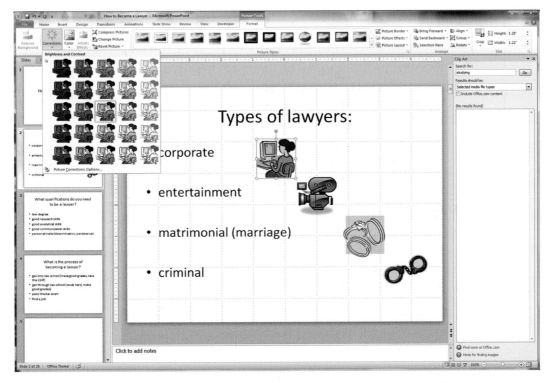

FIGURE 6.37

Compressing Images

When using image files such as color photos, it is very important to reduce or compress the file size of the images. A typical PowerPoint presentation could include images from backgrounds, icons, bullets, clip art, and photos. In addition to these images, the slide presentation would contain text of different sizes and many colors. Add sounds, transition effects, and slide animations to the above list and the file size of the presentation increases considerably. Large PowerPoint presentations with huge file sizes can run extremely slow. Slow presentations are not the most ideal as they can be boring to audience members.

To compress embedded media files (see Figure 6.38):

1. Click the *File* tab.
2. Click **Info.**
3. Click **Compress Media** on the right.
4. Click the level of quality you wish to preserve for the presentation from the options **Presentation Quality, Internet Quality,** and **Low Quality.**
5. A dialog box will display to show you the progress of the compression. Click **Close** when it is complete.

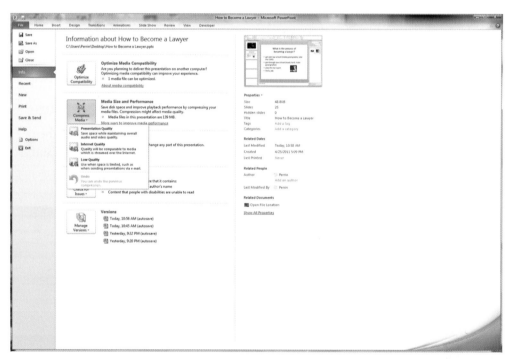

FIGURE 6.38

Adding Shapes

Sometimes the images provided by clip art or pictures do not meet your needs. You can draw your own images in PowerPoint using preset shapes. You can add text to a shape by selecting it and then typing.

To add shapes:

1. Click the *Insert* tab.
2. In the Illustrations group, click **Shapes.**
3. Click to "pick up" the shape that you want to draw. Your pointer appears as a plus sign. See Figure 6.39.
4. Click on the slide, hold down the mouse button, and then drag to draw the shape.

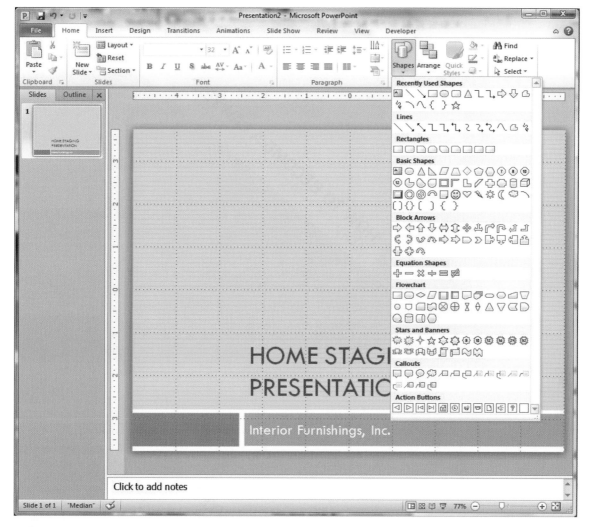

FIGURE 6.39

If you hold down the **Shift** key while you drag to draw a shape, you can constrain the dimensions of the shape. For example, holding the **Shift** key while dragging a circle creates a perfectly round circle; holding it while dragging a line draws a straight line; and holding it while dragging a rectangle draws a perfect square.

Adding Borders

Borders are a good way to make sure objects stand out within a slide. Marisa created the two slides shown in Figures 6.40A and 6.40B for her "How to Become a Lawyer" presentation. She added a border to the subtitle placeholder in Figure 6.40B. Which do you think calls more attention to the subtitle?

To add borders around an object:

1. Click the object to select it.
2. Click the *Home* tab.
3. In the *Drawing* group, click **Shape Outline.**
4. Click the weight drop-down to choose a border thickness.
5. Click the color box to choose a color for the border.

PowerPoint has a variety of preset Quick Styles for images that combine borders, colors, and special effects.

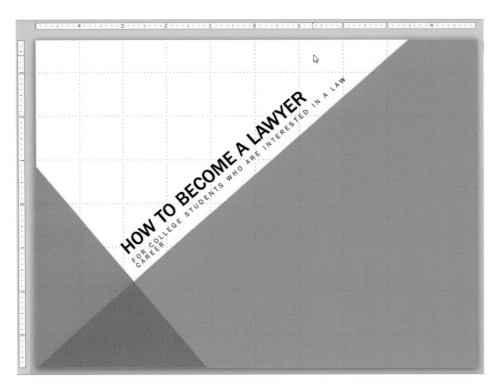

FIGURE 6.40A

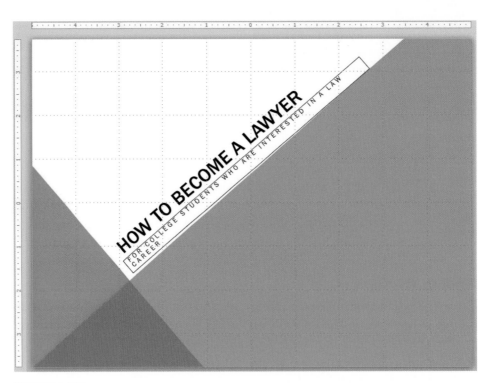

FIGURE 6.40B

To apply a preset Quick Style image:

1. Click an object to select it.
2. Click the *Home* tab.
3. In the Drawing category, click the **Quick Styles** button to show the available border styles.
4. Click a style to apply it to your object.

EXERCISE 6.5: ADDING GRAPHICS

One of your goals with this presentation is to improve your Power-Point skills, so you decide to experiment with images added to slides.

1. Open the STA Presentation.pptx file from the last exercise, if necessary.

2. Add at least two slides that include images—clip art, pictures, SmartArt® diagrams, or shapes—that help communicate the information in your presentation.

3. Add relevant images to at least two of your bulleted list slides.

4. Save the presentation.

5. Close STA Presentation.pptx, or leave it open for the next exercise.

Using the Notes Pane

Notes included in PowerPoint presentations provide your audience with additional information such as references or footnotes that cannot fit onto the slide itself. Or, use them to write a script for the presenter to refer to during the presentation. The presenter may print a hard copy of the notes for distribution or reference.

To add notes to a slide:

1. Display the slide in Normal view or in the Notes Pages view from the *View* tab.
2. Click in the Notes pane at the bottom of the screen and type the notes for that slide.

Working with Slides

Slide Sorter View shows thumbnails of the slides in your presentation and provides a very convenient way to add, delete, and rearrange them. Click the **Slide Sorter View** button on the bottom right side of the status bar or on the *View* tab to change to this view.

To rearrange slides in Slide Sorter View:

1. Switch to Slide Sorter View.
2. Point to the slide you want to move and hold down the mouse button. Drag the slide to a new location.
3. You will notice a vertical line appears as you drag. When it is positioned appropriately, release the mouse button to drop the slide in that location.

As with the other Microsoft Office 2010® applications, it is a good idea to right-click on an element to modify in PowerPoint. The right-click displays a context menu of commands that it makes sense to choose from, depending on what you clicked. For example, you can right-click a slide in Slide Sorter View and choose **Delete Slide** to remove it. Or right-click and choose **Hide Slide** to leave it in the presentation, but skip it when running the slide show.

To add new or duplicate slides in Slide Sorter View:

1. Switch to Slide Sorter View.
2. Right-click on the slide and choose **New Slide.** A blank slide with the same slide layout is added after the slide you right-clicked.
3. You can also right-click on the slide and choose **Duplicate Slide.** Now a copy of the slide is added after the selected slide.

In Normal view, right-clicking on slides in the slide list pane on the left of the screen provides a similar set of commands.

A slide number in PowerPoint is similar to a page number in Word, often appearing in the footer area at the bottom right of the slide. Slide numbers are useful for presentations because they make it easier for audience members to refer to slides when asking questions to the presenter.

To insert a slide number on a slide (see Figure 6.41):

1. Click the *Insert* tab.
2. In the *Text* group, click **Slide Number.**
3. In the Header and Footer dialog box that appears, click the *Slide* tab.
4. Check *Slide Number* to insert the slide number to the bottom right.
5. Slide numbers are usually not displayed on the title slide. Check *Don't show on title slide* to leave the number off.
6. Click **Apply to All,** or **Apply** if you want to display the number on the selected slide only.

FIGURE 6.41

Adding Transitions

Once you finish your slides, you can add transitions between them that instruct PowerPoint how to display each slide when you run the slide show. Transitions are small animations that deliver each slide in a unique and interesting way. It is recommended that you keep transitions consistent within a presentation, changing them only to call attention to an important slide.

Some available transitions in PowerPoint are shown in Figure 6.42.

Cut	After the current slide displays, the next slide comes in quickly.
Fade	After the current slide displays, it fades out and the next slide comes in.
Wipe	After the current slide displays, it leaves the screen as the next slide comes in.

FIGURE 6.42

To add a transition between two or more slides:

1. Select the slide or slides to which you want to add transition effects.
2. Click the *Transitions* tab.
3. Click the **More** button in the bottom right of the *Transition to this Slide* group to display the full gallery of options.
4. Point to a slide transition to preview its effect, then click the one you would like to apply.

Several options for slide transitions are available from the *Timing* group. To apply timing options:

1. Select the slide or slides to which you want to control timing.
2. Click on the *Transitions* tab.
3. In the *Timing* group, click the sound drop-down to add sound effects to slide transitions. Click the duration arrows to set the duration of the slide transition in seconds.

Viewing a Slide Show

Before delivering your presentation, run it as a slide show to evaluate its appearance and practice speaking with it. To run a slide show, click the Slide Show view on the status bar, or click the **Slide Show** button on the *View* tab. For more control, click the *Slide Show* tab and choose a button from the *Start Slide Show* group. To stop a slide show and return to Normal view, press the **Esc** key on the keyboard.

You have several options to advance the slide show manually as it runs.

- *Option #1.* Use the arrow keys (or the **Enter** and **Backspace** keys, or **Page Up** and **Page Down**) on your computer keyboard to advance the slides in the presentation. This approach is suitable if you give your presentation from a lectern or smart podium (laptop connected podium) in front of an audience. If you choose to walk around during the presentation, you will have to come back to the podium each time you advance the presentation.
- *Option #2.* Use the connected mouse to advance the slides in the presentation. This approach is similar to the first option because you have to be near the computer during the presentation.
- *Option #3.* Use a wireless mouse to advance the slides in the presentation. This option provides you with more flexibility while presenting the slide show because you can be a certain distance away from the computer. The limitation is that there cannot be any obstructions between the mouse and computer.

You may choose to run the presentation automatically with the PowerPoint software itself. To do this, you must set up the presentation as a show that will run using settings that you apply.

To set up an automatic slide show:

1. Click the *Slide Show* tab.
2. In the *Set Up* group, click **Set Up Slide Show.**
3. In the Set Up Show dialog box, check the appropriate boxes to apply your desired settings for the show. For instance, under Show type:

   - For a normal speaker-at-a-podium with an audience, choose **Presented by a speaker (full screen).**
   - For a presentation to be viewed on a PC, choose **Browsed by an individual (window).**
   - For a presentation at an exhibit or convention, choose **Browsed at a kiosk (full screen).**

   Under Show options:

   - Check **Loop continuously until 'Esc'** to play the presentation repeatedly until the **Esc** key is pressed.

   Under Show slides:

   - Click **All** to play the entire presentation.
   - Click **From slide # to slide #** to play a portion of the presentation.

   Under Advance slides:

   - Click **Manually** to advance manually with the keyboard or mouse.
   - Click **Using timings, if present** to advance slides after preset times.

EXERCISE 6.6: RUNNING THE SLIDE SHOW

You are ready for the speaking engagement but want to add slide transitions and preview your slide show to see what improvements you can make.

1. Open the STA Presentation.pptx file from the last exercise, if necessary.

2. Add slide transitions to all slides.

3. Run the slide show and make any necessary improvements.

4. Run the slide show for a classmate and incorporate his or her suggestions as you see fit.

5. Save the presentation.

6. Your instructor may ask you to present your slide show in class.

7. Close STA Presentation.pptx.

Printing a Presentation

You can print PowerPoint presentations as handouts and distribute them for an audience to follow along with the presenter, or print the slides themselves on one page each for reference or distribution. These printouts are sometimes called *decks*. You may also want to print the notes of your final PowerPoint presentation as a script for the speaker to follow.

To print the slides of a presentation:

1. Click the *File* tab.
2. Click **Print.**
3. Under Print Range, click **All** to print all of your slides. Or, to print only the slide that is displayed, click **Print Current Slide.** Or, to print specific slides, click **Custom Range,** and then enter the numbers of individual slides or a range of slides.
4. Under Other Settings, click **Color** and click the option that you want.
5. Click **Print.**

To print Notes:

1. Click the *File* tab.
2. Click **Print.**
3. Under Settings, click the arrow next to **Full Page Slides,** then click **Notes Pages.**
4. Click **Print.**

Handouts

Creating handouts with readable slides and a notes section for your audience is important when your goal is to provide appealing materials for your presentation. Audience members will appreciate handouts that do not contain too many pages and at the same time, contain pages with readable text. For instance, if your slides have charts and graphics on them, choose a print layout that involves fewer pages, such as a two per page, three per page, or four per page layout.

To print handouts (see Figure 6.43A and 6.43B):

1. Click the *File* tab.
2. Click **Print.**
3. Click the *Full Page Slides* drop-down list.
4. Under Handouts, click the number of slides to print per page, and whether they should appear in order vertically or horizontally.
5. Click **Print.**

FIGURE 6.43A

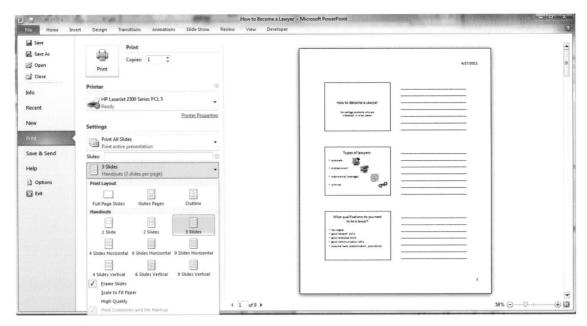

FIGURE 6.43B

ADVANCED TOPICS IN POWERPOINT

Custom Animations

Custom animations in PowerPoint add excitement and movement to objects on individual slides in a presentation. Use the Animation Pane to add animations to selected elements on a slide. You can create animations that affect how objects in a slide will:

- Appear on the screen (entrance)
- Disappear from the screen (exit)
- Move across the screen (motion paths)
- Behave while on the screen (effects)

For example, imagine that Lee Schuster needs to compile an album of his most successful designs to run in the reception area of his interior design business. He decides to experiment with a series of animations to the first slide for a photo album. He bases his new presentation on the six-slide template presentation called "Contemporary Photo Album" that comes with PowerPoint 2010 (see Figure 6.44).

To apply a series of animations to the first slide of the photo album presentation:

1. Select the first slide in the slide list on the left pane of the document window.
2. Click the *Animations* tab.
3. Click on any object in the slide and notice that the options in the *Animations* tab are now active. For this example, Lee applies the following animations: Set the picture to appear on the screen with a special effect called Zoom, and set the title text Contemporary Photo Album to appear with the special effect Float In.
4. Click the picture on the slide to select it.
5. In the *Animation* group, click the small down arrow on the bottom right side of the *Animation* group.
6. Under the Entrance options, click the **Zoom** button to apply this effect to the picture. A small number 1 appears to the left of the picture.

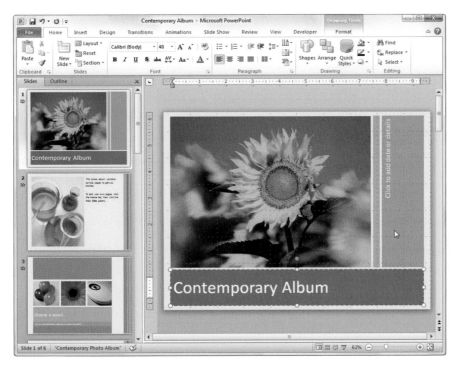

FIGURE 6.44

7. Select the text Contemporary Photo Album at the bottom of the slide.

8. Under the *Animation* group, click the small down arrow on the bottom right side of the *Animation* group.

9. Under the Entrance options, click the **Float In** button to apply this effect to the text. A small number 2 appears to the left of the picture. See Figure 6.45. Next, Lee also wants to add an underlining animation effect to the text Contemporary Photo Album so that after the text floats into the slide, it appears underlined for emphasis.

FIGURE 6.45

10. Click the small number 2 on the left side of the text Contemporary Photo Album. The animation number and object appear in the Animation Pane with a border around them.

11. In the *Advanced Animation* group, click the **Add Animation** button to select the additional animation. In the Emphasis category, click **Underline** to add underlining. A small number 3 appears to the left of the text Contemporary Photo Album on the slide.

Lee will not see the animations until he runs the slide show or previews the animations. To preview the series of animations:

1. Click the *Animations* tab.
2. In the *Preview* group, click **Preview.**

If Lee is not satisfied with the custom animation effect, he can delete it. To delete an animation from a slide:

1. Click the slide containing the animations.
2. In the Animation Pane, click the animation number you wish to delete. (If you are not sure, click the **Play** button in the Animation Pane to preview that particular animation.)
3. With the animation selected in the Animation Pane, click the down arrow to the right of the selected animation. From the drop-down list, click *Remove*.

Copying, Importing, and Exporting Slides

Copy and Import a Slide

When you create a slide presentation, you can insert an existing slide into a new slide presentation instead of creating a slide from scratch.

To import a slide from another PowerPoint presentation:

1. Click on the slide before the place where you want the new slide to appear.
2. Click the *Home* tab.
3. In the *Slides* group, click **New Slide.**
4. Click **Reuse Slides.** The Reuse Slides task pane opens on the right side of the window. See Figure 6.46.
5. Click the **Browse** button at the top of the Reuse Slides pane and choose **Browse File.** The Browse dialog box opens.
6. Navigate to the presentation with the slide(s) you want to reuse.
7. Click **Open.** All of the slides in the imported presentation display in the Reuse Slides task pane.
8. Click the slide(s) that you wish to import into the existing slide presentation. The selected slide(s) from the Reuse Slides pane now appears after the slide you selected in your presentation.

Export a Slide

PowerPoint also allows you to save slides in different formats for use in other types of software programs. For instance, you can save one or more PowerPoint slides from a presentation in Windows Media Video format; graphics formats such as GIF, JPEG, PNG, TFF; or a PDF format.

To save a slide or entire slide presentation into a different format:
1. Click the slide you want to export.
2. Click the *File* tab.

FIGURE 6.46

3. Click **Save As.**
4. In the Save As dialog box, click the drop-down arrow next to *Save as Type* and choose the desired file format from the drop-down list.
5. Type a file name in the File name field.
6. Click **Save.**
7. In the dialog box that appears, click the buttons for **Every Slide** (if you want the entire presentation) or **Current Slide Only** (if you want only one slide). If you choose Every Slide, PowerPoint creates a new folder and adds all the picture files to the folder. If you choose Current Slide Only, PowerPoint saves the picture in the chosen format.

Comment Feature

In PowerPoint, you can insert comments on slides in a presentation. Comments assist with editing. Insert them to provide additional information or alert a colleague of a slide from a shared presentation to be edited. Comments appear like footnotes at the bottom of the page when printed. Inserted comments appear on the slide labeled with your user name and initials followed by the comment number, and the date you inserted the comment. See Figure 6.47.

To insert a comment onto a slide of a presentation:

1. Click the *Review* tab.
2. In the *Comments* group, click **New Comment.**
3. In the small textbox that appears, type in the text for the comment.
4. When finished typing the comment, click anywhere on the slide to exit the comment box.

To edit an existing comment:

1. Click the comment you wish to edit.
2. Click the *Review* tab.
3. In the *Comments* group, click **Edit Comment.** Or, double-click on the comment number.

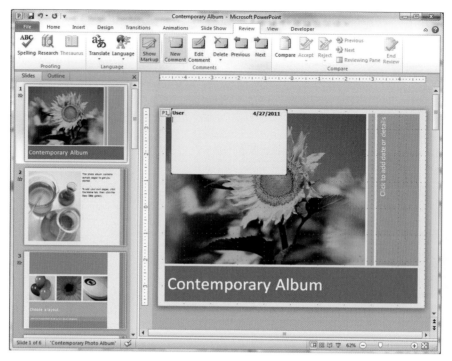

FIGURE 6.47

To delete a comment:

1. Click the comment you wish to delete.
2. Click the *Review* tab.
3. In the *Comments* group, click **Edit Comment** or double-click on the comment number and press the **Delete** key on the keyboard.

INTEGRATION: SENDING HANDOUTS TO WORD

One advantage to using the Microsoft Office suite is the smooth integration of the output from one application into another. For example, PowerPoint has the ability to convert your slide presentation to a handout in Microsoft Word. From Word, you can save it as a Word document, edit and format it using Word features, and then print it or e-mail it to your audience. The PowerPoint slides appear in the Word document as large thumbnails displayed alone on a page or next to blank lines for your audience members to use for notes pages. You choose how many slides will appear on a handout page: one, two, or three for each. To convert a PowerPoint presentation to a Word handout:

1. Click the *File* tab.
2. Select **Save & Send**.
3. Click **Create Handouts**.
4. In the pane on the right, click **Create Handouts**.
5. In the Send to Microsoft Word dialog box, choose a layout option: **Notes next to slides; Blank lines next to slides; Notes below slides; Blank lines below slides;** or click **Outline only** to send the text of your presentation to Word.
6. Click **OK**.

FAST TRACK PRACTICE: CREATING A SALES PRESENTATION

Mark Sonnerheim is a medical equipment salesman for MedStatic Equipment, Inc. and needs to create an effective sales presentation to present his latest sales numbers and information to his superiors at the company's corporate headquarters. The presentation must contain the following information and data arranged in an interesting, manageable format for the audience of senior-level executives.

Slide 1: Title

- Mark Sonnerheim
- MedStatic Equipment, Inc.
- Medical equipment sales report
- Year to date 2011

Slides 2, 3, 4: Medical Equipment Suppliers

- Supplier names
- Supplier location (city and state)
- Supplier equipment
- Number of units supplied to MedStatic

Slide 5: Sales from Medical Equipment

Year	Sales (in millions)
2010	5.4
2009	5.6
2008	4.2
2007	4.1
2006	4.0

Slide 6: Recommendations for Next Year to Save Money

- Increase size of territories for each sales force
- Sales force needs to check in with main offices more frequently to receive assignments
- Add teleconferencing to avoid sales force coming into main office

Slide 7: Closing

- "Thank you" to the audience
- Mark Sonnerheim's contact information
- E-mail: mark.sonnerheim@MedStatic.com

Include the following features in the final sales presentation:

- Appropriate backgrounds, graphics, and bulleted text
- Animations within slides
- Slide transitions
- Headers and footers on each slide

Also, final slides should be:

- Visually appealing
- Professional
- Consistent in the use of fonts, headings, layout, and graphics such as bullets

SUMMARY

Organizations use presentation software to visually communicate business ideas to colleagues, employees, customers, and potential clients. Originally created to run on large mainframe computers, presentation software gained more popularity and use throughout the 1990s as the use of personal computers and digital projectors increased. Like most software booms, there were early forerunners of presentation software, but the Microsoft PowerPoint software quickly became the most popular presentation graphics software on the market.

PowerPoint is a graphics presentation software application that is widely used by many types of businesses and in many industries. Business professionals create attractive and engaging business presentations that include text of all sizes, shapes, colors, and effects. Presentations can also include graphics to engage an audience while imparting valuable information in an easy to understand visual manner. The graphics may be clip art images, pictures, diagrams, charts, tables, and drawn shapes.

PowerPoint slide shows are often enhanced with special effects known as transitions as, within a presentation, one slide replaces the next. Custom animations, as well as sound effects, music, and embedded videos, are added to grab an audience's attention.

Although PowerPoint presentations may contain lots of bells and whistles, it is wise for PowerPoint users to plan and create presentations carefully. Effective presentations are succinct, to the point, and targeted to a specific audience and delivery method. In a professional setting, presentations should use appropriate, relevant graphics and slide transitions. An additional feature of PowerPoint is the ability to print presentations as handouts for audience members. Printouts can include handouts with sections for audience members to annotate.

Mastering PowerPoint is a useful skill in any career you pursue. Basic PowerPoint skills include the ability to enter, edit, and format text on slides using document themes, adding appropriate graphics and special effects, and printing presentations in various formats. More advanced skills include adding custom animations, reusing slides, and adding comments for editing.

KEY TERMS

- animation
- Microsoft PowerPoint
- placeholder
- slide deck
- transitions

Productivity
Software:
Managing
Personal Data

THE POWER OF PERSONAL INFORMATION MANAGEMENT SYSTEMS

Personal information management systems are applications that perform e-mail, event calendar, notepad, and contact management functions as part of a single application. **Microsoft Outlook** 2010® personal data management software, or Outlook, is the most commonly used personal information management system today; it is bundled with Microsoft Office 2010® products and is therefore installed in the vast majority of computers for business and personal use. This chapter will discuss Outlook as it performs "out of the box," but many large businesses purchase customized versions. Outlook and other personal information management systems are part of a larger group of applications known as **productivity software.**

MICROSOFT OUTLOOK
Microsoft Outlook is a personal information manager and e-mail client that is offered as a part of the Microsoft Office software package, Microsoft Exchange Server®, and as a standalone product.

PRODUCTIVITY SOFTWARE
Software that provides users with word processing, database management, spreadsheets, and personal information management applications.

Widespread Business Use

Personal information management systems are an indispensible part of the communications network. Businesses depend on programs such as Outlook to disseminate information to employees, track e-mail messages, and schedule meetings. Millions of people keep track of their personal e-mail, schedule events, and maintain contact databases for personal and business use with personal information management systems.

Personal and business communications are often synchronized among multiple devices, such as work computers, home computers, and smartphones. Today,

KEY CONCEPTS

- The Power of Personal Information Management Systems

- A Brief History of Personal Information Management Systems

- Common Business Tasks That Use Outlook

- Overview of the Outlook Window

- E-mail

- Calendar

personal information systems enable many people to be more productive in nearly every aspect of their lives, as users can now easily synchronize business and personal information. Often, people maintain more than one e-mail account—usually one for work and one or more for personal communication—and keeping track of several e-mail accounts can be time consuming as well as confusing. Personal information management systems can combine multiple e-mail and messaging accounts and calendar applications into a single point of reference.

Microsoft Outlook is by far the leading software for managing e-mail, but there are many other options as well, including:

- MacMail, for Macintosh users (software included with the system)
- Lotus Notes
- Internet service provider-based online e-mail accounts (such as Comcast or AT&T Uverse)
- Free online e-mail accounts, such as Yahoo! Mail, Microsoft Hotmail®, Google's Gmail, and other providers

How much do you depend on personal information systems in your personal and business lives? The traditional concept of going to the office and working a set number of hours in a specified workplace has changed radically in the past several years. Globalization has created new demand for U.S. businesses to expand their hours of operation, and those businesses in turn demand more flexible work schedules from their employees. While the trend toward globalization is hailed as a great step forward for most industries, employees of U.S.-based businesses are forced to redefine the traditional expectations associated with a manufacturing-based economy and its predictable schedules. Personal information management systems are now commonly used to reconcile employees' more flexible, but also less predictable, work schedules with their personal family and leisure activity schedules.

Automated Reminders

Personal information management systems are able to schedule recurring events, such as weekly business meetings, social gatherings and other leisure activities, doctor's appointments, pay dates, or due dates for bills, as well as one-time events. For example, with a personal information management

system such as Microsoft Outlook or Google Calendar™ you can enter appointments or time-sensitive information and set alarms to remind you of those events. When used as a single point of reference for a portable calendar, a personal information management system can also help you plan in advance for time away from work or school, track sick days, or follow up on personal or work-related agenda items.

Central Point for E-mail Access

Because the most popular personal information management systems are preinstalled with most business and home office software packages, many computer users find them "automatically" available on their computers. These personal information systems allow users to receive and send e-mail from any business or personal e-mail account. With the ability to synchronize e-mail, events, and calendars, personal information management systems have become integrated into business and personal lives alike. They are commonly referred to as **personal organizers.**

PERSONAL ORGANIZERS
A generic term for personal information management software and the device on which the applications are installed. Originally, a personal organizer referred to a contact folder, journal, calendar, and notebook all combined within a case or book cover.

Today, personal organizers make up a multi-billion-dollar industry focused on increasing productivity through creating a central reference point that allows the user to view contacts, scheduling, and other information within a single software application. The goal of personal information management software is to place all the information you may need, in the correct format, in a single, easily accessible place.

A BRIEF HISTORY OF PERSONAL INFORMATION MANAGEMENT SYSTEMS

Thirty years ago, a personal information system usually consisted of a set of paper-based calendars—usually at least one for work and one for personal schedules. People who had extremely busy schedules often carried personal planners, which combined a comprehensive calendar, a contact list with addresses and telephone numbers, a calculator, and a paper pad for notes taken during meetings or other functions. Personal planners were critical for synchronizing business and leisure schedules; however, they were only effective if their owners were diligent about using them.

During the late 1980s and early 1990s, simple digital organizers began to emerge. Initially, they took the form of sophisticated calculators, or in a few cases, digital wristwatches. These first digital organizers could store little more than names, addresses, and telephone numbers. Most had a clock function and could set alarms to remind the user about an appointment, but they generally had no text function.

Personal information managers (PIMs) became available during the mid-1990s. They began as bulky calculator-sized devices with small keyboards and tiny monochrome screens. The PIM was a revolutionary development that quickly became indispensible to professionals with their increasingly busy schedules as they combined the functions of the notebook-and-paper personal organizer with digital note-taking and scheduling capabilities.

PERSONAL INFORMATION MANAGER (PIM) A software application that keeps track of personal data, e-mail, calendar events, and contacts.

As the 20th century came to an end, the PIM evolved as an increasingly complex personal information archiving and retrieval system. The PIM was replaced by the end of the decade by the **personal digital assistant (PDA).** The PDA took advantage of innovations in game consoles and laptop computers and offered all the advantages of the PIM in the form of a smaller, more powerful device that also offered a range of software applications designed to interface with personal and office computers. PDAs also introduced touch screens that required a stylus.

PERSONAL DIGITAL ASSISTANT (PDA) A portable handheld device that uses a PIM to keep track of appointments, e-mail and communications contacts, journal entries, and other personal information.

The introduction of the PDA also encouraged the development of advanced PIM software that could be synchronized with home or office computers through network connections. Smartphones began to replace PDAs as mobile personal information management systems in the mid-2000s, with operating systems designed for compatibility with the growing variety of office-related applications that continue to move to the web.

The Rise of Microsoft Outlook

Microsoft Outlook was originally called Outlook for Windows. It ran as two separate programs: Windows Messaging and Windows Schedule+. Before Outlook for Windows was released, scheduling and e-mail were separate applications, but as the PC became standard equipment for most office workers, demand grew for a single application that performed those functions without the need to run separate programs.

Outlook, which was first offered as part of Microsoft Office 97 in response to that demand, included the ability to open and read Microsoft Office documents sent as attached files in the Outlook e-mail window. In 1998, Microsoft released a free version of Outlook to encourage small businesses and home users to use the Outlook product. During the late 1990s and early 2000s, Microsoft Office products were installed in the vast majority of business computers, and with the explosive growth of the Internet as a communications medium, Outlook became the most popular business communications product in the world. In 2003, Outlook was finally offered for sale as a standalone product for users who wanted to use the personal information manager but had no need for the associated Microsoft Office suite of products.

Beginning with Outlook 2007, Microsoft updated its layout and introduced a new tabbed menu system called the Ribbon (see Figure 7.1). The Ribbon uses tabs to access commands related to the active function, and is present whenever an Outlook function such as Calendar, e-mail, or Microsoft Word® is active. The Ribbon also introduced a new feature called contextual tools, which are tabbed tools that appear when a particular item is selected.

FIGURE 7.1

Since the late 1990s, e-mail has become a primary method of communication, and many different e-mail clients remain in use today. Another very popular e-mail client was Outlook Express, which was included with the Microsoft Internet Explorer web browsing application. Outlook Express was created as a simple e-mail client alternative for users who did not need calendar options. It must be stressed that Outlook Express was not part of the Outlook or Microsoft Office suite, and it did not include features such as document conversion, spell check, or calendar, even though its interface was similar to that of Outlook. Due to these limitations and other data loss and security issues that arose, Microsoft replaced Outlook Express with Windows Mail with the release of its Microsoft Windows Vista® operating system. In 2007, Microsoft released Windows Live Mail as the e-mail client for Microsoft Windows 7®and has announced that it will discontinue support for Outlook Express in 2014.

COMMON BUSINESS TASKS THAT USE OUTLOOK

As you know, Microsoft Outlook is included in Microsoft Office, the most commonly used business-related application suite in the world. Outlook is a personal information management system that combines an appointment calendar, an e-mail application, notes, tasks, to-do lists, and contact management within a single main window. Within that window, information is separated into "panes" that correspond to one or more of the functions Outlook controls. Many businesses choose Outlook because of its seamless integration with the Microsoft Office suite of applications, which includes spreadsheets (Microsoft Excel®), databases (Microsoft Access®), presentations (Microsoft PowerPoint®), and word processing (Word).

Outlook allows users to create contact groups, which are filtered lists of e-mail addresses. For example, if you wish to send an e-mail to a specific group of coworkers about a project you are working on with them, such as an upcoming meeting about next quarter's budget, you can create a contact group that contains only the contact information for those coworkers who are involved in the project with you. You can then send an e-mail with attachments, such as any spreadsheets regarding the budget or other documentation to support the purpose of the meeting, directly from Microsoft Excel to that contact group.

Another business use of Outlook is its shared calendar function. Sharing a calendar allows multiple users to view common calendar dates. Continuing the earlier example, once you are ready to schedule the budget meeting on the calendar, you can view your contact group members' schedules and select a time for the meeting that works for all of them. You can then send an invitation to the meeting through Outlook, or if you have created an agenda in Microsoft Word, you can send the agenda and invitation, as well as any other documentation your coworkers need to review, directly from Word. When your coworkers respond to the meeting request, it becomes a part of their calendars.

OVERVIEW OF THE OUTLOOK WINDOW

Navigation Pane

As discussed in the previous section, Microsoft Outlook combines e-mail, calendar, and contacts within a single window. Access these features in a pane on the left-hand side of thewindow, which is called the Navigation Pane. The Navigation Pane allows you to see all of the features of Outlook at a glance from within a specific feature; in other words, you can access your Contacts, Calendar, and Tasks from the Navigation Pane while reading or composing e-mail. Within the Navigation Pane, buttons allow quick access to all the features of Outlook. The standard Navigation Pane has a **Mail** button at the top. Below this button are buttons to access your **Calendar, Contacts,** and **Tasks.** See Figure 7.2.

FIGURE 7.2

Preview Pane

The Preview Pane, which is part of the Reading Pane in Outlook 2010, can be activated to view the text portion of a message without opening the e-mail. This helps prevent the activation of virus or other malware programs by opening e-mail with attachments or HTML code that may be infected. Beginning with Outlook 2007, the Preview Pane was incorporated into the Ribbon as AutoPreview. To activate the Preview Pane in Outlook 2010, click the *View* tab, click *Change Preview,* and activate *Preview.* See Figure 7.3.

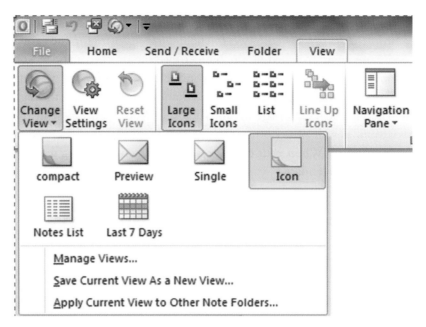

FIGURE 7.3

Reading Pane

In the Reading Pane, the body of a message is displayed along with any graphics and hyperlinks. Resize the Reading Pane by dragging the corners or sides of the message window. You can also deactivate or change the orientation of the Reading Pane by clicking the *View* tab. Then click *Reading Pane* and select the preferred orientation or *Off* to deactivate the Reading Pane.

View Settings

You can also customize the way Outlook displays your messages within the Reading Pane. To change the way messages appear, click the *View* tab in Outlook Mail (see Figure 7.3). Then click *Change View*. This will allow you to select *Compact,* which displays your messages as a group, or *Single,* which will display one message at a time. In the *View* tab you may also select *View Settings*. This allows you to change your default settings of the View such as color, columns, or date received. To save a custom View you have created, click *Change View* and click *Save Current View As a New View*. If you wish to return to the original View Settings at any time, click the **Reset Current View** button at the bottom of the View Settings edit box.

E-MAIL

Electronic mail, or e-mail, as it is commonly known, is a way of writing, exchanging, and reading digital messages. E-mail is now far more popular than "snail mail" as a method of written communication. As you likely already know, e-mail is available to you nearly every moment of your day.

Procedures

An e-mail includes the message body and the header. The header includes the subject of the e-mail, sender and recipient addresses, and date and time information about when the message was sent. E-mail addresses consist of a user name, followed by the "at" (@) sign and the domain name of the computer or server hosting the mailbox where the e-mail will be sent and stored. See Figure 7.4.

E-mails are sent using the standard Simple Mail Transfer Protocol (SMTP). They are received using either the Post Office Protocol (POP) or the Internet Message Access Protocol (IMAP). SMTP, POP, and IMAP server address settings should be configured according to the specifications provided by your Internet service provider (ISP). The mail server allows your e-mail client to send and receive e-mails after verifying your user name and password.

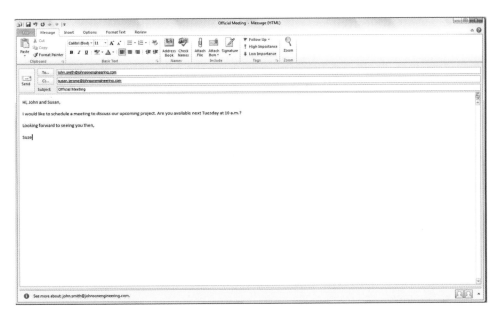

FIGURE 7.4

EXERCISE 7.1: CREATE AN E-MAIL ACCOUNT IN OUTLOOK

Double-click the **Outlook** icon on your desktop or use the *Start* menu in the lower left corner of your computer screen and click the left button of your mouse on the **Start** button, then click **Programs** and select **Microsoft Office**.

1. Click on the *File* tab.

2. Click the *Info* tab in the Navigation Pane. Select the **Add Account** radio button and then click **Next**.

3. Choose the type of server your e-mail account uses according to your ISP's instructions.

4. You may choose to have the program remember your password so you do not have to enter it every time you send or receive e-mail.

5. Microsoft Office may be used to manage multiple e-mail accounts. Use the E-mail Accounts wizard to add multiple accounts for personal and business use.

Composing, Addressing, and Sending an E-mail Message

To choose a recipient:

1. Click on the *Home* tab, then click *New E-Mail.*
2. Alternately, you may use the keyboard shortcut **Ctrl+Shift+M.**
3. Type one or more recipient e-mail addresses, separated by semicolons, in the address box.

Add names from your address book by clicking the **To, Cc,** or **Bcc** icons to open your Contacts and select recipients. "Cc" is the abbreviation for carbon copy and "Bcc" means blind carbon copy. Recipients who receive carbon copies are visible to other recipients, while recipients of blind carbon copies of messages are not.

To compose your message:

1. Type the subject of your e-mail message in the Subject box. It is best to keep the subject of your e-mail short and meaningful so your recipient knows the reason you are sending the e-mail. You can explain in more detail in the body of the message.
2. Type your message in the message body. Outlook is integrated with the Microsoft Office suite and uses Microsoft Word as the word processing editor for e-mail messages. This enables the following features and capabilities of Microsoft Word:

   - Spelling and grammar checking
   - Autocorrecting of common spelling and typing errors
   - Bullets and numbering
   - Tables
   - Themes
   - Formatting
   - Hyperlinks
   - Images

Save a Draft of Your E-mail

Microsoft Outlook automatically saves unfinished messages to the Drafts folder every three minutes. There are two ways to save a message in progress:

1. Click the **Save** icon on the Quick Access Toolbar.
2. Click the *File* tab and click *Save.*

To return to a saved draft and continue composing a message, do the following: In **Mail**, in the Navigation Pane, click **Drafts,** and then double-click the message. After composing your e-mail message, read the message to check for typographical or spelling errors.

Add a Signature

You can personalize your e-mails by adding a signature at the end of each message. In business settings, e-mail signatures are sometimes governed according to a company policy that specifies how employees should identify themselves, usually with their name, company name and contact information, job title, phone, e-mail, and website information, and sometimes brand slogans or privacy messages.

To create a signature (see Figure 7.5):

1. Begin with a new message.
2. Locate the *Message* tab in the *Include* group.
3. Click the **Signature** button and click **Signatures.**

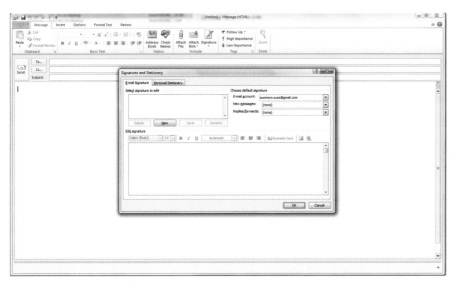

FIGURE 7.5

4. Next, click **New.**
5. Create a name for your signature and click **OK.**
6. The Edit signature box is where you will type the text you want to include in your new signature.
7. If you want to alter the format for your signature, select the text you want to format, and use the style and formatting buttons to change the font style, font size, or font color.
8. When you are finished creating your signature, click **OK.**

Open, Read, Print, and Close an E-mail Message

The Outlook inbox designates messages as "Read" or "Unread." Unread messages appear in bold print font marked by a **closed envelope** icon. When a message is read, the font appears as regular type and the icon changes to an open envelope. To read your message, click on a message in the inbox preview pane to view it in the reading pane below or double-click on a message to open it in a separate window.

If you open and read an e-mail message, you can change its status to Unread by right-clicking the message and clicking **Mark as Unread.** See Figure 7.6.

FIGURE 7.6

If you want a hard copy of an e-mail, you can print it. To print an e-mail message, click the *File* tab and click *Print*. When you finish reading or printing a message, close it by clicking on the X in the upper right corner.

Adding an Attachment

Attachments are used to include files, pictures, or shortcuts in the body of an e-mail message. In the past, documents were often sent to recipients through fax machines because the associated files were too large to be sent in the body of e-mail messages. As printer manufacturers have expanded the functions of their products to include copying and scanning options, and the speed of data transmission has increased dramatically, faxing and fax machines have experienced a sharp decline in use. Most documents can now be printed, scanned, and attached to e-mail messages as graphic images from the desktop. Other software programs such as Adobe Acrobat™ and Adobe Reader™ allow documents or even entire reports to be converted into detailed files with embedded graphics and attached to e-mail messages.

As a best practice, make sure that the recipient is able to receive attachments before you include an attachment in an e-mail message. Download speeds vary significantly and receiving a large attachment could delay the transmission or receipt of other important e-mail messages. As attaching documents has become more popular, many Internet service providers have established limits on the size of e-mail messages sent or received. This is commonly described as a file size limit for attachments. Many online groups and forums do not allow members to send messages with attachments because of capacity issues.

To add an attachment to an e-mail (see Figure 7.7):

1. Begin a new message or open an e-mail message to reply or reply all.
2. Choose a recipient, type in your subject, and write a short message about the file you are sending.

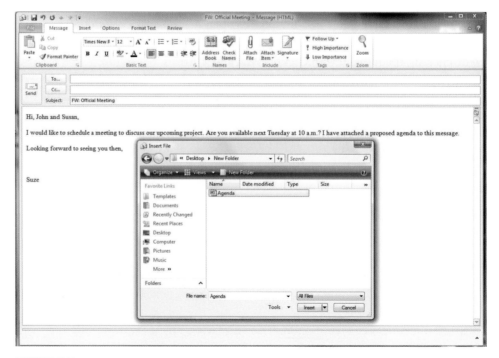

FIGURE 7.7

3. In the Message window, on the *Message* tab, in the *Include* group, click *Attach File*.
4. Browse the location of the file you wish to attach and click **Insert.**
5. Click **Send** to send the e-mail message.

To open and save an attachment:

1. Double-click on the attachment from the Reading Pane or an open message.
2. Click *Save As* on the *Attachments* tab in the *Actions* group or right-click on the icon for the attachment and click **Save As.**
3. Select a location and enter a name for the file in the File Name box.
4. Click **Save.**

Executable files are programs that deliver code instructions to the computer. An .exe file is an executable file; a .bat file is a disk-operating system (DOS) batch-processing file that functions like a program; and .vbs files are virtual basic scripts. You should never open executable file attachments or unexpected attachments from unknown sources. Microsoft Outlook automatically blocks certain types of executable attachments that may contain viruses, such as .exe, .bat, or .vbs file types. File types or extensions describe the kind of program needed to open a particular file. These file types include:

- Text files, such as .docx or .txt
- Audio files, such as .mp3 or .wav
- Spreadsheet files, such as .xlsx
- Database files, such as .db or .sql
- Video files, such as .mov, .mp4, or .mpg
- Image files, such as .eps, .tif, .gif, .jpg, or .bm
- Web files, such as .html or .php
- Data files, such as .ppt or .xml

Reply to an E-mail

To reply to an e-mail:

1. Open an e-mail message.
2. In the *Respond* group, click **Reply.**
3. Choose from the options at the bottom of the pane whether you want to display the original message in your reply.
4. Type your reply in the message box and click **Send.**

Forward an E-mail

Forwarding allows you to send a received e-mail to a new recipient. To forward an e-mail message:

1. Click the **Forward** button in an open e-mail message or choose forward an e-mail message by clicking the *Home* tab, selecting an e-mail message, and then clicking **Forward** in the *Respond* group.
2. Add any additional message in the message box and click **Send.**

Managing Your Inbox

It is important to keep your inbox free of clutter. Sorting through hundreds or thousands of messages to find the one you need wastes time. The best practice for managing your e-mail inbox is to read and process your messages often in order to keep the inbox empty. E-mail messages can be classified as action information or reference information. Action information applies to your calendar or to-do list. In addition to managing e-mail, Outlook can be a very useful tool for task and time management. Reference information is information that you want to keep and look up later. If you do not organize and file e-mail messages, they can accumulate quickly, which can end up wasting your time and your storage capacity.

The keys to managing your inbox are cleaning, organizing, and filtering your e-mail messages. Schedule a regular time to maintain your inbox each week. To keep your inbox clean, regularly delete e-mails you do not need and empty the trash folder. Move messages you want to keep to a labeled folder. Create new folders to file reference information where you can easily retrieve it.

To create a folder:

1. Click the *File* tab and select *New*.
2. You can also press **Ctrl+Shift+E** to create a folder.
3. In the Create New Folder dialog box, indicate what the folder will contain and name the new folder.
4. Create various folders to organize and store messages according to projects, priorities, or people. You can then create Rules to sort your incoming e-mail messages to their appropriate folders.

As a shortcut, you can also right-click on your inbox and select *New Folder*. See Figure 7.8.

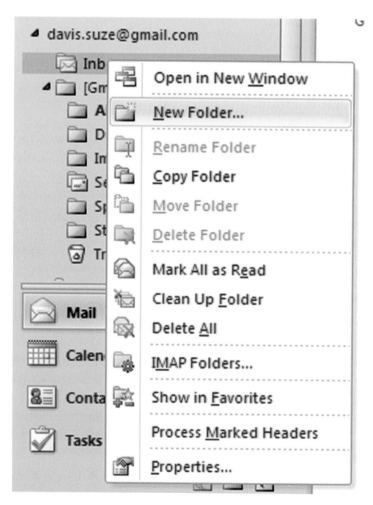

FIGURE 7.8

You can save storage space in your e-mail program by saving attachments to a folder on your computer and deleting the original message.

To save an attachment to a folder:

1. Open an e-mail message containing an attachment.
2. Click on the attachment in the Reading Pane or in the message.
3. Click on the *Attachments* tab in the *Actions* group. Click **Save As** (or right-click the attachment and click **Save As**).
4. The next dialog box will show your folder locations. Choose a location by clicking on a folder.
5. Next, click **Save.**

Conversations

You can also view messages as conversations. Conversations are groups of e-mail messages that have been forwarded or replied to that have the previous messages copied into the body of the message. This allows you to view all of the responses to an e-mail as the conversation progresses, and can be very useful when corresponding with multiple people. To conserve disk space and eliminate redundant messages, you can also use the Conversation Cleanup feature in Outlook 2010. To use the Cleanup command, right-click the desired conversation and select *Conversation Cleanup*. This eliminates all the previous messages in the conversation that are duplicated with each succeeding response.

To manage your e-mail, sort your messages by date, sender, or topic and work your way down the list to process each one. (See Figure 7.9.) As you view each message, use the 4D method to decide what to do:

- Delete
- Do
- Delegate
- Defer

If you do not need the information or can find it somewhere else, delete the message.

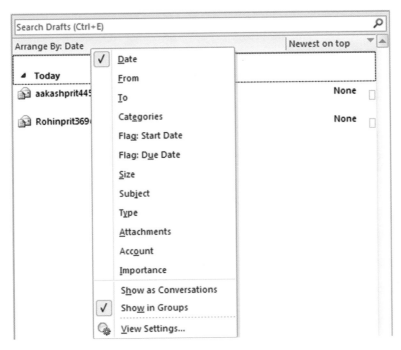

FIGURE 7.9

To delete an e-mail message, select the message, then click the **Delete** button on the *Home* tab or press the **Delete** key on the keyboard. You can select and delete multiple e-mails by pressing the **Ctrl** key and clicking each message. This action highlights the selected messages in blue. Delete the messages. In case you accidentally delete a message you wanted to keep, go to the Deleted Items folder to view deleted e-mails. Move items from the Deleted Items folder by left-clicking and dragging them to the correct folder or by right-clicking the message and choosing the *Move to Folder* option. You should also empty your Deleted Items folder regularly. Look at the messages in the Deleted Items folder to verify that they are all intended for deleting; then right-click on the **Deleted Items** icon in the left-side Navigation Pane and choose *Empty Deleted Items Folder*. See Figures 7.10 and 7.11.

FIGURE 7.10

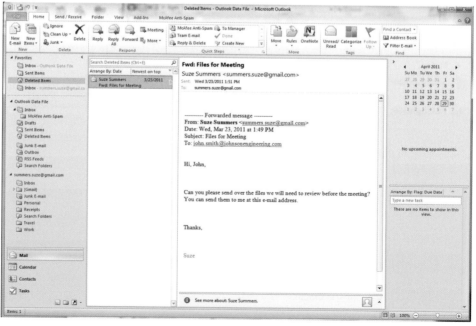

FIGURE 7.11

Address Book and Contact Groups

As you use Outlook, you will find that you need to create an Address Book to help keep track of e-mail addresses and other contact information. If you find that you send frequent e-mails to a specific group of individuals, you may want to create a contact group that automatically adds the names and e-mail addresses of group members into messages.

To create a new contact (see Figures 7.12 and 7.13):

1. Create a new e-mail message.
2. In the *Message* tab, click *Address Book.*
3. Select the *File* menu and then *New Entry.*

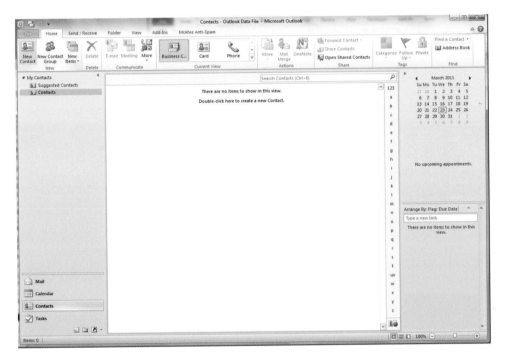

FIGURE 7.12

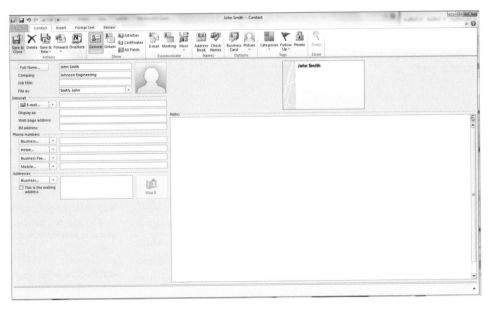

FIGURE 7.13

4. Choose **New Contact** to enter an individual's information.
5. Click on each information box to enter name and other contact information.
6. Click the **Save and Close** icon when you are done entering the information.

To create a contact group (see Figure 7.14):

1. On the *Home* tab, look in *Contacts*.
2. In the *New* group, click *New Contact Group*.
3. Name your Contact Group by typing the name in the Name box.
4. On the *Contact Group* tab, in the *Members* group, click **Add Members.**
5. If you need to create a new contact, open the Add New Member dialog box and enter the person's information.
6. If you have contacts in your address book or in your Outlook contacts you need to add to your new group, click on the *Address Book* drop-down list and click the names you want. Click *Members* to add them to the group.
7. Click **OK.**

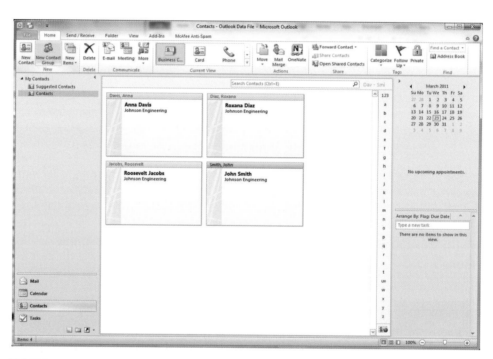

FIGURE 7.14

Security Concerns

You can use e-mail filters to reduce unwanted e-mail and spam. **Spam** refers to unsolicited e-mails sent through bulk distribution lists, generally for the purposes of advertising or promotion. E-mail spam is comparable to junk mail that is sent through the postal service; however, electronic junk mail is cheaper and easier to distribute. Most spam originates from computers infected with viruses or worms that become infected with a **bot,** which is a malicious program code, and become part of a **botnet,** which is an online network of computers controlled by an outside source.

SPAM Unsolicited mass-produced e-mail.

BOT Malicious program code that infects computers, usually gaining access to a system through spam e-mails.

BOTNET An online network of computers controlled by an outside source.

Poor **firewalls** and unsecure passwords can allow infection by bots that may be used to send spam e-mail. This spam appears to come from a user who in fact has no idea that his or her account is generating e-mails. For this reason, you should be careful before clicking a hyperlink or opening unexpected attachments—even when you are reading e-mail messages from addresses you recognize.

FIREWALL A device that follows a set of rules for transmissions coming into a computer system to protect the system from threats such as malware and viruses.

E-mail attachments are a very common way to spread viruses. Common spam topics include pharmaceuticals, pornography, dating, income opportunities, and weight loss plans. The best response to spam and junk e-mail is to delete messages without opening them. Do not reply or attempt to unsubscribe from unknown e-mails.

Images in e-mails can also contain malicious code and can be prevented from being displayed unless they come from a known contact in your address book. Spam filters are used to detect and delete junk e-mail before it reaches your in-box. Unwanted e-mail can be marked as junk mail as it is received or rules can be specified to handle mail from specific sources. In Outlook, right-click on any junk e-mail messages you receive and then select *Junk E-Mail*. Next, click *Add to Junk Senders List*.

Outlook 2010 has several features to protect you from spam, **malware, and viruses.** The Junk E-Mail filter analyzes incoming messages and sends e-mails that may be spam to the Junk Mail folder.

To customize the Junk E-Mail filter:

MALWARE Computer software that works as an independent program that infects a computer's files and programs after being downloaded from what looks like a trusted source.

1. To customize the Junk E-Mail filter, click the *Home* tab.
2. In the *Delete* group, click the **Junk** button. Next, click **Junk E-Mail Options.**
3. You can select the level of protection and customize how junk e-mail is processed, including automatic deletion. In general, automatic deletion is not a good idea because some legitimate e-mail might be filtered as junk and then deleted without notification.

VIRUS Computer software unknowingly downloaded from what looks like a trusted source that is designed to infect a computer's programs and files by using those programs and files to attack others on the system.

The Junk E-Mail filter also disables links and Reply and Reply All to prevent you from accidentally responding to a suspicious e-mail. Another way to avoid spam and e-mail viruses is to set up your e-mail account to display only plain text messages. This will prevent images and **HTML** (hypertext markup language) Internet content from being displayed. Text display options in e-mail messages include plain text, rich text, and HTML. Plain text is just that: only alphabetic and numeric characters are displayed. Formatted, or rich, text allows you to customize style elements, such as font, color, bold print, italics, and text size. HTML offers the most options for formatting and adding pictures or hyperlinks to websites, but they are much larger files than plain text messages and allow hidden code to be attached to the message.

HTML (HYPERTEXT MARKUP LANGUAGE) A markup language that tells the browser what should appear on the web page.

Phishing and Scams

E-mail has transformed written communication, but it has also created new ways for criminals to steal information and assets. **Phishing** is the term for sending fraudulent e-mails, usually to a large number of e-mail users simultaneously, that incorporate a reputable organization's brands and logos in order to steal personal information such as credit card and Social Security numbers, banking information, or passwords. Botnets are

PHISHING The practice of using spam e-mail to elicit a response and obtain a computer user's private information.

commonly used for phishing purposes. For instance, phishing e-mails might appear to come from a bank, government, investment firm, commercial website, charity, or social networking site. The e-mails usually contain a hyperlink directing you to an imitation website that resembles and may contain links back to the legitimate site.

When you reply to e-mails or fill out forms on the Internet, you release your personal information to businesses that may use it to compile large e-mail distribution lists for advertising purposes or resell your information to others. Beware of e-mail messages that come from strangers promising rewards of money or prizes, particularly if the messages are overly familiar or contain many obvious grammar or translation errors. For instance, if the greeting of a message from an unfamiliar person starts with "My Dear," "Beloved," "Dear Friend," and so on, the source is likely to be unreliable. A common scam promises large sums of money related to bank transfers or an inheritance from an unknown relative. Make sure you know the source of an e-mail before clicking on any hyperlink in the message.

Microsoft Outlook 2010 flags potentially dangerous e-mails for you. Messages considered to be phishing may arrive in your inbox, but Outlook will disable their links and block their attachments. You will also be unable to use Reply or Reply All on a flagged message.

If a suspicious message finds its way into your inbox, you can investigate hyperlinks in e-mails before you open them by right-clicking on them to view the source. Check to see if the **Uniform Resource Locator (URL)** address that displays is from the domain that the e-mail claims to represent. A number of websites are specifically designed to educate and inform the public about e-mail hoaxes and scams. For instance, the Federal Bureau of Investigation website maintains a list of current scams on the Internet at http://www.fbi.gov/scams-safety/e-scams. Another website with useful Internet scam information is http://www.snopes.com/fraud/phishing/phishing.asp. The Snopes.com website is a reference dedicated to identifying and correcting misinformation on the Internet.

UNIFORM RESOURCE LOCATOR (URL) The combination of words and numbers of a web address.

E-mail in a Business Setting

E-mail is a very important tool in business, enabling rapid communication among coworkers and customers. However, the convenience and speed of e-mail messages makes it easy to assume a very informal conversational style. An informal tone is acceptable among friends and family members, but professional e-mail correspondence follows certain rules. The rules concerning e-mail communication, or e-mail etiquette, are called **netiquette.** In addition to netiquette, using e-mail at work raises other issues, such as privacy and ownership of e-mails. When you use an e-mail account created by your employer, all e-mail is the property of the company and may be subject to monitoring by your supervisor or your company's information technology department.

NETIQUETTE Informal rules of behavior for communicating on the web.

A good practice is to maintain at least three separate e-mail accounts. Use your professional account only for work-related correspondence. Use a personal e-mail account to write to friends and family members, and use one or more different e-mail accounts for risky online behavior, such as filling out forms for sweepstakes, contests, and newsletters. Free e-mail accounts are available through many providers and are easy to create and use online. If one of these accounts becomes too cluttered with spam, you can create a new one to use for online activity. Make a habit of deleting your **browsing history** and **cache** and closing the browser window anytime you check your e-mail online.

BROWSING HISTORY The record or log of websites a user visits that is kept by a computer.

CACHE A reference to the storage location where a computer's browser can recall files a user has accessed.

In addition, be aware that any work you do on a company computer while at work may be monitored and archived by your employer. E-mail correspondence is admissible evidence in lawsuits, and legal precedent has been established that e-mail records can be used as evidence in criminal and civil courts.

Archiving Programs

Archiving is the process of saving and storing e-mail messages for backup and retrieval. Archiving protects against loss of data by storing copies of old e-mails and can be used to improve the performance of computers and servers. Outlook archives e-mail messages into a personal folders (.pst) file. The Outlook default settings archive e-mail every two weeks. You can alter the settings for how Outlook archives your messages, if you like.

To change how often Outlook archives your messages:

1. Click the *File* tab and select the *Options* tab. Next, click *Advanced*.
2. Under *AutoArchive,* click **AutoArchive Settings.**
3. Check *Run AutoArchive every n days* and decide how often you would like AutoArchive to run.

Netiquette: E-mail Etiquette

Proper netiquette includes using a meaningful subject in the header; addressing the recipient with a personal greeting, such as "Dear Mr. Rodriguez"; using proper spelling, punctuation, and capitalization; and writing short, clear sentences and paragraphs. Following are some additional good practices for professional e-mail correspondence:

- Do not use all capital letters when composing an e-mail message or subject line; that is thought of as "shouting" when you are communicating online.
- Just as is true with face-to-face communication, it is always a good idea to be clear and polite in e-mail communication. Unlike face-to-face or telephone conversations, where your tone of voice or facial expressions can communicate whether you are serious or joking, humor in e-mails may not be professionally appropriate, or it may not be interpreted as you intended.
- Always reply promptly to e-mails.
- Do not send unsolicited attachments or pictures to people, as they may be blocked by the recipient's spam filter and prevent your message from being delivered.
- E-mail is not a private method of communication. Never send protected private information such as account numbers or passwords by e-mail.
- Always be careful about expressing complaints, criticisms, and grievances in e-mail messages, because they can be easily forwarded and copied to other recipients.
- E-mails sent or received through workplace accounts belong to your employer and may be monitored, so remember to be polite and professional in all work e-mail correspondence. Refer to your company's information technology policy for rules and restrictions specific to your workplace.

CALENDAR

Basic Procedures

The Microsoft Outlook Calendar is a tool used to schedule appointments, meetings, all-day events, and tasks. To view the Calendar, click **Calendar** in the Navigation Pane. You can change the view to see day, week, or month views. Scheduling the right kind of entry in your Calendar helps you organize your time more efficiently. See Figure 7.15.

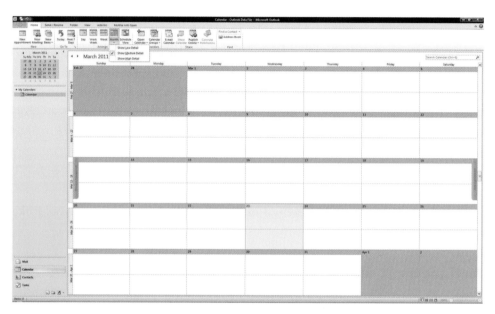

FIGURE 7.15

Appointments

An appointment is for a specified time. Schedule an appointment by moving your mouse pointer over the selected date and time in your Calendar. Click and enter the details of the appointment. You can extend the time required for the appointment by dragging the box down.

To schedule an appointment:

1. Click **Calendar** in the Navigation Pane and click the *Home* tab.
2. Click **New Appointment** in the *New* group.
3. Enter your information in the Subject, Description, and Start/End time fields.
4. On the *Appointment* tab, in the *Actions* group, click **Save & Close.**

As a shortcut, you can also right-click on the appropriate time on your Calendar and select **New Appointment**. See Figures 7.16 and 7.17.

Meetings

A meeting happens at a specific time, like an appointment, but involves you and other people, and can be scheduled by issuing a meeting request through e-mail. Meetings appear in your Calendar and in the Calendars of other meeting participants. A meeting request is sent via e-mail and the meeting shows as tentative in your Calendar. Accepting the meeting request schedules it permanently in your

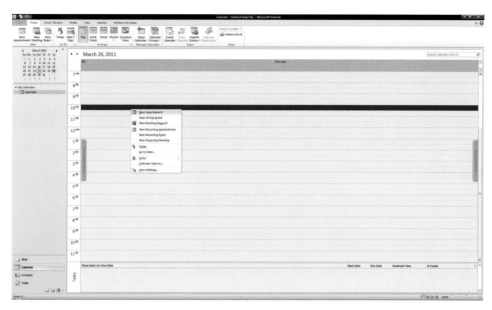

FIGURE 7.16

FIGURE 7.17

Calendar, and declining the request removes it. A meeting entry includes the name of the organizer and the meeting location.

To create a new meeting:

1. Click the *Home* tab.
2. Click **New Meeting** in the *New* group.
3. Enter your information in the Subject and Location fields.
4. Click **Add Others** and select the people you want to invite to the meeting from your Address Book, or type the e-mail address of the person if he or she is not included in your Address Book.
5. In the body of the message you can include attachments along with your invitation.
6. Click **Send** to send the meeting invitation.

You can also request a meeting in response to an e-mail message:

1. Click the message to which you wish to respond
2. In the *Home* tab, click the **Meeting** button. This will automatically invite the sender and everyone listed in the To: box of the original message to attend the meeting.
3. Enter the Location and the Start and End times as you would for a normal meeting request.

Events

An event is an activity that lasts all day, but does not block out time on your Calendar, so you can schedule other events for the same day. Events display at the top of your Calendar. Examples of events are birthdays, conferences, vacations, or holidays. You can specify recurring events, such as birthdays. As a shortcut, you can right-click on the appropriate date on your Calendar and select *New All-Day Event.* See Figures 7.18 and 7.19.

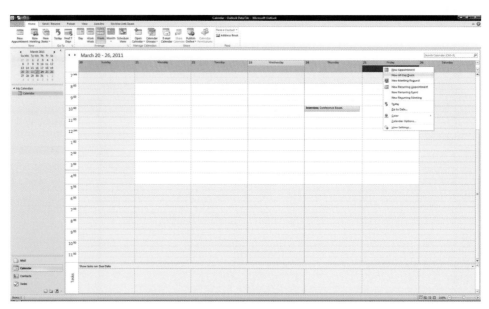

FIGURE 7.18

FIGURE 7.19

Adding Appointments and Events

People can compare their schedules to find convenient meeting times or identify scheduling conflicts using the Calendar's side-by-side or overlay features. Code the border colors of Calendar events to show times when you are busy. This allows you to plan your time and informs other people who view your Calendar when you are available. Busy time is indicated with a solid blue border, while tentatively scheduled events are marked with a striped border. A purple border indicates you are out of the office. Free time is indicated with a clear border. Tentative and free time is displayed as available to other people who view your Calendar. Busy and Out of the Office times are displayed as unavailable to other people who view your Calendar.

To enter your availability in the Calendar:

1. Open the Calendar.
2. On the *Home* tab, in the *New* group, click **New Appointment** or right-click the time you want to block directly on the Calendar grid and click **New Appointment.**
3. On the *Appointment* tab, in the *Options* group, click **Show As** and choose **Free, Tentative, Busy,** or **Out of Office.**
4. Click **OK.**

Outlook automatically sends you a reminder message 15 minutes before appointments and meetings and 18 hours before all-day events. To change when the reminder is sent, double-click on the event to open it. Use the reminder tab to select when or if you want to be reminded about events.

Editing and Deleting Appointments and Events

To change or delete a scheduled event, double-click on the event to open it. You can change a single appointment or a recurring series.

1. To change a single appointment, click on the appointment tab and type changes to date, location, or details; then click **Save & Close**.
2. To change a series, select **Open the Series** in the Open Recurring Item dialog box that appears whenever you open a recurring appointment, meeting, or event. Change options, then click **Save & Close**. You can change the date of an event, appointment, or meeting by dragging it to a different date.
3. Change an all-day event to an appointment by clicking the event to open it. Clear the event box and select times for the appointment.
4. To delete a Calendar item, click on the event or appointment and click **Delete**.

INTERACTION DIVERSITY: ADD ANOTHER COUNTRY'S HOLIDAYS TO YOUR CALENDAR

Business and personal communication has become increasingly international, so it is a good idea to include other nations' legal or cultural holidays in your Calendar. To add holidays celebrated in other countries to your Calendar:

1. Click the *File* tab and click *Options*.
2. Click **Calendar** on the left-hand side. Under **Calendar Options** in the main window, click **Add Holidays** to view a new dialog box with a list of other countries.
3. Check the countries you would like to add to your Calendar and click **OK**.

EXERCISE 7.2: CREATE A RECURRING APPOINTMENT

1. **Open your Calendar.**

2. **On the *Home* tab, in the *New* group, click the New Appointment icon or click directly in the Calendar on the date or time for the first meeting.**

3. **Type the details about the study group such as location and notes.**

4. **Choose the date and time.**

5. **On the *Actions* menu, click the Recurrence icon and select *Weekly* and *Wednesdays*.**

6. **You may choose to end the series at the end of the semester.**

7. **Click the *Attendees* tab to invite other people to attend the study group.**

8. **Check your Calendar for scheduled conflicts by clicking the *Availability* tab.**

Click on a scheduled event to change its time or details. When you double-click to open a recurring event, a message asks if you want to change one instance or the entire series for that event.

Appointment Options

Some events in your Calendar may recur at daily, weekly, monthly, or annual intervals. For example, you might have a weekly study group Wednesdays at 7 p.m. Outlook allows you to create a recurring appointment for events such as study groups. See Exercise 7.2.

Tasks

A Task involves only you and does not require a specific time or date. There are several ways to create Tasks in Outlook. Create a Task from an e-mail message by dragging the e-mail to the Tasks bar. You can then set a beginning, ending, or completion date. In the Tasks creation pane, you can also set a reminder for a follow-up, and set an audible alarm if you wish. This will also show up in your Calendar at the bottom next to the Tasks bar.

To create a new Task:

1. In the *Home* tab, click **New Items**.
2. Select **Task**.
3. Describe your Task in the Subject box and set your Start Date and Due Date.
4. Type any messages or instructions in the message box.
5. Click **Save** & **Close** to set your task in Outlook.

With these tools in the Outlook Calendar, you can enter Tasks and check them off as you complete them. Tasks are viewed in the day or week views of the calendar, and you can also set certain Tasks to recur in the Task dialog box. When a Task is marked as completed, it appears as crossed off and associated with the date it was completed, allowing you to track your accomplishments.

Syncing Outlook, Facebook, Google Calendar, and Yahoo!

You can share calendars over the Internet. Internet calendars share a common file type called iCalendar that uses the .ics file extension. You can synchronize (sync) your Outlook account with other calendars regardless of which program was used to create the calendar and share them among different programs. For instance, Google, Yahoo!, Facebook, or other online calendars can be imported into your Outlook Calendar. Internet calendars may be calendar snapshots or subscriptions. A **snapshot** is a file that can be e-mailed to another person and is not linked to the original calendar or updated.

A **calendar subscription** is a link to another calendar that updates when the other calendar is changed. For instance, you might subscribe to your school or other organization's calendar. The calendar subscription appears as a separate calendar in your Outlook Navigation Pane. You can drag events between calendars to add events to your schedule.

SNAPSHOT A file that can be e-mailed to another person and is not linked to the original calendar or updated.

CALENDAR SUBSCRIPTION A link to another calendar that updates when the other calendar is changed.

INTEGRATION: DRAGGING TO CREATE OUTLOOK ITEMS

You can create items in Outlook using Drag and Drop. For example, you can create a new contact from e-mail by simply clicking the e-mail and dragging it to your Contacts file. This will bring up the Add New Contacts dialog box, where you will see that your new contact's name and e-mail address are already inserted into the New Contact fields. You will also see the e-mail copied into a Notes field in the lower right-hand corner. This has an additional benefit of including any information in the e-mail you may need later in the actual Contact entry. When you finish entering the information you wish to save, click **Save & Close**.

To create a new Calendar item from e-mail, click the e-mail and drag it to the **Calendar** button on the Navigation Pane. This will bring up an Appointment form, and you will see that the Subject field will contain the subject of the e-mail. The body of the e-mail will be copied to the text box so you will have the information contained in the e-mail also. You will need to set a Start Time and an End Time, or if the appointment is scheduled all day you can check the appropriate box. This will automatically insert an appointment into your Calendar and set an alarm to remind you of the scheduled task.

As you can see, Drag and Drop is a convenient way to add information from various Outlook functions to your Calendar and contacts lists, or to paste selected parts of messages or documents to new notes. Outlook is designed to help you manage your personal information more efficiently through shortcuts such as Drag and Drop.

To subscribe to an Internet calendar with your Outlook account:

1. In the *Home* tab, click **E-Mail Calendar** in the *Share* group.
2. Select the dates you wish to share in the Send a Calendar Via E-Mail dialog box and click **OK**.
3. Click to send the calendar dates as a message.

SUMMARY

Effective management of your personal and business information is a very important part of successfully maintaining schedules that can seem overwhelming. The evolution of personal information management systems makes a technologically advanced lifestyle possible, allowing you to integrate all of your communication and information needs into a single point of reference. The busy and often conflicting schedules you keep can seem impossible to maintain without constant reminders throughout the day, and planned meetings or appointments can change at a moment's notice.

As you have learned in this chapter, personal information management systems can dramatically increase your productivity at work as well as provide you with a convenient tool to help integrate your personal and professional lives into a manageable schedule. Comprehensive information management systems that are part of business communication applications give you an additional method to merge several calendars into a single scheduling tool that you can access from multiple devices and locations. The added convenience of creating tasks and to-do lists within the same application ensures that you never miss an appointment or meeting, and the ability to drag e-mail or other information directly into your calendar allows you to see your entire schedule at a glance.

Communication skills and etiquette have become more varied as e-mail has allowed instant correspondence to become commonplace. The use of e-mail for business communication creates the need for proper etiquette and online behavior. In addition, e-mail correspondence increases the need for additional security procedures to prevent malicious activities or espionage. The use of digital media to keep your records drastically reduces the need for physical copies of information, which then fuels the enormous growth in the need to archive records much more frequently than was required in the past. You must track and reference information from multiple sources, and in modern business and personal communication, much of that information must be easily accessible months or even years later. Digital storage is rapidly replacing traditional archiving methods, like filing cabinets or document warehousing, and the amount of information you need to maintain your lifestyle would not be possible without personal information management.

KEY TERMS

- bot
- botnet
- browsing history
- cache
- calendar subscription
- firewall
- HTML (hypertext markup language)

- malware
- Microsoft Outlook
- netiquette
- personal digital assistant (PDA)
- personal information manager (PIM)
- personal organizers

- phishing
- productivity software
- snapshot
- spam
- URL (uniform resource locator)
- virus

Computing in the Future

What do you think the future of computing will reveal? Computers are nearly everywhere in modern society. Our dependency on computers to assist us in daily life has become so great that their presence is no longer noticed. For example:

- Small computers are present in automobiles, household appliances and home electronics, gaming consoles, and medical monitoring equipment.
- The wiring in your home may be part of a computer network that monitors energy use or security needs. Electric utility meters are now equipped with small computers that record average usage and report fluctuations to indicate the need for repairs.
- Cordless telephones are controlled by microprocessors that manage a number of complex functions and user options—all of which would have been inconceivable to telephone users in the 1980s.
- Cash registers, barcode scanners, and credit card transaction terminals all rely on computers to function.
- A **smartphone** contains a tiny but powerful computer capable of executing many tasks that once could only be performed by personal computers.
- Networking with a wireless connection allows you to communicate with both audio and video components without worry.

SMARTPHONE A mobile phone that incorporates advanced features such as web browsing, e-mail, multimedia streaming, video, and photo capture. Most smartphones connect directly to computers to synchronize and update data and contacts using third-party applications.

WHAT TO EXPECT IN THE NEXT FIVE YEARS

As technological innovation continues to improve upon existing systems, we can expect computers to become even more important, now in almost every aspect of our lives. Due to the open and accessible nature of the Internet, we live in a world where distance and language no longer present barriers to learning, entertainment, or commerce. Social networking has introduced the concept of constant contact with large numbers of people using a variety of personal data devices such as cell phones, laptops, slate, and tablet computers.

Within a single generation, computers have become indispensible for everyday living. Just a few decades ago, computers that filled entire rooms and cost millions of dollars performed tasks that can now be accomplished by most cell phones. During the 1990s and early 2000s, the personal computer became affordable for most U.S. households, and the emergence of the World Wide Web allowed nearly instant communication and information exchange.

For example, during the past decade, cellular phones evolved into mobile personal communication devices with Internet access and the ability to instantly download or transmit photographs and video. More recently, smartphones and portable tablet devices began to combine the features of the cellular phone with those of traditional desktop or laptop computers. Microprocessor speeds double approximately every 18 months, and innovations in **parallel processing** are creating increasingly seamless and integrated experiences for businesses and individuals. Parallel processing, also known as massively parallel processing, is a computation method that distributes data to multiple processors to increase the efficiency of complex applications such as large databases or **Software as a Service (SaaS)** providers. The development of parallel processing enhances the ability for Internet content providers such as online gaming sites to provide simultaneous interactions between millions of individual players; other well-known applications of parallel processing technology are online auction sites, search engines, and Cloud-based applications such as web mail. Personal computers will continue to become more powerful as operating systems and applications developers take advantage of multiple-core processing (a more limited application of parallel processing technology).

KEY CONCEPTS

- What to Expect in the Next Five Years

- Cloud Computing in the Future

- Trends in Information Technology and Health

- Trends in Information Technology and Other Industries

- Wireless Magazine and Newspaper Subscriptions

- Hardware Personal Computing

PARALLEL PROCESSING A data processing method used to perform complicated and processor-intensive tasks using multiple processors. This increases the efficiency and speed of overall application performance while decreasing latency issues related to processor workloads. Online gaming, Internet auction sites, data mining applications, and web mail, such as Google's Gmail, all use this technology to enhance users' experiences and achieve near-real-time responses.

SOFTWARE AS A SERVICE (SAAS) Applications accessed on remote servers via an Internet connection. SaaS applications allow access by a browser, run remotely, and close when the remote user completes the task. Examples of SaaS are Google Docs™, chat clients, and video upload services such as YouTube™.

WHAT WILL FUTURE INDUSTRIAL AND PERSONAL COMPUTING NEEDS REQUIRE?

As computers continue to become a bigger part of our daily activities, smaller and more powerful processors, devices manufactured from new materials, and revolutionary new applications will lead the way.

- Personal and business communication will continue to move away from traditional landlines or wired connections. A 2010 report estimated that one in four households in the United States uses wireless phones and the Internet as their primary mode of communication. New applications will enable us to merge communications and information from a variety of sources into a single point of contact, regardless of the source or device used. Smartphones will be able to access databases through secure Internet connections, download and display presentations via a USB or wireless connection, generate spreadsheets, and conduct video conferences. Web-based applications will enable smartphone users to use a standard browser to access Software as a Service, which will enable the smartphone to perform most of the operations of a personal computer from virtually any location.

- Increased access to high-speed wireless networks such as **4G** and **mobile broadband** will drive the need to create and access content with personal devices. 4G, so named as the "fourth generation" of wireless communication standards, will support data transport speeds up to 100-megabits per second (100Mbit/s) over a mobile wireless connection, allowing the users of Apple iPads™ and other handheld tablet computers, as well as smartphones, to view live television, satellite broadcasting, and video chat in real time. Mobile broadband, while not as fast as 4G, will expand high-speed wireless access into areas where cell reception is strong but wired connections are too expensive or impractical to maintain.

- Continued advances in virtualization will allow more opportunities for employees to participate in meetings from various locations. Companies like Cisco, with WebEx, and Adobe, with Adobe Connect, offer this technology for meetings or training purposes.

- Public and private transportation will continue to require more information technology resources to handle increased traffic flow, law enforcement monitoring, and other reporting needs. Navigational systems will merge with **global positioning systems (GPSs)** to assist drivers with directions, including making personalized suggestions for shopping or dining based on the user's previously expressed music and media preferences. Weather and traffic reporting will be more easily accessed via integrated wireless networking systems, enabling commuters to make informed travel decisions or avoid accidents.

- Media delivery will also expand to personal and public transportation, bringing entertainment—and, of course, advertising—to passengers during their travels.

- In 1981, iPv4 was introduced as the Internet protocol (the numerical address that defines location and destination information as you use the Internet) for all Internet users. Since 1981, usage and Internet technology has changed rapidly and the numbers to assign new addresses will run out in the very near future. The old protocol will be replaced by a new one, iPv6. This new protocol allows for a greater number of Internet addresses and other capabilities necessary to support current Internet users and the increasing number of new devices.

4G A popular notation for "fourth generation" mobile communication standards still in development. Eventually, 4G expects to produce transmission speeds at least 10 times faster than current mobile transmission rates.

MOBILE BROADBAND High-speed data transmission and reception using existing cellular phone technology, taking the unused portion of voice transmission bandwidth and making it available for data transmission. It is a practical option for high-speed access in rural or inaccessible areas.

GLOBAL POSITIONING SYSTEM (GPS) A navigation system originally developed by the U.S. military that uses 24 satellites to measure an object's position, speed, and direction. GPS receivers are in widespread use as commercial navigation aids, and many smartphones are also GPS receivers.

Nanotechnology

The emerging **nanotechnology** industry will have a tremendous influence on the evolution of computers and their use in future society. Nanotechnology, strictly defined, is the engineering and production of functional systems at the molecular level. Engineers and chemists have created microscopic machines from molecules that store and discharge energy in a controlled manner to perform very basic tasks. Nanotechnology is still in a very early phase of development, but engineers are developing methods of creating computers out of **carbon nanotubes** that will redefine how information is processed and distributed. Carbon nanotubes are carbon atoms arranged as molecules in the shape of a tiny hollow cylinder. These cylinders are many times stronger than steel and have unique electrical properties. Within the next five years, carbon nanotubes will begin to replace the silicon material currently used for computer memory and storage, resulting in "instant-on" computers with no need for a **boot-up process.** Because many components of computers can fail due to mechanical or thermal problems, the boot-up process verifies that the computer is operational, testing the various parts of the computer each time it is started. The boot-up process is time consuming, but necessary to verify that the memory, hard drives, and graphics components are working properly before the operating system launches. Nanotube materials can allow most of the physical functions of a computer to be performed by much more compact components or by combining multiple functions into a single component, replacing the need for large, heat-generating parts such as hard drives and DVD-ROM drives. These materials are lighter, stronger, and generate much less heat than plastic, metal, and silicon.

NANOTECHNOLOGY The engineering and production of functional systems smaller than 100 nanometers, a measurement that is one billionth of a meter.

CARBON NANOTUBES Carbon molecules, formed into tiny tubes less than 1/100,000 millimeters wide.

BOOT-UP PROCESS The initial procedures that occur before a computer operating system is loaded and the computer can be used.

Advances in nanotechnology will also lead to the creation of fabrics, textiles, and other flexible materials that include embedded software designed to collect information about its user, making it possible to remotely monitor the vital signs of the disabled or the elderly, as well as countless other health care applications. Tremendous amounts of data will be collected and processed by nanocomputers embedded and networked in building materials designed to monitor safety and security. Air quality will be determined by spraying a cloud of **nanosensors** programmed to collect, analyze, and transmit information on a molecular level. Nanosensors are made up of nanotubes or other nanomaterials with the ability to react to other molecules by capturing those molecules and absorbing different wavelengths of light. These reactions are shown through changes in color, a magnetic charge, or another detectable change.

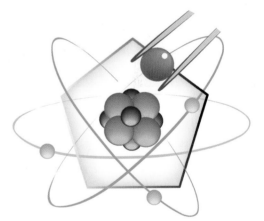

NANOSENSORS Made of nanomaterials, these are used to detect tiny variations resulting from stress cracks in building materials and to analyze the presence of specific gases in the air.

Data Storage

Industry experts estimate that the total amount of digitized data generated by information and entertainment providers doubles approximately every one to two years. Because the storage needs for archiving data have increased significantly since the emergence of the World Wide Web, new solutions are constantly being developed to allow for the expansion of data availability while improving data storage and retrieval.

Historically, digital information, such as databases and other records that required massive amounts of storage space, was housed in physical locations on-site—on hard drives or digital backup devices, such as tape drives, for example. Although physical on-site storage is still common, the Internet now enables users to easily store and share vast amounts of information without archiving most of their data in a single location.

Portable hard drives capable of storing multiple terabytes of data are now available, and **flash drives** with **solid-state memory** can store everything from movies to databases on a device the size of a stick of gum. Developments in nanotechnology will create storage solutions that will replace traditional hard drives with much smaller devices. Continued advancements will also incorporate memory and other components on a single chip, greatly reducing the energy and space needed to run future computers.

Innovations in Information and Entertainment Delivery

During his tenure at Hewlett-Packard, a computer manufacturer, computer scientist Prith Banerjee predicted that by 2015, information and entertainment will be delivered in ways that will no longer be confined to rigid devices such as laptops or smartphones. Flexible displays that consume very little power will allow designers to develop new ways to produce and view content. **Peripheral devices,** such as a computer's mouse and keyboard,

will be replaced by sensors able to interpret speech, touch, and gestures. Banerjee also predicted that "carbon-intensive" information delivery methods, such as magazines and other periodicals, will either be reduced to on-demand services or become digital-only subscriptions.

CLOUD COMPUTING

Cloud computing, which is the concept of off-site, decentralized data storage and retrieval, is commonly referred to as "the cloud." It takes advantage of the increased capability of portable storage and our decreasing reliance on individual archives of data that are commonly available on the Internet or private networks maintained by content providers. Many large information technology companies have massive data centers that provide access to information technology (IT) services such as **raw computing,** data storage, and data retrieval via remote servers. These are provided to customers for a fee, and some companies such as eBay and Amazon offer complete data services such as virtual storefronts with transaction-processing and inventory management.

Processors, servers, and storage reside in multiple locations and are accessed on the Internet without the need for or expense of maintaining an in-house information technology (IT) department. Software as a Service (SaaS), such as database management, data archiving and backup, website design templates, and e-commerce transaction processing, has become a major source of revenue for companies that provide cloud computing services. Media is particularly well-suited to cloud technology, with high-demand video or music accessed by millions of users from a variety of devices. Web mail applications, such as Google's Gmail, Microsoft Hotmail®, and Yahoo! Mail, are an example of an early technology that took advantage of cloud computing. The future of cloud computing is still being defined, but many experts and technology leaders predict that cloud computing and related businesses will generate $120 billion yearly by 2015. Although data security and **bandwidth** concerns will continue to be important issues, the future of the cloud seems to be bright as demand for data and media access continues to expand. The rise of social networking, multimedia, and online gaming has fueled the expansion of access to the cloud, and going forward, innovation will be led by the need to access comprehensive information services from a variety of devices.

Portable Devices and Cloud Computing

Social networking companies, such as Facebook, LinkedIn, and Twitter, and media aggregators, such as YouTube and Hulu, owe their success to the emergence of online technology such as the cloud. People interact with one another online via the web in a variety of ways, including sharing videos and music and playing games online. With the development of such wireless portable devices as tablets and smartphones, many users no longer access the Internet only on personal computers at home or at work.

Outside the United States, the number of people who access the Internet exclusively on these portable devices is much greater. For example, India has an estimated 450 million cell phone users, while only 50 million of its citizens use computers.

Many experts claim that the Internet will expand to become the preferred medium to access information, particularly as access to tools and applications continue to experience demand from smartphone and other mobile users. Within the next five years, Internet computing will become accessible to individuals through local networks that provide services to home media systems, applications, gaming consoles, security systems, and climate control via a variety of devices. These "local" websites will also be able to access other, larger sites through subscription-based services in order to update or add content.

Businesses and Cloud Computing

Cloud computing services will continue to grow as more small and mid-sized companies plan to reduce their hardware and physical location costs. The large companies are already there, as Google, IBM, and Amazon have made large investments in cloud-based architecture. Users can access office documents, use remote servers, and use server-based applications from smartphones, laptops, or personal computers in their home or remote office. As businesses continue to reduce IT power and space requirements, cloud computing will expand to fill the needs of remote users who need access to servers, applications, and other services without using local data centers.

Data management and outsourcing will also migrate to the cloud, with businesses "renting" the servers and applications for specific projects, then renegotiating services and informational needs as required. Outsourcing in particular will become more scalable, as companies will be able to purchase custom services designed to take advantage of short-term computing needs without the expense of building data centers and retaining staff for short- and medium-term projects.

The emergence of the cloud as an outsourcing alternative has prompted Amazon, one of the Internet's largest retailers, to build a **cloud service bureau** that allows clients access to a variety of services, including temporary, short-term high-performance **cluster computing** for high-density networks. Solutions such as cloud service bureaus will expand to allow private local networks to access the cloud on an

CLOUD INTEGRATION SERVICES An emerging technology by which applications help integrate and transfer data between separate clouds.

as-needed basis, maximizing temporary computing needs while maintaining security and cost considerations. Over the next several years, new data management and delivery applications will be developed by small cloud-based companies; these **cloud integration services** will be designed to manage the flow and access of data between various clouds.

Concerns About Cloud Computing

Of course, security and bandwidth issues will continue to be major concerns at the enterprise and provider levels. Privacy concerns and vulnerability to cyber attacks will ensure that traditional desktop computing will not simply fade away; proprietary projects, as well as high-security applications, will ensure the continued need for on-site computing. Some technology experts predict the emergence of hybrid systems that will combine the security of local computing with the convenience of on-demand cloud computing.

Virtualization and iPv6

Virtualization is the creation of a virtual machine or virtual environment that appears to be one system, but in reality may be separated across several systems or environments but run as a single unit. It may even seem like it is running on a client machine. Virtualization can be implemented at a software, operating system, application, memory, storage, data, database, network, or desktop level.

Consider the following example of virtualization: At a school, all the staff members have Microsoft Office 2010® on their desktops, but the actual Microsoft Office applications are not installed on their individual computers. Instead, they are stored on a virtual server. Because it is implemented in this way, the school's information technology department can seamlessly install the latest releases without having to install them on individual machines and impact the school staff.

Internet Protocol version 6 (iPv6) is the latest version for the Internet layer protocol. It was developed to allow for the creation of larger 128-bit addresses, since the current iPv4 is only 32-bit and is fast approaching exhaustion of address assignment availability. This international communication protocol also has many other new features, including integrated network security. It is anticipated that many companies, both large and small, will need to dedicate resources to convert to the new protocol over the next few years.

TRENDS IN INFORMATION TECHNOLOGY AND HEALTH

The near future will also see a massive expansion of information technology in the health care industry. The **Health Information Technology for Economic and Clinical Health Act (HITECH Act),** which is part of the American Recovery and Reinvestment Act of 2009, set aside $19.2 billion to address technology gaps and shortcomings in the U.S. health care industry. The incentives offered through the HITECH Act will encourage health care services vendors to accelerate the conversion of patient health records to a digital form.

HEALTH INFORMATION TECHNOLOGY FOR ECONOMIC AND CLINICAL HEALTH ACT (HITECH ACT) Signed into law by President Barack Obama in 2009 as a part of the American Recovery and Reinvestment Act to provide financial incentives, beginning in 2011 and ending in 2015, to health care firms who "demonstrate meaningful use of electronic health care records."

MEDICAL HOME Also known as a patient-centered medical home, this emerging concept envisions coordinating and directing the patient's health care services, such as surgical procedures, rehabilitation and physical therapy, and mental health services, from a single point of contact.

The Medical Homes Model

The emergence of **medical homes** that concentrate on patient well-being may take the place of traditional hospice or long-term hospital stays for cancer treatment or rehabilitation services such as physical therapy. The medical homes model will rely heavily on networked monitoring and communications between on-site nurses, health care technicians, and physicians to enable those physicians to make better-informed diagnoses in real time. Outpatient surgery centers will no longer need to be located near major hospitals, allowing patients in rural areas increased access to quality health care. Information technology will continue to play an increasingly important role across the health care industry for the foreseeable future, as patients demand better access to their records and health care providers seek to streamline service and accelerate payment schedules.

Electronic Record Keeping

Electronic medical records (EMR) and **electronic health records (EHR)** will become the backbone of access to all health care services, and companies that serve the industry will create new ways to access patients' records to avoid waste, fraud, and inaccurate or incomplete medical reports. This will reduce the risk of dangerous drug interactions and other medical errors.

ELECTRONIC MEDICAL RECORDS (EMR) The individual collected and administered health care records of a single facility or health care provider.

ELECTRONIC HEALTH RECORDS (EHR) The comprehensive or aggregated health care records of an individual, collected from multiple health care providers and facilities.

Telemedicine

The use of **telemedicine** to monitor elderly or disabled patients will become more common as access to broadband and high-speed wireless Internet connections expands. Satellite communications will provide video and medical records access in areas where broadband and wireless communication is unavailable or impossible—particularly in developing countries. Telemedicine and networking applications will expand to include remote diagnostics for acute conditions and maintenance care for patients with chronic conditions such as diabetes. Such advances can improve the overall health of patients in very poor or remote areas. For example, a diabetic patient in a remote area could take advantage of remote examinations via webcam and networked glucose monitoring systems. Such systems allow doctors to observe a patient and make preliminary diagnoses of disease or injury.

TELEMEDICINE The use of telecommunications technology to assist in the diagnosis, treatment, and monitoring of medical conditions. Examples include digital transmission of vital statistics between a patient and a care facility, transmission of x-rays or MRI images to an off-site facility for interpretation, and refilling prescriptions by e-mail.

Telemedicine can allow for early diagnosis of common diabetic complications, such as ulcers from injuries. As a result, lives are saved. Money is saved as well—as much as $2 million per patient, should early intervention prevent amputations due to neuropathy.

Aid workers in remote or isolated areas can use telemedicine to scan a blood sample and then transmit the raw data from a smartphone with satellite or broadband access to a laboratory for analysis. Such versatility is particularly valuable in the event of secondary disease outbreaks following epidemics or pandemics. Some health care technology experts predict that the use of telemedicine will allow doctors in urbanized areas to view, diagnose, and direct treatment from virtually any location. This technology will be instrumental in managing health crises in the aftermath of natural disasters or within refugee camps in areas of armed conflict.

Innovations in remote diagnostics are expected to decrease overall health care costs in the United States by reducing the need for emergency room visits and unnecessary travel to medical centers or physician's offices for routine observation and such monitoring services as blood glucose and high blood pressure in the elderly or chronically ill.

Increased Need for Health Information Technology Specialists

As hospitals, physicians' offices, and insurance companies continue to implement EMR to comply with regulations set forth in the HITECH Act, there will be a tremendous need for IT specialists familiar with constraints imposed by the **Health Insurance Portability and Accountability Act (HIPAA),** as well as data security procedures and general networking administration. Outpatient surgical centers, long-term care facilities, and large physician group practices will experience increased demand for health information technicians during the next several years. Industries specializing in networking technologies will also experience rapid growth as the need to upgrade the existing hardware and networking infrastructure expands. According to United States Bureau of Labor Statistics projections, employment prospects for health care information workers are expected to increase by 20 percent over the next five to eight years.

The HITECH Act will accelerate the rate of the implementation of necessary infrastructure that all sectors of the health care industry will need. Computer and diagnostic hardware will need to be upgraded, and medical facilities' physical networking infrastructure will, in many cases, require significant improvements in order to remain compliant with the new national health care regulations. The next five to eight years will likely feature tremendous growth in remote-diagnostic facilities, where patients' records can be instantly accessed and updated health information can be transmitted simultaneously to a patient's primary care provider, specialists, and insurance provider from third-party facilities.

Electronic Record Security and Cloud Computing

Medical records and health information security will become more important than ever as new health care regulations begin to take effect under the **Patient Protection and Affordable Care Act** and HITECH Act. As patients' medical histories and general health care data are collected and merged into a single data set, a massive—but temporary—need will arise for medical transcriptionists and data entry specialists to collate and review hundreds of millions of records. Employees with additional training and experience in proprietary or specialized applications will be in strong demand and will have opportunities for advancement. Software development companies will create specialized applications to assist in the collection and maintenance of these records; other applications will be developed to facilitate the transmission of combined data, text, and imagery to multiple health care providers and insurance companies.

Health care technologies and information services technologies related to cloud computing represent exciting innovations that can be implemented within existing industries. As the world becomes increasingly technology-driven, many innovations in data security, outsourcing management, and software application engineering will arise. Many services will be automated or outsourced via cloud computing and specialized data centers.

As mentioned earlier, the need for new security applications in health care and web-based transaction processing will spur growth among third-party providers that can monitor activity in real time and generate on-demand reports from a variety of sources. Growth in the information security technology sector will be a combination of analytical applications and real-time monitoring of multiple sources to detect unusual activity. Employees will be required to have broad experience with a variety of software and analytical tools in order to combat fraud.

TRENDS IN INFORMATION TECHNOLOGY AND OTHER INDUSTRIES

Within the next several years, even career paths once considered "low-tech" will require some level of familiarity with basic information technology. Examples include manufacturing and assembly, construction, customer service and care, retail, and many public-service sector jobs, such as postal services and law enforcement.

Construction Management

The construction industry will undergo a dramatic transition from the traditional "blueprint and materials" approach, as technology-intensive applications will take projects from concept to final solution. The construction workforce will also need to acquire basic IT skills related to materials acquisition, project management software, and employment eligibility compliance. Construction site supervisors and project managers will require new sets of reporting and safety-compliance applications designed for mobile devices with the capability to be modified not only locally but also on the construction site as changing conditions or obstacles present themselves.

The next 5 to 10 years will bring an increase in the use of networking infrastructure as a key component in the construction of "intelligent" buildings. Construction managers will work closely with technology specialists and architects to implement increasingly complex networks and sensor technology in buildings. Among other features, this technology will sense and adjust environmental and temperature conditions as needed and secure the buildings.

Energy efficiency is a primary motivation for intelligent building design. As much as 20 percent of the energy consumption in the United States is wasted—largely because of inefficiency that is correctable during construction. Construction managers will continue to hone the efficiency of buildings' shared resources through automation and monitoring networks.

Independent telephone and internal communication networks are another major source of inefficient resource use. The recent downturn in new building construction has made it more practical to update older buildings with high-speed wireless networking technologies that provide common intranets for tenant use. Integrated communications networking within a building will become much more common in the next 5 to 10 years, as tenants demand comprehensive benefits as part of their occupancy requirements. Many of these networks also include on-demand teleconferencing capabilities, which can dramatically cut a company's travel costs. In essence, buildings will become interactive communities, with construction and building management incorporating social networking and "mini-cloud" data capabilities into building design.

Leadership in Energy and Environmental Design Certification

New building and renovation construction projects that incorporate **Leadership in Energy and Environmental Design (LEED)** certification into their site management, new building construction, and major renovations are perhaps the hottest trend in construction today. Projections show that the popularity of LEED certification will continue to grow

LEADERSHIP IN ENERGY AND ENVIRONMENTAL DESIGN (LEED) A certification system developed by the United States Green Building Council that attempts to guarantee certain energy-usage and environmental conservation improvements pertaining to building construction. LEED is recognized as the international standard for energy-efficient and environmentally sustainable building construction and operation.

throughout the coming decade. More and more architects and construction managers will undergo testing to become LEED accredited through the certifying body, **United States Green Building Council (USGBC).** Construction projects that pursue LEED certification focus on conservation of resources during the construction process and also later, as the building is operated and maintained. Electricity, gas, and water conservation; waste management; and shared information technology resources are closely measured during the LEED certification process to promote healthier, more efficient buildings.

In the future, LEED certification standards will be incorporated into most commercial buildings. As these standards become more comprehensive, architects and construction managers will move beyond their traditional role as site supervisors and become vital participants in project management and planning for post-construction building maintenance and systems administration.

Certification

So far, we have discussed many trends in information technology–related industries and the growth opportunities expected to result from these trends. In order to take advantage of the employment opportunities in information technology, prospective employees may acquire one or more specific certifications.

Certification is by no means a new idea, but it has become increasingly important in gaining employment in nearly all sectors of information technology. Certifications do not guarantee a better position, but they have proven valuable to workers who seek new employment opportunities or job advancement. In the past, such basic certifications as **A+** and **Microsoft Certified Systems Engineer (MCSE)** were considered standard for advancement in information technology positions. In the future, these certifications will become basic requirements for entry-level positions, while additional, more specific certifications will be sought for advancement to better-paying jobs in the information technology industry. The next two sections list a number of up-and-coming certifications.

Trends for Future Certification in Information Technology

Technology workers who wish to maximize their earning potential in the field of data security over the next few years should consider becoming a **Certified Information Security Manager (CISM)** or another certification that complies with **ISO/IEC 27001:2005** standards. These certifications will require at least a bachelor's degree in information technology or a masters' degree in computer engineering or a related field. The migration of data and delivery systems to the cloud will require a new standard of data security to protect clients' information from hacking and other malicious activities. Growth in this sector is predicted to be greater than the average rate for information technology in general.

Other certifications include **Certified Information Systems Security Professional (CISSP)** and **Certified Information Systems Auditor (CISA).** These certifications take longer to achieve than vendor-specific certification, and are concerned with comprehensive information technology security expertise coupled with extensive practical experience in information systems auditing and control. Entry-level security programs are also projected to experience growth in the next several years, with CompTIA's **Security+** certification being the most widely accepted.

Vendor-Specific Certification

The future will continue to be bright for all sectors of information technology employment. However, the basic and traditional certifications (such as Microsoft and Cisco Systems) will remain the most common and desired certifications. Microsoft's certification program will continue to expand into the business information technology area with strong growth projected for **Microsoft Certified IT Professional (MCITP), Microsoft Certified Technology Specialist (MCTS),** and **Microsoft Office Specialist (MOS)** certifications in particular. These certifications will continue to be relevant for IT workers who wish to stay up-to-date within the Microsoft platform.

As networking standards continue to grow more complex, the **Cisco Certified Network Associate (CCNA)** certification will help workers seeking advancement in information technology networking positions. CCNA-certified associates will find challenging growth opportunities across the information technology sector as businesses migrate to the cloud. Basic certification such as CompTIA's A+ Hardware Certificate and the **Microsoft Certified Professional (MCP)** for specific products are also excellent entry-level certifications for first-time entrants into information technology.

Online Education

Education is becoming more and more technology-oriented and accessible to anyone with an Internet connection. Online learning drastically reduces costs associated with printing textbooks, maintaining buildings and classrooms, and other overhead. At the same time, it allows students to work at their own pace, according to their schedules. As a result, the next few years will feature an explosion in online learning. Course materials offered today online include computer-based training for industry certifications, online college classes, and basic high-school courses for remote or disabled students. The variety and availability of Internet-based learning will increase dramatically in the coming decade, thus changing traditional education irrevocably.

Shortages in public school funding have forced some high schools to seek online education offerings from other institutions that offer online courses. For example, the state of Virginia's publicly funded project Virtual Virginia offers advanced placement subjects online to high-school students whose schools cannot offer similar courses due to lack of funding or teaching resources. In the future, more programs like these will be offered online so students in other states—or even other countries—will be able to take advantage of online learning.

WIRELESS MAGAZINE AND NEWSPAPER SUBSCRIPTIONS

Another industry in the process of redefinition, due to technology, is publishing. This includes books, newspapers, and magazines—all of which have seen a decline in demand over the past few years. Newspapers, including the *Christian Science Monitor* and the *Detroit Free Press,* among others, are sometimes forced to abandon their printed editions in favor of digital formats. News magazines such as *Time* and *Newsweek* have reduced their number of pages by approximately a third since 2008 in response to lower readership and advertising revenues. The transition from printed newspapers and magazines to digital media online will continue to force fundamental changes in the business models of major traditional periodicals.

Online Access to Print Publications

In the next several years, there will be a dramatic increase in digital wireless devices, commonly called **e-readers.** Booksellers such as Amazon and Barnes & Noble have designed

their own e-readers that allow consumers to purchase and download books and periodicals directly from their stores with a wireless connection. Other companies, such as Kobo, offer book purchases and subscriptions to newspapers and magazines through a proprietary e-reader.

E-READERS Wireless digital devices that allow users to read published content on a tablet, versus buying physical books, magazines, or newspapers.

Although digital newspapers and other periodicals have been offered through a variety of specialized proprietary devices, it is generally expected that within the next decade most periodicals and other print publications will settle on a format that will allow users to download content to a variety of portable devices such as iPads and smartphones. As digital content becomes more interactive, some experts believe that e-readers will add features that resemble those offered by popular smartphone applications, while other experts predict that e-readers will be encompassed by the continued evolution of smartphones and tablet computers. Apple and Samsung have begun integrating the ability to download and read e-books, some with embedded graphics and video capabilities.

Loss of Advertising Revenue

A greater dilemma will face publishers of newspapers and magazines in the near future: the correlation between declining advertising revenue in print magazines and rising demand for free digital content. News will be even more widely available for free—forcing publishers to create new types of content to entice subscribers. Advertising programs will become much more targeted, seeking out very specific demographics based on location and subject matter preferences. Studies have shown that the e-reader audience and those who use e-reader applications on Apple's iPhone or other personal communication devices tend to be technically adept early adopters of new technology.

INTERACTION DIVERSITY: ROBOTS HELP THE AUTISTIC ENTER THE MAINSTREAM

In the future, companion robots may be able to help people with autism hone their interpersonal interaction and communication skills. Autism, which is generally diagnosed in early childhood, is characterized by difficulties with normal social interaction. These difficulties are sometimes quite severe and can accompany a range of communication problems related to verbal interaction, gestures, and physical touch. People with autism are often very intelligent, but even those who are extraordinarily gifted may be prevented from entering the mainstream due to their inability to recognize critical social cues necessary for normal personal interaction. Many people with autism are more comfortable interacting with inanimate or technological objects, because they require very little or no social interaction. These robots can provide a nonthreatening intermediary presence, allowing those with autism to benefit from increased social stimulation and, ultimately, live more fulfilling lives.

University of Notre Dame researchers are experimenting with Nao, a robot who may be able to serve as a nonthreatening intermediary for people with autism. Therapists or instructors can use Nao to interact with an autistic child more closely, thus helping them develop better social communication skills. Robots that are being developed for use as lifelong companions will use voice-to-text technology and advanced artificial intelligence applications to help communicate with the patients they are designed to help.

Even more sophisticated robots that develop attachments to people based on human-like interaction are currently in development. These robots are programmed to remember individuals; in fact, if they are removed from a companion they have become accustomed to, the robots become agitated. As robots learn to adapt and interact more fully with people and their environments, they may provide a long-term solution to those with autism or other severe social disabilities.

HARDWARE PERSONAL COMPUTING

Wireless access to the Internet through mobile broadband and WiFi networks is widespread in the United States, and with the increase in accessibility, the demand for smaller and more powerful personal devices has also increased. Our need to have information or entertainment will fuel innovative solutions to our ever-increasing demand to be "connected all the time." Next, we will examine some possibilities for personal computing in the near future.

Smartphones

As the demand for more powerful personal computing devices continues to increase, manufacturers are developing smartphones that function more as mini-PCs with wireless communication capabilities. This trend toward devices that perform tasks as varied as video chat, office software applications, interactive multimedia, and gaming will continue over the next several years.

With improvements in high-speed wireless access and broadband technology providing ever-increasing bandwidth capabilities, is the device that "does it all" on the horizon? Manufacturers are confident that smartphones with multi-terabyte storage and broadband-capable transmission speeds can be developed at consumer prices by 2015. Strong consumer demand to consolidate personal computing devices with high-speed communications indicates that the merger of these technologies is simply a matter of time.

Current technology enables us to use smartphones like microcomputers for communication with e-mail, text messaging, and access to the Internet. Right now, users of smartphones may use them for live video chat, cameras, video cameras, alarm clocks, mobile music storage devices and players, or personal digital assistants. Consumer technology experts predict that next-generation smartphones will combine the features of the iPad and other tablet personal computers with the ultimate portability of the smartphone. These futuristic "super phones" will connect wirelessly to television monitors, printers, and other personal or business peripherals.

The Future Smartphone Network

In the future, local server connections, or nodes in cloud networks, will provide seamless interaction with entertainment such as online or stored movies, online gaming, and social networking. Users will be able to connect to public **WiFi (wireless fidelity)** networks without taking any action, thus enabling constant immersion in a type of "mega-cloud" architecture supported by high-speed wireless connectivity.

WIFI (WIRELESS FIDELITY) A trademark of the nonprofit Wi-Fi Alliance. The term has come to define the ability of certain devices such as computers, multimedia players, and networking devices to connect to the Internet via a wireless interface.

Home computer networks will continue to serve as the main storage facilities for personal data and media, but they will be able to effortlessly synchronize with and update smartphones, tablets, and other mobile devices. The home network could include personal data devices, entertainment and multimedia service, security monitoring, and remote access from personal wireless devices.

Smartphone Availability

Engineers are confident that eliminating the technological barriers to merging handheld devices, telecommuting into work, and providing the necessary security is just a few years away. According to a report issued by IBM's Almaden Research Center, the research dedicated to making the concept of **pervasive computing** a reality has been underway for a few years now. Of course, major obstacles still exist in terms of battery technology—including lengthy charging times and battery life that is still measured in terms of hours rather than days.

PERVASIVE COMPUTING Also called ubiquitous computing, the concept that computing devices are embedded in everyday objects and communicate constantly with networks and users.

GESTURE-RECOGNITION SOFTWARE Software that can interpret human movement and respond in some way.

Still another possibility is that all-inclusive personal computing on a smartphone level could eliminate the need for input devices, relying instead on custom, flexible displays with **gesture-recognition software.** Personal computing devices seem destined to become smaller, more powerful, and energy efficient through the further refinement of solid-state memory and storage, multicore processing, and shared peripheral devices. Consider that during the 1990s traditional printers, copiers, and fax machines eventually merged into single devices that then could be accessed remotely over a network and used by multiple users. The PDA merged with the cell phone shortly afterward and became the smartphone, with enhanced features inspired by gaming consoles and video cameras. Computer monitors and LCD high-definition televisions have begun to merge, with live broadcasting and other media content now available for download directly to a computer or receiver that allows content to be viewed on different devices via a WiFi connection. As existing personal computing technologies continue to merge functions and capabilities, we will witness the emergence of unobtrusive pervasive computing.

SUMMARY

The future of computing may seem to be ripped from the pages of a science-fiction novel. Some of the predictions that experts in the field are making today will never become reality; more likely, they will be modified to fit better with existing research. New careers will be created as technology continues to change—after all, in 1950, who knew that there would be software engineers?

- Cloud computing will continue to expand, and new networking technologies will enable online learning to become accessible to more of the world's population.
- Building construction will become more efficient and environmentally friendly, and nanotechnology will continue to expand the way engineers integrate computing and information systems.
- Information security will be challenging, as always, in the expanding information networks of the future.
- Digital media will evolve into a form that will reduce or eliminate the newsstand in favor of more environmentally friendly, carbon-neutral digital subscription services.
- Smartphones will develop the capability to function as standalone computing devices and will become the primary delivery method for entertainment, social media, and correspondence.
- Web content will become more immersive, allowing the opportunity to create virtual worlds in which millions of users interact with one another in a socially networked digital world where the barriers of distance and language will no longer matter.

KEY TERMS

- A+
- bandwidth
- boot-up process
- carbon nanotubes
- Certified Information Security Manager (CISM)
- Certified Information Systems Auditor (CISA)
- Certified Information Systems Security Professional (CISSP)
- Cisco Certified Network Associate (CCNA)
- cloud computing
- cloud integration services
- cloud service bureau
- cluster computing
- e-readers
- electronic health records (EHR)
- electronic medical records (EMR)

- flash drive
- 4G
- gesture-recognition software
- global positioning system (GPS)
- Health Information Technology for Economic and Clinical Health Act (HITECH Act)
- Health Insurance Portability and Accountability Act (HIPAA)
- ISO/IEC 27001:2005
- Leadership in Energy and Environmental Design (LEED)
- medical home
- Microsoft Certified IT Professional (MCITP)
- Microsoft Certified Professional (MCP)
- Microsoft Certified Systems Engineer (MCSE)
- Microsoft Certified Technology Specialist (MCTS)

- Microsoft Office Specialist (MOS)
- mobile broadband
- nanosensors
- nanotechnology
- parallel processing
- Patient Protection and Affordable Care Act
- peripheral device
- pervasive computing
- raw computing
- Security+
- smartphone
- Software as a Service (SaaS)
- solid-state memory
- telemedicine
- United States Green Building Council (USGBC)
- web mail
- WiFi (wireless fidelity)

File Management Essentials: File Management Shortcuts

MANIPULATING DESKTOP WINDOWS

Open a Window: Double-click a desktop icon or open a program or application from the *Start* menu.

Close a Window: Click the red X located in the upper right corner of the window.

Maximize a Window: Click the rectangular button located in the upper right corner of the window.

Minimize a Window: Click the dash button located in the upper right corner of the window.

- Manipulating Desktop Windows
- Working with Files and Folders
- Working with Microsoft Office 2010
- The Ribbon Interface

Restore a Window: Click the double square button located in the upper right corner of the window.

Move a Window: Position the pointer at the top of the window banner and drag the window while you hold down the left mouse button.

Resize a Window: Position the pointer at any edge of the window and drag the edge while you hold down the left mouse button.

Switch a Window: Click once on the window to make it active. The active window moves to the top of the window stack.

Windows Explorer Window

The Windows Explorer window is the main file management system for Microsoft Windows 7® operating systems. Click on the **Windows Explorer** icon located in the lower left corner of the Windows 7 screen to open the Windows Explorer window.

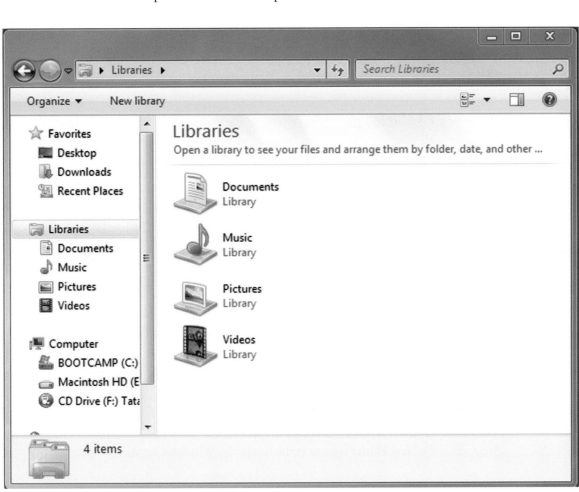

Manipulating Files with Windows Explorer

Windows Explorer allows a user to manipulate files in a number of ways. File modifications you use most often are renaming, moving, copying, and deleting. To perform these tasks, click the *Organize* pull-down menu located in the upper left corner of the window and select one of the file options.

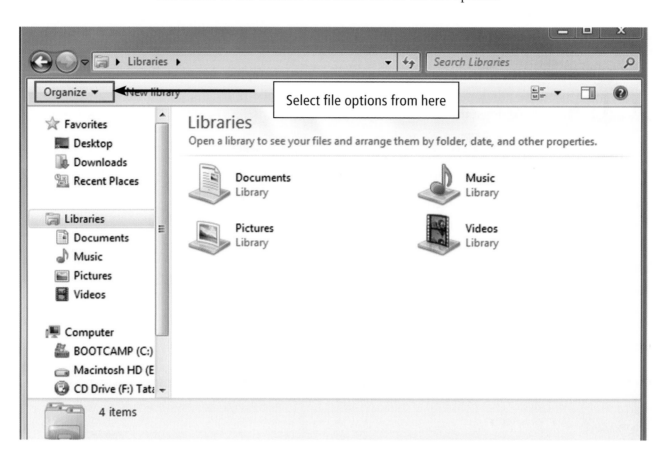

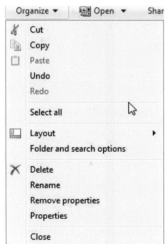

Rename a File: To rename a file, select the file name and click *Rename* from the *Organize* pull-down menu. As you type a new name, the new characters fill the highlighted space. Click outside the highlighted space to enter the new name.

Move a File: To move a file, select the file and click *Cut* from the *Organize* pull-down menu. Select a destination folder or space and then click *Paste* from the *Organize* pull-down menu. The file is copied to the new folder or space.

Copy a File: To copy a file, select the file and click *Copy* from the *Organize* pull-down menu. Select a destination folder or space and then click *Paste* from the *Organize* pull-down menu. The file is copied to the new folder or space.

Delete a File: To delete a file, click on the file and then click *Delete* from the *Organize* pull-down menu. The deleted file moves to the Recycle Bin.

WORKING WITH FILES AND FOLDERS

Creating a New Folder

To create a new folder, click into a library or space within the Windows Explorer window. Next, click the **New Folder** button at the top of the Windows Explorer window.

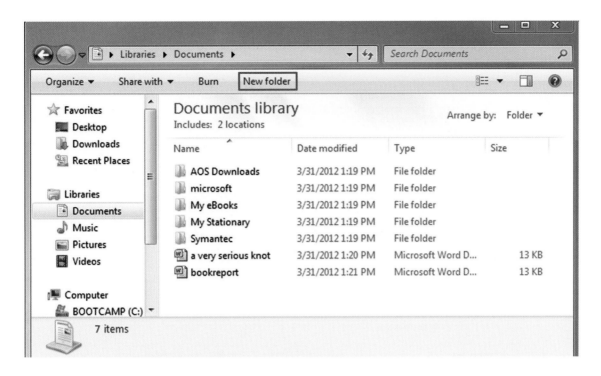

Saving a File to a Folder

To save a file (such as a Microsoft Word® file) to a regular folder:

1. Click the **Save** button under the *File* tab.

2. Type a new filename in the File name section.

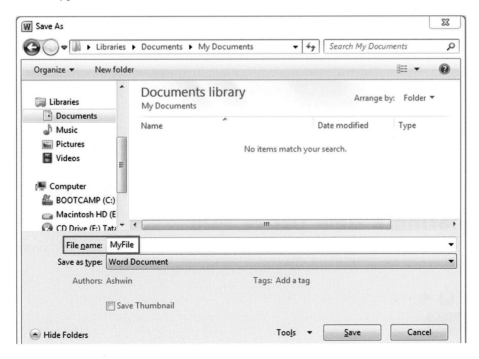

3. Click on categories to locate a folder destination in the Navigation Pane or click on the individual folders listed in the main window.

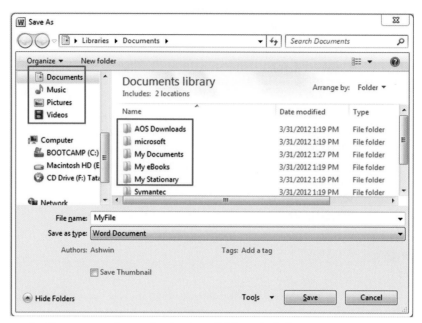

4. Once you select a destination folder, click **Save.**

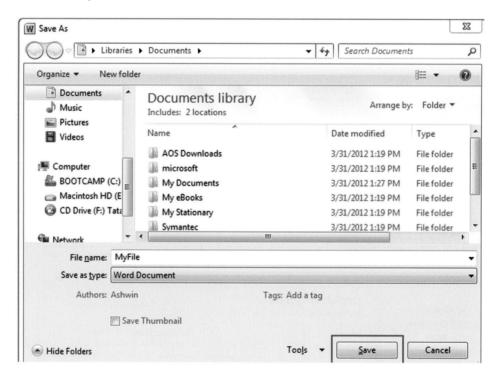

WORKING WITH MICROSOFT OFFICE 2010

Creating a New Office File

To create a new Microsoft Office 2010® file, click the *File* tab at the top left corner of the window. Then, click the *New* tab on the left side.

Depending on your Office application, double-click one of the template options to create a new file.

Opening an Existing Office File

Microsoft Office 2010 offers two options to open an existing Office file: Backstage View or Windows Explorer.

Opening an Existing File Using Backstage View

To open an existing Microsoft Word 2010® word processing software file using Backstage View:

1. Click the *File* tab in the upper left corner of the window.

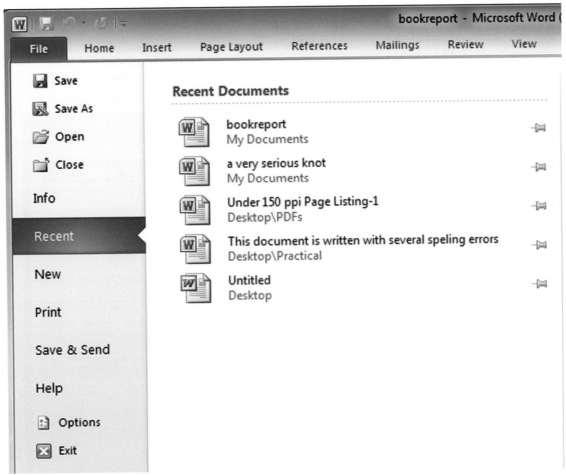

2. Click **Recent.**
3. Locate the file under the Recent Documents listing and double-click the file.

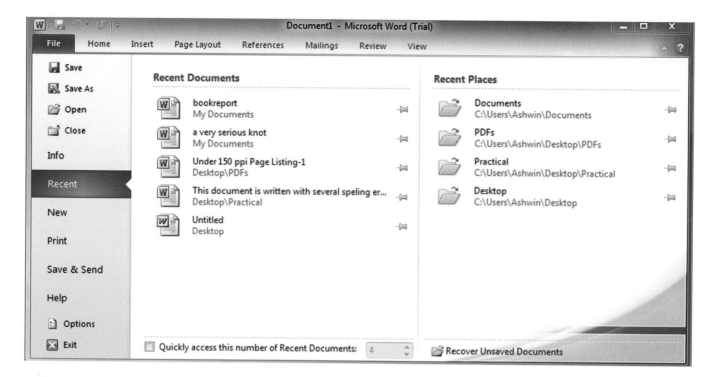

Opening an Existing File Using Windows Explorer

1. Click the Windows Explorer icon in the bottom left corner of the screen.
2. Double-click in the Documents library to search for a file.

3. Double-click the filename to open it.

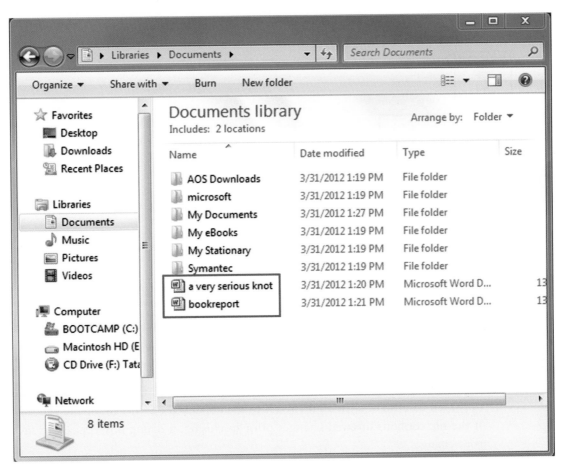

Printing an Office File

To print an existing Microsoft Word file:

1. Click the *File* tab on the Ribbon.
2. Click **Print.**

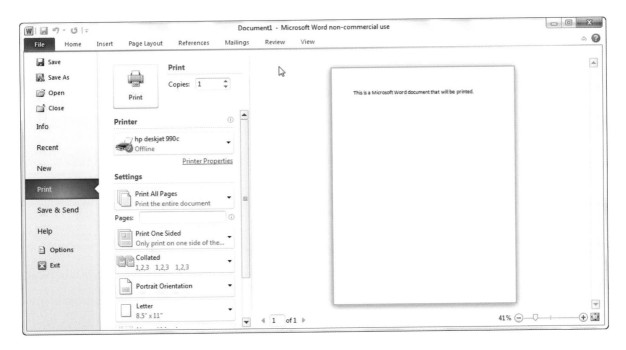

3. Select a printer device and select your printer settings. When finished, click **Print.**

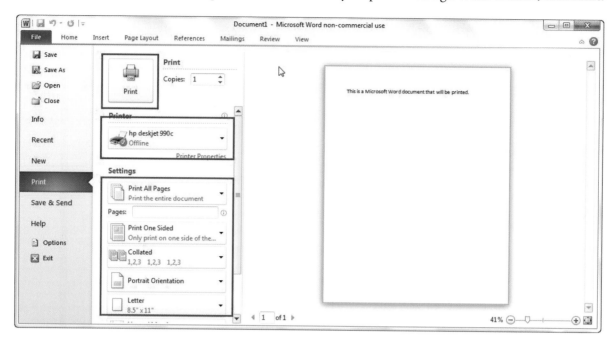

Closing an Office File

To close a Microsoft Word file, click on the *File* tab and then click **Close** in the upper left column or click on the red X in the upper right corner of the file window. If the file contains unsaved changes prior to closing, a dialog box appears to save your changes.

THE RIBBON INTERFACE

Commonly Used Office Commands

The following are commonly used Office features.

Using Cut, Copy, and Paste

- To cut, use the **Ctrl+X** keys.
- To copy, use the **Ctrl+C** keys.
- To paste, use the **Ctrl+V** keys.

Checking Spelling and Grammar

To check the spelling and grammar of a Word document, click the *Review* tab. Next, click the **Spelling & Grammar** button in the upper left corner.

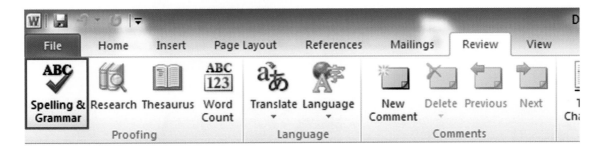

Accessing Office Help

To access Microsoft Office 2010 Help, click the **Help** icon located in the upper right corner of the window.

Internet Essentials: Internet Shortcuts

TYPES OF NETWORKS

The Internet is comprised of two basic networks: the local area network (LAN) and the wide area network (WAN). Each of these networks is briefly described below:

- The local area network (LAN) is a small network of computers that covers a limited geographic area such as a home, school, or office building.
- The wide area network (WAN) is a much larger network of computers that connects multiple LANs together and covers a broad geographic area such as a state or country.

CONNECTING TO THE INTERNET

You can connect to the Internet three basic ways: dial-up, broadband, and wireless. Each of these connections is briefly explained below:

- A dial-up connection is the slowest method for data transfer (56 kilobits per second or slower) and uses a traditional telephone wire.
- A broadband connection is a much faster method for data transfer (64 kilobits to 4 megabits per second) and uses a more efficient wire. There are two types of broadband delivery systems: digital subscriber line (DSL) and cable modem.
- A wireless connection offers broadband performance over radio waves instead of physical wires. The most common type of wireless service is wireless fidelity (WiFi).

KEY CONCEPTS

● Types of Networks

● Connecting to the Internet

● Service Providers

● Websites and Servers

● Navigating the Web

● Web Addresses

● Search Engines and Keywords

● Domain Name Categories

In order to properly connect to the Internet using a dial-up or broadband service, you must connect to a hardware device called a modem (see Figure B.1).

FIGURE B.1

In order to properly connect to the Internet using a wireless service, you must connect to a device called a wireless access point (see Figure B.2).

FIGURE B.2

SERVICE PROVIDERS

Companies called service providers sell Internet connection service plans to consumers. There are three basic types of service providers: Internet service providers (ISPs), wireless Internet service providers, and online service providers (OSPs). Each of these service providers is briefly described below:

■ The Internet service provider (ISP) sells connection plans to individual consumers. Major ISPs include AT&T and Comcast.

■ The wireless Internet service provider sells Internet connectivity in the form of radio waves to individual consumers. Major wireless Internet service providers include T-Mobile, Sprint, and Verizon Wireless.

■ The online service provider (OSP) sells Internet connectivity packages to individual consumers. Services typically include e-mail, news feeds, entertainment, and other specialized content and services. Consumers access these services through an OSP's browser or another provider's browser. Major OSPs include MSN®, AOL, and EarthLink.

WEBSITES AND SERVERS

Websites

Websites are composed of multiple web pages. The home page is the main navigation page that displays when a user enters a web address. The home page is typically organized into separate categories and contains links to redirect the user to separate web pages related to the category.

Web Servers

Specialized computers called servers store web pages for web users. Servers are also referred to as hosts. The Internet is designed as a client-server system and functions when a client (a web browser) asks for something from a server (a specialized computer) and the server delivers the requested information back to the client.

NAVIGATING THE WEB

You access and navigate web content using a software tool called a browser. The browser displays this content in a graphical, user-friendly manner so the user can conveniently locate information quickly. The three major browsers used today are Microsoft Internet Explorer®, Mozilla Firefox, and Google Chrome. The table below displays the pros and cons of each browser.

Microsoft Internet Explorer 9 or Higher

PROS	CONS
Uncluttered interface	Slow installation and operation
Excellent tabs feature	Consumes lots of memory and system resources
Private browsing option	Slower than Chrome and Firefox
Many applications available	
Protects against multiple security threats	
Add-ons available for security	
Excellent parental controls	
Works with virtually all web pages	

Mozilla Firefox 3.6 or Higher

PROS	CONS
Fast, organized, and intuitive	6,000 options available are confusing to users
Very customizable, with over 6,000 options	If one tab crashes all will crash
Uses fewer system resources	Other features require add-ons
Excellent tabs feature	
Offers sticky notes option	
Protects against multiple security threats	

Google Chrome 12.0 or Higher

PROS	CONS
Fast and simple interface	No ad blocking
Many applications available	Minimal options available
Private browsing option	Consumes lots of system resources
Best crash protection	
Excellent tab features	
Protection against multiple security threats	

WEB ADDRESSES

Each website has a unique collection of characters identifying its location or address. This identifier is known as a uniform resource locator (URL) or web address. Each URL is comprised of three elements: the protocol, domain name, and page name. Each URL element is briefly explained below:

- The protocol is a required nomenclature that allows computers to talk to one another. This nomenclature is known as hypertext transfer protocol, or http for short, and is typed into a browser search window before the domain name as http:// (or https:// for secure websites).
- The domain name is an address of a company or entity that exists on the web. An example of a domain name is www.southwest.com.
- The page name is a specific web page a user might be interested in within a company's website. This name follows the domain name of the web address. See Figure B.3.

http://www.southwest.com/flight/

Protocol   Domain Name   Page Name

FIGURE B.3

SEARCH ENGINES AND KEYWORDS

Search Engine

A search engine is an automated database that searches the web and delivers requested information complete with links in response to specific words or phrases. Major search engines in use today include Google, Yahoo!, and Microsoft Bing®.

Keywords

Keywords are specific words or phrases used to narrow a web search when using a search engine. A user types a keyword into the search window of a search engine. A list of relevant keywords one might use to retrieve information about George Washington is listed below:

- George Washington
- First President of the United States
- Founding Fathers
- Revolutionary War

DOMAIN NAME CATEGORIES

A domain name is also used as an identification label placed at the end of a website to establish a realm of ownership, authority, or control on the Internet. Domain names are typically three characters long and identify the following: businesses, schools, government entities, the military, and organizations. The table below lists some common domain names on the Internet.

DOMAIN NAME	PURPOSE
.edu	Reserved for academic institutions
.gov	Reserved for government entities
.mil	Reserved for the military
.museum	Reserved for museums
.org	Reserved for organizations
.com	Reserved for businesses
.info	Available for anyone

Word Essentials: Word Shortcuts

CREATING A NEW DOCUMENT

Use the following steps to create a new document in Microsoft Word 2010® word processing software:

1. Click the *File* tab located at the top left corner of the Word window.

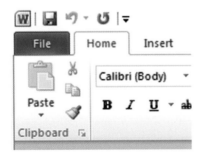

2. Click the *New* tab in the left margin.

3. Double-click the **Blank document** icon.

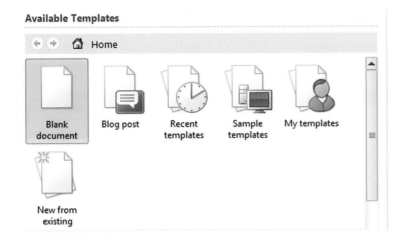

ACCESSING THE HELP FEATURE IN WORD

Use the following steps to access the Help feature in Word:

1. Click the *File* tab located at the top left corner of the Word window.

2. Click the *Help* tab in the left margin.

3. Select the desired topic under the Support heading.

KEY CONCEPTS

- Creating a New Document

- Accessing the Help Feature in Word

- Viewing, Sizing, and Navigating Pages

- Selecting Text

- Editing Text

- Formatting Text and Pages

- Checking Spelling and Grammar

- Inserting Graphics and Tables

VIEWING, SIZING, AND NAVIGATING PAGES

Viewing Pages

There are five viewing options under the *View* tab located at the top of the Word window:

- **Print Layout:** The Print Layout viewing option displays pages in the configuration that will be printed. The Print Layout view is the default view for Word.
- **Full Screen Reading:** The Full Screen Reading viewing option displays pages side by side, like a book. This viewing option is only used for browsing and does not allow for edits to the pages.
- **Web Layout:** The Web Layout viewing option displays pages as they would appear in a web browser or web page.
- **Outline:** The Outline viewing option adds styles and numbering features to help organize the page layout.
- **Draft:** The Draft viewing option displays pages in a simplified format without graphics or margins.

Sizing Pages

Use the following steps to size pages in Word:

1. The Zoom feature is under the *View* tab located at the top of the Word window. Click the **Zoom** icon.

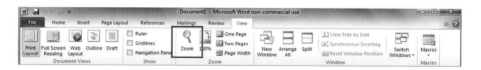

2. From the Zoom pop-up window, select the sizing options desired.

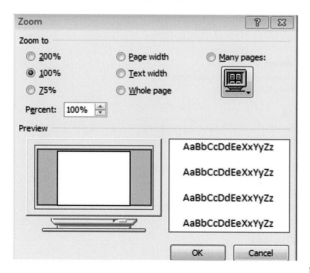

3. You can also size pages with the sliding zoom tool located at the bottom right corner of the Word window.

Navigating Pages

The following table provides some basic keyboard shortcuts for navigating a Word document.

KEYBOARD KEY(S)	MOVEMENT OF CURSOR
Home	Moves to the beginning of the current line
End	Moves to the end of the current line
Page Up	Moves up one page
Page Down	Moves down one page
Up Arrow	Moves up to the previous line
Down Arrow	Moves down to the next line
Right Arrow	Moves one character to the right
Left Arrow	Moves one character to the left
Ctrl+Home	Moves to the beginning of the document
Ctrl+End	Moves to the end of the document

SELECTING TEXT

The following are several methods for selecting (highlighting) text in Word.
Use the following steps to select text using the left mouse button:

1. Position the cursor at the beginning of the text you want to select.
2. Hold down the left mouse button and drag to the end of the text you want to select.
3. Release the left mouse button.

Use the following steps to select text using the **Shift** key and left mouse button:

1. Position the cursor at the beginning of the text you want to select and click the left mouse button.
2. While holding down the **Shift** key, click the left mouse button at the end of the text you want to select.

The following table offers additional options for selecting text in Word.

SELECTION PREFERENCE	REQUIRED ACTION(S)
Word	Double-click anywhere in the word
Paragraph	Triple-click anywhere in the paragraph
Paragraph	Move your cursor into the left margin of the document and double-click
Sentence	Hold down the **Ctrl** key and click anywhere in the sentence
Document	Move your cursor into the left margin of the document and triple-click
Document	Press **Ctrl+A** on your keyboard

EDITING TEXT

The following are basic text editing functions used in Word:

- Insert text
- Delete text
- Replace text
- Cut and paste text
- Copy and paste text
- Find and replace text

To insert text, click the cursor where you want to insert text and type new text.

To delete text, click the cursor to the left of the text to be deleted and press the **Delete** key. Or, click the cursor to the right of the text and press the **Backspace** key.

To replace text, select the text and type new text in its place.

To cut and paste text, use the following steps:

1. Select the text to move.
2. Click the *Home* tab at the top left side of the Word window.

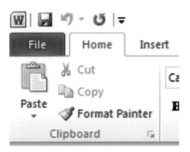

3. Select **Cut** from the Home toolbar.

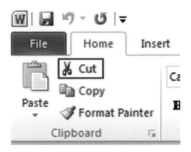

4. Click the cursor where you want to insert text.
5. Select **Paste** from the Home toolbar.

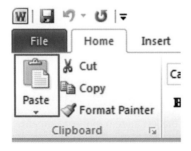

To copy and paste text, use the following steps:

1. Select the text to copy.
2. Click the *Home* tab at the top left side of the Word window.

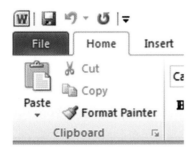

3. Select **Copy** from the Home toolbar.

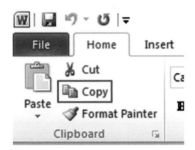

4. Click the cursor where you want the text to be inserted.
5. Select **Paste** from the Home toolbar.

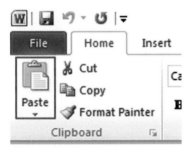

To find and replace text, use the following steps:

1. Click the *Home* tab at the top left side of the Word window.

2. Select **Replace** from the home toolbar.

3. In the *Find what* box, enter the text that you want to replace and Word will search your document.

4. In the *Replace with* box, enter the new text.

5. Click the **Find Next** button to locate the text from your search.

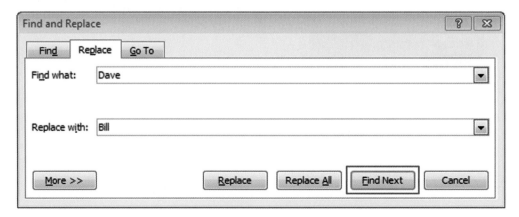

6. Click the **Replace** button to replace a single instance of the selected text.

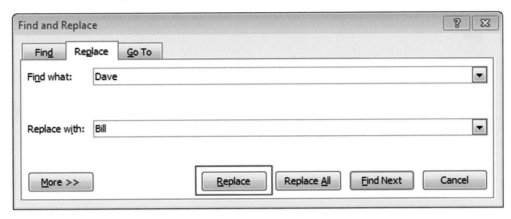

7. Click the **Replace All** button to replace all instances of the selected text.

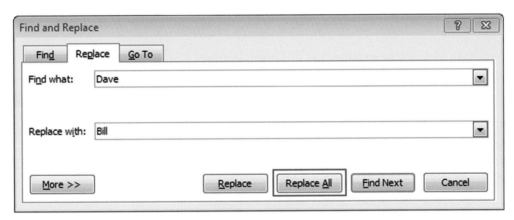

8. Click the **Find Next** button to skip the current selected instance and proceed to the next instance.

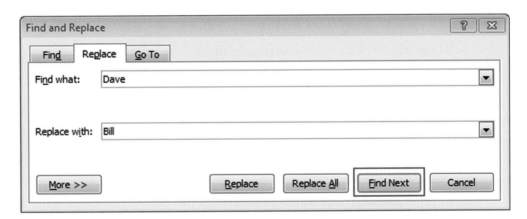

FORMATTING TEXT AND PAGES

The following is a summary of the menu locations for formatting text and pages in Word.

To format **fonts** in Word, use this group of menu options:

To format **paragraphs** in Word, use these groupings of menu options:

To format **justification,** use this group of menu options:

To format **line spacing,** use this menu option:

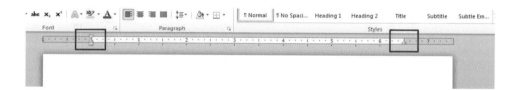

To adjust **margins,** move the indentation markers on the ruler.

To adjust **tabs,** click the tab button on the upper left side of the page.

To incorporate **bullets and numbers** in lists, use this grouping of menu options:

To format **pages,** use this grouping of menu options:

CHECKING SPELLING AND GRAMMAR

Use the following steps to check spelling and grammar in a document:

1. Click the *Review* tab located at the top center of the Word window.

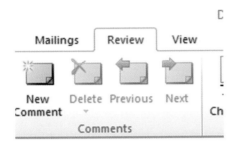

2. Click on the **Spelling & Grammar** icon on the far left side of the toolbar.

3. Select the spelling and grammar options appropriate for your document.

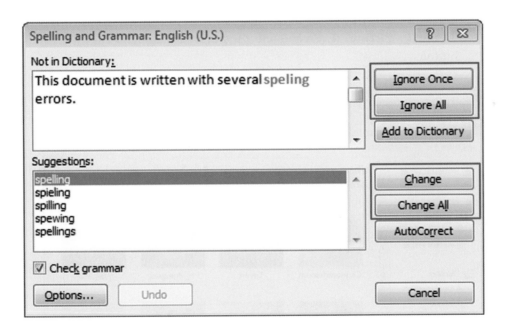

The following list briefly explains the basic spelling and grammar options:

- **Ignore Once:** Ignores the current misspelled word and moves on to the next misspelled word.
- **Ignore All:** Ignores all of the same occurrences of the misspelled word.
- **Change:** Corrects the misspelled word based on the selected suggested spelling.
- **Change All:** Corrects all of the same occurrences of the misspelled word based on the selected suggested spelling.

INSERTING GRAPHICS AND TABLES

Inserting Graphics

Use the following steps to insert graphics into a document:

1. Click the *Insert* tab located at the top center of the Word window.

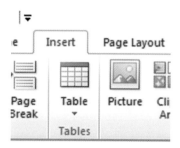

2. Position and click your cursor in the document where you want to place the graphic.
3. Select one of the six graphical element icons in the *Illustrations* grouping.

4. To insert a **Picture,** search and select the desired image and click the **Insert** button.

5. To insert **Clip Art,** search for the clip art on the right side of the document and click on the image.

6. To insert **Shapes,** click on the **Shapes** icon and select a shape. Click in the document to insert the shape.
7. To insert **SmartArt®,** select a graphic category in the left-hand column. Select a graphic in the center window and click **OK.**

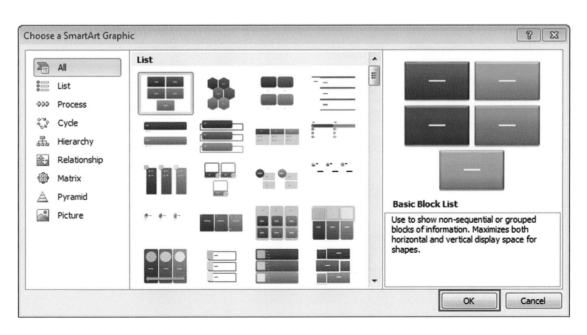

8. To insert a **Chart,** select a graphic category in the left-hand column. Select a chart configuration in the center window and click **OK.**

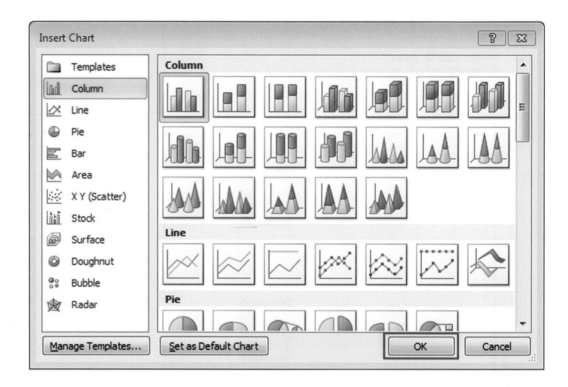

9. To insert a **Screenshot,** click on the **Screenshots** icon and select an image.

Inserting Tables

Use the following steps to insert tables into a document:

1. Click the *Insert* tab located at the top center of the Word window.

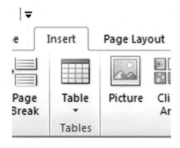

2. Click the **Table** icon in the toolbar and then select **Insert Table.**

3. In the Insert Table pop-up window, enter the number of rows and columns and then click **OK.**

Excel Essentials: Excel Shortcuts

CREATING A NEW WORKBOOK

Use the following steps to create a new workbook in Microsoft Excel 2010® spreadsheet software:

1. Click the *File* tab located at the top left corner of the Excel window.

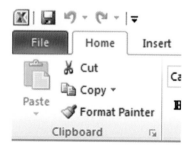

2. Click the *New* tab in the left margin.

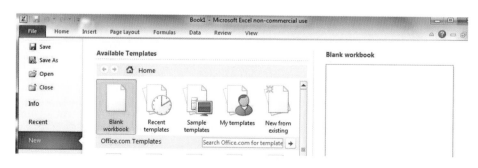

3. Double-click the **Blank workbook** icon.

Available Templates

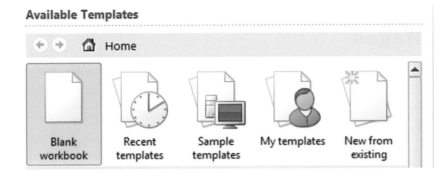

ACCESSING THE HELP FEATURE IN EXCEL

Use the following steps to access the Help feature in Excel:

1. Click the *File* tab located at the top left corner of the Excel window.

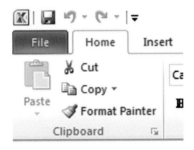

2. Click the *Help* tab in the left margin.

3. Select the desired topic under the Support heading.

KEY CONCEPTS

- Creating a New Workbook

- Accessing the Help Feature in Excel

- Viewing, Sizing, and Navigating a Worksheet

- Entering and Editing Data in Cells

- Inserting and Deleting Rows and Columns

- Formatting Cells

- Adjusting Rows and Columns

- Copying and Pasting Data in Cells

VIEWING, SIZING, AND NAVIGATING A WORKSHEET

Viewing Pages

Under the *View* tab located at the top of the Excel window are three basic viewing options:

- **Normal:** The Normal viewing option displays the worksheet with cells, rows, and columns all visible. The Normal view is the default viewing option for Excel.
- **Page Layout:** The Page Layout viewing option displays the page margins, headers and footers, and page breaks of the worksheet.
- **Page Break Preview:** The Page Break Preview viewing option allows the user to adjust the pages prior to printing.

Sizing Pages

Use the following steps to size pages in Excel:

1. Under the *View* tab located at the top of the Excel window is the Zoom feature. Click on the **Zoom** icon.

2. From the Zoom pop-up window, select the sizing options desired.

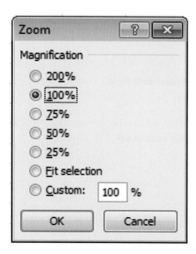

3. You can also size pages with the sliding zoom tool located at the bottom right corner of the Excel window.

Navigating Pages

The following table provides some basic keyboard shortcuts for navigating an Excel worksheet.

KEYBOARD KEY(S)	CELL MOVEMENT
Up, Down, Right, and Left Arrow keys	Moves to cells above, below, right, and left of current cell
Enter	Moves one cell below current cell
Tab	Moves one cell to the right of current cell
Shift+Tab	Moves one cell to the left of current cell
Ctrl+Home	Moves to cell A1
Ctrl+End	Moves to lower right cell of worksheet

ENTERING AND EDITING DATA IN CELLS

Entering Data

Use the following steps to enter data into an Excel worksheet with and without the Formula bar.

To enter data with the Formula bar:

1. Click any cell.
2. Type the data into the Formula bar at the top of the worksheet and then click the **check** icon.

3. To remove data before entering, click the **delete** icon.

To enter data without the Formula bar:

1. Click any cell.
2. Type your data.
3. Press the **Enter** key to enter the data and move down one cell. (**Note:** You can also use the navigation keys listed in the table above.)
4. To remove data before entering, press the **Esc** or **Backspace** keys.

Editing Data

Use the following steps to delete, replace, or modify data within an Excel worksheet. To delete data:

1. Select the cell.
2. Press the **Delete** key.

To replace data:

1. Select the cell.
2. Type over the contents with new data.
3. Press the **Enter** key.

To modify data:

1. Select the cell.
2. Click inside the Formula bar window to make editing changes and then click the **check** icon.

3. You can also double-click on the cell and make changes directly inside the cell.

INSERTING AND DELETING ROWS AND COLUMNS

Inserting Rows and Columns

Use the following steps to insert rows and columns in an Excel worksheet:

1. Select a row or column by holding down the left mouse button and dragging the cursor across the row or column.
2. Click the *Home* tab located at the top left corner of the Excel window.

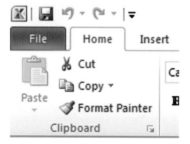

3. Click the down arrow below the **Insert** icon and select either **Insert Sheet Rows** or **Insert Sheet Columns.** A new row or column appears to the left of the selected row or column.

Deleting Rows and Columns

Use the following steps to delete rows and columns in an Excel worksheet:

1. Select a row or column by holding down the left mouse button and dragging the cursor across the row or column.
2. Click the *Home* tab located at the top left corner of the Excel window.

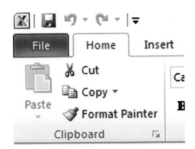

3. Click the down arrow below the **Delete** icon and select either **Delete Sheet Rows** or **Delete Sheet Columns.** The selected row or column is deleted.

FORMATTING CELLS

Use the following steps to format data within cells in an Excel worksheet:

1. Click on the cell you want to edit.
2. Click the *Home* tab located at the top left corner of the Excel window.

3. Click the **Format** icon located in the toolbar and select **Format Cells.**

4. To format **Numbers,** select the appropriate category and modify, and then click **OK.**

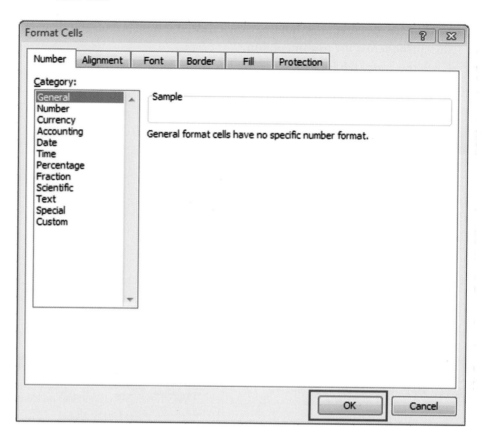

5. To format **Alignment,** select and modify the appropriate settings (including selecting *Wrap text,* for example), and then click **OK.**

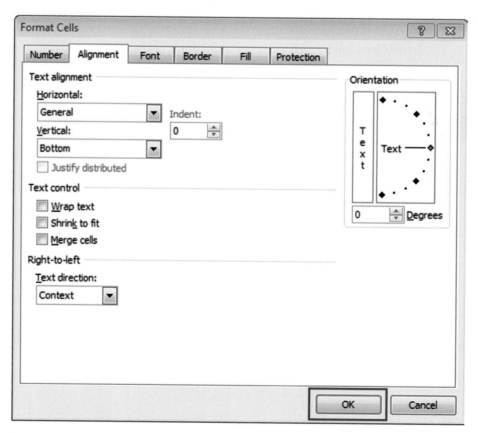

6. To format **Fonts,** select and modify the appropriate font size and style, and then click **OK.**

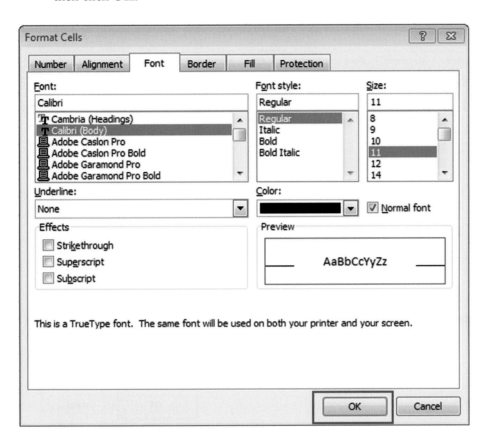

7. To format **Borders,** select and modify the appropriate style and color, and then click **OK.**

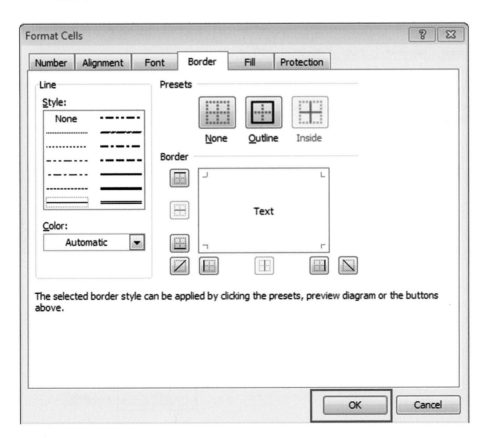

8. To format **Fills,** select and modify the appropriate color, effect, and pattern, and then click **OK.**

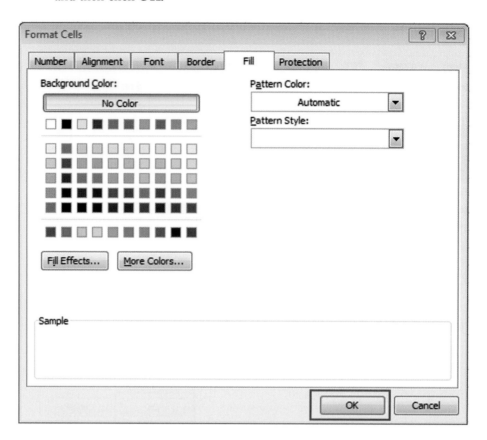

9. To format **Protections,** click the appropriate security settings and then click **OK.**

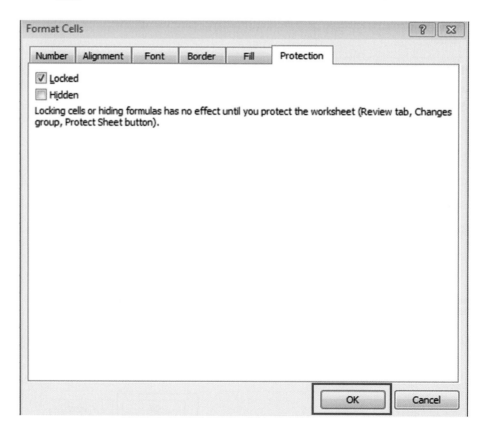

ADJUSTING ROWS AND COLUMNS

Adjusting Rows

Use the following steps to adjust rows in an Excel worksheet:

1. Select a row by holding down the left mouse button and dragging the cursor across the row.
2. Click the *Home* tab located at the top left corner of the Excel window.

3. Click the **Format** icon located in the toolbar and select **Row Height.**

4. In the Row Height pop-up window, enter the new row height number and then click **OK.**

5. You can also manually adjust the row height by placing the cursor inside the number margin on the border between the numbers and dragging while holding the left mouse button.

Adjusting Columns

Use the following steps to adjust columns in an Excel worksheet:

1. Select a column by holding down the left mouse button and dragging the cursor across the column.
2. Click the *Home* tab located at the top left corner of the Excel window.

3. Click the **Format** icon located in the toolbar and select **Column Width.**

4. In the Column Width pop-up window, enter the new column width number and then click **OK.**

5. You can also manually adjust the column width by placing the cursor inside the letter margin on the border between the letters and dragging while holding down the left mouse button.

COPYING AND PASTING DATA IN CELLS

Use the following steps to copy and paste data in cells:

1. Select the data you want to copy.
2. Click the *Home* tab located at the top left corner of the Excel window.

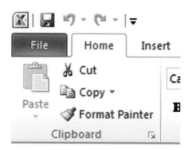

3. Click **Copy** located on the left side of the toolbar. The selected data becomes surrounded by an animated marquee pattern. (**Note:** The copy command can also be performed by using the **Ctrl+C** keys on the keyboard.)

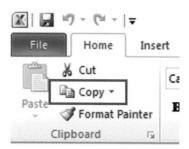

4. Click the upper left corner cell of the section where you want to paste data.
5. Click **Paste** on the left side of the toolbar. The selected section appears in the new location. (**Note:** The paste command can also be performed by using the **Ctrl+V** keys on the keyboard.)

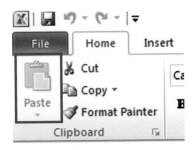

PowerPoint Essentials: PowerPoint Shortcuts

CREATING A NEW PRESENTATION

There are two ways to create a new presentation with Microsoft PowerPoint 2010® presentation software. You can base your presentation on a template or base your presentation on a theme.

To create a presentation based on a template, use the following steps:

1. Click the *File* tab on the Ribbon.

2. Click *New*.

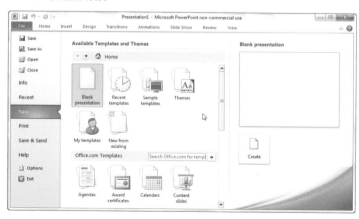

3. Select an available template under Available Templates and Themes.

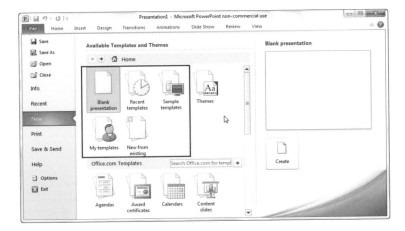

4. Click **Create.**

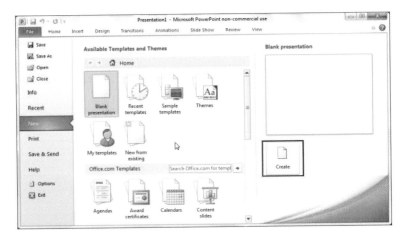

To create a presentation based on a theme, use the following steps:

1. Click the *File* tab on the Ribbon.

2. Click *New.*

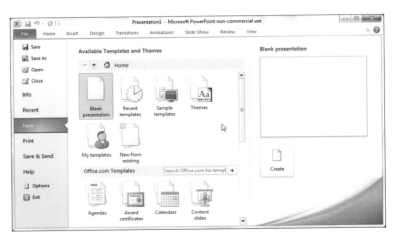

KEY CONCEPTS

• Creating a New Presentation

• Entering, Selecting, and Editing Text

• Formatting Slides

• Adding and Deleting Slides

• Viewing a Slide Show

• Printing a Presentation

3. Select **Themes** under Available Templates and Themes.

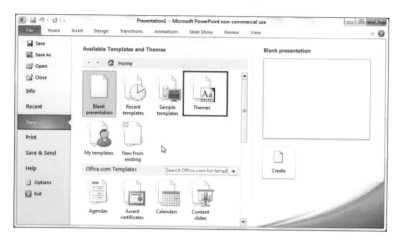

4. Click **Create.**

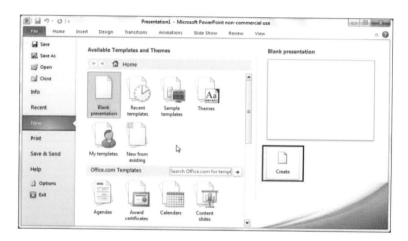

ENTERING, SELECTING, AND EDITING TEXT

Entering Text

To enter text into a PowerPoint slide, click inside the text placeholder box and begin typing.

Selecting Text and Objects

Hold down the left mouse button and drag over the text or double-click on a word to select text in PowerPoint. Triple-click inside a paragraph to select the entire paragraph.

To select an object in PowerPoint, click on the object. To select multiple objects, press the **Shift** key as you click on each object.

Editing Text

Editing text in the PowerPoint application is similar to editing text in the Microsoft Word 2010® word processing software application. To insert a word into an existing sentence, click to place the insertion point of the new word and type the new word. To delete individual characters, click the insertion point at the right of the letter and press the **Backspace** key. To delete a word, select the entire word and then press **Delete** or **Backspace.** To replace text, select the text and type over it.

FORMATTING SLIDES

You can format slides in PowerPoint a number of ways.

To change the theme of a presentation, use the following steps:

1. Click the *Design* tab.

2. In the Themes section, select a desired slide design. Click the down arrow to the right of the theme selections to view more slide choices.

3. Click a slide design to apply the theme to the entire presentation.

To change the appearance of existing characters, use the following steps:

1. Select the text you want to format.
2. Click the *Home* tab.

3. Under the Font section, use the appropriate menu options to format the selected text.

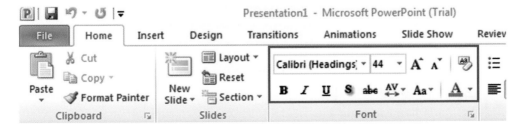

To change the appearance of existing paragraphs, use the following steps:

1. Select the paragraphs you want to format.
2. Click the *Home* tab.

3. Under the Paragraph section, use the appropriate menu options to format the paragraphs.

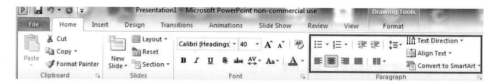

To change the background style of a presentation, use the following steps:

1. Click the *Design* tab.

2. Click on the **Background Styles** button on the right side of the Ribbon.

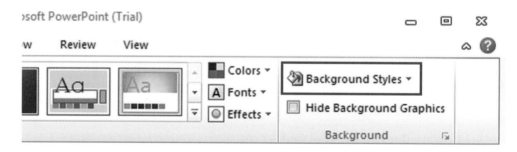

3. Click on a desired background style from the gallery.
4. For more background options, click the **Format Background** button.

5. Modify the fill settings to achieve the desired effect. Then, click **Apply to All.**

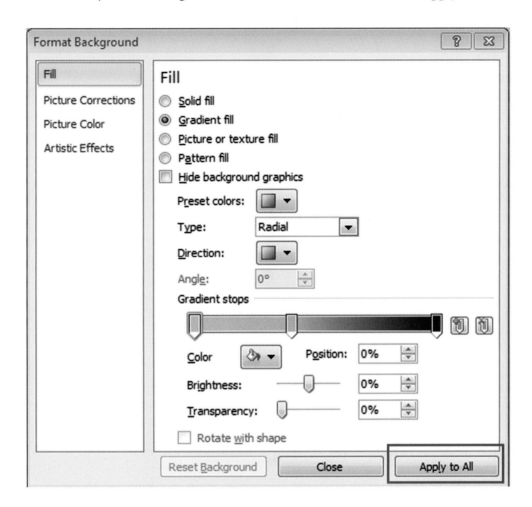

ADDING AND DELETING SLIDES

To add a new slide to a presentation, use the following steps:

1. Click the *View* tab. Then, click **Normal.**

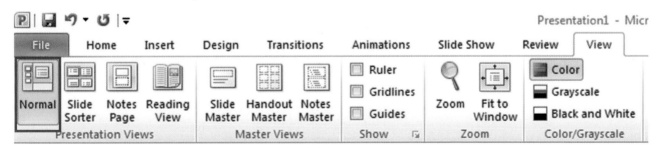

2. Click the *Home* tab.

3. In the Slides pane on the left side of the window, click the slide thumbnail of the slide preceding the slide you will insert.

4. Click the down arrow inside the **New Slide** button.

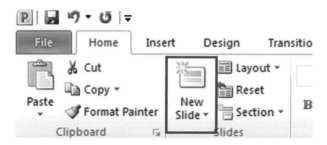

5. Select and click a desired slide layout from the list of slides.

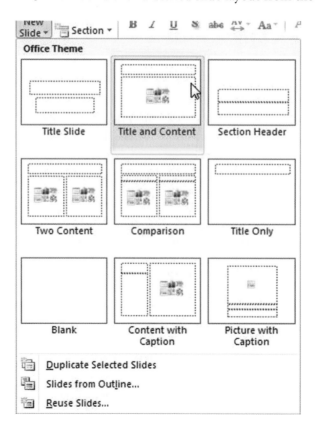

To delete a slide from a presentation, use the following steps:

1. Click the *View* tab. Then, click **Normal.**

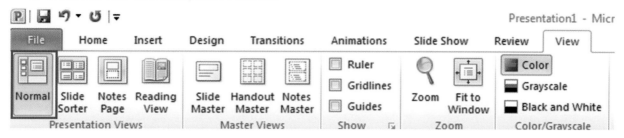

2. In the Slides pane on the left side of the window, click on the slide thumbnail you want to delete.

3. Press the **Delete** key.

VIEWING A SLIDE SHOW

PowerPoint allows the user to advance slides either manually or automatically when presenting a slide show.

To advance slides manually, use the following steps:

1. Click the *Slide Show* tab and then click **From Beginning.**

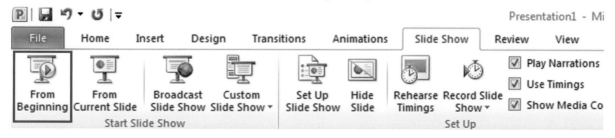

2. To advance the slides, press the left and right arrow keys or **Enter** (page up) and **Backspace** (page down) keys.
3. To terminate the slide show at any time, press **Esc.**

To advance slides automatically, use the following steps:

1. Click the *Slide Show* tab and then click the **Set Up Slide Show** button.

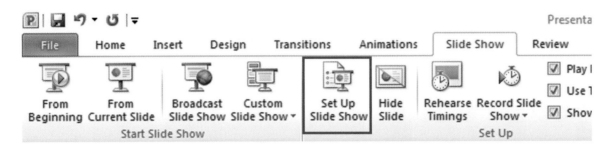

2. Select the appropriate slide show settings in the dialog box and click **OK.**

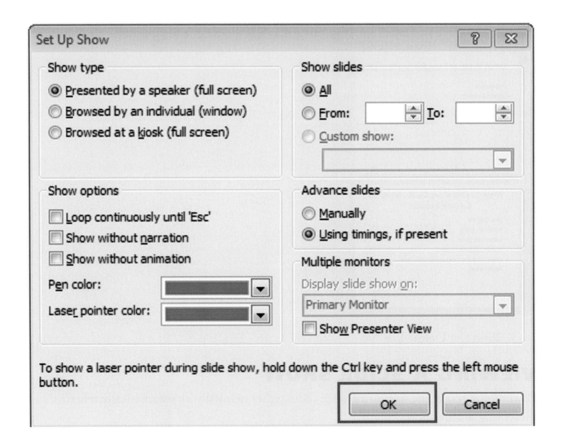

PRINTING A PRESENTATION

The two most common ways to print a presentation in PowerPoint is to print out each slide on a full page or as a handout with multiple slides on one page.

To print a presentation with one slide on each page, use the following steps:

1. Click the *File* tab.

2. Click *Print.*

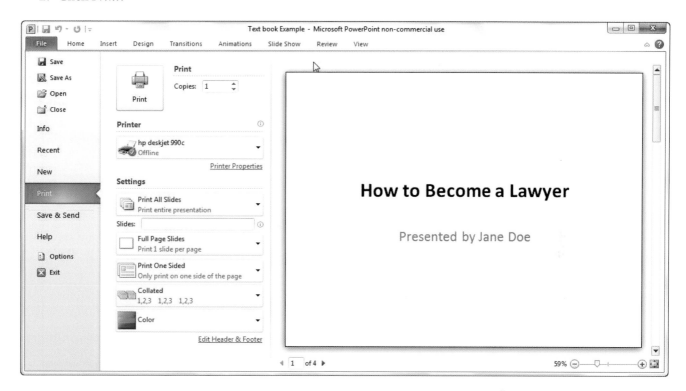

3. Select **Print All Slides** and then click **Print.**

To print a presentation as a handout, use the following steps:

1. Click the *File* tab.

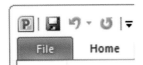

2. Click *Print*.

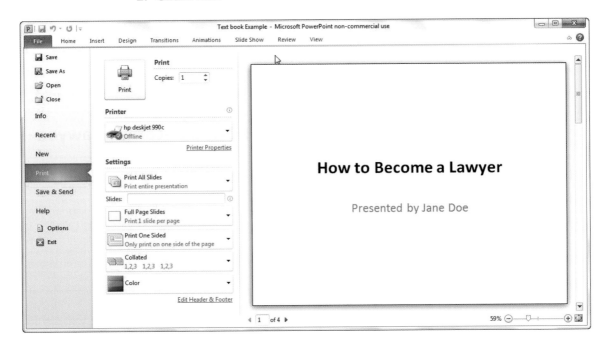

3. Click **Full Page Slides.**

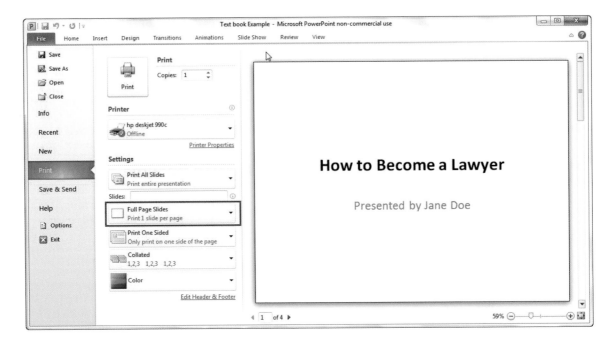

4. Select the appropriate slide layout configuration under Handouts.

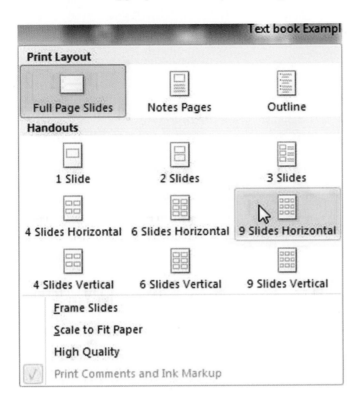

For information on adding notes to a presentation, see Using the Notes Pane in the chapter, "Productivity Software: Presentations."

APA Style

APA style is a set of rules and guidelines for manuscript preparation based on the psychology literature that was developed by the American Psychological Association (APA). APA style is a standard format for academic research writing and is used extensively in the social sciences. The *Publication Manual of the American Psychological Association* (2010) is the style's official guide. The information in this chapter comes from the sixth edition of the *Publication Manual* and its affiliated website.

The *Publication Manual* provides guidelines for formatting a research paper and referencing sources. It provides specific information about organizing the content of the research paper; using effective writing style and avoiding bias in language; employing Standard English grammar and punctuation; and using tables, figures, and graphs to illustrate a research paper. The *Publication Manual* also guides authors through the process of submitting papers for publication. The purpose of this chapter is to focus on the guidelines the *Publication Manual* sets forth for most undergraduate papers.

The *Publication Manual* also includes detailed information about documenting sources—giving credit to the sources that were used to prepare a manuscript. Following these guidelines can help a writer avoid plagiarism. Every type of source used

- Formatting a Paper

- References and Internal Citation Style

in a research paper must be cited, from journals and books to music and videos. The APA's website (http://apastyle.org) and its accompanying blog (http://blog.apastyle.org) are among the best resources for the most up-to-date information on citing electronic sources.

FORMATTING A PAPER

Each research paper should have four core components:

- Title page
  - Includes the title of the work, running head, and byline
  - May also include school and instructor information
- Abstract
  - Provides a short summary of research and findings
- Body text
  - Includes an introduction with a background of literature consulted, method of research, results, and a discussion of the results
- References
  - Includes all sources referenced in the paper

The following basic guidelines should be used when formatting a paper:

- Use 8½ × 11 in. (22 × 28 cm) paper (standard)
- Use double spacing between lines
- Use a 12-point serif font, such as Times New Roman
- Number each page on the right-hand side at the top of the page
- Use 1-inch margins on each side
- Indent the first line of each paragraph to ½ in. (1.3 cm)
- Align the text to the left, leaving the right margin ragged and unjustified
- Present a title page, abstract, body text, and references, in that order

Some papers may feature other collateral items, such as appendices, author notes, footnotes, tables, figure captions, and figures. They should be placed in this sequence after the references.

Organization is important to help the reader follow the flow of ideas from existing research to original findings. The APA has established common formatting styles to create uniformity in published material that is recognizable to a broad readership. Perhaps most important is that writers remember to not worry about perfectly formatting the paper in APA style until the revision stage. Becoming preoccupied with formatting early on will slow writing progress.

Title Page

The title page includes the title of the paper centered in the upper third of the page. This is followed by a byline, which includes the author's name. In the upper-left corner of the title page, the running head (see the next section for more information) should be identified. Also include a page header that includes the running head to the left and the page number in the upper-right corner.

Running Head

The research paper's title page should include a page header, called a running head, that will appear on each page of the document. Usually a shortened version of the paper's title (two to three words, no more than 50 characters) is used as the running head. For example, if the title of the document is "Everything You Need to Know about APA Citations," an appropriate running header might be "APA CITATIONS." The running head should be flush left in all caps. In the top-left corner of the title page, type "APA CITATIONS" flush left and the page number flush right.

Abstract

An abstract is a summary of the research paper and its findings. It is an extremely important paragraph that allows readers to immediately determine if they are interested in reading the paper. This section begins on page 2 with the header "Abstract" centered on the page with an initial capital A followed by lowercase letters. Abstracts should be brief and usually range between 150 and 250 words. The text should be flush left (without an indention) beneath the title and Arabic numerals should be used for any numbers.

Headings

Using levels of headings provides a hierarchy for the sections in a paper; in effect, they provide the reader with an outline of the paper. Avoid use of only one subsection heading or one subsection within a section. The same level of heading should be given to all topics of equal importance (e.g., Method, Results). At least two subsection headings should be used within a section; otherwise, none should be used. A heading structure for all sections should use the same top-to-bottom progression, regardless of the number of levels of subheading. APA style uses five possible levels of headings, which follow each other sequentially. Thus, if only one level is used, use Level 1; if two are used, use Levels 1 and 2 (the most common combination in most research papers), in that order; if three are used, use Levels 1, 2, and 3, in that order, and so on.

Level 1: Centered, boldface, initial capital letters on important words; on the line above the paragraph

Example:

BASIC FINDINGS

Level 2: Flush left, boldface, initial capital letters on important words; on the line above the paragraph

Example:

Demographic Analysis

Level 3: Indented, boldface, sentence-case heading followed by a period, on the same line of copy as the beginning of the paragraph that follows.

    Demographic analysis. The demographic analysis shows that among participating physicians…

Level 4: Indented, boldface, italicized, sentence-case heading followed by a period, on the same line of copy as the beginning of the paragraph that follows.

Demographic analysis. The demographic analysis shows that among participating physicians…

Level 5: Indented, italicized, sentence-case heading followed by a period, on the same line of copy as the beginning of the paragraph that follows.

Demographic analysis. The demographic analysis shows that among participating physicians…

Punctuation and Spacing

Punctuation provides the pace for a sentence and tells the reader where to pause (commas, colons, or semicolons), stop (periods, question marks, or exclamation points), or deviate (parentheses, dashes, or brackets). The different kinds of punctuation in a sentence usually designate different kinds and lengths of pauses. Modern word-processing programs provide the appropriate space for each character, so hit the space-bar only once after commas, colons, and semicolons. Do not add extra spaces around dashes, parentheses, or brackets.

APA style suggests—but does not require—two spaces after punctuation marks at the end of a sentence in draft manuscripts. Because requirements vary across publications, when submitting a manuscript for publication, consult the publication's style guidelines regarding spacing after end punctuation.

Following is a quick guide to some punctuation rules required in APA style.

Period

Periods are used in reference lists after the author's name, the year, the title of a book or article, and the close of the reference; an exception to this close-reference rule is references that end in a website address (electronic references), which do not end with a period.

When in-text citations are used at the end of a sentence, the period should follow the citation. When in-text citations appear at the end of a long, indented quote, periods should not follow the in-text citations. In that case, the period appears at the end of the quote but before the in-text citation. See "Quotations of 40 Words or More," which appears later in this section, for an example.

Colon

Colons appear between the publication location and the publisher listed in individual references. In text, a colon should not be used after an introductory clause that is not a complete sentence. If two independent clauses are separated by a colon, capitalize the word that begins the second clause.

Semicolon

Although semicolons are usually used to separate two independent clauses (complete sentences), a semicolon should also be used to set off items in a series when one or more of these items already includes commas, regardless of whether the items are complete sentences—for example, "The sisters were challenged to ride a bike for two hours; juggle a ball, a book, and a toy car for 10 minutes; and walk on a treadmill for 30 minutes."

Comma

In in-text citations, a comma should be used to set off the year of publication within parentheses. In text, use a comma between all elements in a series of three or more items, including before *and* and *or*.

Quotation Marks

Double quotation marks should be used in the following situations:

- To introduce a word or phrase that is used as slang, a coined expression, or an example of irony
- To identify an article or chapter title in a periodical or book when the title is mentioned in text
- To reproduce or cite material from a published source (only up to 40 words)

Double quotation marks should not enclose quotations of 40 words or more.

Quotations of 40 Words or More

Quotations of 40 words or more should be in a paragraph by themselves, should be indented five spaces without the customary first-line indent, and should not include quotation marks. These block quotations should also be followed by a citation that includes a page number. The citation is presented after the closing punctuation of the block quotation. If the quoted text contains quotation marks, double quotation marks should be used. Note the following example:

> Candy manufactured at the offshore facility was tainted, but testing of product made domestically revealed that it was safe. Representatives from the manufacturer claimed that the company was unaware of any problems with ingredients or machinery at the offshore plant prior to the discovery of the poisoned product. (Bradenforth, 2007, p. 238)

Italics

Use italics for introduction of a new, technical, or key term (but only on first use of the word; do not italicize the word again if it is used in subsequent sentences). Also use italics in the following instances:

- Letters used as statistical symbols
- Periodical volume numbers in the reference list
- Anchors on a scale (e.g., a survey asks respondents to rate customer service on a scale of *1* to *5*).

Parentheses

Parentheses are used in the following circumstance:

- To set off reference citations in text
- To separate letters that identify terms in a series within a sentence or paragraph
- To enclose the citation or page number of a direct quote
- To introduce an abbreviation
- To enclose numbers that represent formulas, equations, statistical values, or degrees of freedom
- Avoid use of back-to-back parenthetical text.

Hyphens

A hyphen should not be used on common fractions used as nouns (e.g., Two thirds of the students missed class); however, a hyphen should be used when the fraction is used as a descriptor (e.g., The student council requires a two-thirds majority to pass a new rule). Hyphens should also be avoided in compounds in which the first word is an adverb (e.g., The nearly vetoed legislation has finally passed) and in situations where there is no possible way a compound term could be misread without it (e.g., The health care industry lobbied Congress for this law). Do not use a space before or after a hyphen.

Dashes

APA distinguishes em dashes (two hyphens placed side by side with no space in between: —) from en dashes (which are slightly longer than a hyphen: –). Note that some word-processing programs include em dash and en dash symbols, often a combination of keystrokes or accessible from the symbols menu. As shown in the examples in the paragraphs that follow, do not add spaces before or after em dashes and en dashes.

An em dash should be used to either highlight a clause or to indicate a diversion from the sentence's primary clause (e.g., The test subjects—who were unaware of the change—disliked the nature of the treatment).

An en dash is used between words of equal weight in a compound adjective (e.g., "medication–nutrient interaction") and between page ranges (e.g., 112–114).

Using Numbers in a Document

Generally, APA style uses numerals to express numbers 10 and larger and words for numbers one through nine. One primary exception to this rule is when a number greater than 10 begins a sentence. In this case, the word should be spelled out (e.g., Forty-eight men were surveyed).

There are several exceptions in which numbers less than 10 are listed in numeric form, generally related to presenting a specific quantity measurement, such as in the following instances:

- When the numbers precede a unit of measurement or a percentage symbol
- When the numbers are used for a mathematical or statistical function
- When used to represent time, dates, ages, scores, or points on a scale
- When placed in a numbered series, parts of book chapters or tables, or in a numbered list of four or more
- When included in a research paper's abstract

If the number of days, months, or years are an approximation, write out the numbers (e.g., The ships takes approximately eight days to reach Portugal). A zero should be written before decimals and numbers that are less than one, except in decimal fractions where the number cannot be greater than one. Plurals of numbers should be written by adding -s or -es, without an apostrophe.

Abbreviations

APA style recommends minimal use of abbreviations, as they can often cause more confusion than clarification and can hinder reader comprehension. Generally, an abbreviation should be used only if (a) it is well known and a reader would be familiar with it, or (b) it saves considerable space and prevents repetition.

A writer must decide whether to spell out an expression or group name every time or spell it out initially and abbreviate it thereafter. If abbreviating, the term must be written out completely the first time, followed by its abbreviation in parentheses. Afterward, the abbreviation can be used without any further explanation.

Do not write out standard abbreviations for units of measurement on first use, but do not use the abbreviation if a specific measurement is not given (e.g., It was 3 cm in length; It was measured in centimeters).

A sentence can begin with an abbreviation or acronym that appears in all capital letters but not if it is all lowercase letters. Some abbreviations are accepted as words in APA style and do not require explanation, including the following well-known terms: IQ, REM, ESP, AIDS, and HIV.

Periods are used with abbreviations for initials of names (e.g., William S. Sanderson), to abbreviate the United States when used as an adjective (e.g., U.S. Navy), in identity-concealing labels for study participants (e.g., participants S. P. and J. M.), and with Latin and reference abbreviations (e.g., i.e., etc.).

Periods should not be used with abbreviations of state names, capital letter acronyms, or metric and nonmetric measurements; one exception is the abbreviation for inch (in.), which includes a period because of the likelihood of its confusion with the word "in."

In general, use Latin abbreviations only in parenthetical material and use the English translations of Latin abbreviations in running text (e.g., use "e.g." in parentheses and use "for example" in text). However, "et al." (and others) and "v." (for versus) should be used for citations, both parenthetical and in text (APA, 2010, pp. 106–111).

Percent and Percentages

The symbol for percent (%) should be used only when it is preceded by a numeral (e.g., 5%). The word "percent" should not be spelled out after a numeral. When a number is not given, the word "percentage" should be used (e.g., a significant percentage of women in the group preferred the reformulated product). In table headings or legends, use a percent symbol in lieu of the word "percentage" to conserve space.

Lists

Elements or ideas in a series can be enumerated to clarify their relationship. This is particularly important when a sequence is lengthy or difficult to understand. Three different forms are possible: a within-sentence list, a numbered list, or a bulleted list. Example of a within-sentence list:

The student's three choices were (a) living in the dorm with a roommate, (b) living alone in the dorm, or (c) living at home.

Listing within a Sentence with Internal Commas

When listing items within a paragraph or sentence with items that include commas, use lowercase letters in parentheses and semicolons, as shown in the following example:

■ The respondents were broken into three groups: (a) high communication apprehension, scoring more than 35; (b) moderate communication apprehension, scoring between 18 and 35; and (c) low communication apprehension, scoring below 18.

Numbered Lists

To list paragraphs in a numbered sequence, such as itemized conclusions or successive steps in a procedure, number each paragraph or sentence with an Arabic numeral followed by a period, as shown in the following example:

1. We divided the study sample into three groups based on income.
2. We further subdivided these three groups into subgroups based on race/ethnicity.
3. We calculated the average monthly income for each of these subgroups.

Bulleted Lists

Numbered lists may imply an unintended and unwanted hierarchy such as chronology or importance. In such cases, a bulleted list, as shown in the following example, is an option:

The physicians were asked questions about the following factors:

- How long they have been in practice
- How many patients they see per week on average
- How many of those patients have private insurance

Each item in the bulleted list should be indented. Items in a bulleted list may be complete sentences or parts of a longer sentence introduced with a colon, but all items in the list should be parallel (e.g., they should all start with the same part of speech or same conjugation, form, or tense of a verb).

REFERENCES AND INTERNAL CITATION STYLE

Proper documentation of sources includes two important steps: creating a reference list and using internal citations. APA guidelines require a structured reference list and parenthetical in-text citations of each source listed in the references. It is critical to carefully follow APA guidelines for placement and style of citations and references. Footnotes and endnotes are occasionally used, but they are secondary to parenthetical citations. Content footnotes are used to clarify or expand on information in the text, and copyright permission footnotes are used to identify the source of quotations. Neither type should be used in place of parenthetical citations in an APA-style research paper.

Citation Style

For parenthetical citations, include author name(s) and year of the publication. If using a direct quotation or paraphrasing a particular passage, the page number must also be included. APA style offers a variety of acceptable citation formats. Example 1 illustrates an effective way to mention the authors in the text of the sentence; it is particularly useful if the writer wishes to describe the cited author in some way. The style of Example 2 results in a complete statement without using the cited author's name in the sentence. Example 3 shows a direct quote from the reference material coupled with mention of the author's name in the sentence. Example 4 combines a direct quote and a complete statement that does not mention the author's name in the sentence.

Example 1:
According to Booth, Colomb, and Williams (2003), you should avoid plagiarism.

Example 2:
You should avoid plagiarism (Booth, Colomb, & Williams, 2003).

Example 3:
According to Booth, Colomb, and Williams (2003), "In all fields, you plagiarize when you use a source's words or ideas without citing that source" (p. 202).

Example 4:
Many authorities have commented on the topic, but this is one of the most effective descriptions: "In all fields, you plagiarize when you use a source's words or ideas without citing that source" (Booth, Colomb, & Williams, 2003, p. 202).

If a source has two to five authors, use all the names of the authors in the first citation, but in later citations, refer to secondary authors with the abbreviation "et al." If a source has six or more authors, in all citations—including the first—list only the first author followed by "et al." and the date (e.g., Smith et al., 2007). Note that if citing the same source more than once in the same paragraph, it is not necessary to include the year in the succeeding citations. See Example 5 for an illustration.

Example 5:
Plagiarism can harm your career (Booth et al., 2003). Several prominent historians have lost credibility because they had plagiarized from the works of others (Weaver et al., 2009). It is best to create your own original content and exercise caution when quoting and summarizing the content of others (Booth et al.).

Some citation styles do not meet the criteria listed previously, including the following:

- Personal communications
- Anonymous works
- Works without publication dates
- Classical works

See Figure 2 for examples of these unusual styles.

Reference Style

The APA reference style is preferred for many reasons, but primary among them is that APA style is perhaps the most common form of organizing, citing, structuring, and verifying information in universities today. APA reference style provides all the basic building blocks that make it easier to learn other styles, such as MLA, Turabian, and Chicago style, and underscores the importance of professionalism and rigor in writing. All references should be listed in alphabetical order by the first authors' last name or, if no author is listed, by the title of the source.

Assembling a Reference List

An APA reference list is more than just a simple listing of works cited. Each type of reference—a journal article, a book, a website, or a newspaper article, for example—has its own unique style. The idea behind the reference list is to give readers as much information as possible to seek out the references and gain a deeper understanding of the logic expressed in the paper by reading them. The following are general guidelines for an APA reference list:

- Sources should be arranged alphabetically by the author's last name. If there is no identified author, alphabetize the reference listing by the first main word of the title, excluding "A," "An," or "The."

REFERENCE TYPE	IN-TEXT CITATION STYLE	REFERENCE STYLE	EXPLANATION
Personal communications that include letters, memos, e-mail, nonarchived discussion groups, personal interviews, and telephone conversations	S. H. Hanson (personal communication, January 1, 2007), or (S. H. Hanson, personal communication, January 1, 2007)	Not included in reference list	Cite personal communication in the text only
No publication date given	(Hamilton, n.d.)	Hamilton, G. (n.d.). *Hope is the verb*. Boston, MA: Cambridge Press.	When no date is given, write n.d. in parentheses for in-text and reference list mentions
A work with no identified author, not designated as anonymous	("College Bound," 2007)	College bound. (2007). *Journal of Teacher Education, 45*(3) 26–31.	In the reference list, alphabetize by title
Works with group authors	(American Psychological Association, 1994)	American Psychological Association. (1994). *The APA manual of style*. Washington, DC: Author.	Alphabetize group authors, such as associations and universities, by the first significant word of the name
A work's author is designated "anonymous"	(Anonymous, 2007)	Anonymous. (2007). *Let's build bridges*. New York, NY: Prentice Hall.	In the reference list, only a work that is explicitly identified as written by "Anonymous" includes the word, which is alphabetized as such.
Classical works	(Plato, trans. 1938), or (Freud, 1931/1997)	Not required	Reference entries are not required for major classical works. That includes ancient Greek and Roman works and the Bible. In cases of the Bible, identify which version was used in the first in-text citation—for example, "(1 Cor. 13:1) [King James Version]."

FIGURE APA.2 APA Citation Style for Unusual References

- Double space or leave one blank line between each line of type in a reference list.
- The first line of a reference is set flush left, but any subsequent lines in the same reference are indented one-half inch (known as the hanging indent).
- Periods separate most parts of a reference, including (a) after the author name(s), (b) after the date, (c) after the closing parenthesis for the date of publication, and (d) at the end of the reference (except for an electronic reference, which requires no period). Periods should also be used after the first and middle initials of each author.
- Commas are used between the author's last name(s) and initials; to separate authors; between the book or periodical title and the volume number; after an issue number and before a page number; and between a volume number and page number. A colon is used to separate the city of publication and the publisher's name.
- The author's names in a reference should be listed as last name first, followed by a comma, and then the first and middle initials, and finished with a period. When there are eight or more authors, list only the first six and abbreviate the remaining authors using ellipsis points ("…"), followed by the final author. If a group or

entity is the author, spell out its full name as the author. If a second author of a book or magazine is listed with the word "with," he or she should be listed in the reference in parentheses—for example, "Porter, J. (with Rutter, K. L.)." To reference an edited book, list the editor's name in the author position and follow it with the abbreviation "Ed." or "Eds." in parentheses. If there is no author, the title of the work should be moved to the beginning of the reference.

- The year the work of a reference was copyrighted should follow the authors' names (or title, if there are no authors), appear in parentheses, and have a period at the end outside of the parentheses. For magazines, newspapers, or newsletters, the year, followed by the exact date (month and date) of the publication should be listed in parentheses. If no date is available, "n.d." should be written in parentheses and should be followed by a period.

- The title of an article or chapter comes after the date, followed by the title of the work, periodical, or book. Only the first word of the title and subtitle (if there is one) should be capitalized. The title should not be italicized or have quotation marks around it. All nonweb references should end with a period. Web-based references should include as much of the previously listed information as possible and the digital object identifier (DOI) if available or the web address of the source. If the last item in the reference is a DOI or a website address, it should not end with a period.

- The city of publication follows the title of any book or brochure. Regardless of how well-known a city is, write a comma and the appropriate two-letter abbreviation for the state or territory that is used by the U.S. Postal Service. Spell out country names. A colon should follow the city, state, or country of publication. If the publisher is a university that has the same name as the state or province (e.g., Ohio State), do not repeat the state or province in the publisher location.

- The publisher's name follows the city of publication. The name of the publisher should be as brief as possible, eliminating terms such as "Inc.," or "Co.," but the words "Books" and "Press" should be kept in the reference. If two or more publisher locations are given, give the first listed or the publisher's corporate office, if specified. A period should follow all listings.

- "Page" and "pages" should be cited as "p." and "pp." in instances where book chapters are listed. Periodical page numbers go at the end of the reference, following the title of the journal, and "p." or "pp." is not used. Book page numbers go between the title and the city of publication. All page numbers should include the entire article or chapter, and the beginning and end numbers should be separated by an en dash. Page numbers for entire books are not listed.

- Appropriate abbreviations for use in reference section and in-text citations include the following:
  - chap. = chapter
  - ed. = edition
  - Rev. ed. = revised edition
  - 2nd ed. = second edition
  - Ed. (Eds.) = editor (editors)
  - Trans. = translator(s)
  - n.d. = no date
  - p. (pp.) = page (pages)
  - Vol. = volume (as in Vol. 4)
  - Vols. = volumes (as in four volumes)

- No. = number
- Pt. = part
- Suppl. = supplement
- Tech. Rep. = technical report
  - U.S. states and territories should be indicated with the appropriate two-letter abbreviation used by the U.S. Postal Service. City names and country names should not be abbreviated (APA, 2010, p. 187).

Examples of References

Refer to the *Publication Manual* or its companion website (http://apastyle.org) if citing a resource that is not included among the examples that follow. Different sources have different requirements and rules. Books, journal articles, magazine articles, websites, and other sources each have particular requirements that give proper credit and help readers locate the reference material. If any part of the reference is not included, this amounts to failure to properly credit a source. The following 11 examples illustrate some of the more common reference styles.

Example 1: A book with a single author.

Klein, N. (2000). *No logo*. New York, NY: Picador.

Book author: The author's last name is listed first, followed by the author's first and middle initials (if applicable). The period that follows the initial is also the period that follows the first element (author's name) of the References citation.

Date of publication: The year the book was published is included in parentheses, followed by a period.

Book title: The title is italicized with all words except the first in lowercase. If there is a colon in the title, the first word following the colon is also capitalized. If the book has several editions, the edition of the text goes in parentheses following the title. This element is followed by a period.

Publication information: For all cities, include the state (e.g., Newbury Park, CA), even if the city is well known. A colon is placed after the state and followed by the name of the publisher. Omit superfluous terms such as "Publishers," "Co.," or "Inc.," but keep the words "Books" or "Press."

Example 2: A book with two to seven authors.

Rubin, R. B., Rubin, A. M., & Piele, L. J. (2000). *Communication research: Strategies and sources* (5th ed.). Belmont, CA: Wadsworth.

Book author: The author's last name is listed first, followed by the author's first and middle initials (if applicable). A comma follows the name of the first author, even when there are only two authors to list. Type "&" before the last author is listed. Authors are listed in the order they are listed on the book cover.

Date of publication, book title, and publication information: Follow the format applied in Example 1.

Example 3: A book with eight or more authors.

Brown, L. V., Ecks, T. Z., Walters, F. A., Zim, A., Ricks, J., Bynum, C. T., ... Olsen, L. (2007). *Research methods for undergraduate students*. New York, NY: Text Press.

Book author: The author's last name is listed first, followed by the author's first and middle initials (if applicable). With more than seven authors, list only the first six authors and abbreviate the remaining authors using ellipsis points ("..."), followed by the final author. Do not type "&" before the final author.

Date of publication, book title, and publication information: Follow the format applied in Example 1.

Example 4: An article with only one author in a scholarly journal.

> Kramer, M. W. (2005). Communication in community theatre groups. *Journal of Applied Communication Research, 33,* 159–182.

Article author: The author's last name is listed first, followed by the author's first and middle initials (if applicable).

Date of publication: The year the article was written is included in parentheses, followed by a period.

Article title: The article title is not italicized nor enclosed in quotation marks, and only the first word of the title and the subtitle should be capitalized. The title is followed by a period.

Journal title: The journal title is italicized and all words in the title are capitalized except articles and prepositions ("a," "the," "and," "an," "of").

Publication information: Provide the volume number (in italics) and the page numbers (not italicized) of the article. If the periodical uses successive pagination in its volumes, it is not necessary to include the issue number. If the pagination is not successive, the issue number should be included in parentheses and not italicized—for example, *Consulting Psychology Journal: Practice and Research, 45*(2), 10–36.

Example 5: An article with multiple authors in a scholarly journal.

> Rosenfeld, L. B., Richman, J. M., Bowen, G. L., & Wynns, S. L. (2006). In the face of a dangerous community: The effects of social support and neighborhood danger on high school students' school outcomes. *Southern Communication Journal, 71,* 273–289.

Article author: The author's last name is listed first, followed by the author's first and middle initials (if applicable). Type "&" before the last author is listed. Authors are listed in the order they appear on the article. With more than seven authors, list only the first six authors and abbreviate the remaining authors using ellipsis points ("..."), followed by the final author. Do not type "&" before the final author.

Date of publication, article title, journal title, and publication information: Follow the format applied in Example 4.

Example 6: A magazine article.

> Marano, H. E. (2004, August). Rock around the doc. *Psychology Today, 9,* 47–52.

Article author: The author's last name is listed first, followed by the author's first and middle initials (if applicable).

Date of publication: The year and month the article was written is included in parentheses as "(year, month)."

Article title: The article title is not italicized, and only the first word of the title and subtitle should be capitalized.

Periodical title: The periodical title is italicized, and all words in the title are capitalized except articles and prepositions ("a," "the," "and," "an," "of").

Publication information: Provide the volume number (italics) and the page numbers of the article (not italicized). If the periodical uses successive pagination in its volumes, do not add the issue number. If the pagination is not successive, the issue number should be included in parentheses and not italicized—for example, *Communication Connection*, *2*(2), 3–7.

Example 7: An online magazine or news article.

Marano, H. E., & Schwartz, B. G. (2004, August). Rock around the doc. *Psychology Today, 9,* 47–52. Retrieved from http://www.psychologytoday.com

Article author, date of publication, article title, periodical title, and publication information: Follow the format applied in Example 6.

Retrieval information: The rule for electronic resources is to list the information that will help readers find the resource. Do not include the date the document was retrieved unless there is an expectation that the material cited will change over time. Some documents include a digital object identifier (DOI), which is a number that provides a consistent means to find an online document. If the cited publication has a DOI, it is usually prominently displayed at the top of the online document. If the research document includes a DOI, include it at the end of the reference, after the page numbers. For example, Marano, H. E., & Schwartz, B. G. (2004, August). Rock around the doc. *Psychology Today, 9,* 47–50. doi:10.1187/0142-9052.78.1.298. If no DOI is available, give the home web page for the periodical, not the specific link to the article. Web pages often disappear or change, and this avoids citing expired web addresses.

Example 8: An article from a newspaper database.

Russell, P. R. (2007, May 11). Saving energy is a hot topic: Energy to develop ways to conserve. *New Orleans Times-Picayune,* p. Money 1. Retrieve0d from www.timespicayune.com

Article author: Follow the format applied in Example 7.

Date of publication: The year, month, and day the article was written are included in parentheses (year, month, day).

Article title, periodical title: Follow the format applied in Example 6.

Publication information: Follow the format applied in Example 7.

Retrieval information: The rule for electronic resources is to list the information that will help the reader find the resource. Do not include the name of the database where the article was found; instead list the newspaper's home web page address. Do not close the web page address with a period.

Example 9: An article from a newspaper with one author and nonconsecutive page numbers.

McBride, J. (2007, May 30). Pantex crew returns today: Guards union ratifies 5-year pact. *Amarillo Globe-News,* pp. A1, A6.

Article author: Follow the format applied in Example 7.

Date of publication: Follow the format applied in Example 8.

Article title, periodical title: Follow the format applied in Example 6.

Publication information: For newspapers, include the section and page number. Unlike journal citations, newspaper references do require a "p." or "pp." before the section and page number(s). If the pages are not continuous, list the page on which the article begins, insert a comma and a space, and then list the page where the article continues (e.g., pp. A1, A6).

Example 10: An article with no author, from a newspaper.

> Asarco gets approval to auction land in Salt Lake City. (2007, May 30). *Amarillo Globe-News,* p. D6.

Article author: If an article has no author, do not write "Anonymous." The article title is placed first. It is not italicized, and only the first word of the title and subtitle should be capitalized.

Date of publication: Follow the format applied in Example 8.

Article title, periodical title: Follow the format applied in Example 6.

Publication information: Follow the format applied in Example 7.

Example 11: An Internet source.

> How to publish with APA. (n.d.). Retrieved from American Psychological Association website: http://www.apastyle.org

Heading title: Websites and web pages often do not have identified author(s). In such a case, the website section heading is used at the beginning of the reference. It is not italicized, and only the first word of the title and subtitle should be capitalized.

Date of publication: A date is also not often available, so it is acceptable to reference that there is no date identified by typing (n.d.) after the heading title.

Internet site title: Identify the publisher of the resource as part of the retrieval information.

Retrieval information: The rule for electronic resources is to list the information that will help readers find the resource. Only include the complete web page address if the home page of the organization housing the document does not have a search function or if the website is large and hard to navigate, making it unlikely that the reader will be able to find the document from the home address. Do not close the web page address with a period.

Example 12: A picture from a website.

> Pollock, J. (1953). *Greyed rainbow* [Painting]. Retrieved from http://www.artic. edu/aic/collections/artwork/83642?search_id=1

Artist or photographer: Follow the format applied to authors in Example 6.

Title: The title of the picture is italicized and only the first word of the title should be capitalized. The title is followed by the medium (e.g., painting, photograph, etc.) in brackets.

Retrieval information: Follow the format applied in Example 8.

Example 13: A picture from a book.

Pollock, J. (1953). *Greyed rainbow* [Painting]. In E. G. Landau, *Jackson Pollock*
   (p. 230). New York, NY: Abradale Press.

Artist or photographer: Follow the format applied to authors in Example 6.

Title: Follow the format applied in Example 12.

Book author and title: The word "In" is followed by the author's name. First and middle initials (if applicable) precede the author's last name, which is followed by a comma. The title of the book is italicized and only the first word and any proper nouns are capitalized. The page number(s) or plate number for the artwork is set in parentheses and is not italicized.

Publication information: Follow the format applied in Example 1.

GLOSSARY

A

A+ A certification demonstrating basic technical proficiency with computer systems, offered by the Computing Technology Industry Association (CompTIA), requiring at least 500 hours of hands-on experience, the ability to identify and troubleshoot computer components and their configuration, networking knowledge, and familiarity with basic computer security.

absolute cell address A spreadsheet application code, represented by a dollar sign, indicating a cell address that should not be altered.

activation key A combination of letters and numbers a user must enter before using software. These access codes serve as an intellectual property protection for the software developer, granting a license to the user and preventing multiple downloads.

adapter card A card that adds additional functions to a computer by plugging into the motherboard.

add-ons Software downloaded to add a feature to another product; can also refer to hardware peripherals.

Advanced Research Projects Agency Network (ARPANET) The first network communications system.

animation Movement of graphics, images, or words used in a Microsoft PowerPoint® presentation.

application software These computer programs are designed to help users complete tasks on their computers or smartphones.

B

AutoSum A button in Microsoft Excel® that allows quick access to the SUM function.

AVERAGE A Microsft Excel® function that averages values or the contents of a range of cells.

Backstage View A new feature in Microsoft Office 2010® that allows users to manage files, set options, adjust data, print, and e-mail documents from one location.

bandwidth A common term for the amount of data that can be transmitted through a network connection. Bandwidth is also used to describe relative Internet connection speed for DSL and cable modems. Bandwidth is usually measured in megabits per second (Mbps).

blog An online journal or diary where an individual records his or her thoughts.

bookmark An electronic marker for a website.

boot-up process The initial procedures that occur before a computer operating system is loaded and the computer can be used.

bot Malicious program code that infects computers, usually gaining access to a system through spam e-mails.

botnet An online network of computers controlled by an outside source.

broadband service Internet service that ranges from 64 kilobits per second to 4.0 megabits per second.

browsing The process of performing a search of online categories in order to find a website or web page.

C

browsing history The record or log of websites a user visits that is kept by a computer.

bullet points Content that is indented and begins with a large dot; frequently used to set off lists.

byte The basic measurement unit of computer storage and memory, equivalent to one character of text.

cache A reference to the storage location where a computer's browser can recall files a user has accessed.

calendar subscription A link to another calendar that updates when the other calendar is changed.

carbon nanotubes Carbon molecules, formed into tiny tubes less than 1/100,000 millimeters wide.

central processing unit (CPU) The main system of a computer that controls and carries out its functions.

Certified Information Security Manager (CISM) A certification granted by ISACA (formerly Information Systems Audit and Control Association). CISM requires management experience in addition to several years' hands-on experience designing, improving, and implementing information security at the enterprise level.

Certified Information Systems Auditor (CISA) A certification granted by ISACA that requires at least five years' experience in an information technology auditing, control, or finance environment; passing of the CISA examination; and maintaining technological relevancy through continuing education.

Certified Information Systems Security Professional (CISSP) A certification granted by the International Systems Security Certification Consortium. CISSP requires a minimum of five years' hands-on experience in an information security setting, successful completion of the CISSP exam, a criminal background investigation, and an endorsement from a CISSP in good standing. A CISSP must be recertified every three years through the completion of continuing professional education credits or retaking the CISSP exam.

Cisco Certified Network Associate (CCNA) A certification granted by Cisco Corporation that demonstrates the ability to configure, install, and maintain medium-size networks that require routing or switching.

citation A quote from a larger work.

cloud computing Services and applications provided over the Internet that provide individuals and businesses readily available infrastructure to share documents, resources, and software. Social networking sites (Facebook, LinkedIn) and online gaming (World of Warcraft, Second Life) also use this technology.

cloud integration services An emerging technology by which applications help integrate and transfer data between separate clouds.

cloud service bureau Any outsourced or third-party firm that provides Software as a Service (SaaS) or other remote application-based computing services.

cluster computing The use of clusters of computers to process large amounts of data. Some uses for cluster computing are climate modeling, weather forecasting, predicting the spread of epidemics, and processing data generated by scientific research.

command A command is the language of the computer, telling the program or application what function to perform.

condition argument The value of the IF function in Microsoft Excel® that is the value you want to test.

conditional formatting A feature in Excel that allows users to format values and text based on chosen criteria. Options include colors, bolding, font changes, and adding shapes to highlight the data so that it stands out from the other values on the worksheet.

context-sensitive command These shortcut menu choices appear as a user right-clicks on the computer screen.

COUNT A Microsoft Excel® function that tallies (counts) the number of cells in a range.

COUNTA A Microsoft Excel® function that tallies the number of cells in a range not including blank cells.

COUNTBLANK A Microsoft Excel® function that tallies the number of cells in a range that are blank.

COUNTIF A Microsoft Excel® function that tallies the number of cells in a range that satisfy criteria.

credibility Whether or not a source provides reliable, accurate information, checked and verified by experts.

D

data mining The practice of searching large amounts of electronic data to find patterns.

database application A computer program that allows users to enter large amounts of data for complex record keeping, sorting, and manipulating as needed.

dial-up service Slow Internet service, defined as 56 kilobits per second or slower. Dial-up service also ties up the existing land-based phone line in a home or office.

dialog box A window that appears during the use of a computer application. The window contains a question or requests confirmation of an action the user must reply to before continuing.

digital subscriber line (DSL) A service providing users Internet access through a phone line or television cable with either a DSL modem or cable modem.

domain name The words or numbers, known as IP addresses, that identify a website.

download The transfer of a file from the Internet to your computer.

E

e-commerce The buying and selling of goods online.

e-mail Electronic mail.

e-readers Wireless digital devices that allow users to read published content on a tablet, versus buying physical books, magazines, or newspapers.

editing Correcting text by inserting, replacing, or deleting.

electronic health records (EHR) The comprehensive or aggregated health care records of an individual, collected from multiple health care providers and facilities.

electronic medical records (EMR) The individual collected and administered health care records of a single facility or health care provider.

ExpressCard A data storage plug-in for PCs.

F

fill handle The small box that appears in Microsoft Excel® on the bottom right of a cell when you select it.

fill series Created in Microsoft Excel® when data being copied suggests that it is part of a sequence, such as the name of a month or day of the week.

firewall A device that follows a set of rules for transmissions coming into a computer system to protect the system from threats such as malware and viruses.

flash drive A small, portable data storage device that uses solid-state memory, also called flash memory, to store data. It connects to any USB-capable computer.

4G A popular notation for "fourth generation" mobile communication standards still in development. Eventually, 4G expects to produce transmission speeds at least 10 times faster than current mobile transmission rates.

font A typeface design, such as Times New Roman or Verdana.

format painter A command on the *Home* tab that provides access to document formatting styles.

formatting Changing the appearance of text by changing its size, color, typeface, and so on.

function key One of the 12 keys located at the top of the computer keyboard, labeled F1 through F12. They are used to perform shortcut functions.

functions Predesigned formulas created for Microsoft Excel®.

G

gadget Standard specific programs on the computer's desktop such as the clock, calendar, or weather.

gesture-recognition software Software that can interpret human movement and respond in some way.

global positioning system (GPS) A navigation system originally developed by the U.S. military that uses 24 satellites to measure an object's position, speed, and direction. GPS receivers are in widespread use as commercial navigation aids, and many smartphones are also GPS receivers.

graphical user interface (GUI) A way to manipulate a computer system by interacting with graphics (icons, buttons, menus, and so on) instead of by typing in commands.

H

hard copy A printed copy of a document.

hard disk drive The permanent storage on a computer.

hardware The physical parts of a computer. This includes internal and external parts, such as the hard drive, memory, keyboard, and mouse.

Health Information Technology for Economic and Clinical Health Act (HITECH Act) Signed into law by President Barack Obama in 2009 as a part of the American Recovery and Reinvestment Act to provide financial incentives, beginning in 2011 and ending in 2015, to health care firms who "demonstrate meaningful use of electronic health care records."

Health Insurance Portability and Accountability Act (HIPAA) This 1996 act ensures continued access to health care plans in the event of a job change or loss and established standards governing the privacy of medical records.

home page The first page in a group of pages on a website that describes the site's purpose and provides the navigational structure for moving through the website.

hypertext markup language (HTML) A markup language that tells the browser what should appear on the web page.

hypertext transfer protocol (HTTP) The defining protocol for how a server is accessed.

I

IF function A function in Microsoft Excel® that checks the data in a cell, compares it to some set criterion, and returns a value (or text) based on whether the data meets or fails to meet the criterion.

input device A device that provides information for the computer to process.

Internet The Internet is a digital network of computers spanning the globe.

Internet service provider (ISP) A company that sells Internet connectivity to individuals.

ISO/IEC 27001:2005 An international standard developed by the International Organization for Standardization (ISO) and the International Electrotechnical Commission (IEC) that attempts to establish procedures and guidelines for information security management systems. Certification under ISO/IEC 27001:2005 is regarded as a requirement for other information security certifications.

K

key Tips A Windows Ribbon feature allowing a user to use the keyboard keys instead of a mouse to switch tabs or activate commands from the Quick Access Toolbar.

keywords A term or group of terms used to find information on the web.

L

Leadership in Energy and Environmental Design (LEED) A certification system developed by the United States Green Building Council that attempts to guarantee certain energy-usage and environmental conservation improvements pertaining to building construction. LEED is recognized as the international standard for energy-efficient and environmentally sustainable building construction and operation.

local area network (LAN) A small group of connected computers.

M

malware Computer software that works as an independent program that infects a computer's files and programs after being downloaded from what looks like a trusted source.

MAX A Microsoft Excel® function that returns the largest number in a range of cells.

medical home Also known as a patient-centered medical home, this emerging concept envisions coordinating and directing the patient's health care services, such as surgical procedures, rehabilitation and physical therapy, and mental health services, from a single point of contact.

memory card A data storage device used in digital cameras and smartphones.

menu A graphical collection of options that appears on your desktop so you can perform a function on your computer.

metropolitan area network (MAN) A large group of connected LANs that connect users in a geographical area, such as a city or campus.

Microsoft Access® The database creation and management program in the Microsoft Office suite.

Microsoft Certified IT Professional (MCITP) A certification granted by Microsoft Corporation encompassing several different certification paths. The number of courses and examinations are dependent upon the Microsoft products chosen.

Microsoft Certified Professional (MCP) A catch-all term for technology professionals who have attained one or more certifications related to Microsoft products.

Microsoft Certified Systems Engineer (MCSE) A certification granted by Microsoft Corporation. Requires completion of seven courses covering network design, configuration, and maintenance using Microsoft Server 2000® and Microsoft Server 2003®.

Microsoft Certified Technology Specialist (MCTS) A certification granted by Microsoft Corporation. MCTS certification is product and technology specific, with approximately 20 specialties offered. MCTS certification in one or more technological specialties is required for certification as MCITP and MCSE.

Microsoft Excel® The spreadsheet program in the Microsoft Office suite.

Microsoft Office 2010® A suite of computer programs created and distributed by Microsoft that includes word processing, spreadsheet, presentation, and database software.

Microsoft Office Specialist (MOS) A certification granted by Microsoft Corporation that shows expertise in all areas of Microsoft Office: Word, Excel, Access, and PowerPoint.

Microsoft OneNote® The muti-user collaboration program in the Microsoft Office suite.

Microsoft Outlook® Microsoft Outlook is a personal information manager and e-mail client that is offered as a part of the Microsoft Office software package, Microsoft Exchange Server®, and as a standalone product.

Microsoft PowerPoint® Presentation software in the Microsoft Office suite of products. The software provides the user the ability to create professional-looking presentations with graphics, sound, animations, and movie clips.

Microsoft Publisher® The desktop publishing program in the Microsoft Office suite.

Microsoft Word® The word processing program in the Microsoft Office suite.

MIN A Microsoft Excel® function that returns the smallest number in a range of cells.

mobile broadband High-speed data transmission and reception using existing cellular phone technology, taking the unused portion of voice transmission bandwidth and making it available for data transmission. It is a practical option for high-speed access in rural or inaccessible areas.

modem A hardware device that allows users to connect to a network.

monitor The screen or display of a computer.

motherboard The large circuit board of a computer where peripherals attach.

MS-DOS® An early computer operating system for the IBM PC.

N

nanosensors Made of nanomaterials, these are used to detect tiny variations resulting from stress cracks in building materials and to analyze the presence of specific gases in the air.

nanotechnology The engineering and production of functional systems smaller than 100 nanometers, a measurement that is one billionth of a meter.

netiquette Informal rules of behavior for communicating on the web.

network A group of connected computers.

network drive A location on a server where networked users can access shared files by mapping to the specific location where they reside.

new media Content not traditionally delivered in digital form that is now found online, such as music, movies, newspapers, or books.

O

online service provider (OSP) A company that sells Internet connectivity and services such as e-mail, news feeds, and proprietary content to individuals. Users can access the Internet through the OSP's browser or another provider of their choice.

open source Computer code that is free and available for anyone to use.

operating system The system software provided to a computer user by the computer manufacturer. Popular operating systems include Microsoft Windows® and the Apple Macintosh's OS.

optical disc A data storage device in the form of a CD or DVD. It is called optical because the reading and writing capabilities rely on light, in the form of a laser, to access or store data on a disc.

output device A device that accepts information from a computer and does something with it such as a monitor, printer, speaker, or headphones.

P

page name The part of a URL that defines which page you are viewing on a website.

parallel processing A data processing method used to perform complicated and processor-intensive tasks using multiple processors. This increases the efficiency and speed of overall application performance while decreasing latency issues related to processor workloads. Online gaming, Internet auction sites, data mining applications, and web mail, such as Google's Gmail, all use this technology to enhance users' experiences and achieve near-real-time responses.

Patient Protection and Affordable Care Act A sweeping national health care law, passed in 2009, that restructures many aspects of the delivery and compensation of health care in the United States. Also referred to as the "Affordable Care Act."

peripheral device Any device connected to a computer such as a printer, monitor, keyboard, computer mouse, or WiFi antenna.

personal area network (PAN) A very small space that contains all the connected devices in proximity to an individual.

personal digital assistant (PDA) A portable handheld device that uses a PIM to keep track of appointments, e-mail and communications contacts, journal entries, and other personal information.

personal information manager (PIM) A software application that keeps track of personal data, e-mail, calendar events, and contacts.

personal organizers A generic term for personal information management software and the device on which the applications are installed. Originally, a personal organizer referred to a contact folder, journal, calendar, and notebook all combined within a case or book cover.

pervasive computing Also called ubiquitous computing, the concept that computing devices are embedded in everyday objects and communicate constantly with networks and users.

phishing The practice of using spam e-mail to elicit a response and obtain a computer user's private information.

platform The hardware and operating system of a computer.

placeholder A space on a Microsoft PowerPoint® slide designated by a dotted outline for text insertion.

point A unit of measurement for sizing text in word processing programs.

pointing Clicking on a cell or dragging over a range of cells for use in a formula.

pointing device An input device that moves the computer's cursor around or is used to click to choose a function. Examples include the computer's mouse and the pointing stick or touchpad on a laptop.

pop-up blocker Software that limits or removes pop-up advertisements from your screen.

presentation application A computer program that allows users to create a show to display for an audience with the ability to include media. One example is Microsoft PowerPoint®.

processor The computing center of a computer where all information is processed.

productivity software Software that provides users with word processing, database management, spreadsheets, and personal information management applications.

protocol The set of rules governing how computers communicate with one another.

Q

Quick Access Toolbar A group of frequently used commands on the Windows Ribbon interface. You can customize the set of commands it displays.

R

random access memory (RAM) The temporary storage on a computer.

range A block of cells in Excel.

raw computing The processing of data by a computer, such as filing or filtering. Raw computing is also a common term for processing very large amounts of data by dedicated computer systems or clusters of computers.

Recycle Bin A location on the desktop, represented by a wastepaper basket icon, where files appear after you delete them. In this location, you can retrieve deleted files or permanently delete them.

relative addressing A function of Excel that copies the cell references relative to the location of the formula when a formula is copied or moved.

rootkit A computer virus that attacks a computer's internal storage system.

S

Scale to Fit A feature in Microsoft Office® that allows users to shrink the font size in a document so that it prints on a single page.

scroll bar Sliding control tools on the bottom and side of the computer window that allow you to navigate within your document.

search engine An automated database that delivers a list of links as a response to a specific keyword request from the user.

Security+ An information security certification granted by CompTIA. Security+ requirements include two years' experience in an information technology security setting and successful completion of the Security+ examination. Security+ is also an elective certification for MCSE certification.

server The host computer that delivers web pages and other applications to your browser.

shortcut The graphical icons on your desktop for programs you access frequently or those you choose to access directly from your desktop.

slide deck A common term used for a collection of Microsoft Power-Point® slides that form a working or finished presentation.

smartphone A mobile phone that incorporates advanced features such as web browsing, e-mail, multimedia streaming, video, and photo capture. Most smartphones connect directly to computers to synchronize and update data and contacts using third-party applications.

snapshot A file that can be e-mailed to another person and is not linked to the original calendar or updated.

social engineering The usually criminal practice of manipulating a person into providing sensitive information online.

social network An online community.

software A program that is not a physical device that directs the computer to perform certain tasks.

Software as a Service (SaaS) Applications accessed on remote servers via an Internet connection. SaaS applications allow access by a browser, run remotely, and close when the remote user completes the task. Examples of SaaS are Google Docs™, chat clients, and video upload services such as YouTube™.

software upgrade A change in an application or new feature added to a software program that a developer releases, usually on the Internet, for users to add.

solid-state memory A storage solution that uses electric charges to read and write data.

spam Unsolicited mass-produced e-mail.

spider The program used by search engines to look for requested content on the web.

spreadsheet application A computer program that allows a user to create worksheets with data in rows and columns to sort and manipulate as needed. One example is Microsoft Excel®.

status bar This is a row of information about the current application that appears at the bottom of the document window.

storage device A device that keeps a computer's information, even when the machine is off, until the user decides to delete the information; examples include hard disk drives, CDs, DVDs, and online storage.

SUM An Excel function that totals values or the contents of a range of cells.

system software Software that operates a computer hardware's most common tasks such as transferring data between components or sending data to display on the computer's monitor.

T

task bar Appears at the bottom of the computer desktop screen and displays all running programs, frequently used programs, diagnostics, and the date and time.

telemedicine The use of telecommunications technology to assist in the diagnosis, treatment, and monitoring of medical conditions. Examples include digital transmission of vital statistics between a patient and a care facility, transmission of x-rays or MRI images to an off-site facility for interpretation, and refilling prescriptions by e-mail.

transitions An option in Microsoft PowerPoint® that allows you to choose different effects when you move to another slide during a presentation. These effects include a slow fade, a spiral effect, or a wipe from top to bottom.

Trojan horse A computer virus disguised as a normal program that infects a computer after being downloaded from an e-mail, pop-up advertisement, or downloaded software.

trolls People who intentionally disrupt online discussions.

U

uniform resource locator (URL) The combination of words and numbers of a web address.

United States Green Building Council (USGBC) A nonprofit organization formed in 1993, dedicated to the development of environmentally responsible and energy-efficient building construction and maintenance. USGBC was the principal architect of LEED.

USB flash drive A small data storage device, also known as a thumb drive, designed to plug into a computer's USB port. Some drives hold more than 32GB of data.

utility program Computer software that maintains the system for maximum performance. Examples of utility programs are a computer's antivirus program or the regular data backup.

V

value_if_false argument The value of the IF function in Microsoft Excel® that is what you want to happen if the condition is not met.

value_if_true argument The value of the IF function in Microsoft Excel® that is what you want to happen if the condition is met.

virus Computer software unknowingly downloaded from what looks like a trusted source that is designed to infect a computer's programs and files by using those programs and files to attack others on the system.

virus protection program Software installed on a computer that runs regular checks of programs and files, alerting the computer's owner of any viruses.

W

Web 2.0 The evolution of the Internet from a place to consume information to a place to participate in content creation such as social networks, blogs, and wikis.

web browser The software used to access websites on the Internet.

web mail Internet-based e-mail accessed via a browser or other web-based application. Web mail is accessed and stored on remote servers in the cloud.

what-if analysis Testing various scenarios by re-entering spreadsheet data in order to recalculate formulas and thus gauge the impact of proposed changes.

wide area network (WAN) A large, often global group of connected computers.

WiFi (wireless fidelity) A trademark of the nonprofit Wi-Fi Alliance. The term has come to define the ability of certain devices such as computers, multimedia players, and networking devices to connect to the Internet via a wireless interface.

WiFi access point A location from which WiFi radio waves travel so that people can access the Internet.

Windows Explorer The main file manager for Windows 7® operating systems, providing the graphical user interface.

wireless Internet service provider A company that provides Internet connectivity through radio waves.

wireless local area network (WLAN) A group of connected computers with access to a signal over radio waves, such as WiFi.

word processing A computer program that allows a user to create documents with text. One example is Microsoft Word®.

World Wide Web (web) A collection of Internet sites that provide text, graphics, sound, video, and other digital content.

worm Standalone malware that infects a computer after being downloaded from an e-mail, pop-up advertisement, or downloaded software.

WYSIWYG (what-you-see-is-what-you-get) A computer system with the ability to show a document's editing and formatting changes on the screen as they are made.

PHOTO CREDITS

Chapter 1: Opener, p. 2: © iofoto (Fotolia); p. 4: © sellingpix (Fotolia); p. 5: © Marion Wear (Fotolia); p. 6: © Yuri Arcurs (Fotolia); p. 8, top: © Vicky (Fotolia); p. 8, bottom: © Yuri Arcurs (Fotolia); p. 9: © Yuri Arcurs (Fotolia); p. 10: © Pavel Losevsky (Fotolia).

Preface Opener, p. VI: © Sebastian Duda (Fotolia); p. VII, top: © iQoncept (Fotolia); p. VII, bottom: © iQoncept (Fotolia).

Chapter 1 Opener, p. 2: © Dash (Fotolia); p. 3, top: © soupstock (Fotolia); p. 3, bottom: © rudybaby (Fotolia); p. 5, top: © daboost (Fotolia); p. 5, bottom: © Mardis Coers (Fotolia); p. 7: © pressmaster (Fotolia); p. 8, top: © jim (Fotolia); p. 8, bottom: © cphoto (Fotolia); p. 11: © Sublimages (Fotolia); p. 12: © bagpereira (Fotolia); p. 14: © Thomas Pajot (Fotolia); p. 17: © iQoncept (Fotolia); p. 18: © Francesco Bisignani (Fotolia); p. 20: © A1Stock (Fotolia); p. 22: © endostock (Fotolia).

Chapter 2 Opener, p. 24: © verte (Fotolia); p. 24, bottom: © Scanrail (Fotolia); p. 27, left: © Dudarev Mikhail (Fotolia); p. 27, right: © Ivan Hafizov (Fotolia); p. 28: © Yuri Arcurs (Fotolia); p. 29, top: © Paul Pirosca (Fotolia); p. 29, bottom: © alphaspirit (Fotolia); p. 31: © HaywireMedia (Fotolia); p. 32: © Sirgunhik (iStockphoto); p. 33: © Sven Bähren (Fotolia); p. 34: © gunnar3000 (Fotolia); p. 36: © Paul Fleet (Fotolia); p. 38: © Luminis (Fotolia); p. 40: © gunnar3000 (Fotolia).

Chapter 3 Opener, p. 42: © Taras Livyy (Fotolia); p. 43: © jim (Fotolia); p. 44, top: © Andrey Zyk (Fotolia); p. 44, bottom: © chagin (Fotolia); p. 45: © Feng Yu (Fotolia).

Chapter 4 Opener, p. 82: © kristian sekulic (iStockphoto); p. 83: © Lisa F. Young (Fotolia); p. 120: © goodluz (Fotolia).

Chapter 5 Opener, p. 138: © goodluz (Fotolia); p. 139, top: © nyul (Fotolia); p. 139, bottom: © Jim Barber (Fotolia); p. 140: © Kati Molin (iStockphoto); p. 158: © FrankU (Veer).

Chapter 6 Opener, p. 188: © nyul (Fotolia); p. 189: © pressmaster (Fotolia); p. 190, top: © Dmitry Goygel-Sokol (Fotolia); p. 190, bottom: © Anatoly Tiplyashin (Fotolia).

Chapter 7 Opener, p. 236: © olly (Fotolia); p. 237, top: © Anton Balazh (Fotolia); p. 237, bottom: © JJAVA (Fotolia); p. 238: © Barry Barnes (Fotolia); p. 239: © Elenathewise (Fotolia).

Chapter 8 Opener, p. 264: © James Thew (Fotolia); p. 265, middle: © Amy Walters (Fotolia); p. 265, lower-left: © daboost (Fotolia); p. 265, lower-right: © AZP Worldwide (Fotolia); p. 267: © lapencia (Fotolia); p. 268: © goodluz (Fotolia); p 269: © kastock (Fotolia); p. 271, top: © bloomua (Fotolia); p. 271, bottom: © Kurhan (Fotolia); p. 273: © auremar (Fotolia); p. 276: © Uwe Annas (Fotolia); p. 277: © AlienCat (Fotolia).

Appendix A Opener, A-2: © Scanrail (Fotolia).

Appendix B Opener, C-2: © Yuri Arcurs (Fotolia); B-3, top: © tuulijumala (Fotolia); B-3, bottom: © bagpereira (Fotolia).

Appendix C Opener, C-2: © Elenathewise (Fotolia).

Appendix D Opener, D-2: © Elenathewise (Fotolia).

Appendix E Opener, E-2: © Yuricami (Fotolia).

INDEX

A

Absolute cell address (Excel), 166
Access. *See* Microsoft Access
Activation key, 15
Adapter card, 5
Add-ons, 31
Address book (Outlook), 251–252
Addressing, in Excel, 165–166
Addressing e-mail (Outlook), 244
Advanced Research Projects Agency
  Network (ARPANET), 26
Alignment
  in Excel, 152
  in Word, 103–104
Amazon, 269, 276
Animations
  customizing in PowerPoint, 228–230
  defined, 190
Anonymity, online, 37
A certification, 274
A Hardware Certificate, 275
Apple, 3, 276
Apple Macintosh, 4, 13
Applications, 16–17. *See also* Microsoft
  Office 2010; *specific applications*
  graphics, 18
  software suites, 17
  web, 14
Appointments (Outlook), 256–260
Archiving e-mail (Outlook), 255
ARPANET (Advanced Research
  Projects Agency Network), 26
Attachments, e-mail, 246–247
Autism, 277
AutoCorrecting, 79
AutoFilter (Excel), 174
Automated reminders, 237–238
AutoSum (Excel), 162–163
AVERAGE function (Excel), 161

B

Background formatting (PowerPoint),
  209–212
Backing up, 12
Backstage View, 70, A-7–A-8
Bandwidth, 269
Banerjee, Prith, 268
Bar chart, 174
Barnes & Noble, 276
Berners-Lee, Tim, 28
Blogs, 33

Bookmark, 30
Boot-up process, 267
Borders
  in Excel, 155
  in PowerPoint, 221
Bot, 252
Botnet, 252
Bricklin, Dan, 139–140
Brightness, of PowerPoint
  images, 219
Broadband service, 27, 266
Browse button, 72–73
Browsers, 26, 31
Browsing, 35
Browsing history, 255
Bulleted lists, 108–109
Bullying, online, 37
Buying computers, 20–21
Byte, 6

C

Cache, 255
Calendar (Outlook), 256–261
  adding appointments and events,
    258–259
  appointments, 256–260
  editing and deleting appointments
    and events, 259
  events, 258–259
  meetings, 256–258
  sharing, 261, 262
  Tasks, 260–261
Calendar subscriptions, 261, 262
Carbon nanotubes, 267
CDs, 10–11
Centered text, 104
Central processing unit (CPU), 6, 42
Certification trends, 274–275
Certified Information Security
  Manager (CISM), 274
Certified Information Systems Auditor
  (CISA), 275
Certified Information Systems Security
  Professional (CISSP), 275
Character formatting (Word),
  100–102
Charts and graphs (Excel), 174–179
  embedded, 176–177
  modifying, 177–179
  types of, 174
CISA (Certified Information Systems
  Auditor), 275

Cisco Certified Network Associate
  (CCNA), 275
CISM (Certified Information Security
  Manager), 274
CISSP (Certified Information Systems
  Security Professional), 275
Citations, 36, 37
Closing
  files, 74, A-9–A-10
  windows, 54, 55, A-2-1
Cloud computing, 268–270
Cloud integration services, 270
Cloud service bureau, 269
Cloud storage, 10
Cluster computing, 269–270
Color, in Excel worksheets, 156
Column chart, 174
Columns (Excel)
  adjusting, 154, D-11–D-12
  deleting, 149–150, D-7
  inserting, 149–150, D-6
Columns (Word), 128–129. *See also*
  Tables (Word)
Commands (Office 2010), 53,
  78–80, A-10–A-11
Comment feature (PowerPoint),
  231–232
Communication, electronic, 25
Communications devices, 12
Compressing files, 67–68
Compressing images (PowerPoint),
  220
Computers, 4–22
  basic operations, 5
  buying, 20–21
  defined, 2, 4
  hardware, 5–12
  networks, 18–19
  shutting down, 44, 45, 47
  software, 13–18
  starting and operating, 44–46
  types of, 4
Computing, 2–3
  future of, 264–279
  pervasive, 278
  raw, 268
Condition argument (Excel), 182
Construction management, 273
Contact groups, e-mail (Outlook),
  251–252
Context-sensitive menus, 76
Contrast
  in Excel worksheets, 156
  of PowerPoint images, 219

Copy and paste
  in Excel, 164–169, D-12–D-13
  from Excel to Word, 184
  text, in Word, 98–99
Copy command, 78, A-10
Copying. *See also* Copy and paste
  files, 58
  PowerPoint slides, 230
Copyrighted images, 219
Copyright infringement, 15
COUNTA function (Excel), 162
COUNTBLANK function (Excel),
  162
COUNT function (Excel), 161
COUNTIF function (Excel), 162
CPU (processor/central processing
  unit), 6, 42
Credibility, of online sources, 35–36
Custom animations (PowerPoint),
  228–230
Cut command, 78, A-10
Cutting text, 98–99
Cybercrime, 39

D

Database applications, 17
Data mining, 38
Data storage, future of, 267–268.
  See also Memory
Dates, in Excel, 182
Deleting
  calendar appointments and
    events, 259
  Excel rows and columns, 149–150,
    D-7
  files, 58
  Word table columns and rows, 126
Delivery, innovations in, 268
Design tab (Excel), 177
Desktop (Windows 7), 50–51
Desktop computers, 4, 20
Dialog boxes, 53, 77
Dial-up service, 27
Digital subscriber line (DSL), 12
Discussions, online, 38
Document files, 57
Document formatting (Word),
  111–116
Document Information Panel, 79–80
Domain names, 26, 31, 35–36, B-6
Download, 13–14
Drafts of e-mail, saving, 244
Dragging, to created Outlook
  items, 261
Drive letters, 9
DSL (digital subscriber line), 12
DVDs, 10–11

E

Ease of Access (Windows 7), 48
E-commerce (electronic commerce), 25
Editing
  calendar appointments and
    events, 259
  data in Excel, 148–151, D-6
  text, 76, 97–100, 204–205,
    C-6–C-9
Education, online, 275–276
Electronic commerce (e-commerce), 25
Electronic health records (EHR), 271
Electronic medical records
  (EMR), 271
Electronic Numerical Integrator and
  Computer (ENIAC), 3
E-mail (Outlook), 242–255
  adding attachments to, 246–247
  adding signature to, 244–245
  address book and contact groups,
    251–252
  archiving, 255
  in business settings, 254–255
  composing, addressing, and
    sending, 244
  conversations, 249–250
  creating e-mail account, 243
  forwarding, 247
  managing inbox, 247–249
  netiquette, 254, 255
  opening, reading, printing, and
    closing, 245–246
  personal organizers for, 238
  phishing and scams, 253–254
  replying to, 247
  saving drafts of, 244
  security, 252–253
  spam, 39
Embedded charts and graphs (Excel),
  176–177
EMR (electronic medical records), 271
ENIAC (Electronic Numerical
  Integrator and Computer), 3
Entering
  Excel data, 148, 150–151, D-5
  PowerPoint text, 203, 206
  text, 76, 92–95
Entertainment software, 16–17, 25
Envelopes, 132–133
E-readers, 276
Ergonomics, 12
Events, calendar (Outlook), 258–259
Excel. *See* Microsoft Excel
Excel window, 142
Exporting slides, 230–231
ExpressCard, 9, 10
External hard drives, 8–9

F

File extensions, 66–67
File formats, 66
File management, A-2–A-11
  manipulating desktop windows,
    A-2–A-4
  Ribbon interface, A-10–A-11
  working with files and folders,
    A-4–A-6
  working with Microsoft Office 2010,
    A-6–A-10
Files
  closing, 74
  compressing and zipping, 67–68
  copying, 58
  creating, 69–71
  deleting, 58
  formats of, 66
  moving, 58
  in Office 2010, 69–74
  opening, 72, 73
  organizing within folders, 59–63
  printing, 73–74
  renaming, 58
  saving to folders, 63–68, A-5–A-6
  types of, 57–58
  working with, A-4–A-6
File-sharing software, 15
File size, for PowerPoint
  presentations, 192
Fill handle (Excel)
  copy and paste with, 166
  fill series with, 167–168
Fill series (Excel), 167–168
Filtering lists (Excel), 174
Find and Replace, 78
  in PowerPoint, 205
  in Word, 99
Firewalls, 253
Flash drives, 9, 10, 268
Flash memory storage, 9–10
Floppy disk drives, 9
Folders (Office 2010)
  creating, 61–62, A-4–A-5
  expanding and collapsing, 62–63
  organizing files within, 59–60
  saving files to, 63–68, A-5–A-6
  working with, A-4–A-6
Folders, e-mail (Outlook), 247–249
Folder window, 62
Fonts, for PowerPoint
  presentations, 192
Footers
  for Excel worksheets, 171
  in Word documents, 114–115
Footnotes (Word), 115–116
Format Painter, 78

Format tab (Excel), 179
Formatting (Excel)
  cells, D-7–D-10
  Conditional, 179–181
  numbers, 152–154
  text, 151–157
Formatting (PowerPoint), 206–212
  background, 209–212
  paragraph, 209
  themes, 206–209
Formatting (Word)
  character, 100–102
  page and document, 111–116
  paragraph, 101, 103–108, 111
  saving as a style, 110–111
  text, 110–116, 119–120, C-9–C-10
Formula bar (Excel), 143–144
Formulas (Excel), 158–164
  AutoSum, 162–163
  building formulas, 158–160
  functions, 160–162
Forwarding e-mail (Outlook), 247
4G, 266
Frankston, Bob, 140
Function keys, 45–47
Functions (Excel formulas), 160–162
Future of computing, 264–279
  certification in IT trends, 274–275
  cloud computing, 268–270
  companion robots, 277
  data storage, 267–268
  health IT trends, 270–272
  industry IT trends, 273–274
  innovations in delivery, 268
  nanotechnology, 267
  in the next five years, 265
  online education, 275–276
  publishing trends, 276
  requirements for, 266
  smartphones, 277–278

G

Gadgets, 51
Gesture-recognition software, 278
Gigabyte, 6
Global positioning systems
  (GPSs), 266
Google Chrome, 30, B-5
Go To, 78
GPSs (global positioning systems), 266
Grammar Checking, 79, 95, 117–119,
  A-10–A-11, C-11
Graphical user interface (GUI),
  8, 13, 44
Graphics (Office 2010), 79
Graphics (PowerPoint), 214–223

adding borders, 221
adding shapes, 220–221
compressing images, 220
correcting images, 219
images, 214–217, 219
movie clips, 217–218
pictures, 218
sound clips, 218
Graphics (Word), 121–123
  inserting, 121–122, C-12–C-14
  resizing, 122–123
  wrapping text around, 123
Graphics software, 18
Graphs (Excel). See Charts and
  graphs (Excel)
Gridlines (Excel), 155
Guest Account (Windows 7), 48–50

H

Handouts (PowerPoint)
  creating, 227–228
  sending to Word, 232
Hanging indents, 108
Hard disk drives, 6, 8–9
Hardware, 5–12
  communications devices, 12
  defined, 5, 28, 42
  input devices, 7
  Internet, 28
  output devices, 6–7
  peripherals, 6
  storage devices, 8–12
  system unit, 5–6
Headers
  for Excel worksheets, 171
  for Word documents, 114–115
Health Information Technology for
  Economic and Clinical Health Act
  (HITECH Act), 270
Health Insurance Portability and
  Accountability Act (HIPAA), 272
Health IT trends, 270–272
Help
  Excel, 141–142, 146–147, D-3
  Office 2010, 80, A-11
  PowerPoint, 193–194, 202
  Word, 87–88, 91, C-3
Help and Support (Windows 7),
  53–54
HIPAA (Health Insurance Portability
  and Accountability Act), 272
HITECH Act (Health Information
  Technology for Economic and
  Clinical Health Act), 270
Holidays, on calendar, 259
Home page, 29

HTML (hypertext markup language),
  253
HTTP (hypertext transfer
  protocol), 31

I

IBM, 3, 278
IF function (Excel), 181–182
Images (PowerPoint), 214–217, 219
  compressing, 220
  copyrighted, 219
  correcting, 219
Importing slides, 230
Indents (Word), 107–109
Industry IT trends, 273–274
Inkjet printers, 8
Input devices, 6, 7
Inserting (PowerPoint)
  images, 214–217, 219
  movie clips, 217–218
  pictures, 218
  sound clips, 218
Inserting (Word)
  graphics, 121–122, C-12–C-14
  table columns and rows, 125–126
  tables, C-14–C-15
  text, 93–94
Inserting graphics and symbols
  (Office 2010), 79
Inserting rows and columns (Excel),
  149–150, D-6
Intellectual property, 36
  copyrighted images, 219
  copyright infringement, 15
Intel Pentium, 6
Internet, 18–19, 24–40, B-2–B-6
  accessing, 26–28
  connecting to, B-2–B-3
  defined, 24
  history of, 26
  networks, 18–19, B-2
  power of, 24–26
  security, 39
  service providers, B-3–B-4
  social issues with, 37–38
  Web 2.0, 32–34
  web research, 33–37
  and World Wide Web, 28–32
Internet Explorer, 29, 30, B-4
Internet service providers (ISPs),
  26, 27
IPv4 (Internet Protocol version 4), 266
IPv6 (Internet Protocol version 6),
  266, 270
ISO-IEC 27001:2005, 274
ISPs (Internet service providers), 26, 27

J

Justified text, 104

K

Keyboard, 6, 7
  function keys, 45–47
  repeat rate, 120
Keyboard shortcuts, 45–47
Key Tips, 75
Keywords, 33–35, B-6
Kilobyte, 6
Kobo, 276

L

Labels (Excel)
  formatting, 151–157
  too wide for cell, 149
Labels (Word), 132–134
Laptop computers, 4, 21
Laser printers, 8
Layouts, slide (PowerPoint), 212–214
Layout tab (Excel), 177–178
Leadership in Energy and Environ-
  mental Design (LEED), 273–274
Left-aligned text, 104
Licensing software, 15
Line chart, 174
Line spacing (Word), 104
Lists (Excel), 173–174
  filtering, 174
  sorting, 173
Lists (Word), 108–109
Local area network (LAN), 19, 26
Lotus 1-2-3, 140

M

Magazines, 276
Mail Merge, using Excel workbook
  as data source for, 134
Mainboard, 5
Malware, 39, 253
MAN (metropolitan area network), 19
Margins
  for Excel worksheets, 170
  for Word documents, 112
Mattessich, Richard, 139
MAX function (Excel), 161
Maximizing windows, 54, 55, A-2
MCITP (Microsoft Certified IT
  Professional), 275
MCP (Microsoft Certified
  Professional), 275

MCSE (Microsoft Certified Systems
  Engineer), 274
MCTS (Microsoft Certified Technol-
  ogy Specialist), 275
Medical homes model, 270–271
Meetings, on calendar (Outlook),
  256–258
Megabyte, 6
Memory
  flash memory storage, 9–10
  future for, 267–268
  random access memory, 6
Memory card, 9, 10
Menus, 52
  context-sensitive, 76
  shortcut, 76
Metropolitan area network (MAN), 19
Microsoft Access, 69, 71
Microsoft Certified IT Professional
  (MCITP), 275
Microsoft Certified Professional
  (MCP), 275
Microsoft Certified Systems Engineer
  (MCSE), 274
Microsoft Certified Technology
  Specialist (MCTS), 275
Microsoft Excel, 68, 139–186
  adjusting columns, D-11–D-12
  adjusting rows, D-11
  business tasks using, 139
  charts and graphs, 174–179
  Conditional Formatting, 179–181
  copying and pasting in, 164–169,
    D-12–D-13
  copying and pasting to Word
    from, 184
  creating workbooks in, 140–141,
    146–147, D-2–D-3
  data/labels too wide for cells in, 149
  dates in, 182
  deleting rows and columns,
    149–150, D-7
  editing data in, 148–151, D-6
  entering data in, 148, 150–151, D-5
  Excel application window, 142
  formatting cells, 151–157,
    D-7–D-10
  Formula bar, 143–144
  formulas, 158–164
  Help, 141–142, 146–147, D-3
  IF/THEN functions, 181–182
  inserting rows and columns,
    149–150, D-6
  lists, 173–174
  monthly billing report with,
    184–186
  named ranges in, 182–183
  navigating in, 144–145, D-5

printing worksheets, 169–172
  Ribbon, 142–143
  selecting in, 145
  sizing pages, D-4
  status bar, 146
  using Access vs., 71
  using workbook as Mail Merge
    data source, 134
  viewing pages, D-4
  worksheet area, 144
  worksheet design, 147–148
Microsoft Internet Explorer, 29,
  30, B-4
Microsoft Office 2010, 68–80
  common commands, 78–80
  conventions for working with dialog
    boxes, 77
  creating files, 69–71
  file management, A-6–A-10
  Ribbon, 74–75
  shortcut menu, 76
  working with text, 76–77
Microsoft Office Specialist
  (MOS), 275
Microsoft OneNote, 69
Microsoft Outlook, 68, 69
  business tasks using, 240–241
  calendar, 256–261
  defined, 236
  dragging to create items in, 261
  e-mail, 242–255
  Navigation Pane, 241
  origin of, 239–240
  Preview Pane, 241–242
  Reading Pane, 242
  view settings, 242
Microsoft PowerPoint, 68, 188–234
  adding borders, 221
  adding shapes, 220–221
  adding slides, 212–214, E-7–E-8
  adding transitions, 224–225
  background formatting, 209–212
  business tasks using, 189
  changing slide layouts, 212–214
  comment feature, 231–232
  compressing images, 220
  copying and importing slides, 230
  correcting images, 219
  creating handouts, 227–228
  creating new presentations, 193–196,
    202, E-2–E-4
  creating sales presentations, 233–234
  custom animations, 228–230
  defined, 188
  deleting slides, E-9
  editing text, 204–205, E-5
  entering text, 203, 206, E-4
  exporting slides, 230–231

Microsoft PowerPoint (*Continued*)
  formatting in, 206–212, E-5–E-7
  graphics, 214–223
  Help, 193–194, 202
  images, 214–217, 219
  movie clips, 217–218
  Notes Pane, 223
  paragraph formatting, 209
  pictures, 218
  planning presentations, 190–192
  PowerPoint window, 196–198
  printing presentations, 226–227,
    E-10–E-13
  selecting in, 203–204, E-5
  sending handouts to Word, 232
  sound clips, 218
  status bar options, 200
  themes, 206–209
  viewing slide shows, 225–226,
    E-9–E-10
  views, 198–202
  working with slides, 223–224
Microsoft Publisher, 68, 69
Microsoft Word, 68, 84–136
  alignment, 103–104
  bulleted and numbered lists, 108–109
  character formatting, 100–102
  columns, 128–129
  copying and pasting from Excel
    to, 184
  creating documents, 84–85,
    C-2–C-3
  document formatting, 111–116
  editing text, 97–100, C-6–C-9
  entering text, 92–95
  envelopes, 132–133
  graphics, 121–123, C-12–C-14
  Help feature, 87–88, 91, C-3
  indents, 107–108
  labels, 132–134
  line spacing, 104
  navigating pages, C-5
  page formatting, 111–116, C-9–C-10
  paragraph formatting, 101,
    103–108, 111
  paragraph spacing, 104–105
  saving formatting as a style, 110–111
  selecting text, 95–96, C-5
  sizing pages, C-4
  Spell and Grammar Checking,
    117–119, C-11
  status bar, 89–91
  tables, 124–128, C-14–C-15
  tabs, 105–107
  text formatting, 100–116, 119–120,
    C-9–C-10
  viewing pages, C-4
  Word application window, 85–87

MIN function (Excel), 161
Minimizing windows, 55, A-3
Mobile broadband, 266
Mobile devices, 4
Modem, 26, B-3
Modifying charts and graphs (Excel),
  177–179
Monitors, 6, 8
Monthly billing report project,
  184–186
MOS (Microsoft Office
  Specialist), 275
Mosaic, 29
Motherboard (mainboard), 5
Mouse, 6, 7
  keyboard alternatives to using, 45–47
  operating, 45
  pointer speed, 120
  using, 44–46
Movie clips (PowerPoint), 217–218
Moving
  files, 58
  windows, 55, A-3
Mozilla Firefox, 30, B-5
MS-DOS, 3, 4
Music files, 57, 218

N

Named ranges (Excel), 182–183
Nanosensors, 267
Nanotechnology, 267
Navigating
  Excel worksheets, 144–145, D-5
  the web, B-4–B-5
  websites, 32
  Word pages and documents, 93, C-5
Navigation Pane (Outlook), 241
Navigation software, 42–80
  Microsoft Office 2010, 68–80
  operating system, 43–44
  saving files into folders, 63–68
  starting and operating the computer,
    44–46
  starting programs with Start menu,
    52–54
  starting Windows 7, 46–51
  working with files and folders, 59–63
  working with Windows 7, 54–59
Netbooks, 4
Netiquette, 37, 254, 255
Netscape Navigator, 29–30
Network drive, 64
Networking, 19
Networks, 18–19
  defined, 26
  on Internet, B-2
New media, 25

Newsletters, creating, 135–136
Newspapers, 276
Notebook computers, 4
Notes Pane (PowerPoint), 223
Numbered lists, 108–109
Number formatting (Excel), 152–154

O

Office 2010. *See* Microsoft Office
  2010
Office Help, 80
OneNote, 69
Online discussions, 38
Online education, 275–276
Online service providers (OSPs),
  26, 27
Opening
  files, 72–73, A-7–A-9
  windows, 54, 55, A-2
OpenOffice suite, 80
Open source, 30
  Mozilla Firefox, 30
  OpenOffice suite, 80
Operating systems, 15–16, 43–44
  defined, 54
  MS-DOS, 3
  and pointer speed, 120
  for today's computers, 44
Optical discs, 10–11
O'Reilly, Tim, 32
Orientation
  of Excel worksheets, 169–170
  of Word document pages, 112–113
OSPs (online service providers), 26, 27
Outlook. *See* Microsoft Outlook
Output devices, 6–7

P

Page name, 31
Pages (Excel)
  navigating, D-5
  sizing, D-4
Pages (Word)
  formatting, 111–116, 119–120,
    128–129, C-9–C-10
  navigating, C-5
  sizing, C-4
  viewing, C-4
PAN (personal area network), 19
Paper orientation (Word), 112–113
Paragraph formatting
  (PowerPoint), 209
Paragraph formatting (Word), 101,
  103–108, 111
  alignment, 103–104

indents, 107–108
spacing, 104–105
tabs, 105–107
Parallel processing, 265
Paste. *See* Copy and paste
Paste command, 78, A-10
Paste Special command, 78
Patient Protection and Affordable
    Care Act, 272
PCs (personal computers), 3, 9
PDAs (personal digital assistants), 239
Peripheral devices, 6. *See also*
    specific devices
    defined, 268
    in the future, 268
Personal area network (PAN), 19
Personal computers (PCs), 3, 9
Personal digital assistants (PDAs), 239
Personal information management
    systems, 236–240. *See also* Microsoft
    Outlook
Personal information managers
    (PIMs), 238–239
Personal organizers, 238
Pervasive computing, 278
Phishing, 39, 253–254
Picture files, 58
Pictures (PowerPoint), 218
Pie chart, 174
PIMs (personal information
    managers), 238–239
Placeholders (PowerPoint slides),
    199
Platforms, 4–5
Pointer speed, 120
Pointing
    in Excel, 158
    in Word, 93
Pointing device, 7. *See also* Mouse
Pop-up blockers, 31
Portable computers, 20
Portable devices, cloud computing
    and, 269
Positioning text, 93–94
PowerPoint. *See* Microsoft PowerPoint
Preinstalled software, 13
Presentation applications, 17, 190.
    See also Microsoft PowerPoint
Preview Pane (Outlook), 241–242
Printer, 8
Printing
    e-mail, 245
    envelopes, 132–133
    Excel worksheets, 169–172
    files, 73–74, A-9–A-10
    labels, 132–134
    PowerPoint presentations, 226–227
Print publications, 276

Privacy of personal information, 37, 38
Processor (CPU), 6, 42
Productivity software, 17, 80. *See also*
    Microsoft Office 2010
    defined, 236
    navigation (*See* Navigation software)
    personal information management,
    240 (*See also* Microsoft Outlook)
    presentation applications, 17, 190
    (*See also* Microsoft PowerPoint)
    spreadsheets, 17, 138–140 (*See also*
    Microsoft Excel)
    word processing, 83–84 (*See also*
    Microsoft Word)
Protocol, 31
Publisher, 68, 69
Publishing trends, 276

Q

Quick Access Toolbar, 75

R

Random access memory (RAM), 6
Raw computing, 268
Readability, of PowerPoint presenta-
    tions, 192
Reading Pane (Outlook), 242
Recurring appointments, 260
Recycle bin, 51
Relative addressing (Excel), 166
Reminders, automated, 237–238
Renaming files, 58
Repeat rate, key, 120
Replying to e-mail (Outlook), 247
Research, online, 33–37
    browsing, 35
    citations, 36–37
    credibility of sources, 35–36
    keywords, 33–35
    online, 25–26
    procedures, 33
    search engines, 33
Resizing
    windows, 55, A-3
    Word graphics, 122–123
    Word table columns and rows,
    126–127
Restoring windows, 55, A-3
Ribbon (Excel), 142–143, 165
Ribbon (Office 2010), 74–75,
    A-10–A-11
Right-aligned text, 104
Robots, for the autistic, 277
Rootkits, 39
Rotating text (Excel), 152

Rows (Excel)
    adjusting, 154, D-11
    deleting, 149–150, D-7
    inserting, 149–150, D-6
Rows, table. *See* Tables (Word)

S

SaaS (Software as a Service), 265
Sales presentations, 233–234
Samsung, 276
Saving
    drafts of e-mail, 244
    files, 67
Scale to Fit (Excel), 170–171
Scams, e-mail, 253–254
Screen resolution
    changing, 59
    setting, 16
Scroll bars, 55–56
Search engines, 33, B-6
Security
    e-mail, 252–253
    Internet, 39
Selecting
    in Excel, 145
    in PowerPoint, 203–204
    text, 76–77, 95–96, C-5
Servers, 14, 29, B-4
Service providers, 26–27
Shapes (PowerPoint), 220–221
Shared folders, saving files to, 64–67
Sharing, calendar (Outlook),
    261, 262
Shortcut menu, 76
Shortcuts (desktop), 51
Shutting down computers, 44, 45, 47
Signature, e-mail (Outlook),
    244–245
Sizing pages
    in Excel, D-4
    in Word, C-4
Slide deck (PowerPoint), 191
Slides and slide shows. *See* Microsoft
    PowerPoint
Smartphones, 4
    defined, 264
    in the future, 277–278
    platforms, 4–5
Snapshot, 261
Social engineering, 39
Social issues, with Internet usage,
    37–38
Social networking, 33
Social networks, 25
Software, 13–18, 42–43
    add-ons, 31
    application, 16–17

Software (*Continued*)
 buying, 21
 categories of, 54
 defined, 5, 29, 42
 entertainment, 16–17
 graphics, 18
 installing, 13–14
 Internet, 28
 licensing, 14
 system, 15–16
 upgrades, 14
 user interfaces, 13
 utility programs, 16
 web browsers, 29–30
Software as a Service (SaaS), 265
Software piracy, 15
Software suites, 17
Software upgrades, 14
Solid state drive, 9, 10
Solid-state memory, 268
Sorting lists (Excel), 173
Sound clips (PowerPoint), 218
Sources
 citing, 35–36
 credibility of, 35–36
 research, 25–26
Spacing, in Word, 104–105
Spam, 39, 252
Spell Checking, 79, 117–119,
  A-10–A-11, C-11
Spiders, 33
Spreadsheet applications, 17
Spreadsheets, 138–140. *See also*
 Microsoft Excel
Start button, 51
Starting
 the computer, 44
 programs with the Start menu,
  52–54
 Windows 7, 46–51
Start menu, 52–54
Status bar (Excel), 146
Status bar (PowerPoint), 200
Status bar (Word), 89–91
Status bars, 56
Storage devices, 8–12
 backing up, 12
 flash memory storage, 9–10
 hard disk drives, 8–9
 optical discs, 10–11
 web-based cloud storage, 10
Style, saving formatting as, 110–111
SUM function (Excel), 161
Switching between windows, 55, A-3
Symbols, inserting, 79
Syncing calendars, 261, 262
System software, 15–16
System unit, 5–6

T

Tables (Excel). *See* Lists (Excel)
Tables (Word), 124–128
 deleting columns and rows, 126
 design options for, 127–128
 entering text into, 124–125
 inserting, 125–126, C-14–C-15
 resizing columns and rows, 126–127
Tablet computers, 4, 20
Tabs (Word), 105–107
Task bar, 51
Tasks (Outlook calendar), 260–261
Telemedicine, 271
Templates (PowerPoint), 194–195
Terabyte, 6
Text (in general)
 copying, 98–99
 cutting, 98–99
 editing, 76, 97–100
 entering, 76, 92–95
 global Find and Replace, 99
 pasting, 98–99
 positioning, 93–94
 selecting, 76–77, 95–96
Text (PowerPoint)
 editing, 204–205
 entering, 203, 206
Text (Word)
 editing, C-6–C-9
 entering into tables, 124–125
 selecting, C-5
 wrapping around graphics, 123
Text formatting (Excel), 151–157
Text formatting (Office 2010), 77
Text formatting (Word), 100–116,
 119–120, C-9–C-10
 alignment, 103–104
 bulleted and numbered lists, 108–109
 character formatting, 100–102
 columns of, 128–129
 indents, 107–108
 line spacing, 104
 paragraph, 101, 103
 paragraph spacing, 104–105
 saving formatting as a style, 110–111
 tabs, 105–107
Themes (PowerPoint), 195–196,
 206–209
Thesaurus, 79
Threats, 39
Touchpad, 7
Track Changes (Word), 130–131
Transitions (PowerPoint), 190,
 224–225
Trojan horses, 39
Trolls, 37
Turning on the computer, 44

U

Uniform resource locators (URLs),
 31, 254
Uninstalling software, 13
United States Green Building Council
 (USGBC), 274
Upgrades, software, 14
URLs (uniform resource locators),
 31, 254
USB flash drive, 9, 10
User interfaces, 13
USGBC (United States Green
 Building Council), 274
Utility programs, 16

V

Value_if_false argument (Excel), 182
Value_if_true argument (Excel), 182
Values (Excel), 151–157
Version control, 67
Video files, 58, 217–218
Viewing pages (Word), C-4
View(s)
 in Office 2010, 78
 in Outlook, 242
 in PowerPoint, 198–202
Virtualization, 270
Viruses, 39, 253
Virus protection programs, 39
VisiCalc, 140

W

WAN (wide area network), 19, 26
Warranties, computer, 21
Web. *See* World Wide Web
Web 2.0, 26, 32–34
Web addresses, 31, B-5
Web applications, 14
Web-based cloud storage, 10
Web browsers, 29–30
Web pages, 29
Web research, 33–37
Web servers, B-4
Websites, 29, B-4
 creating/publishing, 32
 credibility of, 35–36
 navigating, 32
Welcome screen (Windows 7), 46–48
What-if analysis, 138
What-you-see-is-what-you-get
 (WYSIWYG), 84
Wide area network (WAN), 19, 26
WiFi (wireless fidelity), 12, 27–28, 278
WiFi access points, 28
Wikipedia, 35

Windows
  folder, 62
  manipulating, A-2–A-4
  working with, 54–55
Windows 7
  desktop, 50–51
  Ease of Access, 48
  Guest Account, 48–50
  Help and Support, 53–54
  keyboard alternatives to using
    mouse, 45
  starting, 46–51
  Welcome screen, 46–48
  Windows Explorer, 56–59
  working with, 54–59
Windows Explorer, 56–59
  manipulating files with, A-4
  opening files from, 72–73, A-8–A-9
  Windows Explorer window, A-3

Windows PC, 4, 13
Wireless fidelity. *See* WiFi
Wireless Internet service providers,
  26–28
Wireless local area network
  (WLAN), 19
Word. *See* Microsoft Word
Word processing, 17. *See also*
  Microsoft Word
  for common business tasks, 83
  history of, 83–84
Workbooks (Excel)
  creating, 140–141, 146–147,
    D-2–D-3
  defined, 140
  as Mail Merge data source, 134
  themes, 155–156
Worksheets (Excel)
  completing, 172

design of, 147–148
  navigating, 144–145
  printing, 169–172
  worksheet area, 144
Workspace, ergonomic design of, 12
World Wide Web (web), 28–32.
  See also Internet
  defined, 28
  history of, 26
Worms, 39
Wrapping text around graphics
  (Word), 123
WYSIWYG (what-you-see-is-what-
  you-get), 84

Z

Zipping files, 67–68

Notes